Praise for Kirk Ellis and *They Kill People*

"Kirk Ellis, a true connoisseur of cinema, deftly uses an iconic movie as a jumping-off point for a much larger study of America's disturbing obsession with guns and our propensity not only for violence but for celebrating and romanticizing it. Ellis's argument—that gun culture is central to our national identity—is hard to dismiss. *They Kill People* is a supple and far-ranging narrative that examines our country's long, sordid trigger-happiness through the lens of film. You can't read it without wondering, on multiple levels, *What the hell's wrong with us?*"—Hampton Sides, *New York Times* bestselling author of *Blood and Thunder* and *The Wide, Wide Sea*

"Kirk Ellis has written a vibrant, astute, and vastly entertaining account of the making of one of the greatest American movies of the modern era. But *They Kill People* is not just an excellent movie book. It's also the story of a country struggling to escape the death grip of the Great Depression, its myths, its mortal wounds, and its obsession with fast cars, lethal weapons, and murderous celebrity outlaws. Ellis understands that while history doesn't repeat itself, it often rhymes, and he deftly connects the dots between the roaring '30s, the rebellious '60s, and our own troubled decade."—Glenn Frankel, Pulitzer Prize–winning journalist and author of *Shooting Midnight Cowboy: Art, Sex, Loneliness, Liberation, and the Making of a Dark Classic*

"Kirk Ellis examines the disturbing roots of this country's obsession with guns and outlaws in a book that's as rollicking as it is alarming. A brilliant exploration of how a fascination with violence reveals the darkest reaches of our American identity."—Betsy Gaines Quammen, author of *True West: Myth and Mending on the Far Side of America*

"Released amid the social turmoil of 1967, *Bonnie and Clyde*'s counterculture depiction of two bank robbers during the Great Depression began a New Wave of Hollywood filmmaking and changed the industry's rating system. Almost a half century later, Kirk Ellis's compelling, dramatic reassessment of this unusually influential film demonstrates that *Bonnie and Clyde* is as relevant as ever. Packed with fascinating behind-the-camera stories—such as how star/producer Warren Beatty fought for the film's re-release after Warner Bros. sensed the threat it posed and dumped it—this major study entertains as much as it enlightens."—David Morrell, *New Yok Times* bestselling author of *First Blood*

"Ellis brings his award-winning writing and sharp eye for history to a brilliant and thought-provoking exposé of America's obsession with guns and violence. Through the spectacle of real-life criminals Bonnie and Clyde and the Hollywood myth makers who made them legendary, Ellis serves up a haunting, irresistible, and riveting tale. I could not put it down!"—Kate Clifford Larson, author of *Walk with Me: A Biography of Fannie Lou Hamer*

"With *They Kill People*, Kirk Ellis has delivered an important work for fans of Arthur Penn's classic and seminal movie *Bonnie and Clyde*, plus a compelling account of the real-life Texas criminals who inspired it. This exquisitely written book captivated me. I read it two sittings. It's that good."—W. K. Stratton, Western Heritage Award–winning poet and author of the *Los Angeles Times* bestseller *The Wild Bunch: Sam Peckinpah, a Revolution in Hollywood, and the Making of a Legendary Film*

"In *They Kill People*, Kirk Ellis leads the reader through our history of gun-fueled outlawry with entertaining enlightenment."—Bryan Cranston, producer/star of *Breaking Bad*

☞ They Kill People

That's a wrap. The final curtain image from the 2023 London revival of Frank Wildhorn and Don Black's *Bonnie and Clyde* musical. Arthur Penn would have approved. Author photo.

THEY KILL

High Road Books

Albuquerque

Bonnie and Clyde, a Hollywood Revolution, and America's Obsession with Guns and Outlaws

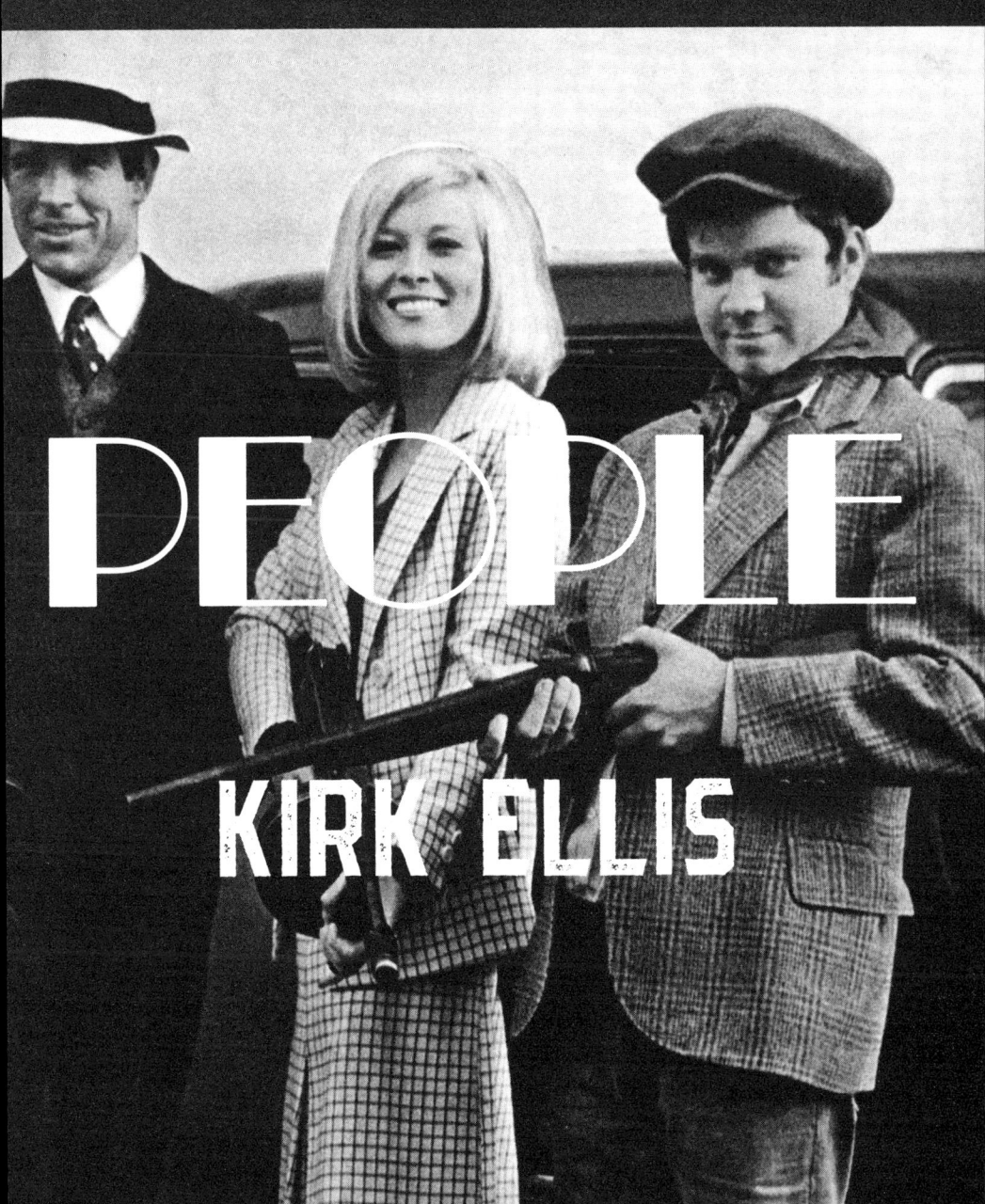

PEOPLE
KIRK ELLIS

© 2026 by Kirk Ellis
All rights reserved. Published 2026
Printed in the United States of America

ISBN 978-0-8263-6937-6 (cloth)
ISBN 978-0-8263-6938-3 (ePub)

Library of Congress Control Number: 2025944335

Founded in 1889, the University of New Mexico sits on the traditional homelands of the Pueblo of Sandia. The original peoples of New Mexico—Pueblo, Navajo, and Apache—since time immemorial have deep connections to the land and have made significant contributions to the broader community statewide. We honor the land itself and those who remain stewards of this land throughout the generations and also acknowledge our committed relationship to Indigenous peoples. We gratefully recognize our history.

Cover illustration and title page: *Bonnie and Clyde* cast publicity photo, Warner Bros./Courtesy of Everett Collection.
Designed by Isaac Morris
Display type: Adorn, Bartender, Broadacre, and Condor
Composed in: Adobe Jenson Pro 10.75 | 16

For Sheila, as always

The United States of America was born
with a gun in her hand.

—Richard Mack, founder of the Constitutional Sheriffs and
Peace Officers Association

 Contents

INTRODUCTION. "Who Shot Him?"   xv

1. "Ambush"   1
2. "Dumbbells"   11
3. "Lightning in a Bottle"   21
4. "The Bloody Massacre"   32
5. "Anything Goes"   42
6. "Blood Always Surprises Me"   50
7. "I Steal"   65
8. "Infringed!"   82
9. "An Argument Every Night"   95
10. "A Couple of Kids"   118
11. "Cold, Dead Fingers"   136
12. "What's Wrong with These Guys?"   147
13. "We're in the Money"   164
14. "A .45 Slug in the Gut"   181
15. "Fadin' Away"   197
16. "Trail's End"   209
17. "Martyrs"   226
18. "A Squalid Shoot-'Em-Up"   242

19. "He's Nothing but a Little-Bitty Fart"   260
20. "Opening the Bloodgates"   277
EPILOGUE. "Made in America"   294

AFTERWORD AND ACKNOWLEDGMENTS   301
NOTES   305
SELECTED BIBLIOGRAPHY   349
INDEX   357

Introduction

"WHO SHOT HIM?"

On April 13, 1882, a six-foot, three-inch peacock strode on to the stage of the Tabor Opera House in Leadville, Colorado.

Twenty-seven-year-old Oscar Wilde, a few years away from becoming one of the most celebrated authors and playwrights in the world, had come to the Rocky Mountain West as an advance man for the D'Oyly Carte Opera Company. His mission: to promote the American tour of *Patience*, the latest sensation by *H.M.S. Pinafore* and *The Pirates of Penzance* authors Gilbert and Sullivan. A thinly disguised caricature of Wilde (billed in the cast of characters as "Reginald Bunthorne, a Fleshly Poet") featured prominently in this musical satire about the arts-for-art's-sake aesthetic movement then sweeping across Britain.

At the time of Wilde's arrival in America, "the young nation's biggest celebrity was dime novel hero Buffalo Bill," according to historian Preston Lewis. Wilde's sojourn to the United States lasted nearly a year and garnered even more publicity than William F. Cody himself. "At the very least," Lewis wrote, "Wilde was the first celebrity who became famous for merely being famous, launching the superficial celebrity culture that permeates American popular culture to this day."[1]

Leadville had not been on Wilde's original itinerary. But he could not resist an invitation from mining tycoon Horace A. W. Tabor, one of America's richest men, to declaim on the subject of art and beauty at Tabor's newly built Italianate music hall. "I was told that if I went there, they would be sure to shoot me or my traveling manager," Wilde recalled. "I wrote and told them that nothing they could do to my traveling manager would intimidate me."[2] Wilde had reason to fear bad reviews. A sign over the piano in a Leadville saloon read, "Please Do Not Shoot the Pianist; He Is Only Doing His Best." (Wilde later declared it "the only rational method of art criticism I have ever come across."[3])

Like so many entertainers making their first visit to the Rockies' higher altitudes, Wilde succumbed to what a local doctor termed "a case of light air" and confined himself to his room at the Clarendon Hotel. A capacity crowd of curiosity seekers, some of whom had paid the unheard of price of $1.25 for reserved seats, fidgeted nervously as the scheduled performance hour came and went. When Wilde finally stepped out from the wings, his appearance did not disappoint: color-coordinated dress coat, knee breeches, and stockings (possibly purple, or green or yellow) ornamented with silver-buckled patent-leather pumps and his trademark broad-brimmed hat; a giant sunflower beamed from his lapel.

Still too fragile to deliver his customary lecture, Wilde came armed with a copy of the autobiography of sixteenth-century Florentine sculptor and goldsmith Benvenuto Cellini, from which he began to read passages verbatim. The baffled audience grew increasingly restless. One miner leaped to his feet to demand why "Mr." Cellini couldn't be there to speak for himself.

"He's dead," Wilde explained.

The miner let this information sink in. Then he asked:

"Who shot him?"

~:·~

Guns made America.

Guns *are* America.

America's story is inextricably bound with the weapons that have become as iconic—as identifiably *American*—as the men and women who wielded them.

Brown Bess.

Sharps rifle.

Colt .45.

Winchester '73.

Thompson submachine gun.

.44 Smith & Wesson.

The AR-15—"America's gun."

The American vernacular itself has been weaponized. An honest person is called a "straight shooter." A lucky one "dodges a bullet." Determined people "set their sights" and "stick to their guns." Gamblers "take the long shot." Optimists "look for a silver bullet." A hesitant person is "gun-shy." Fools go off "half-cocked" and sometimes "shoot from the hip." We "get the drop on" our rivals and enemies. Stressful situations make us "sweat bullets." Astonishing sights "blow us away." Travel companions "ride shotgun," while "hired guns" attend to unpleasant tasks.

No ethos is more deeply ingrained in the American psyche than that of The Outlaw: those Legendary Rebels who raise a middle finger to Established Society and embark on a fatal career of so-called Resistance to Authority and Redistribution of Wealth.

The United States of America owes its very existence to an act of rebellion. Contrarianism is deeply ingrained in our national DNA. "Resist much," advised Walt Whitman in one of his *Songs of Insurrection*. "Obey little."

American popular culture is rife with the names of the notoriously disobedient. Frank and Jesse James: vicious borderland bushwhackers remade as Western gunslingers. Billy the Kid: a buck-toothed psychopath given a new, redemptive identity in a sordid New Mexico range war. Wyatt Earp: a canny entrepreneur and onetime brothel-keeper lionized for his role in a one-horse-town shootout of no particular importance.

"Outlaws play better after the fact," admits Bob Boze Bell, publisher of *True West* magazine, "when the blood's dried and you don't have to look at the autopsies, you can just look at the 'glory.'"[4] Western historian Mark

Lee Gardner, whose work includes reassessments of both Jesse James and Billy the Kid, notes how "we sympathize with these individuals because of their backstory. They've got to have that tragedy that sends them down this different path. The myth redeems them. Yet when you put the myth next to the cold, hard reality, sometimes they don't live up to the hype."[5]

Far from it.

"By conventional means of measuring history, the gunfighters of the Old West are of scant importance," one account of frontier violence rightly maintains. "They left no political or socioeconomic legacy, little that would justify even inclusion in a history textbook. Their impact is instead cultural, as symbols beloved or reviled, most notably in our entertainments, [and] maybe in our firearms as well; one is tempted to sense their presence in the way children play with toy guns."[6]

For a citizenry whose republic was established as a nation of laws, not men (John Adams's immortal phrase), twenty-first-century Americans retain an alarming admiration for lawbreakers. "A lot of [us] want to feel [we]'re being oppressed by somebody or something," observes true crime writer Jeff Guinn, "and we're going to give credence to the goodness of people who don't necessarily have good intentions, just because they're confronting people we don't like."[7]

Outlaws are seductive. They appeal to our darkest hidden desires. Especially in an era when individual initiative has been subsumed by corporate consolidation, outlaws make our most outrageous Robin Hood fantasies come true. But also, as the advertising for *Bonnie and Clyde* famously proclaimed:

"THEY KILL PEOPLE."

And when they do, it's almost always with guns.

~:·:~

Numbering just 4 percent of the global population, America holds 50 percent of all guns in civilian hands globally: 393 million according to a 2018 survey, for an average of 120.5 firearms per one hundred people—a private-ownership rate that ranks as the highest in the world. In the years during and immediately following the COVID-19 pandemic, Americans purchased more than *60 million firearms*; a 2020 ABC News investigation estimated that the US firearms industry accounted for $63.5 billion in combined revenues.[8]

In late June 2024, US Surgeon General Vivek H. Murthy declared gun violence a public health crisis. In his 39-page advisory, Murthy noted that deaths caused by guns rose to a three-decade high in 2021, driven by increases in homicides and suicides. Citing 2015 data from the World Health Organization showing that the United States displayed a firearm-related death rate 11.4 times higher than 28 other high-income nations, the surgeon general concluded, "We're clearly the outlier, and not in a good way."[9]

Historian Richard Hofstadter first identified the United States as a "gun culture" in an influential 1970 essay, mincing few words. "Many otherwise intelligent Americans," he wrote, "cling with pathetic stubbornness to the notion that the people's right to bear arms is the greatest protection of their individual rights and a firm safeguard of democracy. No other democracy in the world observes any such 'right.'"[10] Hofstadter expanded on this thesis in his documentary history of America from first settlement to the assassination season of 1968. "Every aspect of violence in our history," he and coauthor Michael Wallace concluded, "has been exacerbated by the fact that ours is a gun culture—a thing without parallel among independent nations of the world."

"What is most exceptional about . . . Americans," the authors added, "is not the voluminous record of their violence, but their extraordinary ability, in the face of that record, to persuade themselves that they are among the best-behaved and best-regulated of peoples."[11]

For a time, the everyday slaughter of the early 1930s crime wave shocked America out of that national complacency. Clyde Barrow and Bonnie Parker were black-and-white bit players in that red-heavy Technicolor extravaganza. Resurrected in a landmark 1967 film made during the apocalypse of Vietnam and a time of unprecedented urban unrest that set American cities ablaze, they became cinematic and fashion icons of a decade that uncomfortably mirrored their own.

Arthur Penn's *Bonnie and Clyde* broke every rule in the Old Hollywood playbook and redefined the portrayal of on-screen violence, sex, and criminality. Nearly sixty years after it exploded on to American screens, the film retains the power to shock, amaze, and provoke. The movie's resonance goes well beyond its peerless filmmaking. *Bonnie and Clyde* taps into a dark wellspring in the American psyche. Produced in a time of great social upheaval, with a country divided under a deeply polarizing president, the film confronts troubling questions about America's propensity to violence and its obsession with guns.

"*Bonnie and Clyde* was one of those absolutely fortunate films where I made the movie I wanted to make, and it turned out to be a big hit,"[12] Penn said. "It hasn't aged," he reflected on the occasion of his film's fortieth anniversary. "I don't know why it hasn't, but it hasn't. You watch it today, and it sort of invents itself before your eyes."[13]

The reason why is the subject of this book.

~:•:~

In the wake of the assassinations of Martin Luther King Jr. and Robert F. Kennedy in the late spring and early summer of 1968, the year *Bonnie and Clyde* scored ten Oscar nominations, historian Arthur Schlesinger Jr. asked, "How many more such murders before we strive . . . to identify the violent impulses in American life?"[14] Arthur Penn ventured an answer to that question at the film's 1967 Montreal Film Festival premiere. "I think violence is part of the American character," Penn said. "It began with the Western, the frontier. America is a country of people who act out their views in violent ways."[15]

And so we begin with a scene of violent death.

1

"AMBUSH"

> You've read the story of Jesse James —
> Of how he lived and died;
> If you're still in need
> Of something to read
> Here's the story of Bonnie and Clyde.
> —Bonnie Parker

Highway 154, Bienville Parish, Louisiana.
Wednesday, May 23, 1934, 9:15 a.m.

Nobody came prepared for the goddamned mosquitoes.

They're eating Frank Hamer and his six-man posse alive in this thicket on the side of a miserable country road in the northwestern corner of Louisiana. Collectively the lawmen wield two Browning automatic rifles, a pair of Remington Model 8 .35-caliber big-game rifles and two Colt .45 semiautomatic pistols each, none of them of any use against blood-sucking insects. Hamer carries the most lethal hardware: a Remington Model 11 shotgun and Colt Monitor machine rifle with a twenty-shot magazine, designed to inflict maximum carnage with minimal effort. Today is meant to mark the end of a 102-day manhunt that has carried the former Texas Ranger repeatedly across the Midwest and Southwest; 1,397 miles in the first two weeks of February alone.

The stakeout location has been carefully chosen. The high vantage point offers unobstructed half-mile perspectives in both directions; moss-covered trees on the south side of the road completely conceal the posse from the view of approaching motorists. A confidential informant has assured Hamer that his quarry is bound to pass by en route to their latest hideout. Eighteen hours of waiting have taken their toll. "We look like the wrath of God," thinks Dallas County deputy Ted Hinton, detailed to the posse along with partner Bob Alcorn as the only men among them who can positively identify their targets on sight. "Unshaven, eyes bloodshot, and feeling the wear of no sleep."[1]

As if the plague of mosquitoes isn't enough, grumbling stomachs are a constant reminder that, in their haste to establish a position, none of the lawmen have remembered to pack any food. To lessen the monotony, they talk about their next meal. So far, all the traffic they've encountered along this lonely rural stretch is a solitary school bus and the occasional logging truck; folks here in the Depression-era Louisiana backwoods are prone to harvesting telephone poles, stripping them, and selling them as lumber. Nine o'clock has come and gone; by 9:10, the posse is all but resigned to the fact that this is yet another false lead.

"Let's give it another thirty minutes, and then throw the coffee on the fire and call in the dogs,"[2] Hinton suggests—no matter that they've forgotten the coffee as well.

Five minutes later, everyone hears it.

The whine of a Ford V-8 motor.

"Singing like a sewing machine,"[3] Hamer thinks.

Costing between $500 and $600 (unless it's stolen) and packing an impressive 75 horsepower, Henry Ford's latest sensation is the sleekest automobile on the market, with a streamlined, backward-slanted silhouette to emphasize its capability for speed. Readily sustaining 60 miles per hour, in the hands of a capable driver the V-8's 221-cubic-inch engine can be pushed to 75 or 80, outrunning every other vehicle on the road, including police cars. "I can make any other car take a Ford's dust," writes one satisfied Chicago customer named John Dillinger in a testimonial letter. "For sustained speed and freedom from trouble the Ford has got every other car skinned," enthuses another. "Even if my business hasn't been strictly legal it don't hurt to tell you what a fine car you got in the V-8."[4]

Behind the wheel of the freshly stolen tan 1933 Ford V-8 B-400 convertible now approaching the waiting posse sits one of those letter-writing fans: twenty-four-year-old Clyde Chestnut Barrow. Riding shotgun, crippled by a leg injury sustained in a terrible crash the year before, is Barrow's companion for the last four years, twenty-three-year-old Bonnie Elizabeth Parker. Both hail from neighboring parts of West Dallas, Texas. Minutes later, their car will also be found to contain three Browning automatic rifles, two sawed-off shotguns, a variety of Colt semiautomatic pistols, one hundred Browning automatic magazines, and three thousand rounds of ammunition, together with fifteen sets of stolen license plates, suitcases full of clothes, a stack of true crime periodicals, a makeup case and a saxophone, along with a copy of *The Saga of Billy the Kid* by Walter Noble Burns.

For the past two years, in the company of a rotating supporting cast of accomplices, the Barrow Gang has perpetrated a string of small-town (and almost always small-time) robberies and ransom-less kidnappings, leaving the bodies of nine murdered lawmen scattered over four states; most recently, two highway patrolmen gunned down on Easter Sunday in Grapevine, Texas. Their most daring escapade is barely four months old: a daylight breakout of five inmates, including several former associates, from the notoriously brutal Eastham Farm prison colony on the outskirts of Houston (a.k.a. "The Bloody 'Ham'"), where Clyde once served time—a sentence, says another former inmate, that transformed him from "a schoolboy into a rattlesnake."[5]

Beneath their camouflage of dried brush and vines, the posse readies its arsenal. There will be no announcement of their presence. No "Stop in the name of the law!" or "Put up your hands!" (Hamer and the others will maintain otherwise.) Hamer's orders, issued by general manager of Texas prisons Lee Simmons and authorized by Governor Miriam "Ma" Ferguson in direct response to the Eastham breakout, are unequivocal: "Put 'em on the spot and shoot everyone in sight."[6] All that remains is a positive identification. Hinton's Dallas partner Bob Alcorn raises a pair of field glasses to his eyes.

"It's him, boys," Alcorn announces quietly. "This is it—it's Clyde."[7]

Sixteen seconds later, it's all over.

The first shots—most likely fired with a Remington Model 8 rifle by Prentiss Oakley, an understandably jittery young Bienville Parish deputy—strike Clyde in the head, killing him instantly. All six officers open fire, emptying their magazines in less than three seconds, then reloading. Forensic reports testify to one hundred and sixty-seven rounds being launched at point-blank range, perforating the V-8's steel-reinforced double door panels and whizzing through the open driver's-side windows. Coroner's records list seventeen entrance wounds on Clyde's body and forty-one on Bonnie's, including those from the .30–06 steel-jacketed rounds from Hinton's BAR that stitch a line up Bonnie's left side and blow her red go-to-meeting hat off her head and into the back seat, splintering her jaw along the way.

"I literally could not have heard thunder," Hinton later writes. "My head was ringing from the cannonade of bullets and the clank of steel-jacketed metal tearing steel."[8] Their automatic weapons spent, the posse blasts away with pistols and shotguns—and keeps blasting long after the riddled V-8 has rolled to a final stop in a ditch a short distance away. Even then, the lawmen can't be sure that Barrow and Parker are really finished; Clyde's ability to survive a shootout has already become a part of Texas legend. Drawing his personally inscribed Colt .45 pistol, "Old Lucky," Hamer cautiously approaches the vehicle.

"Be careful, Cap!" shouts Maney Gault, another former Texas Ranger. "They may not be dead."

"If they're not, they soon will be," Hamer assures him.[9]

Only "a bunch of wet rags"[10] awaits the posse inside the V-8. Clyde's head dangles grotesquely through the spokes of the steering wheel, blood and brains leaking through his exposed skull; a 16-gauge sawed-off shotgun is wedged between his left leg and the driver's side door. Bonnie's head is slumped between her knees. One hand still clutches a half-eaten sandwich. A blood-spattered *True Detective* magazine rests in her lap; a nickel-plated Colt .45 semiautomatic pistol, cocked and ready, sits concealed beneath it. The ambush has come so suddenly, so unexpectedly, that neither has had a chance to get off a single shot. Now, their killers gawk at them through the windshield's pockmarked, shatterproof safety glass—another of Ford's dandy innovations, made-to-order for fast-moving larceny.

For decades, none of the members of the posse will speak of the events leading up to the the barrage that shattered that spring morning and ended the lives of what one modern crime historian has called "a shark-eyed multiple murderer and his deluded girlfriend."[11] Bienville Parish sheriff Henderson Jordan, whose own painstaking investigation led to the tip that sealed Clyde and Bonnie's fate, will never forget how Bonnie "screamed like a panther" when shots first rang out, or how the death car "looked like where hogs had been slaughtered"[12]; but he, like Hamer, like Hinton and Alcorn and the rest, will never express regret for their role in an extrajudicial execution.

"I hated to bust a cap in a woman," Hamer will grudgingly admit, "but if it [hadn't] been her it would've been us."[13]

The acrid smell of gun smoke remains heavy in the air when Hinton remembers the sixteen-millimeter amateur movie camera he's brought along for the occasion, "as a friend had suggested I should if ever we came upon Clyde and Bonnie and there was time to make pictures. The movies," Hinton is absolutely sure at the time, "would show how it was when it happened, so there would be no doubt, even if the landscape should change someday, exactly how it had been on this morning in May 1934, when Clyde and Bonnie had died as she predicted they would, side by side."[14]

Little did he know.

Albertson Ranch, Triunfo, California
Tuesday, January 3, 1967

Killing Clyde and Bonnie in real time took less than half a minute. Killing them on screen takes four days—and this low-budget Warner Bros. production is already three days over schedule.

Director Arthur Penn feels the pressure. After three months of location shooting in small-town central Texas—including some of the actual places plundered by the Barrow Gang—the forty-four-year-old veteran of television, stage, and film, with a Tony Award and a Best Director Oscar nomination behind him, knows he and his collaborators are on to something, and he won't be easily dissuaded. The ambush scene isn't even in the script, which calls for the sequence to be related in a series of still photographs, accompanied by the sounds of gunfire. Penn knows instinctively that isn't the right ending. "We [have] to turn them into legends," he thinks, "move from reality into a new degree of experience."[15] Somewhere along the line, Penn has had a vision for the fade-out to his film. The whole sequence has dropped into his head, dreamlike, inspired by the breathtaking, almost ethereal action sequences of Akira Kurosawa's 1954 *Seven Samurai*. "It's a kind of spastic ballet," he explains to his star, Warren Beatty, who also happens to be making his debut as a producer.

"I don't know what the fuck that means," replies Beatty, unimpressed—and likely skeptical of the cost.

"Just trust me on this one," Penn implores Beatty in one of their daily work-stopping creative arguments. "I know what I want."[16]

What Penn wants will emerge as one of the most influential scenes in the history of American filmmaking, the moment when the factory system of the old Hollywood moguls and the outmoded Production Code that dictated on-screen morality collapsed against the onslaught of a new generation of artists and a society in the midst of a seismic upheaval. Achieving the director's vision, however, is proving to be a slow-motion agony here on a

Warner Bros. movie ranch location far removed from the actual events that occurred in Bienville Parish.

Four synchronized cameras running at different speeds are lined up to record Clyde and Bonnie's death throes. Penn has instructed his truculent cameraman, Burnett Guffey, to capture the same action from different angles to ensure a constant match that will enhance the lyricism he intends to extract from the violence. Because of the length of time necessary to wire both the prop Ford V-8 and the actors with pyrotechnic "squibs" designed to replicate the impact of gunshots (along with the gallons of stage blood required to render them realistic), only two takes are possible each day, one in the morning, the other in the afternoon. Every repetition further reduces the limited inventory of first-time costume designer Theadora Van Runkle and causes debut art director Dean Tavoularis to wonder that he may not have been able to wrangle quite enough vintage automobiles for this shoot.

As the minutes click past—and time is money when it comes to making films, especially on a chintzy $1.8 million budget like this one—Penn waits as special effects technician A. D. Flowers painstakingly attaches a strip of synthetic flesh to Beatty's forehead. When the first off-screen shots are fired, the strip will be yanked away by invisible wires; Penn intends the effect to recall the by-now infamous Zapruder film of President John F. Kennedy's assassination in Dallas three years earlier. Meanwhile, costar Faye Dunaway's left leg is tied to the emergency brake of the prop Ford V-8. So many wires dangle from her face and body she feels as if she resembles "an escapee from a mad scientist's laboratory."[17] When the squibs detonate, she'll perform a St. Vitus's dance of death, then slump forward out of the car without falling, caught in grotesque suspended animation, her blond hair brushing the ground.

This hasn't been an easy shoot for the twenty-five-year-old actress, forced to lose weight before principal photography and reliant on diet pills and Coca-Colas to maintain her daily energy. Her on-screen heat with Beatty is incendiary, but it's a different story on set. By now—at this crucial moment when Penn's vision calls for Clyde and Bonnie to exchange one last, loaded glance before high-velocity bullets tear them apart—Dunaway and Beatty can barely stand to look at each other. In these situations, a good director does what needs to be done. Instead of having his principal actors exchange looks directly, Penn stands in their respective eye lines for individual close-ups that, in split-second crosscuts, will prove electrifying to young audiences and transform cheap hoodlums into romantic martyrs.

Penn has no illusions about the story he's telling. "These two people were killers," he says flatly. "They seemed to have almost no conscience."[18] But he also says, "the justice meted out by the forces of law and order . . . seems to me far worse than the crimes they're avenging."[19]

Bonnie and Clyde has come together in an atmosphere of all-pervasive violence.

On August 1, 1966, shortly before production on the film began, a clean-cut, twenty-five-year-old white man by the name of Charles Whitman ascended the University of Texas Tower in Austin and committed what was then the largest mass murder in American history. Armed with a 6 mm Remington rifle with a 4× scope (with which he did most of the killing), a .35-caliber Remington carbine, a .357 Magnum Smith & Wesson revolver, a 9 mm Luger pistol, and seven hundred rounds of ammunition, Whitman killed sixteen people and wounded thirty-one others in just over ninety minutes before being fatally shot by two Austin police officers. The unprecedented killing spree put an "ordinary" face on murder to an American public already reeling from the slaughter of the Clutter family of Kansas by a pair of violent ex-cons (dramatized in book and film of Truman Capote's *In Cold Blood*) and the shocking close-quarter slayings of eight student nurses in Chicago by a psychotic drifter, Richard Speck.

Something in the fabric of the "traditional American way of life" was coming unhinged.

Penn had already tapped into that current in his previous film, *The Chase* (1966), made for Columbia Pictures and producer Sam Spiegel in the shadow of the 1965 Watts riots. The story of a manhunt that takes place over the course of a single day in a Texas town ripe with social and sexual tensions, the movie was badly compromised in production, but nonetheless emerged as what one critic called "a dissection of the violence oppressing America."[20] The film's seething, hothouse atmosphere and soap-opera story, scripted by Lillian Hellman, is underlaid with a sense of boiling ferocity that bubbles into moments of unexpected savagery, then erupts into a junkyard Götterdämmerung that sees an entire population transformed into a lynch mob.

The Chase served as a dry run for the themes Penn is now bringing to this Barrow Gang story by a couple of first-time New York writers, David Newman and Robert Benton. It is an angry, unforgiving film, devoid of redeeming characters (even Marlon Brando's principled sheriff is deeply compromised), full of gun-toting, alcohol-fueled vigilantes. At the climax, with order finally restored, a Jack Ruby–like avenger assassinates the fugitive. That ending wasn't scripted either: Penn, Brando, and Robert Redford, playing the fugitive, Bubber Reeves, improvised it on the spot. The image is depressingly familiar: As Brando's sheriff escorts Redford's prisoner through a crowd of townspeople, a figure on the jailhouse steps unloads a concealed weapon into Redford's guts.

The movie flopped. Penn is determined to make sure this one doesn't.

Assistant director Jack Reddish double-checks Beatty and Dunaway's marks and calls "Last looks!" Makeup man Robert Jiras, hair stylist Gladys Warren, and their teams scurry around another of Tavoularis's soon-to-be-pulverized prop Ford V-8s, making last-minute adjustments. Director of photography Guffey readies his quartet of cameras to roll in unison. Special effects chief Flowers mans the electronic board that will set off his explosive charges in pre-timed sequence. Penn takes a seat next to the principal "A" camera. In this era before the regular use of video monitors and instant playback, a director can only rely on his own eyes.

The waiting is finally over. Four days of shooting are about to reach their culmination.

Maybe.

A silence falls over the Albertson Ranch. The ritual roll call of production begins.

"Speed," calls sound recordist Robert Miller.

"Set," chimes in Guffey.

"It was one of those insane moments where, as a director, you're saying to yourself, 'I see it this way, I see it no other way, so I'm not going to economize,'" the director thinks, "and meanwhile, you can see people whispering on the set, 'This guy is nuts. What the fuck is he doing?'"[21]

A beat, then Arthur Penn launches what he dearly hopes will be the final take.

"Action!"

2

"DUMBBELLS"

> The Americans are certainly hero-worshippers, and
> always take their heroes from the criminal class.
> —Oscar Wilde

Clyde Barrow and Bonnie Parker sealed their love with a gun.

On the late afternoon of March 11, 1930, then nineteen-year-old Bonnie smuggled a .38-caliber Colt pistol to twenty-year-old Clyde in the McClennan County jail in Waco, Texas, where he awaited transfer to the Texas state prison in Huntsville. Clyde—a.k.a. Elvin Williams, Jack Hale, and Roy Bailey—had been fingered for a string of two burglaries and five car thefts, each carrying a two-year sentence. Taking into account Clyde's status as a first-time offender, his guilty plea, and his youth (Clyde claimed to be eighteen, and there were no official records to prove otherwise), the jury had recommended the terms be served concurrently rather than consecutively.

54th District Court judge R. I. Monroe seemed inclined to uphold the jury's ruling, but over a week after the trial, no final sentence had been forthcoming, and Clyde had begun to reconsider the prospect of even two years—make it eighteen months for good behavior—in prison. When a fellow inmate let slip he knew where a weapon to facilitate an escape could be obtained, Clyde turned for help to the one person he believed could do the job: his girlfriend of two months, Bonnie.

The youngsters had met in January at a West Dallas home where Bonnie, whose waitressing job at one of Dallas's most popular cafés evaporated with the onset of the Depression, had been earning a few desperately needed dollars as a housekeeper and where Clyde was an occasional visitor. By all accounts, the attraction between them was instantaneous. Parker family lore relates how Clyde, "a likable boy ... [who] looked more like a law student or a doctor than a bandit"[1] first endeared himself to Bonnie by strapping on an apron and whipping up a batch of hot chocolate, one of his favorite guilty pleasures. No matter to Bonnie that she was married to Roy Thornton, a good-looking but faithless grifter she'd hitched herself to at fifteen, now doing a five-year stretch for robbery. No matter to Clyde that she refused to file for divorce. Kicking a man when he was down wasn't Bonnie's style; she'd still be wearing Roy's ring on that fatal late spring day in Louisiana four years later.

Something about Clyde and Bonnie just clicked. Maybe it was their shared love of flashy clothes, fast cars, and furious living. More likely it was the fierce determination each saw in the other to rise above their deprived upbringings: Clyde's in the squalor of the shantytown encampments beneath the Oak Creek Viaduct, a dismal causeway spanning the Trinity River bottomlands that cut though Dallas; Bonnie's in neighboring Cement City, a slightly more "upscale," dirt-street industrial town erected in the shadow of oil refineries and foundry smokestacks that belched clouds of toxic air into the surrounding neighborhoods.

"I'm a loser, just like Clyde," Bonnie confided. "Folks like us just haven't got a chance."[2]

Bonnie had been present for Clyde's arrest in early February, which took place in the Parker family living room. Clyde, who'd been sleeping on the couch at the behest of Bonnie's mother, Emma, after a long night of courting her daughter, answered the door himself. So it's only natural that Bonnie would now be here in the Waco jail, sweet-talking the guard on duty to allow her one last visit before her "husband" (she's got the ring, after all) is sent down to Huntsville. The pistol is secured under the front of her dress, inside a belt cinched over her slip; Bonnie knows from previous visits she's unlikely to be subjected to a body search. Retrieving the weapon from the address Clyde provided hasn't been easy. For one thing, Bonnie is "scared to death of guns."[3] No matter what the papers—let alone the motion picture people—have to say about it later, Bonnie will rarely pick up a firearm from this moment on; on one of those few occasions, she nearly blows off her own foot by accident.

Clyde harbored no such inhibitions. "[He] loved guns from the time I can remember," Barrow's older sister Nell told a ghostwriter shortly after his death, "and always played with them. Toy guns, if he could get them; if not, he'd use a stick for a gun."[4] As a little kid, Clyde worshipped the Western actor William S. Hart, whose stalwart, poker-faced portrayals set the prototype of the "good bad man." His two greatest heroes were Jesse James and William Bonney, otherwise known as Billy the Kid—bandits "forced into breaking the law by a corrupt regime," as Bonnie and Clyde biographer Jeff Guinn explains. "And not only do they fight back instead of meekly taking whatever kind of oppression may be involved, but [they] use their banditry to contribute to people in need."[5]

From an early age, Clyde cultivated an interest in firearms, abetted by an industry that had lately targeted the preteen and teenage male demographic. "There isn't a boy in your town who doesn't want to own a Winchester rifle!" a March 1921 company ad to gun retailers enthused, urging dealers to "Put a Winchester Rifle Into the Hands of Every Youth in Your Town. When the boy and girls arrive at the age of twelve years, they become your prospects."[6] A 1927 Sears-Roebuck catalog included five pages of firearms, ranging from Remington and Winchester small-bore carbines to a 12-gauge Browning semiautomatic shotgun (price: $56.95, or $980 today).[7]

Clyde brought something else to these childhood games: a forceful personality married to a mercurial temper. "Clyde was a control freak,"[8] historian John Neal Phillips says flatly, an opinion borne out by Nell Barrow. "Clyde was going to be the big shot if we played," his sister remembered, "and if I kicked about it, we didn't play."[9] Size may have had a lot to do with it. Even by the physical standards of the era, Clyde was short, standing five feet seven inches (some sources reduce him to five feet four) and weighing a scrawny 125 pounds. To lend himself stature, Clyde took to giving his middle name as "Champion" rather than Chestnut; FBI wanted posters issued a day before his death still used that name.

A stylish appearance helped as well. Relatives recalled Clyde always looking "immaculate, even after days spent on the road, fleeing from the law."[10] Fashionable clothes cost money, and for a little while at least, Clyde held those odd jobs available to a high school dropout: clerk at the Brown Cracker & Candy Co., laborer at the Proctor & Gamble soap factory, usher at the Palace Theater, glazier for the United Glass and Mirror Co., where he earned something of a reputation crafting church windows. Far easier for Clyde and older brother Marvin, known as "Buck" for his deerlike ability to outrun pursuers, to take what they wanted, whether that meant stealing chickens, heisting automobiles, or liberating the occasional filling-station safe.

Even more than guns, Clyde Barrow loved automobiles. "The love affair with the gun and the love affair with the automobile are both intrinsic to the American idea of freedom," notes historian Paul Andrew Hutton. "Think about all the freedom [you have] when you're a kid and you get that first car."[11] Clyde was no exception. With his hard-won earnings, Clyde purchased a used Pontiac speedster for fifty dollars and quickly ran the old rattletrap into the ground. His first brush with "the laws" (period slang for the police) came when, at sixteen, he rented a more stylish roadster to impress a girlfriend and her mother, then neglected to return it on schedule; the rental agency declined to press charges. Clyde's paying gigs included a stint at the A&K Auto Top and Paint Shop, where he likely familiarized himself with every vehicle then on the road. Fords quickly became a personal favorite, not only for their style and engineering but also for their easy access.

In her epitaph for the bandit couple, Bonnie would claim that she knew Clyde "when he was honest and upright and clean."[12] But by the time of their meeting in January 1930, Clyde was already a wanted man and had been a "person of interest" to Dallas-Fort Worth police for half a decade, one of the "usual suspects" routinely hauled in "on suspicion," grilled and detained whenever a car theft or robbery occurred. Early mug shots of Clyde in the collections of the Texas/Dallas History and Archives Division are those of a jug-eared kid with Brilliantine hair, older than he appears, who looks more suited to Our Gang than a criminal gang: the *Waco Times-Herald* coined the nickname "Schoolboy" Barrow in its coverage of the trial that finally landed him in jail.

While no charges resulted from those early roundups, the continual on-the-job harassment by police made it all but impossible for Clyde to hold down steady employment. It may have been true that Bonnie had no inkling of Clyde's illicit activities, but everyone in the Barrow clan knew what he was up to—and understood his reasons for doing it. "At an early age, [Clyde] wanted things [he] couldn't have," said his younger sister Marie, "and that seemed the best way to get 'em—go out and take something or another."[13]

Wanting things you couldn't have. Bonnie Parker knew something about that.

Though her own mother considered her "an average girl with an average young girl's existence—not too much sorrow and not too much fun,"[14] Bonnie saw her world very differently. "When I'm on Broadway and I have my name in lights, you'll be sorry you talked to me like this," she warned anyone who doubted her ambitions.[15] A born show-off, Bonnie craved the spotlight, whether by singing "He's a Devil in His Own Home Town" as a three-year-old Sunday-school girl "resplendent in starched bow and ruffles," turning somersaults and cartwheels in the middle of an elementary school performance (in blackface, no less), or bringing home first prize in a local spelling bee.

Bonnie made her presence known in other ways, too: pummeling a pair of female classmates for stealing her pencils, or holding a razor to the throat of a love-struck kid for some undisclosed infraction. All of which only increased her legion of admirers. Bonnie "had a lot of 'fellers' in grade school—boys who thought she was too cute for anything," remembered a cousin. "[She] always had a book satchel full of chewing gum, candy bars and . . . mashed-up apples some little boy had brought her."[16]

Contemporary accounts of the adult Bonnie's vivacity are remarkably consistent. Everyone at the time agreed that published photographs failed to do justice to her looks. "Bonnie could turn heads," remembered then-postal worker Ted Hinton (fated to be one of Bonnie's assassins), who frequented Marco's Café, where Bonnie worked as a waitress. "[She] was perky, with taffy-colored hair that glistened red in the sun, and a complexion that was fair and tended to freckle."[17] Others—among them Clyde Barrow—were struck by her blue eyes and impeccable sense of style. Clyde's sister Nell considered Bonnie "an adorable thing, more like a doll than a girl," with "the loveliest skin I've ever seen without a blemish on it" and "dimples that showed constantly."[18] Like Clyde, Bonnie was an outsize personality for her physical stature, a tiny creature standing only four feet eleven inches and weighing between eighty-five and ninety pounds. (The Collingsworth County Museum in Wellington, Texas, preserves one of the adult Bonnie's dainty white leather gloves, small enough to fit a child's hands.)

The bobbed hair that "kinked all over her head like a baby's,"[19] the bee-stung lips—Bonnie derived her sense of self from her obsessive consumption of popular culture. A dedicated reader of movie-fan magazines such as *Photoplay* and *Motion Picture Weekly*, she sought escape in the exploits of screen sirens Vilma Banky in *A Night of Love*, Florence Vidor in *Afraid to Love*, Virginia Valli in *Marriage*, and—her favorite—"It Girl" Clara Bow in *The Primrose Path*. Though modern historians betray a tendency to categorize her as a "flapper," Bonnie's closest screen equivalents are actually those spunky, fierce working-girl heroines (any number of them waitresses) played by Joan Blondell and Barbara Stanwyck in the daring, even scandalous, pictures now known as "pre-Code films," which pushed the limits of acceptable screen content and put women at the forefront of the narrative. It's absolutely no coincidence that the best of those films were produced and released by Warner Bros., which a generation later would immortalize Bonnie's romance with Clyde Barrow—and, in the best pre-Code tradition, award her top billing.

Pre-Code women give as good as they get from the predatory men who surround them. "I'm A.P.O.—ain't puttin' out," Blondell's "pop-eyed hash slinger" tells a leering brakeman at a seedy rail station café counter in a striking moment from the 1931 William Wellman film *Other Men's Women*. By Ted Hinton's account, Bonnie herself took a page from those sorts of wisecracks. "Several of the men my age flirted with her," he reflected, "and Bonnie could turn off the advances or lead a customer on with her easy conversation."[20] Sex was always on the table. Bonnie's trendy wardrobe hinted at something more than generous tips; gossip reached mother Emma that Bonnie was "the biggest 'hotcha' girl in town."[21] While law enforcement historian John Boessenecker insists that Dallas police knew Bonnie to be a professional streetwalker but never arrested her ("So long as she didn't roll her johns we let her alone," according to one source), most others agree that if a trick was turned, it was occasional—and opportunistic.[22]

It's not much of a stretch to imagine Bonnie sitting in a darkened picture show—sometimes with a date, frequently with a girlfriend, often alone—projecting herself into the determined, take-no-prisoners women on screen. (Faye Dunaway's Bonnie does the same, taking refuge in *Gold Diggers of 1933* after the brutal murder of a bank official; the next scene finds her preening before a mirror in the gang's dingy hotel bathroom, trying out Ginger Rogers poses and humming *Gold Diggers*' signature tune, "We're in the Money.") For all her popularity, Bonnie found life outside the movies and magazines unfulfilling. On New Year's Day, 1928, in the wake of what would prove to be her final estrangement from Roy Thornton, Bonnie began her first and only diary. The entries conclude abruptly barely two weeks later, with a date (*"Tuesday, Jan. 17, 1928 —"*) and nothing else. In between, Bonnie's sense of longing is overwhelming. "Sure am lonesome." "I wonder what tomorrow will bring." "Stayed home all day and slept." "Blue as usual. Not a darn thing to do." "What a life!"

One plaintive phrase occurs repeatedly: "Why don't something happen?"[23]

Almost two years to the day after Bonnie closed the cover on her diary, something finally *did* happen.

Bonnie Parker met Clyde Barrow.

Now she's here in on the third floor of the McClellan County jail, across the bars from Clyde. Checking to make sure they're unobserved, she reaches into the front of her dress. Her fingers touch the steel of the Colt .38. Bonnie hands the pistol to Clyde. Clyde calls her "the sweetest baby in the world."[24] He tells her he loves her. Maybe there's time to steal a kiss. Then Bonnie turns on her fashionable heels, heads downstairs, and sashays out the same way she came in, once more turning the duty guard's head as she passes. Jean Harlow couldn't have managed it any slicker.

Talk about excitement.

Throughout Clyde's incarceration, Bonnie had kept up a daily stream of letters. Like her diary entries, the letters abound with cries of loneliness ("I am so blue I could die") embellished with theatrical flourishes straight out of a good Ruth Chatterton women's melodrama ("I laid my head down... and sure did boohoo. I imagine I sure looked funny with Maybelline streaming down my face.") But there are also flashes of sassy, pre-Code backtalk. "I want you to be a man, honey, and not a thug," she reproaches Clyde at one point. Another letter warns him: "Please don't ever do anything to get locked up again. If you ever do, I'll get me a railroad ticket fifty miles long and let them tear off an inch every thousand miles, because I never did want to love you and I didn't even try. You just made me." This coming only one line after her breathless admission, rife with subliminal sexual excitement: "I never knew I cared for you until you got to jail."[25]

Bonnie waited anxiously for word from her fugitive lover. She spent whole days at the Barrow house, talking nonstop about Clyde, trying to convince herself and anyone else who would listen that Clyde wasn't a bad boy; he just never had a chance. When this mess was all over and Clyde was safely away, she vowed she'd get a divorce and marry him. Days passed anxiously, and then a whole week. When Bonnie finally received word, it came not from Clyde himself but from front-page headlines in the local papers.

BABY THUGS CAPTURED gloated the *Waco News Tribune* (which listed Clyde's age as seventeen). The *Waco Sunday Tribune* went one better: WACO'S DUMBBELL BANDITS, CAPTURED IN OHIO, BACK IN M'CLENNAN COUNTY JAIL. Turns out Clyde and his cellmates, employing a relay of stolen cars, managed to hightail it north to the village of Middletown, south of Dayton, where they knocked off a dry cleaner's shop and the depot office of the Baltimore & Ohio Railroad (total haul: sixty bucks) before becoming hopelessly lost in the countryside on their way out of town. Unknowingly doubling back into Middletown, the bumbling bandits stumbled on to the scene of their own robbery, where a couple of alert cops recognized their license plate.

Never again would Clyde Barrow travel anywhere without a map.

However much hilarity "Schoolboy" Barrow's ignominious return provoked among newspaper readers, 54th District Court Judge Monroe saw only cause for alarm. "I have lost my patience trying to help these men who keep getting into trouble," he intoned at the sentencing hearing. "They get on the sympathies of juries . . . then they break jail. I think it would be good thing to save you boys from the chair," he insisted, addressing his remarks primarily to Clyde. "You are liable to go 'round here shooting a police officer—if you can shoot straight."[26] Saving Clyde from the electric chair meant a fourteen-year sentence: all seven two-year terms now to be served consecutively, not concurrently. Clyde was bound for the Texas State Penitentiary with a new alias: Prisoner No. 63527.

Known to prisoners as "The Walls," the state pen was a decaying Civil War relic that once held notorious frontier killer John Wesley Hardin; by 1930, it housed eighteen hundred inmates in a facility designed for fewer than twelve hundred. Overcrowding had reached such epidemic proportions that prisoners were forced to sleep in corridors or in the open yard; anywhere there was room for a blanket. Bedbugs infested the three-story building, which lacked sewerage and running water; buckets used for toilets in the four-man cells only added to the general stench. "If I had a dog that I thought anything of, I wouldn't want him kept in the Texas penitentiary under present conditions," remarked Texas governor Dan Moody around this time. "I'd kill him before I'd put him down there to stay."[27]

Men were routinely killed like dogs in "The Walls," some by one another, more by the guards and the trustees known as "building tenders." Conditions were unspeakably worse at the Eastham Prison Farm thirty-five miles outside Huntsville, one of several agricultural facilities where inmates were shipped to work the cotton fields that added to the prison system's coffers. Texas law decreed convicted felons to be "slaves of the state," and authorities worked them with antebellum brutality. Newly installed prison system general manager Lee Simmons had outlawed some of the more egregious tortures—hanging by chains from windows, ladders, or the ceiling, for instance—but plenty of abuses remained. Punishment, not rehabilitation, was the overriding philosophy. The Texas prison system constituted "a crime against society, a crime against the taxpayer and a crime against humanity," Texas state senator Thomas B. Love blustered to the *Houston Press*. The system "as it now is breeds crime instead of suppressing it. It is making confirmed criminals out of youths."[28]

Clyde Barrow emerged living proof of that accusation. Two years elapsed before he next saw Bonnie Parker. When he did, the transformation from schoolboy to rattlesnake would be complete. For the rest of their lives—doomed to last a scant seventeen months—the couple spent most of their time together on the road, at high speed. "Their wanderings had no aim or focus," observed reporter Bryan Burrough in his definitive account of the 1930s crime wave, *Public Enemies*. "It makes their story a jerky, alinear narrative, a string of scattered episodes with no discernable arc."[29]

Clyde Barrow and Bonnie Parker needed a screenwriter to rectify that. As luck would have it, when one finally came along three decades later, he hailed from just around the corner in Texas.

3

"LIGHTNING IN A BOTTLE"

> Real is good. Interesting is better.
> —Stanley Kubrick

Had it not been for Gloria Steinem, *Bonnie and Clyde* might never have been written.

In the spring of 1963, a few years before achieving national prominence as a leader of the women's liberation movement, Steinem exercised her female prerogative by breaking up with Robert Benton, a wise-ass editor for *Esquire* magazine, where she occasionally freelanced. The rejection drove Benton to find solace in the darkness of the New Yorker Theater on Broadway and West 88th Street. There he watched—over and over and *over* again—the latest French New Wave sensation, *Jules and Jim*, François Truffaut's plangent account of an ill-fated World War I–era Bohemian ménage à trois. "It was like a life raft," Benton recalled of the experience, "because [the movie] was about somebody surviving."[1] In the film's climax, Catherine (Jeanne Moreau), the woman loved equally by Jules (Oscar Werner) and Jim (Henri Serre), drives herself and Jim off a bridge into a river. The final scene finds Jules burying his friends' ashes in Paris's Père Lachaise Cemetery.

Presumably, Benton found the whole tragic tale cathartic.

The future cowriter of *Bonnie and Clyde* grew up in Barrow Gang country: Waxahachie, Texas, the largest town in Ellis County, where Clyde's family worked as sharecroppers. Benton's father, Ellery, a telephone company employee, claimed to have attended both Clyde's and Bonnie's funerals, and

Benton grew up in an era when the outlaws remained a part of the town's living memory. "You'd go to a Halloween party as a kid and some boy would always be dressed as Clyde and some girl would be dressed as Bonnie," Benton remembered. "Nobody dressed up as Dillinger."[2] Faced with extreme dyslexia that made it painful for him to read or write for more than a few minutes at a time, Benton cultivated a talent for illustration. "It was very difficult for me to understand ... and in turn communicate things through reading, but I discovered I could do it through drawing,"[3] he explained. Consequently, Benton learned the art of storytelling not from books, but from the movies his father took him to on an almost nightly basis when homework became too taxing. "I found it easier for me to follow visual narrative in a movie than ... on a page," he said. "It occurred to me that if I were going to write at all, I should try it for the screen."[4]

The first in his family to graduate from college (University of Texas Class of 1953, with a bachelor of fine arts), Benton enrolled at Columbia University in New York City intending to study art history but dropped out after a single semester. His talents as a graphic designer attracted the interest of *Esquire* editor Harold Hayes, who hired Benton as an assistant art director; within a year, Benton had become full art director. The position put him in sophisticated company: in addition to onetime muse Steinem, the magazine's writers included Norman Mailer, Tom Wolfe, Gay Talese—and David Newman, a like-minded satirist from the University of Michigan, where he edited the campus's humor magazine. The two formed an immediate bond. Newman's talent with words complemented Benton's visual acuity.

"[David would] ask me to design a story he was writing, I'd bring him in to write the text for something I was working on,"[5] Benton told journalist and film writer Mark Harris, who described the two men, both then in their early thirties, as "a slightly Mutt-and-Jeffish pair." Benton was "low-key, precise, bespectacled," Newman "impulsive, hyperkinetic, unruly."[6] In other words: a perfect match.

Benton and Newman (or Newman and Benton—the many drafts of *Bonnie and Clyde* alternated their names on the title page) achieved a kind of celebrity for fashioning *Esquire*'s "Dubious Achievement Awards" and the magazine's lists of "Who's In/Who's Out." The snarky approach reached its pinnacle in a July 1, 1964, cover story, "The New Sentimentality." Essentially a paean to style over content, Newman and Benton's article relegated Eisenhower-era values like "Patriotism, Love, Religion, Mom, The Girl" to the dustbin of history and celebrated an emerging sensibility that "has to do with you, really just you, not what you were told or taught, but what goes on in your head, *really*, and in your heart, *really*."[7] The authors declared Jean-Paul Belmondo and Jean Seberg, stars of Jean-Luc Godard's trendsetting (now embarrassingly dated) 1960 film *Breathless* (*A bout de souffle*), to be "The Key Couple of the New Sentimentality." The time had passed for John Wayne, Grace Kelly, Rodgers and Hammerstein, and even Jackie Robinson; Humphrey Bogart and Marilyn Monroe survived as "Transitional Figures."[8]

With more than a half century's hindsight, the essay reads very much as a supremely arrogant Manifesto for a New Generation. "We felt . . . that an entirely new culture was taking hold in America, but nobody had tried to define or codify it. We did," Newman wrote in 2000. "What we were talking about was what is now known as 'the Sixties.' But as we were in the midst of living through them at the time, we didn't have a chronological name for what was happening."[9]

"The New Sentimentality" would inform every scene in the duo's script for *Bonnie and Clyde*. The story "is about style and people who have style," Newman continued, "people whose style set them apart from their time and place so they seemed aberrant to the general run of society."[10] Benton and Newman themselves were insatiable consumers of the "aberrant" (for Hollywood) cinema culture then electrifying New York's art house cinemas. "The talk was of Truffaut, Godard . . . Bergman, Kurosawa, Antonioni, Fellini and all the other names that fell like a litany,"[11] Benton wrote. A couple of lifelong movie aficionados, Benton and Newman occupied most of their office time at *Esquire* talking films. "As long as [the managing editor] saw us in conference, he assumed we were doing our job,"[12] Benton joked.

Very quickly, the duo landed on the story of "two Texas desperadoes named Bonnie Parker and Clyde Barrow."[13] Inspiration came in the form of John Toland's recently published *The Dillinger Days* (1963), one of the first comprehensive accounts of the crime wave that swept Middle America during the Depression. In decades of subsequent interviews, both Newman and Benton referred to a "footnote" in the book that described the Barrow Gang as "not only outlaws, but outcasts"—making them perfect exemplars of "The New Sentimentality." Clyde and Bonnie actually play prominent supporting roles to Dillinger in the book, as do "Pretty Boy" Floyd, the Barker family, Machine Gun Kelly, and "Baby Face" Nelson. The line that inspired Benton and Newman occurs early in the main text, with a rather different emphasis: the Barrow outfit's inability as outsiders to profit from political or legal connections, "unlike the better-organized gangs."[14]

The Dillinger Days leaves something to be desired as source material. Rightly acclaimed for his Pulitzer Prize–winning accounts of World War II Germany and Japan, Toland's Dust Bowl underworld epic suffers from sloppy scholarship. The Dillinger material is rich in incident, but the author appears to have done no original research whatsoever on Clyde and Bonnie, relying instead on the lurid *True Detective* accounts that flourished after their deaths, at times even adopting the breathless style of pulp magazines. In Toland's telling, Clyde harbored "homosexual tendencies," helped to "satisfy Bonnie's sexual aberrations," and "enjoyed sharing her pleasures."[15] (New Wave ménage à trois, anyone?) Not that any of this mattered to the fledgling screenwriters. The historical Clyde and Bonnie were beside the point. What fascinated them as trendsetters was the notion of "'instant celebrities,' people who became famous by doing nothing except being famous."[16]

As Newman recalled, this was the era when "Andy Warhol was giving parties at The Factory . . . the whole fifteen minutes of fame bit." His and Benton's take on Clyde and Bonnie "was that they wanted to be celebrities.

They saw in each other the mirror of their own ambitions . . . someone who validated an image of what they could be."[17]

In a preface to their treatment, Benton and Newman explained, "This is a movie about two people, lovers, movers and operators." If the pair were "here today, they would be hip. Their values have become assimilated into much of our culture." Not the robbing and killing part, of course, but "their style, their sexuality, their bravado . . . their delicacy, their cultivated arrogance, their narcissistic insecurity." What made them beautiful "is that they didn't know it. They knew they had something to say, but they went about it in a way which inevitably brought doom. But even in the light of their brief lives, we can see they were not squares. Al Capone, he was a square. Clyde Barrow, no."[18]

For Newman and Benton, *Bonnie and Clyde* was "a movie about criminals only incidentally. . . . They are not crooks. They are people, and this film is, in many ways, about what's going on *now*."[19]

The "New Sentimentality" had always been, in Benton's words, "a set of ideas in search of a movie."[20] Now, he and Newman believed they had found that movie. Only one problem: they had "no knowledge at all of the movie business,"[21] or how to write a script. But they knew someone who did—or, at least, who talked a good game: their friend Peter Bogdanovich, then a twenty-five-year-old critic curating a six-month Alfred Hitchcock retrospective at the Museum of Modern Art. Bogdanovich provided a crash course in the art of filmmaking courtesy of the Master. "It was an education in pure cinema," recalled Benton. "There wasn't a day spent in the writing that didn't include at least one discussion of what [Hitchcock] would have done."[22]

Not only Hitchcock: Truffaut's *Shoot the Piano Player* (*Tirez sur le pianiste*, 1960) provided inspiration with its "wonderful combination of comedy and bleakness, gangsterism and humanity."[23] Working sometimes in the office, but mainly at night, with Lester Flatt & Earl Scruggs and the Foggy Mountain Boys' rendition of "Foggy Mountain Breakdown" playing full blast on Benton's high-fidelity stereo, he and Newman generated not a screenplay, but a seventy-five-page treatment: essentially a full shooting script minus the dialogue that included precise cuts, dissolves, camera setups, and music cues (including, naturally, "Foggy Mountain Breakdown").

Considering the changes eventually wrought in the material as it worked its way through development and into production, what remains admirable about *Bonnie and Clyde* from a script standpoint is how much the movie adheres to the vision Newman and Benton (as they were finally credited) first laid down. The writers recognized the art in this form of storytelling relies on exclusion, not inclusion. "We had decided early on that . . . certain figures of considerable historical importance in the true history had to be eliminated, certain adventures altered or dropped, certain facts ignored and certain legends adhered to,"[24] Benton said. Most controversially, Newman and Benton composited the Barrow Gang's many sidekicks into a single character, C. W. Moss, originally conceived as a muscular lunkhead turned on as much by the promise of bisexual hijinks as he is by the endorphin high of robbery and murder. In the script, he's a "1931 version of a rock 'n' roll hood: blond, surly and not very bright."[25]

As originally conceived, both the beginning and ending of the film were meant to consist of actual still photographs of Clyde and Bonnie—first as young people in their prime, then as victims of the ambush. Dispensing with backstory, the main action pairs them when a half-naked Bonnie catches Clyde attempting to hot-wire her mother's car. "Before they speak, they have become co-conspirators,"[26] reads the script, which meticulously details Bonnie's feelings of social imprisonment and Clyde's reckless abandon. Firearms and sex go hand in hand. When Clyde first shows off his .45-caliber revolver, Bonnie "touches it in a manner almost sexual, full of repressed excitement"[27]; later, the couple has unconsummated sex on a bed full of guns.

Bonded by an impromptu grocery store robbery, the two outcasts embark on a comical crime spree, soon joined by Clyde's brother Buck ("a chubby, jovial, simple, big-hearted man") and his wife Blanche ("a young hausfrau, no more and no less, inclined to panic").[28] It's all "Mack Sennett stuff,"[29] the script dictates at one point; "almost in the style of a cartoon,"[30] at another. Just good fun—until it isn't. After a successful small-town bank robbery, a "dignified, white-haired, celluloid-collared man, obviously a bank official,"[31] leaps onto the running board of the gang's car. Clyde fires through the window. In a stage direction that would forever change the course of American filmmaking, Newman and Benton wrote:

Close-up (special effects).

The face of the man explodes in blood. Then he drops out of sight.[32]

It's all downhill for the protagonists from here, in the best tradition of the Warner Bros. pre-Code James Cagney/Edward G. Robinson gangster films Newman and Benton meant both to salute and subvert. Enjoying a brief respite from pursuit in Joplin, Missouri, Clyde and Bonnie make use of Blanche's camera to stage portraits of themselves that will become media sensations. The idyll ends in a shootout with local authorities, one of the three major gun battles the script describes in meticulous detail. The Joplin confrontation puts lawman Frank Bryce on their trail. "Tall, strong, contemptuous of almost everyone and particularly women and criminals," Bryce possesses "some hidden evil" that "sometimes shows in his face"[33]—especially after the gang apprehends and humiliates him with compromising snapshots.

Events hurtle to their inexorable conclusion. Run to ground at a tourist motel in Platte City, Iowa, the gang's attempt to shoot its way to freedom results in Buck's being shot in the head and Blanche blinded by flying glass (all historical). A sense of approaching death falls over the story and characters, culminating in Clyde and Bonnie's betrayal by C. W. Moss and their ambush in the Bienville Parish woods. "We never see BONNIE and CLYDE dead," the script specifies, "though for a moment we discern their bodies slumped in the car."[34] The story ends instead on the faces of the lawmen, "horror and shock at what they have just done.... Slowly, slowly the men begin to edge closer to the car to see the result."[35]

From time to time, Benton and Newman's geeky cinematic preoccupations appear in the treatment and the 157-page first-draft script. Setting the scene for a shootout, they write, "that by this light [the gang] looks like a troupe of traveling players, living out of their caravan, pursued by death. A certain *Seventh Seal* quality for just the first moment."[36] Pushing the Ingmar Bergman reference even further, a reunion scene with Bonnie's family is meant to have "the visual quality of the image [at] the end of *Wild Strawberries*—a magic, isolated landscape seen from a distance, lit by a bright sun."[37] In his personal copy of the first-draft script for *Bonnie and Clyde*, producer/star Warren Beatty drew a large question mark on the margins of this passage—as in, "What the fuck does that mean?"

To their credit, the writers understood the difference between a shooting script and a "reading" script designed to attract investors. They also had a keen sense of their audience among New York City's independent cinema elite and benefited from their *Esquire* pedigree. Producer Elinor Wright Jones, whose husband Tom Jones (not the Welsh singer) coauthored the long-running Broadway hit *The Fantasticks* and knew Benton from his University of Texas days, optioned the treatment for $1,700 based on a reading in Benton's apartment. All shared a love of the French New Wave and a particular affection for François Truffaut. How great, they thought, if Truffaut himself could be persuaded to direct.

Be careful, the saying goes. *You may get what you wish for.*

Jones slipped a copy of the treatment to her friend Helen Scott, director of New York City's French Film Office, who had just collaborated with Truffaut as translator on a series of interviews with Alfred Hitchcock later enshrined as *Hitchcock/Truffaut*, the book that transformed the consummate Hollywood craftsman into an auteur. "At first I thought [the story] was too American for you," Scott wrote Truffaut in an enthusiastic cover letter, "but there are a thousand nuances that make it something special."[38] Truffaut apparently agreed, once he had the script translated into French. Though he spoke little English, the director was nonetheless seeking a property to make his English-language debut.[39] Scarcely a month after receiving Scott's introduction, Truffaut arrived at the Hotel Drake in Manhattan with a translated copy of the treatment, "a document that may not seem important to the rest of the world," Benton later admitted, "but convinced us at first look that we would stay in movies for the rest of our lives."[40]

Over the course of the next three days, the former *Cahiers du cinema* critic provided the screenwriters with their second and more influential crash course in movie storytelling. Truffaut found "the issue of historical accuracy even less compelling than Benton and Newman did."[41] The director had broken the treatment up into what he called "unities," blocks of sequences "that stood as emotional and dramatic entities." Most importantly, Truffaut "demonstrated to us the difference between 'real time' and 'film time,' pointing out where we had goofed somewhat in sacrificing the emotional curves of the film for factual or actual purposes."[42] Always the consummate humanist, Truffaut recognized themes in the treatment unremarked by Benton and Newman. "Bonnie and Clyde were most vulnerable when they were most ordinarily human," Truffaut told them. "When engaged in bank robbing and the like, they handled situations fairly well. . . . But when they chose to settle down and behave like regular folks . . . *then* the laws would find them and blast them back onto the run."[43] Truffaut urged the writers to play up the story's intertwining of sex and violence, and offered concrete structural suggestions that found their way unchanged into the finished film—notably the intercutting between the outlaws and lawman Frank Bryce (eventually to become Frank Hamer) as Bonnie reads her lovers' ballad to Clyde in a third-act moment of emotional and sexual release.

Dazzled by Truffaut's engagement, Benton and Newman took a leave of absence from *Esquire* and spent their newly earned option money on a trip to Texas to "really get into it." Their purpose was threefold: to scout potential locations; find firsthand accounts of the real outlaws, and "hear as many Texas accents as possible." Benton found the trip "a delight."[44] They met a woman Clyde had thrown rocks at in third grade. They "spent a memorable afternoon with two old ladies in Waxahachie" who told them a joke about a man who put whiskey in his sick mother's milk that emerged word-for-word into the finished script. They paid homage at Clyde's and Bonnie's graves, the latter "in a well-kept cemetery near Love Field where the manager told us that people came all the time."[45] Everywhere they went, they dispatched postcards to Truffaut.

The director had proved instrumental in the evolution of the *Bonnie and Clyde* script. Like most directors, however, he also proved capricious, juggling multiple projects and awaiting the best offer. By August 1964, a first-draft screenplay was on its way to Truffaut. A month later, producer Jones received what ranks as one of the all-time-great rejection letters. "I want you to know that, of all the scripts I have turned down in the last five years," Truffaut wrote, "*Bonnie and Clyde* is the best." He hoped that Jones would understand his reasons, "and that David Newman and Robert Benton will understand them."[46] *Fahrenheit 451*, an adaptation of Ray Bradbury's novel scripted by none other than François Truffaut, would mark the director's one and only English-language venture, not *Bonnie and Clyde*.

Not to worry, the director assured the devastated producer and writers. He had a backup in mind: his iconoclastic pal Jean-Luc Godard.

That didn't work out so well, either.

Godard professed liking the script and was willing to make it. "Three weeks from now," in Benton's recollection. In New Jersey, in January, on a four-week shooting schedule. That the story was set in Texas, in summer, was irrelevant. "We can make the film anywhere," Godard insisted in a meeting with the writers and producer Jones. "We can make it in Tokyo."[47] Attempts to reason with Godard fell on deaf ears. "I'm talking cinema and you're talking meteorology,"[48] Godard exclaimed, promptly bolting the room. In the intervening decades, Benton and Jones would blame themselves for the meeting's unfortunate turn, but in retrospect the conversation says much more about Godard's lackadaisical, even dismissive, attitude toward his chosen profession; his best film, a movie about filmmaking released just before this encounter, is tellingly titled *Contempt* (*Le mepris*, 1963).

A last-minute conference with the writers the next day proved no more successful. "Call me when the script reverts to your ownership,"[49] Godard told Benton and Newman, moments before boarding a flight back to Paris for preproduction on the science-fiction/film noir pastiche *Alphaville* (1965). "At this point," Benton wrote, "an emotion that can only be described as acute despair set in."[50] The subsequent months "dragged on, with flickers of interest from sources uninteresting to us, rejections from people we never thought would say yes in the first place."[51] Mostly, they said no with a vengeance. Producer Jones left one meeting at United Artists with the feeling that "[we'd] spit on the flag." Remarked one scandalized executive, "I mean, you've got naked women and homosexuals and violence—are you out of your minds?"[52]

At this nadir, Benton remembered the script "went into a drawer . . . literally nobody wanted to do it. David and I would laugh and tell each other that we'd be eighty years old, out on the street, and still peddling *Bonnie and Clyde*."[53] It wouldn't take quite that long—less than two years, in fact. When the right moment came, the script hadn't changed.

America had.

4

"THE BLOODY MASSACRE"

> The essential American soul is hard, isolate, stoic and a killer. It has never yet melted.
>
> —D. H. Lawrence

For a nation founded on the rule of law, the United States of America has over its relatively brief history evinced an alarming propensity for violence.

"We like to think of ourselves as a peaceful, tolerant, benign people who have always lived under a government of laws, not men," former John F. Kennedy presidential adviser Arthur Schlesinger Jr. wrote in a 1968 essay titled "Violence as an American Way of Life." "Yet this is by no means the only strain in our tradition. For we have also been a violent people. When we refuse to acknowledge this other strain, we refuse to see our nation as it is."[1] To back up his judgment, Schlesinger cited Federal Bureau of Investigation statistics reporting a 16-percent increase in violent crime from 1966 to 1967, along with a doubling in arrests for possession of "dangerous weapons" in the first six months of 1968 alone—this not counting the riots in Washington, DC, Newark, Cleveland, Detroit, and Los Angeles that swept across America in the years spanning *Bonnie and Clyde*'s production and release. In the Newark riots alone, twelve thousand bullets resulted in twenty-six casualties, seven hundred injuries, and fifteen hundred arrests.[2]

According to the FBI, gun assaults skyrocketed 77 percent in the four years from 1964 through 1967, while Department of Justice estimates put

4,585,000 firearms in the hands of 42.5 million Americans, more than a fifth of the total population.[3] "We cannot blame the epidemic of murder exclusively on deranged and solitary individuals who are separate from the rest of us," Schlesinger concluded, referencing among others Charles Whitman, whose Austin rampage directly preceded the movie's production. "We must recognize that the destructive impulse is in us and that it springs from some dark intolerable tension in our history and institutions."[4]

As Arthur Penn put it years later, "You have to search high and low for a period of American history that *wasn't* violent."[5]

"This American land . . . has always been particularly fertile ground for violence," Senator Chris Murphy (D-Connecticut) writes in *The Violence Inside Us*. "A predilection for violence exists inside every human, but America's practice of violence is unique. It is definitional. And it is persistent."[6] The perspective isn't the exclusive domain of liberal lawmakers. "More than any other nation in history, the United States has been shaped by the gun," echoes Chris Kyle in *American Gun*. (Kyle's exploits as a decorated US Navy SEAL sniper in Operation Iraqi Freedom were dramatized in Clint Eastwood's 2014 film *American Sniper*, the most successful war film in history, with a worldwide gross of over $500 million.) "Colonists used firearms to secure their land, then turned them on the King and his men to win their war on independence. Cowboys and plain folk used revolvers and rifles to survive in the West."[7]

Cultural historian Richard Slotkin characterized our national history as one of "regeneration through violence" in his three-volume, seventeen-hundred-page rendering of the American frontier experience and its transformation into legend. Slotkin quoted verbatim the 1886 program for William "Buffalo Bill" Cody's Wild West, which hailed the bullet as "the pioneer of [American] civilization, for it has gone hand-in-hand with the axe that clears the forest, and with the family Bible and schoolbook." Cody's triumphalist text went even further in its celebration of the firearm. "Deadly as has been its mission in one sense, it has been merciful in another," the program declared. "Without the rifle ball we of America would not be today in the possession of a free and united country, and mighty in our strength." For Slotkin and other late twentieth-century observers of the American cultural scene, what is distinctively American about this history of violence is not its kind or level of intensity, but "the mythic significance we have assigned [to it]."[8]

Small wonder, then, that colonial America's first acknowledged work of art is a firearm.

The Metropolitan Museum of Art's American Wing accords pride of place in its lofty atrium entrance to a display of exquisitely crafted, custom-made rifles and pistols dating from the late seventeenth to the twentieth centuries. A placard dedicated to "The Artistry of the American Longrifle" notes that the muzzle-loading weapon, developed in southeastern Pennsylvania by immigrant German gunsmiths, constitutes "the first distinctly American art form created by European settlers in North America." Beyond its elaborate workmanship in finely tooled wood and steel, the long rifle also represented a significant technical advance over Old World musketry. Special grooving in the bore of the barrel (known as "rifling") caused a projectile to spin on its axis, increasing stability and enabling accuracy at a range of over two hundred yards, more than double that of a smoothbore musket. A necessity for hunting and self-defense in the contested wilderness areas that constituted much of the early colonial landscape, "Pennsylvania" or "Kentucky" rifles became an indispensable part of American identity.

"Before its founding the United States was a land where individuals owned and used guns, which became badges of civic responsibility and manhood, summoned in defense of self and community,"[9] journalist and historian John Bainbridge Jr. observes at the outset of *Gun Barons*, his chronicle of the legendary industrialists—among them Samuel Colt, Oliver Winchester, and Eliphalet Remington—who transformed the individual craft of weapon-making into an impersonal assembly line. The gunmakers themselves recognized and exploited this fundamental American truth. "The good people of this world are very far from being satisfied with each other,"

Colt lamented, "and my arms are the best peacemakers."[10] Long before the dawn of the Western genre that would enshrine and fetishize Colt's arms, the personification of an American as "a man with a gun" found glorification in the colonial era.

An estimated 60 percent of early eighteenth-century American households possessed a firearm; rates in southern colonies were markedly higher, rising to 81 percent of slave-holding estates.[11] George Washington personally owned fifty guns. Thomas Jefferson, fascinated by their mechanical properties, recommended them to his fifteen-year-old nephew as a means of self-improvement. "While [the gun] gives a moderate exercise to the body, it gives boldness, enterprise and independence to the mind," he wrote in a letter. "Let your gun therefore be the constant companion on your walks. Never think of taking a book with you."[12]

The most lasting visual representation of the events leading up to the American Revolution commemorates—even glorifies—violence.

On March 5, 1770, a Boston mob bent on provocation harassed a lone British sentry outside the city's custom house. The Sons of Liberty under the direction of Samuel Adams had artfully manipulated emotions, already running high after the forced quartering of British troops. British captain Thomas Preston rushed to the sentry's defense with seven grenadiers, bayonets fixed and muskets primed. After a series of circumstances never satisfactorily explained, Preston's soldiers fired into the mob; five men fell dead. Thanks to efficient lawyering by struggling local attorney John Adams (Samuel's cousin), Preston and his men escaped a murder charge.

Whatever the verdict, a widely circulated broadside headlined "THE BLOODY MASSACRE" proved more persuasive in setting public opinion. Engraver Paul Revere freely plagiarized an existing composition to propagate an alternative reality: British redcoats standing outside "Butcher's Hall" gleefully fire into a crowd of well-dressed gentlemen as a lone woman in widow's black looks on in horror. Revere revels in the gory slow-motion details: one man lies with half his head shot off (specially hand-tinted copies emphasized the red); another bleeds out on the cobblestones while two men carry a third dribbling blood from his groin. Nearly two centuries later, in the script for John Ford's *The Man Who Shot Liberty Valance* (1962), this sort of propagandistic historical appropriation would become known as "printing the legend"; a visual through line runs from Revere's engraving to barroom representations of Custer's Last Stand, the Gunfight at the O.K. Corral, the Death of Billy the Kid—and to the "ballets of death" that conclude both *Bonnie and Clyde* and Sam Peckinpah's *The Wild Bunch* (1969).

"This country is born out of rebellion, and there's an emphasis on individualism. All that is compounded by the frontier movement," says Paul Andrew Hutton, whose historical inquiries have encompassed Custer, Wyatt Earp, and Billy the Kid alike. "The kind of people who are moving west are essentially outliers, otherwise they wouldn't be going."[13]

Throughout the half century of westward expansion between the Louisiana Purchase and the Civil War, European travelers to America invariably commented on the prevalence of firearms. On a research trip that formed the basis for his classic study *Democracy in America* (1835), French aristocrat Alexis de Tocqueville expressed astonishment at the presence of multiple weapons in nearly every household he encountered. A decade later, during a nationwide American speaking tour, Charles Dickens compiled pages of newspaper accounts of gun murders, which he published unedited in his first nonfiction book, *American Notes for General Circulation* (1842). (The author found the local habit of public tobacco spitting only slightly less reprehensible than gun violence.)

American travelers in their own country made similar observations. "There are probably in Texas about as many revolvers as male adults,"[14] worried thirty-year-old Fredrick Law Olmstead, not yet a famed Yankee architect, but a roving correspondent in the pre-secessionist South for the *New York Daily Times*. Taking no chances, the undercover reporter fortified himself with a Sharps carbine, capable "in sure hands"[15] of firing eighteen times a minute with a range over a thousand yards. A century and a half later, travel writer Tony Horwitz, who retraced Olmstead's journey, found the situation in Texas unchanged.

In the wake of the Civil War—a fraternal genocide that claimed the lives of nearly 10 percent of the adult white male population of the United States and those of over an estimated million slaves—the already well-armed frontier experienced an exponential increase not only in the number of available firearms but also in the men who knew how to use them, as alienated veterans sought new opportunities. "The Civil War breeds a whole generation of alienated killers," says historian Hutton. "Men who have killed, who are accustomed to it and have an exaggerated sense of honor."[16]

"Before the war," writes Bryan Burrough in *The Gunfighters: How Texas Made the West Wild*, "[guns] had been seen as utilitarian, used mostly to kill varmints. Afterward, when the freeing of enslaved Blacks caused white Southerners to fear for their safety, they were increasingly viewed as items of self-defense and intimidation." More than that: "Some suggest gun use allowed defeated Southerners to reclaim a measure of their own wounded masculinity."[17] For Civil War historian Christopher Matthew Culbert, "The West" functions as a kind of dumping ground where "bloodthirsty Confederates" are "commemoratively excommunicated" to a place where they can be "reincorporated (and 'made safe') via a process that moves them west and buries them there—allowing them to become larger-than-life legends of American machismo."[18]

Legends like Jesse James. Or Clyde Barrow's idol, Billy the Kid.

Jesse James grew up in the disputed Kansas-Missouri borderlands that witnessed some of America's most savage violence in the years leading up to the Civil War. Renegade bands on both sides of the slavery question participated in a series of escalating atrocities that more than earned the region the name "Bleeding Kansas." Jesse came of age as a protégée of the infamous (and possibly unhinged) pro-slavery marauder William "Bloody Bill" Anderson. His older brother Frank had ridden with Anderson and Confederate guerrilla leader William Quantrill in an August 1863 attack on the Unionist town of Lawrence, Kansas, resulting in the wanton butchery of 150 unarmed men and boys; some sources place a barely sixteen-year-old Jesse among the raiders. Young Jesse participated enthusiastically in what came to be known as the Centralia Massacre the following September, when Anderson's forces ambushed a train carrying twenty-four Union soldiers on leave from the war. Forcing the unarmed men to strip naked, the bushwhackers took their sergeant hostage, then shot the others at close range and mutilated the bodies.

"[These bushwhackers] came out of the woods on the jump, riding like Comanches," *True West* publisher Bob Boze Bell says of these raids. "They carried between two to eight pistols, and they'd ride with the reins in their teeth, firing twelve shots, then grabbing two more pistols. They were killing machines—and I mean that literally." Teenage killing machines, "children, really," says Bell. "When they were done killing everybody, they cut off heads and put them on other bodies and laughed about it. They took scalps and attached them to their bridles."[19] ("If Jesse James lived in the 21st century, he would be regarded as a terrorist," adds historian Samuel Kilborn Dolan. "There's no way around that."[20]) Outgunned by the pistol-wielding rebels, the 39th Missouri Infantry Regiment sent in retribution for Centralia suffered near-total devastation, losing 123 of its 147-man force to Anderson's 80 guerrillas. Frank James claimed Jesse fired the shot that dispatched the Union commander, US Army Major Andrew Johnston.

None of this savagery mattered to Missouri journalist and ex-Confederate veteran John Newman Edwards, who set the pattern for the Jesse James legend in *Noted Guerrillas*, published in 1879. Writing at the end of the Reconstruction era, Edwards reframed James's subsequent train-and-bank-robbery exploits as the so-called "Lost Cause" fought by other means. Slavery never factors into Newman's revisionist account of Confederate veterans seeking regeneration and redemption on a new frontier. "What else could Jesse James have done?" Edwards asked in his hagiographic history, which frames the bushwhacker's post–Civil War life as "one eternal ambush . . . one unbroken and eternal hunt."[21]

In terms Clyde Barrow could appreciate, Edwards lauded Jesse and his cohorts as "outlaws . . . but not criminals, no matter what prejudiced public opinion may declare or malignant partisan dislike make noisy with retaliation."[22] Edwards established the relationship between an outlaw and his gun that became a defining characteristic. Before a battle, he wrote, "a guerrilla takes every portion of his revolver apart and lays it on a white shirt . . . as carefully as a surgeon places his instruments on a white towel. In addition, he touches every piece as a man might touch the thing that he loves."[23]

What John Newman Edwards did for Jesse James, Walter Noble Burns did for Billy the Kid, a.k.a. William Bonney, a.k.a. William Antrim, a.k.a. Henry McCarty, second son of an Irish immigrant mother, born in New York City but uprooted to southern New Mexico Territory at a time of gangland warfare in Lincoln County, where rival factions competed for control of the beef and mercantile trade. Bushwhackers had become "regulators," employed by rival monopolies to eliminate troublesome interlopers. In Burns's telling of the story, the killing of Billy's patron and surrogate father figure, independent rancher John Tunstall, sets the young outlaw on a trail of revenge against corporate forces led by cattleman John Chisum. When vigilante war breaks out, President Rutherford B. Hayes appoints former Union general and future *Ben-Hur* author Lew Wallace as territorial governor, with a mandate to end the range war and bring Billy the Kid to heel. Wallace in turn appoints onetime buffalo hunter, bartender, and cowboy Pat Garrett as Lincoln County sheriff.

The yearlong pursuit ends outside a northeastern New Mexico ranch house, where Garrett puts a bullet through the heart of the unarmed twenty-one-year-old renegade, ending the career of "a genius [who painted] his name in flaming colors with a six shooter across the sky of the Southwest."[24] That, at least, is the version of the story Clyde Barrow devoured—so much so that a copy of Burns's book lay in the back seat of his stolen Ford V-8 when another state-appointed lawman carried out his executive orders. Doubtless Clyde saw himself reflected in Burns's portrait of Billy as a young man with an "air of easy, unstudied, devil-may-care insouciance," someone "who dressed neatly and took not a little care in making himself personable."[25] Even those who hated Billy, Burns wrote, "admitted his absolute fearlessness.... Nothing excited him. He had nerve but no nerves."[26] For William Bonney as well as Clyde Barrow, "every hour in his desperate life was the zero hour, and he was never afraid to die."[27]

Burns subtitled his account *The Thrilling Life of America's Original Outlaw*. "[Billy the Kid] is the perfect teenage rebel: he distrusts all authority," says Paul Andrew Hutton. "Because all the authority is sweltering in corruption, he fights against it. And he keeps fighting when everyone gives up. The Lincoln County War finally ends, but he keeps going. He won't stop." More than the Jesse James popularized by John Newman Edwards, Billy the Kid "is the perfect Robin Hood character," says Hutton. "He's fighting against The Machine that's coming into The Garden to destroy everything. It's one of the appeals of Jesse James, too: he's robbing trains, he's robbing insurance companies, and he's robbing banks. It's all the forces that in the Gilded Age are destroying the old agrarian perfection."[28]

Embodied by the apocryphal folkloric hero Robin of Locksley and his historical eighteenth-century Scottish counterpart Rob Roy MacGregor, the "social bandit" famously robs from the rich to give to the poor. He is "what all peasant bandits should be, but in the nature of things, few of them have the idealism, the unselfishness or the social consciousness to live up to their role, and perhaps even fewer can afford to," observed British social historian Eric Hobsbawm in his groundbreaking study, *Bandits*, originally published in 1969. (Outlawry scholarship likely owes its existence to the 1967 release of *Bonnie and Clyde*.) Hobsbawm characterized the "noble robber" as "the righter of wrongs, the bringer of social justice and equity. His relationship with the peasants is that of total solidarity and identity."[29]

In a trajectory typical not only of Jesse James and Billy the Kid but also Newman and Benton's Clyde Barrow, the social bandit "begins his career as a victim of injustice... rights wrongs... takes from the rich to give to the poor...

never kills except in self-defense or just revenge . . . [and] is admired, helped and supported by his community." Perceived as invulnerable, he "becomes the target of oppressors" and "dies by treason."[30] Hobsbawm saw Clyde Barrow and Bonnie Parker as historical throwbacks, "heirs of Jesse James . . . not typical criminals of the 1930s. . . . The nearest the really modern strong-arm man gets to the rural life," Hobsbawm wryly observed of the Barrow Gang's contemporaries, "is a barbecue on a country estate gained by urban crime."[31]

Clyde Barrow and Bonnie Parker weren't just hoodlums or outcasts. They were frontier outlaws in the best American tradition.

5

"ANYTHING GOES"

> The moral importance of entertainment is something
> which has been universally recognized
> —Motion Picture Production Code of 1930

It's one of the least-known aspects of *Bonnie and Clyde* that everyone initially saw the film as a low-budget Western in 1930s dress.

Never one for decisiveness as an actor or producer, Warren Beatty hesitated to purchase the script because "it was too much like a western, and westerns weren't fashionable at the time,"[1] according to his then-lover Leslie Caron. Screenwriters Robert Benton and David Newman acknowledged the similarities outright in the cover letter they drafted to François Truffaut with their original treatment. "In the early 1930s America saw (and enjoyed) a revival of crime and criminal style that it had last seen in the wild west: the time of the desperado," they enthused. "In many ways, their origins were similar. All had their heyday in the Midwest and Southwest, areas hit hard by the times. They came not from criminal societies, but from poor backgrounds.... [T]hey ran from place-to-place executing daring robberies, knocking over banks, stores, gas stations, living from day to day, killing at random. And they killed often."[2]

It didn't help that the country was awash in readily available firearms. The misguided social experiment known as the Eighteenth Amendment to the US Constitution (ratified in January 1919 and not repealed until December 1933), which outlawed the manufacture, transport, and sale of intoxicating liquors, inaugurated a Prohibition era epitomized by the widespread use of the Thompson submachine gun. Colloquially known as the "Tommy gun," "the chopper," "the Chicago typewriter" and "the annihilator," the weapon was invented by US Army ordinance officer John Taliaferro Thompson to clear trenches in World War I—hence its other nickname, "the trench broom."

The Thompson arrived too late for its appointed purpose but found a ready market in the Roaring Twenties and the Great Depression. Manufactured by Colt and capable of firing one thousand .45-caliber rounds per minute, the gun retailed for $175 ($2,000 today) and could be purchased in sporting goods stores or via mail order; Chicago mobster Al Capone demonstrated the Tommy's efficiency with spectacularly gory results in the St. Valentine's Day Massacre of February 1929. Testifying before Congress almost a decade later, Colt's vice president maintained that "[our broker] was a bit careless in their methods of merchandising."[3]

Thirty-six-year-old J. Edgar Hoover, the nation's top cop as director of the Bureau of Investigation (not yet the FBI), found his agency overwhelmed, not just by the nationwide crime spree but also by public sentiment. "People no longer respect respectability," Hoover told *The National Police Officer* in July 1931. "Our problem today is whether the forces of government or outlawry must dominate. You must be either with or against the government. There is no middle ground. . . . Citizens of this country must become enemies of crime."[4]

Hoover had been particularly unsettled by the many gangster films then flooding American movie screens. In the first six months of 1931 alone, Edward G. Robinson had incarnated Capone as *Little Caesar* and James Cagney had played *The Public Enemy* in a film that continues to shock for its unrelenting violence. Cagney's character, the ruthless Irish hood Tom Powers, is cut to pieces in a climactic shootout and collapses into a gutter, gasping, "I ain't so tough"; his trussed-up corpse arrives upright on the doorstep of his mother's house, where it collapses face-first on to the floor as a Victrola plays a scratchy recording of "I'm Forever Blowing Bubbles."

A year later, Howard Hawks's *Scarface*, written by the prolific Ben Hecht, produced by Howard Hughes and starring Paul Muni as yet another Capone composite, Tony Camonte, outdid both of its predecessors in stirring outrage. Anticipating by a generation the initial critical barrage against *Bonnie and Clyde*, Hollywood trade papers shot down Hawks's film for its bold juxtaposition of violence and comedy (to say nothing of the implied incestuous love affair between Camonte and his sister). "It should never have been made,"[5] declared a front-page editorial in *Film Daily*. Audiences responded in sizable numbers, further enticed by Hughes's canny promotion. Retitling the film *Scarface: The Shame of a Nation*, the producer added an exculpatory written preface, stating, "The purpose of this picture is to demand of the government, 'What are you going to do about it?' The government is your government. What are YOU going to do about it?'"

The gangster films of the early 1930s—a particular specialty of Warner Bros., which found the genre ideally suited to its stripped-down, fast-paced house style—were the most provocative manifestations of the trend toward sensationalistic storytelling that prevailed in the years during which the movie industry made the costly transition from silent films into "all-talking pictures." To circumvent local and state censorship following a series of sex and drug scandals in the mid-1920s (one of which unjustly ended the career of Roscoe "Fatty" Arbuckle, then a bigger box office draw than Charlie Chaplin), Hollywood studios closed ranks to develop a Production Code designed to appease the nation's moral guardians. A list of dos and don'ts codified in June 1927 proscribed a host of forbidden behaviors, from "pointed profanity" (lip readers beware) to "illegal traffic in drugs," "sex perversion," "miscegenation," "ridicule of the clergy," "men and women in bed together," and "excessive or lustful kissing." Also included were "the use of firearms" and "sympathy for criminals."

A later 1929 iteration, drafted by *Motion Picture Herald* editor Martin Quigley, a Catholic layman, and Jesuit priest Daniel A. Lord, further restricted acceptable screen content. "No picture should lower the standards of those who see it," the soon-to-be-enshrined Code announced. "This is done: (a)

When evil is made to appear *attractive*, and good is made to appear *unattractive*; [and] (b) When the *sympathy* of the audience is thrown on the side of crime, wrong-doing, evil, sin."[6] Quigley and Lord insisted on a system of what they called "compensating moral values." Virtue was to be rewarded, sin punished. "In the end," read the Code's working principles, "the audience [must] feel that *evil is wrong* and *good is right*."[7] As one latter-day observer memorably phrased it, the Production Code amounted to "a Jewish-owned business selling Catholic ideology to a Protestant America."[8]

For nearly four and a half glorious years from the full-time adoption of sound in 1929 until July 1934, the studios broke these yet-to-be implemented rules with lustful abandon in their desperate attempt to lure Depression-era audiences back into their theaters. The films made in that brief open window before threats of government regulation forced the industry to impose the Code's draconian restrictions (hence the term, "pre-Code") represent one of the only times in which motion picture artists in America felt unfettered in their storytelling—an era not to be matched until the late 1960s, under very similar circumstances, when *Bonnie and Clyde* inaugurated an equally brief period of personal cinematic expression. "In language and image, implicit meanings and explicit descriptions, elliptical allusions and unmistakable references, pre-Code Hollywood cinema points to a road not taken," wrote Thomas Doherty in his definitive history of the era, *Pre-Code Hollywood: Sex, Immorality and Insurrection in American Cinema*.[9]

Literally anything was possible in pre-Code movies. Frank Capra's lavish melodrama *The Bitter Tea of General Yen* (1933) casts Barbara Stanwyck as Megan Davis, a missionary in war-torn Shanghai—dialogue describes her as the daughter of "one of the finest old families in Puritan New England"—who finds herself irresistibly drawn to a Chinese warlord (played by Danish actor Nils Asther in yellowface). "Don't forget, this is a white woman," an old Asia hand at one point warns General Yen. "That's all right," he replies. "I have no prejudice against color." "We're all one flesh and blood," Megan preaches to Yen at the outset of their destined-to-be-unrequited romance. "Do you really mean that?" the general challenges. Megan proves her fidelity to her beliefs—and to General Yen—by taking on the robes and makeup of a Chinese courtesan.

Transvestism in pre-Code cinema is no more a taboo than interracial romance. In *Blonde Venus* (1932), Marlene Dietrich wears both black tie and tails *and* a gorilla suit. Screenwriters and directors excelled in devising narratively organic ways for their stars of both sexes to strip down to the essentials. Dolores del Rio's island girl ogles a nearly naked Joel McCrea as he shimmies up a palm tree in the South Seas romance *Bird of Paradise* (1932); moments later, the couple share an outrageously suggestive drink of coconut milk, white liquid spilling over their lips and across their faces. Barbara Stanwyck and Joan Blondell specialized in playing scenes dressed in lacy lingerie, exemplified by their bedtime pillow talk in *Night Nurse* (1931). Onetime drill sergeant Busby Berkeley excelled in choreographed pageants of hundreds of skimpily clad chorus girls that would make a psychiatrist blush: *42nd Street* (1932), *Gold Diggers of 1933*, and the completely berserk *Dames* (1933).

Sometimes, clothing itself was optional. Clark Gable and Jean Harlow trade wisecracks in the scorching *Red Dust* (1932) while Harlow bathes nude in a water barrel. Rising nearly waist high, her back to the camera, Harlow's brash hooker taunts Gable's sweaty rubber plantation owner to scrub her back. "One more occurrence like this and you'll live in that shack across the river," Gable warns. "I will not! And if you think I give a f–– ," Harlow manages to blurt out before she's pushed underwater. (In a legendary outtake, Harlow stood upright in all her glory after director Victor Fleming called "Cut," gleefully announcing, "This one's for the guys in the lab!") The original version of *Tarzan and His Mate* (1934) included an underwater nude scene, with Olympic swimming champion Josephine McKim body-doubling for costar Maureen O'Sullivan. Restored to prints, DVDs, and Blu-Ray copies of the film, the moment still draws audible gasps of disbelief from viewers.

Even more than sex, crime paid the biggest dividends. MGM, that most decorous and well-behaved of studios, contributed the particularly vicious *Beast of the City* (1933), in which the personal vendetta between a crusading police chief (the always stalwart Walter Huston) and a slick racketeer with a suspiciously foreign accent (the normally avuncular Jean Hersholt) turns an entire metropolis into a war zone; the climactic New Year's Eve gun battle in a crowded speakeasy leaves the entire principal cast dead or dying. At the other end of the spectrum, Ernst Lubitsch's *Trouble in Paradise* (1932), arguably the greatest romantic comedy ever made, clothes its criminals in evening dress rather than fedoras and overcoats. Down-on-their-heels but always elegant crooks Herbert Marshall and Miriam Hopkins set their sights on perfume heiress Kay Francis amid opulent Paramount sets where, as one thief says to another, "Prosperity is just around the corner."

Beyond their frank depiction of sex and violence, which was bad enough, the pre-Code films also challenged the prevailing social order, calling the traditional role of the sexes into question and casting a critical eye on the state of the nation. Warner Bros. excelled in both themes, especially with director William "Wild Bill" Wellman at the helm. Over the course of the pre-Code period, Wellman directed an astonishing two dozen films, unique in their subversive power. *Female* (1933, finished by Michael Curtiz), cast Ruth Chatterton as the head of a major automobile manufacturer; hard-as-nails with her all-male board, she relaxes privately with a seemingly endless stable of fresh studs culled from the junior staff. *Wild Boys of the Road* (1933) offered an unstinting look at the plight of teenagers driven into vagrancy by economic hardships. Shot largely on location, the film retains its potency with episodes of boxcar rape and a rail yard mishap that severs one character's leg.

Heroes for Sale (1933), by far the bleakest of Wellman's and Warner Bros.' pre-Code efforts (and that's saying something), follows the tribulations of World War I veteran Tom Holmes, played by Richard Barthelmess, whose morphine addiction costs him his job and his hometown reputation. Trying to put his life back together in Chicago, Holmes returns to prison after a get-rich-quick scheme backfires; released into the midst of mid-Depression America, he becomes a member of the great unemployed, a victim of "red"-baiting goon squads. The movie's bleak final scene finds Holmes on the march to nowhere with a hobo army. "It's the end of America," says one;

a hurriedly shot soup-kitchen coda, tacked on after the election of Franklin D. Roosevelt the prior November, does little to mitigate the despair.

Eventually, it all became too much for the newly formed Catholic Legion of Decency, which spearheaded a crusade to disinfect "the pest hole [i.e., Hollywood] that infects the entire country with its obscene and lascivious motion pictures."[10] The end came with Fox's *Baby Face*. Conceived by former Warner Bros. head of production Darryl F. Zanuck and starring Barbara Stanwyck in the best role of her pre-Code career, the movie's compact seventy-five minutes encompass incest, patricide, serial seduction, and murder; a young John Wayne features among the title character's throwaway sexual victims. The Legion urged parishioners across the country to take a pledge promising "to remain away from all motion pictures except those which do not offend decency and Christianity." Philadelphia cardinal Denis Dougherty took things a step further in June 1934, demanding an outright Catholic boycott on *all* motion pictures "under pain of sin."[11] Bloviating congressmen took up the cry, raising the specter of national censorship and possible industry regulation under the National Recovery Act.

Faced with a threat to their monopoly on production, distribution, and exhibition of their product, the studios did what today's multinational entertainment conglomerates still do best: cave to their critics. On June 13, 1934, the Motion Picture Producers and Distributors of America (MPPDA) established the Production Code Administration (PCA), known as "The Breen Office," after its first director, Joseph I. Breen. A staunch Irish Catholic personally appointed by MPPDA president Will Hays, Breen came to the top censor's job with a thoroughgoing contempt for both the motion picture industry and its overwhelmingly Jewish executives, whom he regarded as "people whose daily morals would not be tolerated in the toilet of a pest house. [They] seem to think of nothing but making money and sexual indulgence." In Hollywood, Breen wrote to a Catholic pastor, "the vilest kind of sin is a common indulgence . . . and the men and women who engage in this sort of business are the men and women who decide what the film fare of the nation is to be. . . . Ninety-five percent of these folks are Jews of an Eastern European lineage," he estimated, adding "[t]hey are, probably, the scum of the scum of the earth."[12]

The anything-goes honeymoon was officially over. Henceforth, all movies would require a PCA seal of approval. Offending films still in release when the Code went into effect in January 1935 were withdrawn from theaters. Some would be issued seals after substantial editing. Others were deemed permanently objectionable. Cutting their losses, studios melted the negatives for their silver content and had existing prints destroyed. Too many pre-Code titles remain lost films, most notoriously *Convention City* (1933), whose ad copy invited audiences to "join the daffy doings of one of those convulsive conventions where big business makes hey-hey!"[13] Footage from the set prompted studio chief Jack Warner to dispatch a memo to producer Hal Wallis, demanding him to "put brassieres on Joan Blondell and make her cover up her breasts because, otherwise, we are going to have these pictures stopped in a lot of places. I believe in showing their forms, but for Lord's sake, don't let those bulbs stick out."[14] Surviving publicity stills show an all-but-naked Blondell strategically posed in a train caboose.

For the next twenty years, the Breen Office exercised absolute control of what American audiences could and could not see on screen, "advising" studio production heads on which literary properties might be acceptable, examining scripts for questionable content, and demanding wholesale cuts in finished films. American cinema would never quite recapture the exuberance, the daring, and the sheer devil-may-care risk of those all-too-brief early sound years. It would take another existential industry crisis in the late sixties for Hollywood to break free from its self-imposed moral guardians. And it would take someone who came from outside the industry to lead the way. Someone trained in a medium that was truly breaking boundaries.

Someone from television.

6

"BLOOD ALWAYS SURPRISES ME"

> I like violence. I think it makes good movies.
> —Arthur Penn

In retrospect, only one director was ever the right choice for *Bonnie and Clyde*: Arthur Penn.

Only one person disagreed:

Arthur Penn.

Unbeknownst to writers Robert Benton and David Newman, producer Elinor Jones, who shared an attorney with the director, slipped Penn a copy of the seventy-five-page treatment in early 1964, before setting her sights on François Truffaut. Penn gave the story scant attention. "I was caught up in so many other projects, I just didn't take it seriously," he admitted to film writer Mark Harris. "I was sent that movie, but it wasn't 'that movie.' Yet."[1]

Penn still didn't take it seriously a year later, when Jones submitted the finished script during preproduction of *The Chase*. This time, the director didn't bother to respond directly, leaving the honors to an assistant. "Arthur thinks that the material is rich and engaging and that the writers are cinematically hip—what a rare pleasure," the note read. "But. Though it's not really like *The Chase*, it's nevertheless just enough like it to be unfeasible as a project for Arthur."[2] Another year brought a third and final rejection, this one owing to scheduling conflicts. Deep into Broadway rehearsals for *Wait Until Dark* in early 1966, Penn fought off the advances of the film's new producer, Warren Beatty, who had acquired the rights to the script in November 1965.

For Penn, *No* meant "No"—at least, until it didn't.

One of the most versatile and most articulate talents ever to make his mark in Hollywood, Arthur Penn, like so many of his protagonists, cultivated a reputation for stubbornness and contrarianism. "I would like to knock a lot of heads together, and that's how I do it in my films,"[3] he once said. "It's in my nature to be an outsider and to struggle against the Establishment, whatever form that takes."[4] In a career that spanned over half a century, Penn found himself drawn to "outsider" protagonists: not only Clyde Barrow and Bonnie Parker, but also Billy the Kid in *The Left Handed Gun* (1958); Helen Keller in *The Miracle Worker* (1962); Arlo Guthrie and his not-so-merry band in *Alice's Restaurant* (1969); Jack Crabb, the picaresque Everyman who becomes *Little Big Man* (1970); *Night Moves'* (1975) burnt-out private detective Harry Moseby; even iconoclastic illusionists Penn Jilette and Teller in the late-career *Penn and Teller Get Killed* (1989).

"The only people who really interest me are the outcasts from society," Penn insisted. "The people who are not outcasts . . . seem to me good for selling breakfast food." More than that, "society would be wise to pay attention to the people who do not belong in it if it wants to find out where it's failing."[5]

Penn worked in nearly every genre, yet no matter how disparate, his films are linked by uniquely national preoccupations. "His films have nothing in common," observes the director's biographer Nat Segaloff, "except [that] they explore the American character, the good and the bad of it."[6] Penn himself acknowledged the connection. "I have always equated the American temperament with the kinetic temperament. Americans act out what they feel. They apply it," he told fellow director Curtis Hanson. "The whole mythology of the country is based on that—the West; the Western; the great men of action—which seems to me the basic stuff of which movies are made, the best of them."[7] (In the same interview, Penn listed William Wellman's *The Ox-Bow Incident* [1943] and Howard Hawks's *Red River* [1948], both dark variations on the traditional Western, among the films that exerted the most profound personal influence.) Penn's preoccupation with Americana stemmed from visceral concerns. "I am worried about what is happening in [this] country," he said in 1972 at the height of the Vietnam War. "And maybe worry is a very good source from which to try to make art."[8]

From the beginning, critical assessments of Penn have underestimated him as one of the medium's most influential filmmakers.

In *The American Cinema*, the 1968 manifesto that (dubiously) popularized French auteur theory, critic Andrew Sarris listed Penn among the purveyors of what he called "Expressive Esoterica," those "unsung directors with difficult styles or unfashionable genres or both."[9] David Thomson praised Penn as "one of the best directors in America and the filmmaker with the most acute sense of what the audience dreamed and feared" in his *Biographical Dictionary of Film*, but nonetheless faulted many of the movies for being "clinical allegory dressed up in period clothes."[10] Ted Sennet, for one, got it mostly right in his compendium *Great American Directors*: "On the whole," he wrote, "[Penn] has revealed a dark vision—an America where violence can explode in a moment's notice and in the unlikeliest places. . . . [He] is committed to making us see what we, as Americans, have become—and perhaps moving us in the direction of what we can be."[11]

Born in Philadelphia in September 1922 to a Russian-Jewish family, Penn endured a disjointed youth when his parents divorced in the depths of the Depression, shuttling between households with his brother Irving (later to become an acclaimed photographer). "It was a pretty fragmentary childhood," Penn said. "I was really quite a rebellious and obstinate youngster, always ready to put up a fight."[12] That aggression found an outlet in World War II, where Penn served in the 106th Infantry Division, experiencing firsthand the hardships of the Battle of the Bulge in the brutal winter of 1944–1945. "We were in the King's Hunting Lodge in the Ardennes Forest. And *boom!* come the Germans,"[13] Penn recounted to biographer Segaloff. Two of the 106th's three divisions capitulated in the battle that claimed the lives of more than 75,000 Allied soldiers but ultimately frustrated Adolf Hitler's attempt to regain control of the European theater of war.

Chased out of the Ardennes with his unit, Penn followed the reconstituted 15th Army across the Rhine into Germany and remained there after the Nazi surrender. The slaughter he witnessed proved transformative. "To my mind, the Second World War really cut violence loose in every terrible and unimaginable way," Penn said. "I saw enough violence during the war to make me think it wasn't something we could ignore or sanitize."[14] The violence persisted in occupied Europe, when drunken troops were responsible for most of the disturbances. Penn found himself transferred from Berlin to Saint-Cyr-le-Chatoux outside Paris as part of the US Army's Soldiers' Shows unit, designed to provide occupying troops with diversion from less meritorious activities. "The incoming army should not be playing around with *frauleins*," read the official instructions.[15]

Alan Campbell, the gin-swilling husband of renowned wit Dorothy Parker, served as Penn's commanding officer. His colleagues included Joshua Logan, already an acclaimed stage director, and a budding playwright named Paddy Chayevsky. "There were writers and there were movie stars," Penn remembered, "but the main thing was they brought over a hundred American actresses to be in the shows."[16] Penn toured with Soldiers' Shows from town to town throughout Germany and stayed after the war's end to head the army's Wiesbaden-based entertainment unit. "I was running things without any supervision, plus I was getting a check from the U.S. government."[17] (Never again was he to obtain such good terms.) Penn's repertoire consisted of prewar chestnuts like *My Sister Eileen*, the aspirational story of two small-town Ohio sisters with big Manhattan ambitions, and an unauthorized knock-off of the Leonard Bernstein-Betty Comden-Adolph Green musical *On the Town*. "We'd make up a story that we could use that was partly their story, but we weren't paying royalties or anything like that,"[18] Penn admitted.

The director's most memorable "theatrical" experience, however, came as a spectator to the Nuremberg trials that exposed the full horror of Nazi genocide. For several days, Penn listened to the testimony of Hitler Youth leader Baldur von Schirach and the cross-examination led by American attorney Telford Taylor. Over sixty years later, Penn could still paint a vivid picture of the proceedings. He remembered "fat little Hermann Goring ... now skinny with flesh dangling" and the "smallish room" holding no more than "a couple hundred spectators." Penn found the experience "amazing"—and revelatory. "That was the absolute heart of the Nazi Party. I was staring right into it."[19] From that close encounter emerged one inescapable conclusion: "Violence is innate to human beings."[20]

Penn's wartime experience at the head of Soldiers' Shows made him a natural for the world of live drama then flourishing on broadcast television. Fresh from a GI Bill-funded college education at North Carolina's experimental Black Mountain College (whose other alumni include John Cage, Merce Cunningham, Elaine and Willem de Kooning, Buckminster Fuller, Walter Gropius, and Robert Rauschenberg), Penn arrived in New York City in the spring of 1950. NBC hired him on the spot—as a cue-card holder for Milton Berle. Penn's ability to placate and tame the insecure and often abusive "Uncle Miltie" earned him a promotion to stage manager and then associate director on *The Colgate Comedy Hour*, headlined by Dean Marin and Jerry Lewis, in which capacity Penn had the responsibility to prepare the blocking of each shot before it went on air to a national audience.

Live TV directors literally "call the shots" as they happen, editing in their heads as they go along; sitting in a studio control room is to witness a scene of barely controlled pandemonium. "They called it the Golden Age of television, though it wasn't that golden when we were doing it," Penn recalled. "The tensions and pressures were enormous. You needed the talent but also the physical stamina to survive it. . . . Young guys would crack up or have a heart attack or smoke themselves into oblivion because the pressure was too great."[21] Penn's big break came when *Colgate*'s regular director, Kingman Moore, suffered a hemorrhage and slumped over the control panel. The former cue-card holder, who knew that week's show by heart, rushed in to take over, bringing the broadcast to a successful close while medical personnel hustled Moore out of the control room and into an ambulance.

From 1953 to 1958, Penn directed forty-five live TV dramas, first for *Philco Television Playhouse* in New York, then switching coasts to the acclaimed *Playhouse 90* in Los Angeles. (Penn wasn't alone in being prolific: John Frankenheimer, Sidney Lumet, Delbert Mann, and others accomplished similar outputs.) The broadcasts featured original scripts by Horton Foote, Rod Serling, Tad Mosel, Robert Alan Arthur, Arnold Shulman, and Penn's wartime colleague Paddy Chayefsky, and showcased the cream of Actors' Studio "Method" talent, among them Paul Newman and Anne Bancroft, with whom Penn would later work in feature films. Rarely seen today outside of archival kinescope screenings at the Paley Center for Media in New York City and Los Angeles, the programs proved a fertile training ground.

"The real skill I learned working on live television was to be able to walk into a room or onto a set and immediately see the interesting angles," the director recalled. "The placement of the camera never intimidated me."[22] Penn's live TV experience also left him with a lifelong appreciation of the actor's craft—so much so, that he joined the Actors' Studio himself at the invitation of cofounder Paula Strasberg. With his gravely baritone voice and rugged, charismatic looks—like Roy Scheider in his prime—the director's on-camera persona is the equal to that of his stars in countless production stills, interviews, and retrospective commentaries over the years.

Among the featured scripts on the *Philco Television Playhouse* was "The Death of Billy the Kid," written by Gore Vidal, which charted the friendship between William Bonney and Pat Garrett. Vidal's intention was "to show not so much Billy himself as the people who created 'Billy the Kid.'"[23] Penn didn't direct that episode; Robert Mulligan did. When Mulligan turned down the chance to direct a feature-film adaptation for Warner Bros., producer Fred Coe and star Paul Newman, who had played Billy on television, turned to Penn instead. Penn didn't care for Vidal's original script. Working with regular *Playhouse 90* writer Leslie Stevens, the director fashioned a tale that "skirted between the fanciful play-acting and the violence of the west."

Penn didn't hesitate to alter facts to suit the story. "I figure myth is anybody's fair game," he says on the DVD commentary track for *The Left Handed Gun*. "You can do whatever you want with myth."[24] Elsewhere, Penn declared "I don't have a lot of faith in history."[25] Having attended the Nuremberg trials, the director was "very concerned about the way belief in certain myths (let's say—that Adolf Hitler was a god and Aryans were the master race) can be destructive."[26] Like *Bonnie and Clyde* but in embryonic form, *The Left Handed Gun* evinces Penn's fascination with and skepticism of the mythmaking process. It is a film that reconstructs an existing legend while dismantling it at the same time.

His craft forged in the breakneck pace of live TV drama, Penn didn't flinch at the movie's meager $400,000 budget or its twenty-three-day shooting schedule on dilapidated sets left over from the studio's 1939 period drama *Juarez*. "I was much less intimidated going into film than I might have been had I not had that experience in TV where the choice of camera angles and how to work with actors [was part of the process]," Penn explained to a London *Guardian* interviewer a half century later.[27] Youthful arrogance aside, Penn still had a lot to learn about making his way on a film set, and he credited *Left Handed Gun* assistant director Russ Saunders for his professional advice. (Saunders would later serve as *Bonnie and Clyde*'s production manager—and play the role of the ill-fated bank official.)

"What I remember was his saying to me, when Paul passed the camera on that first shot, 'Say, cut! Say, *cut!*'" Accustomed to staging long takes for the camera to accommodate the exigencies of live television, Penn learned from Saunders the importance of coverage from multiple angles. "He said, 'Break it into pieces because you'll never be able to cut it.'"[28] Nevertheless, Penn's newfangled ideas incurred the wrath of veteran studio cameraman J. Peverell Marley. In a production scenario that would repeat itself on the set of *Bonnie and Clyde*, the director of photography for such warhorses as *The Volga Boatman* (1926), *The Count of Monte Cristo* (1934), *The Hound of the*

Baskervilles (1939), and *The Pride of the Marines* (1945) objected to Penn's specificity in lens choices and his unconventional staging.

Penn particularly remembered one day when "another crew [member] went by us while [Marley] was practicing his golf swing, and said, 'How's it going, Pev? And he said, shaking his head, 'I got one-a-them TV guys.'" Initially flabbergasted by his cameraman's arrogance, Penn quickly pivoted. "It was briefly stunning. And then it was, 'Go fuck yourself.'"[29]

Despite the difficulties, Penn found his maiden feature-film experience liberating. "We enjoyed a degree of freedom that was not characteristic of that period," he says with genuine wonder on his commentary track for *The Left Handed Gun*. That freedom ended the last day of shooting, when "a man came up to me and said, 'Hello. My name is Folmer Blangsted. I'm the most creative editor in Hollywood, and I'm going to edit your picture.'" Penn had every expectation he would oversee the cutting of his own movie—after all, he'd edited forty-five pieces of live television in his head, in real time. But the very next day, "I tried to drive onto the lot at Warner Bros. and I had no parking space—it was gone!" At that point, "I thought, movies are not for me. This isn't what I do."[30] Penn returned to New York City, where he embarked on a third career as a successful stage director, winning plaudits for *Two for the Seesaw*, *Toys in the Attic*, *All the Way Home*, *An Evening with Mike Nichols and Elaine May*, and *The Miracle Worker* (all hits), the last of which would lead to a return to filmmaking.

Despite the unwanted but inevitable studio interference, *The Left Handed Gun* remains, among Penn's early films, the one that most closely points the way to *Bonnie and Clyde*. It is an astonishingly assured debut, displaying the director's dark lyricism and his gift for startling deep-focus images. In a sequence that drove cameraman Pev Marley to the point of mutiny, Penn has Newman's Billy draw the plan for a shootout on the steam-coated glass of a hotel window overlooking a main street, then dissolves into a perfectly matched image of the actual gunfight, collapsing the normal transition into a single image. Also present are the abrupt tonal shifts from comedy into unexpected bursts of realistic violence. After Newman's Billy the Kid blasts deputy Bob Ollinger (played by Denver Pyle, the future Frank Hamer) with a double-barreled shotgun, a young girl points and laughs at Ollinger's empty boots lying upright on the ground—this a decade before Sam Peckinpah made such scenes a visual leitmotif in *The Wild Bunch* (1969).

Even in its Folmer Blangsted–edited version, the movie still incurred the wrath of the Production Code Administration, not only for its violence but also for the sexual innuendo that underlies Billy's relationship with his best friend's wife and the clearly homosexual attraction the outlaw holds on his dime-novel follower, a Southern huckster named Moultrie played by the androgynous Hurd Hatfield (best known for *The Picture of Dorian Grey* [1945]). A pivotal scene involves Moultrie's sadomasochistic beating at Billy's hands, leading to Moultrie's betrayal of his idol to Pat Garrett. The final confrontation is no less suggestive, with its clear implication of suicide-by-lawman in the way the unarmed Billy turns into Garrett's bullet. Penn intended the film to end with black-draped, candle-holding peasant women emerging from their adobes to mourn the folk hero; the studio replaced that with a "happy" ending in which Garrett's wife, materializing from nowhere, takes the sheriff in her arms and tells him, "You can come home now." Fade out.

Thematically as well as stylistically, *The Left Handed Gun* anticipated Penn's treatment of the Barrow Gang. The film's subtext concerns the dynamic between fame and notoriety: in Penn's words, "How a boy of no particular history emerges as a figure in American life. . . . The character [of Billy] is someone very uncertain of his own identity but knows his own power. That's miles away from a conventional western hero."[31] Such unconventionality more or less assured the movie's American box office failure on its release in May 1958 but guaranteed its discovery in Europe. Relegated to the bottom half of double bills in the United States, where critics considered it too much a modern story ("as if people in the old west were conspicuously different,"[32] Penn grumbled), the film earned the director a prize for Best First Film from the Belgian Critics' Association nearly three years after its initial release and began the mutual love affair between Penn and the French nouvelle vague.

"I got an overdose of rapture,"[33] the director blushed in retrospect of the experience, which introduced him to both François Truffaut and Jean-Luc Godard, little imagining they'd all be in the running for the same job shortly thereafter. According to Penn, the "*Cahiers du cinema* guys" declared him "an American *Nouvelle Vague* director and kind of absorbed me into their ranks."[34] (Andrew Sarris agreed, calling Penn "the American Truffaut"[35] after *Bonnie and Clyde* was released.)

New Wave techniques manifested themselves in Penn's second film, *The Miracle Worker* (1962). Penn had directed William Gibson's teleplay as a live broadcast for *Philco* and had overseen the fully fleshed-out play's triumphant Broadway production, which starred Anne Bancroft and Patty Duke. The two actresses received Academy Award nominations for their roles in the film version, which Penn thoroughly reconceived for the new medium. Bancroft won Best Actress, and Penn received an Oscar nomination for his direction (David Lean took the prize for *Lawrence of Arabia*). He and producer Fred Coe made *The Miracle Worker* independently, outside the system, and Penn was determined to stay there. His head filled with European accolades, the director overreached with *Mickey One* (1964), the story of a second-rate comic on the lam from the Chicago mob.

Penn envisioned the film as "the ultimate McCarthy paranoia picture"[36] but it emerged with "an excessive degree of obscurity about it. . . . I'm astonished at how derivative it is of European films," Penn admitted to a British Film Institute audience in 1981. "The symbolism almost makes me a little queasy."[37] (Seen today, when its flashy technique and elliptical storytelling have long been appropriated and refined, the film is actually quite entertaining.) *Mickey One*'s importance in the evolution of *Bonnie and Clyde* rests in its being the director's first collaboration—make that clash—with the film's star, Warren Beatty. The two equally stubborn artists partnered as producers on the film shortly after their first meeting, but failed to find a collaborative middle ground.

"I didn't know what the hell Arthur was trying to do and I tried to find out," Beatty claimed. "I'm not sure [Arthur] knew himself."[38] Penn's version: "I wasn't going to entertain compromise no matter what Warren was asking for. It was really a struggle of wills."[39] Quite a struggle, indeed: for a climactic scene where Mickey performs alone in a starkly lit room for an unknown audience that may include his assassin, Penn put Beatty through a grueling sixty-nine takes.

As sometimes happens when creative personalities collide, both Penn and Beatty emerged from their confrontation with a feeling of mutual respect. Beatty proved a steadfast friend to Penn in the "dysfunctional period" that ensued after the director's stormy return to studio filmmaking with *The Chase*. "I was sick of movie shenanigans, and mostly sick of myself for abdicating responsibility,"[40] Penn said of the experience. "It was terrible making a film with so many technicians around. . . . If you have an idea, it immediately gets filtered down, like smoke in a filter[ed] cigarette. All the people around you think they know exactly how your idea should be presented, but what finally comes out of their very precise efforts is not your idea at all, but the archetypal, commonplace, banal Hollywood idea."[41] (He wasn't wrong.)

"C'mon, forget *The Chase*," Beatty told Penn, who replied, "The hell with this. I've got another life. I work in the theater. Why don't I go back to New York and just do that?"[42] Which Penn promptly did, taking on *Dial "M" for Murder* author Frederick Knott's latest thriller *Wait Until Dark*, the story of three murderous thugs who torment a blind woman in her apartment in their hunt for a stash of heroin. Starring Lee Remick and Mitchell Ryan, the play ran on Broadway for the whole of 1966, totaling 374 performances. When Warner Bros.—which seems to appear everywhere in this story—bought the film rights and cast Audrey Hepburn in the lead, Hepburn asked Penn to direct her. But she had competition for his services.

Warren Beatty had sneaked a read of Benton and Newman's script on location in Chicago, courtesy of bilingual Canadian costar Alexandra Stewart, who happened to be François Truffaut's favored Bonnie Parker as well as his current bedmate (at least until she met Beatty). Intrigued by the unconventional telling of the story, the actor tracked the rights to the script "like a hawk," ultimately acquiring the material for $75,000 the very day Elinor Jones's option lapsed.[43] By that time, Truffaut had definitively passed on the project. As he had on two previous occasions, Beatty went to Penn, but Penn again turned down the offer. "When he sent me the script, I said, 'Gee, I don't think so. I don't really want to do a film about a couple of bums essentially.'"[44]

Of all people, Penn should have been the last to underestimate Beatty's powers of persuasion. "I'm going to lock myself in a room with Arthur, and I won't let him out until he reads through the picture,"[45] the actor told Abe Lastfogel, the William Morris agent he shared with Penn. And that's pretty much how it happened. "I didn't stand a chance," Penn conceded of their meeting over lunch at Dinty Moore's in New York. "I had capitulated by the time Warren finished his complicated order for a salad."[46]

At that point, Penn thought it a good time to read the script.

Really *read* it.

And he had a few notes.

From the beginning, Benton and Newman had insisted on the ménage à trois. However strong the writers' convictions, Benton recalled, "within fifteen minutes sitting alone with Arthur, we agreed to take it out. His reasons were so logical and so strong."[47] Penn's argument boiled down to a simple equation: "People will say, 'Of course they're gangsters—they're a bunch of sexual freaks.'" The writers saw the logic. "In most gangster movies, there's a moment when the audience can stand outside, at arm's length from the characters," Benton agreed. "We were careful *not* to do that. We wanted their affection for the characters to remain."[48] The writer later confessed that by this time "we ... began to realize that we didn't know the first thing about what living in a practicing *ménage a trois* was really like.... We had just ignored that in our quest for an off-beat love affair."[49]

Fired up again after years of rejection, the writers set about transforming wheelman C. W. Moss from the oafish stud of their original character description into a kind of playful kid brother to Clyde and Bonnie and recalibrating the script's transition from light to darkness. The sexual elephant in the room dispensed with, Penn and the writers "talked and moved in the direction of a simpler tale, one of narcissism, of bravura and, at least from Clyde's point of view, of sexual timidity."[50] Appreciating Newman and Benton's "New Sensibility," where Style Equals Content, Penn acknowledged, "We [didn't] have a story of very strong characters. They're relatively shallow, rather empty people as far as we know. Nice enough, and with certain problems, but we don't have a moral dilemma which would help us understand what the characters are going through in their interior lives."[51] Rather than burden the script with unnecessary exposition (as inevitably happens in today's development meetings), Penn encouraged the writers to embrace the superficiality.

"I thought in terms of cartoons," he explained, "each frame changing. Here we laugh, here we cry, here we laugh again."[52] In Penn's mind, "It was to start as a jaunty little spree in crime, then turn serious, and finally arrive at a point that was irreversible."[53] More accomplished at cinematic storytelling than he had been in the days of *The Left Handed Gun*, the director intended the constant clash of tones as "a distancing device [to] keep bumping the viewer out of the picture, forcing you to back away and contemplate the fact that you are watching a myth unfold with all of the attendant ramifications."[54]

The screenwriters understood the creative hierarchy. "If there's one thing we have learned beyond any question in the movie business, it is this: once there is a director, he is the boss. The absolute boss," Benton wrote in an essay about the genesis of *Bonnie and Clyde*. "And so it should be ... because if he's any good, the picture will profit. If he's not, you're stuck with a lousy director."[55] Reflecting on the film a decade after its initial release, Benton told interviewer Philip Porcella that Penn "certainly earned a writer's credit on the picture. He'd be gracious enough not to take it, but his contribution was enormous."[56]

Penn also made clear to Newman and Benton that "a gangster film was not really where my interests lay. . . . I felt it should be a story with a broader social theme than a flick about two '30s bank robbers whose pictures I remembered as a couple of self-publicizing hoods holding guns, plastered across the front page of the *Daily News*."[57] The romantic legend on its own was not enough. "This is really a story about the agricultural nature of the country," Penn realized. "Those banks out there were farmers' banks, and then the farmers couldn't pay their mortgages and eventually the banks took over the farms. . . . [A]ll of that wasn't in the script. But I thought it could be."[58] The director drew on his own childhood memory of the country's "paralysis . . . the universality of fear."[59]

He told his collaborators, "If this film isn't embedded in the Depression, if that era isn't presented in detail, it won't make sense."[60] Penn personally conceived the scene where Clyde and Bonnie, having slept the night in an abandoned farmhouse, encounter the farm's dispossessed owner and a black field hand the next morning and encourage the farmer to shoot up his foreclosed home in a symbolic act of revenge. The film's infrequent but meaningful departures into social realism, like its shockingly brutal violence, anchor the characters in a landscape that deliberately recalls both John Steinbeck's 1939 novel *The Grapes of Wrath* and John Ford's 1940 film adaptation, itself inspired by the Farm Security Administration photographs by (among others) Walker Evans, Dorothea Lange, and Carl Mydans.

Penn saw a through line from the 1930s to the 1960s in the disparity between rich and poor in America and the widespread generational alienation. "The film is political in that it deals with . . . that moment when young people felt excluded from a society that was destroying itself economically. Bonnie and Clyde decided to do something and make a change. They were experiencing an identity crisis, something that today's young generation well understands."[61] For Penn, it was absolutely "vital to me that the film be a new American Gothic. The movie was released into a world where kids were burning draft cards and feeling beset by their own government."[62] *Bonnie and Clyde*'s box office results more than validated Penn's instincts. "We rang a big bell with [that] film," he stated with justifiable pride in 2008. "A very big social bell. We had no idea how it would reverberate around the world."[63]

Significantly, the script's level of violence never came into question. Benton and Newman had been unstinting in the graphic quality of the story's various shootouts; describing one moment where Bonnie takes a bullet in the shoulder, the script reads, "We must see this bullet clearly, we must see it go in her flesh so that we can feel it," adding that "her scream is pure animal pain."[64] Penn enhanced this element as the material proceeded into production. "Let's face it," the director told the press at *Bonnie and Clyde*'s 1967 Montreal Film Festival premiere. "Kennedy was shot. We're in Vietnam, shooting people and getting shot. We have not been out of a war for any period of my lifetime. Gangsters were flourishing during my youth. I was in the war at age eighteen, then came Korea, now comes Vietnam." (Less than nine months later, both Martin Luther King Jr. and Robert F. Kennedy fell to assassins' bullets.)

Maybe the screenwriters hadn't landed Truffaut, but they'd found someone who shared Truffaut's sensibility—who knew Truffaut *personally*. They'd written a French New Wave script, and now Arthur Penn was prepared to apply that vision to a distinctly American canvas. Writers and director were, in the hackneyed industry phrase, "on the same page."

Their producer would be a different story.

7

"I STEAL"

> "We rob banks."
> —David Newman and Robert Benton,
> "Bonnie and Clyde" screenplay

On November 9, 1932, in the darkest days of the darkest year of the Great Depression, Warner Bros. released *I Am a Fugitive from a Chain Gang*, based on the real-life adventures of Robert E. Burns, an escaped convict from a Georgia penal colony. Trailers for the film promised "Fiction Has Never Matched This Story for DRAMATIC INTENSITY ... THRILLING LOVE INTEREST ... TERRIFIC SUSPENSE!" Studio chief Jack Warner predicted in a memo that the picture "will make us some enemies,"[1] but nonetheless encouraged his marketing department to crank out sensational taglines. Promised one poster: "Warner Bros.' defiant masterpiece will have conscience-stricken America talking in its sleep!"[2] To ensure absolute authenticity, fugitive Burns, under the payroll alias "Richard M. Crane," sat in on story conferences with screenwriters Howard J. Green, Brown Holmes, and Sheridan Gibney, producer Hal B. Wallis, and director Mervyn LeRoy.

"We arranged a room for [Burns] on the lot, had his meals brought in, and only a very few people were privy to the fact of his presence,"[3] LeRoy recounted in his autobiography. The meetings proved understandably tense. According to Gibney, "Burns would jump upon hearing gunfire emanating from productions shooting on nearby sets." When the convicted felon heard police sirens, "he hid behind furniture and cowered against a wall." The writer settled Burns's nerves by assuring him, "Don't worry. It's only a movie."[4] It all made for great copy.

For once, the film lived up to the hype. *I Am a Fugitive from a Chain Gang*—shortened from the original title, *I Am a Fugitive from a Georgia Chain Gang*, to avoid antagonizing Southern theater owners and shield the studio from lawsuits—became one of the year's biggest box office hits, grossing $1.5 million on a $195,845 budget and earning a Best Picture nomination. Studio mainstay Paul Muni, who became "Scarface" the same year for independent Howard Hughes, plays James Allen, a combat veteran returning from the crucible of World War I to find no opportunity but a life of vagrancy. Accompanying a fellow hobo into a diner, he becomes an unwilling accomplice to an armed robbery that lands him a ten-year sentence on a chain gang.

Director LeRoy depicts the horrors of Allen's incarceration with (for the time) uncharacteristic frankness and unrestrained brutality. Prisoners are chained together in segregated bunks, subjected to beatings with a thick leather strap, and forced to abase themselves before trustees during their daily rock-breaking routine. Driven to extremes, Allen engineers an escape with the help of a black inmate and embarks on a legitimate career in Chicago under an assumed name, only to land back in the same hellhole when his real identity is uncovered. Allen's sanity cracks, and the film descends into a maelstrom of violence and retribution climaxing in Allen once again on the run.

I Am a Fugitive's legendary closing scene finds Allen a grizzled transient haunting the street outside his onetime fiancée's house. "I haven't escaped," he tells her, moving slowly back into the darkness. "They're still after me. They'll always be after me. No friends—no rest—no peace. Keep moving—that's all that's left for me." "How do you live?" she asks. "I steal!" comes the reply from the pitch darkness, as the sound of fast-receding footsteps echoes over the closing title card. In interviews and his autobiography, director LeRoy maintained that this shocking fade-out resulted from happenstance, when "as we were doing the last rehearsal . . . before we went into the take, the fuse on the big klieg lights blew out."[5] Whatever the circumstances (in interviews, LeRoy also claimed the blackout was premeditated), the movie's finale "knocked everybody for a loop," the director remembered.

In one of the rare instances where Hollywood storytelling influenced political reform, *I Am a Fugitive*'s release prompted nationwide outrage. "Editorials were written in dozens of leading newspapers," LeRoy claimed. "Committees were formed, petitions were circulated, congressmen were flooded with letters and telegrams."[6] Georgia's legislature undertook a re-evaluation of the state's prison system, prompting chain-gang warden J. Harold Hardy to file a one-million-dollar lawsuit against Warner Bros. for the film's "vicious, brutal and false attacks."[7] Fugitive Burns remained at large—but only for a little while. Recaptured in December after making too many promotional appearances on behalf of the film, Burns once again became a prisoner, this time in New Jersey, whose sympathetic governor refused to extradite him back to Georgia.[8]

Like Muni's wronged veteran in *I Am a Fugitive*, Clyde emerged from nearly two years of imprisonment on February 2, 1932, a changed, embittered man. "[He] seemed like he just got meaner or something," his younger sister Marie recalled. "He just didn't care anymore about anything."[9]

In many ways, Clyde's prison experience mirrored that of countless other convicted Texas felons in the same era. Upon arrival at the Eastham Prison Farm's Camp No. 2, the sight of a half dozen handcuffed convicts, forced to stand atop narrow oak barrels, greeted the "dumbbell bandit." Nearby, "a pair of thin arms groped through the tiny air vents of [a] sweat box," according to Ralph Fults, a fellow inmate and future Barrow Gang member whose memoir provides the sole eyewitness account of Clyde's prison years. "Another man, stripped to the waist, was tied to a tree; his back bore the marks of a railroad trace chain."[10] Winchester-carrying mounted guards and truncheon-wielding trustees enhanced the newcomers' welcome with a random beating they called a "tune-up."

Work in the cotton and cornfields that supplied the Texas prison system with a steady stream of income was backbreaking; Clyde and Fults joked about their "eight-hour days—[from] eight in the morning [until] eight in the evening."[11] Guards ran down laggards on horseback and subjected troublemakers to lashings with "The Bat," a wood-handled, oiled leather strap ranging from eighteen inches to three feet, applied with sometimes crippling force to the naked backs and buttocks of spread-eagled men. While newly appointed Texas prison system manager Lee Simmons had (at least on paper) abolished some of the more nefarious "deterrents," he encouraged and defended vigorous application of the bat. "Gentlemen, it's like using spurs on an old horse," he told a reform-minded state legislature. "When you've got your spurs on, the old horse will do the job."[12]

Even more than most young offenders, Clyde had a personality that made him a poor prisoner. "Imagine somebody who wants to be in control of everything—and you have no control over anything,"[13] ventures Bonnie and Clyde historian John Neal Phillips, who authored Fults's story and stands by its veracity. Clyde eventually found less taxing work in the kitchens, where he became easy prey for a six-foot, two-hundred-pound trustee named Ed Crowder, considered depraved even by Eastham standards. According to Fults, Crowder repeatedly raped Clyde in the prison dormitory for over a year. Clyde exacted revenge, luring the lumbering trustee into the urinals and smashing in Crowder's skull with a length of pipe. At that time, no penalties existed in Texas for convicts killing one another; by prior arrangement with Clyde, an older inmate serving a life sentence took the rap for Crowder's murder. Facing the remainder of a fourteen-year sentence and desperate to spring himself from the degradations of the Eastham farms, Clyde took the only guaranteed way out. On January 27, 1932, he persuaded an inmate on a work detail to lop off the first two toes of his left foot with an axe. The mutilation had its intended effect, springing Clyde from "The Bloody 'Ham" to the Huntsville infirmary.

News of Clyde's conditional pardon arrived six days later.

From the moment her son had been incarcerated, Cumie Barrow had ceaselessly lobbied Texas governor Ross Sterling, pleading leniency for her son on the grounds of a youthful indiscretion. The effort had finally borne fruit—a few days too late. Clyde "came home to us on crutches,"[14] his sister Nell remembered. He returned with something else: an unshakable determination never to return to prison; "the laws" would have to kill him instead. True to form, Clyde's first request was for a new set of clothes, preferably including a silk shirt and kid gloves. "Nobody but bootleggers and gangsters wear silk shirts," Nell protested. But Clyde insisted: he had someone he needed to impress. "I'm going to doll up . . . and go over [to] see if Bonnie will still speak to me."[15]

He found Bonnie at home in her mother's parlor—sitting with a new beau. "The instant she looked up and saw Clyde," as mother Emma Parker told the story, "it was just like he'd never been away at all. She jumped up . . . and she went right into Clyde's arms."[16] The jilted beau picked up his hat and quietly retreated out the front door. Bonnie hadn't exactly been a faithful correspondent in the seventeen months of Clyde's imprisonment; no letters after an early flurry in 1930 (if any) have come to light. Her innate ennui had taken hold again, and her romantic attention had begun to stray, much to Mrs. Parker's satisfaction.

Clyde's reappearance on the Parker family doorstep, crutches or no crutches, shattered whatever remaining hopes Emma may have harbored for her daughter's future. "If you want to go with Bonnie, that's all right with me," she told Clyde. "But I want you to get a job first."[17] Clyde's family wanted the same thing. For a while, Clyde attempted to oblige them. Since his arrest, the Barrows had added a two-pump filling station to the front of their threadbare home on Eagle Ford Road (what passed for West Dallas's main street), where a cooler offered soft drinks and bologna, colloquially known as "South Dallas Round Steak"; a freshly dug well provided water, and bootleg hooch could be found under the counter. Clyde talked of plans to open up an automotive parts store on the available land next door to the filling station. Ambition took money, and money required a job.

Things didn't work out as planned.

In 1930, the year Clyde entered the Eastham prison fields, 1,350 banks failed, taking $853 million ($15.8 billion today) in deposits with them. A year later, another 2,294 banks closed their doors, culminating in the $200 million ($3.7 billion) collapse of the Bank of the United States in New York City. A full one-quarter of the nation's work force was left unemployed, "with no prospects and no safety net,"[18] as journalist Timothy Egan recounted in his harrowing chronicle of the period, *The Worst Hard Time*. By 1932, nearly a third of all Midwestern and Southwestern farmers faced foreclosure, and one in twenty had lost their land entirely. The first of the dust storms that would lay waste to American agriculture had begun in September 1930, sweeping across Kansas, Oklahoma, and the Texas Panhandle. A month before Clyde's release, a ten-thousand-foot-high dust cloud, pushed by sixty-mile-an-hour winds, rose in Amarillo and traveled north to Colorado, blackening the sky and swamping the countryside in mountains of dirt.

"The earth is on the move," observed one astounded sharecropper. "Look at the land: wrong side up."[19]

The man-made natural disaster on top of the man-made financial crisis prompted nationwide feelings of resentment and rage and provided the explosive backdrop to the crime wave that followed. "The general public held banks and politicians—and for some reason law-enforcement officers—responsible for the conditions of the Depression," says John Neal Phillips. "Anybody who could make fools of them was just fine."[20] (Similar sentiments prevailed in the 1967–1968 season of *Bonnie and Clyde*'s release.) Clyde needed no socioeconomic reasons to hate cops. As before his imprisonment, he found his attempts to secure the precious few jobs available repeatedly frustrated by Dallas police dropping into the workplace to detain him for "routine questioning." Hounded out of the city, Clyde accepted a construction job in Worcester, Massachusetts, his sister Nell lined up for him. Two weeks later, he was back home, nearly "dead [from] lonesomeness. If I've got to hide and run away from the law all my life, I want to be around where I can slip back and see my folks,"[21] he explained.

Clyde's efforts at going straight had come to a dead end. There were other ways to make money.

Throughout March and April 1932, Clyde and Fults (who had won parole six months before Clyde) perpetrated a string of robberies "notable mostly for bad decisions and worse luck."[22] Written accounts of these early thefts can be as comical as the early, bungled heists in *Bonnie and Clyde*. "Their misadventures would have constituted slapstick comedy," biographer Jeff Guinn agrees, "if lives hadn't been at stake."[23] Styling themselves "The Lake Dallas Gang," Clyde, Fults, and an eighteen-year-old neighborhood thug named Raymond Hamilton launched their criminal enterprise virtually in their own backyard, with a raid on the Simms Oil Refinery a few blocks away from the Barrow family filling station. Even at this embryonic stage, the operation demonstrated the careful advance planning and thorough reconnaissance Clyde would make a personal obsession. There was only one problem: the would-be criminal masterminds found the payroll safe empty.

The Lake Dallas Gang had better luck farther afield in Lawrence, Kansas, where after a careful two-day stakeout of the First National Bank, Clyde and his associates followed the bank president inside as he opened the doors and came away with $33,000; making up for their thwarted refinery heist, the gang had managed to locate one of the few banks in the region with money still left in the safe. Clyde would never hit it so rich again—and accomplished it all without a shot being fired.

That wasn't on account of any shortage of hardware.

The gang armed themselves with .38-caliber Saturday Night Specials, .45 revolvers, and an array of shotguns, all readily and legally available in local hardware stores. Clyde perfected what he called his "whippit gun," a Remington Model 11 semiautomatic shotgun cut down on both ends; slung by a loop under the right shoulder beneath an overcoat, the "whippit," true to its nickname, could be whipped into place in a split second. "There was a lot of psychology to that [sawed-off shotgun],"[24] Fults recalled with some amusement. Clyde used some of his share from the Lawrence job to upgrade the gang's arsenal, even trying out an over-the-counter Thompson submachine gun, which he quickly discarded for its incessant malfunctioning. He found weapons more to his taste in National Guard armories, which became frequent targets.

Clyde took a particular liking to the Browning automatic rifle—BAR for short. Manufactured like the Tommy gun for use in World War I, the weapon did not become standard military ordinance until 1938, but saw action in the early thirties criminal underworld. Clyde preferred the original Winchester M1918 model to all the later refinements. A massive weapon weighing 16 pounds with a barrel length of 24 inches, the M1918 could fire 500–650 rounds of armor-piercing Springfield .30–06 rounds per minute. Cartridge magazines came in 24- or 48-round versions, which could be emptied with a single pull of the trigger; Clyde later improved the firing capacity by fusing together multiple magazines. Bullets traveled at a speed of 2,822 feet per second, with an effective range of 1,500 yards and a maximum range of 5,000 yards. The BAR literally spit fire but packed powerful recoil requiring control on the part of the triggerman.

"Anyone who has ever fired that weapon knows that it will take off and you'll find yourself firing straight up if you're not holding on tight,"[25] attested Dallas deputy Ted Hinton, who wielded a BAR as part of Frank Hamer's posse. In short, a big gun for a pint-sized outlaw like Clyde Barrow.

On these early jobs, Clyde indulged what became a frequent pastime: kidnapping seriously outgunned lawmen and taking them on a multistate high-speed joyride, then turning them loose in the middle of nowhere. Police chief James T. Taylor of Electra, Texas, became the first peace officer to be escorted on an enforced road trip when he encountered Clyde and Fults acting suspiciously outside a gas company warehouse. Clyde relieved Taylor of his service revolver, hustled him into a stolen Chevy, and abandoned him at a ranch outside town. When the Chevy ran out of a gas a few miles later, Clyde commandeered the vehicle of mailman W. N. Owens when he happened on the scene. In a Depression-era twist worthy of a Warner Bros. pre-Code film, Owens asked what his captors planned to do with his mail truck. "Leave it in plain sight," Clyde told him. Owens had another suggestion: "You guys would be doing me a big favor if you just burned it up."

"Burn it?" Fults asked.

"Yeah," said Owens. "That way the government 'll have to buy me a new one."[26] Clyde and Fults obliged.

Not every encounter with "the laws" ended so comically. Clyde became wanted for murder in the death of Atoka County, Oklahoma, undersheriff Eugene Moore, gunned down in a July shootout in the small hamlet of Stringtown, where Clyde, Fults, and Hamilton, flush from a recent robbery, called undue attention to themselves at a local hoedown; county sheriff Charles Maxwell suffered serious wounds in the encounter. To his own family, Clyde pleaded innocence, blaming Hamilton for the fatal shots. But the Stringtown incident made him eligible for the death penalty, a fate Clyde would spend what remained of his life trying to outrun.

Clyde also claimed a case of mistaken identity in two other murders: those of Hillsboro, Texas, shopkeeper John Bucher in April, 1932 and Sherman, Texas, grocery store owner Howard Hall that October.[27] In her ghostwritten recollections, Nell Barrow urged readers to "understand, if you can, we never believed anything bad we heard about Clyde until he told us with his lips.... We realized [he] was restless, unhappy and not at all like he had been before he went to prison.... We would have objected with our last breaths to his taking to the road and living by what he could steal.... I fully realize all of these things and I'm not excusing Clyde," she insisted. "I'm just telling."[28]

If anything, Emma Parker's willful blindness exceeded that of the Barrow family. Shortly after Clyde's return from prison—after his $33,000 First National Bank score in Lawrence, in fact—Bonnie told her mother she'd landed a job demonstrating cosmetics for a Houston-based company and would soon be leaving home. "I never had any reason to believe that Bonnie would deceive me and I believed what she told me," Emma recounted. "Two days later I heard from her. She was in jail in Kaufman [Texas]!"[29]

Instead of pushing wholly imaginary makeup and face creams to River Oaks socialites, on April 19 Bonnie joined Clyde and Fults on a joyride to nearby Tyler. There, the Lake Dallas Gang hot-wired a Buick and a Chrysler for use in an upcoming robbery. Clyde, with an excited Bonnie riding beside him, pushed the Chrysler to speeds in excess of ninety miles per hour on the return trip. The outing took an unexpected turn halfway back. A night watchman in Kaufman caught Clyde and Fults attempting to break a hardware store padlock, attracted by the weapons inside. In the ensuing chase, a violent thunderstorm caused the Chrysler to sink to its running boards in the clay muck of the county road.

Forced to flee on foot, Clyde, Bonnie, and Fults next commandeered a pair of mules from a farmhouse, which they rode until Clyde managed to hot-wire another car a few miles farther on. Their luck was short-lived: with fuel prices running a whopping eighteen cents a gallon (the equivalent of three dollars today), most automobile owners in the Depression only kept a few gallons of fuel in their tanks at a time; Clyde's latest acquisition was no exception, leaving the gang stranded on the highway after a few minutes. By now, a sizable posse of townspeople and farmers had taken up the trail. Clyde and Fults found refuge in a creek-bed ditch, a sopping wet and thoroughly miserable Bonnie hugging the ground between them. Unrelenting gunfire ricocheted from every direction. Fults took a round in his left arm; Bonnie nearly fainted from her first close-up view of a man being shot. At that point, Clyde made an unexpected decision.

He ran like hell.

"If I make it, I'll get [help] and come back for you both,"[30] Clyde told Bonnie and Fults. He made a break for a line of bushes flanked by two posse members, both too busy reloading their guns to notice his escape. What Bonnie might have thought about the sight of her lover's decidedly unromantic departure she never revealed. What happened next comes courtesy of Fults's memoir. "They ain't got nothing on you," Fults reminded Bonnie. "Reload my gun [for me] and get the hell out of here before you get your head blown off. . . . Tell them we kidnapped you. Tell them anything you like."[31]

Bonnie needed no further prodding. Leaving Fults with the reloaded gun, she slipped over the embankment straight into the hands of waiting lawmen; Fults was captured scant minutes later—and immediately mistaken for Pretty Boy Floyd, to whom he bore a passing resemblance. After spending a miserable night in a one-cell country hoosegow, Bonnie was transferred to the Kaufman jail to await indictment. "Only a mother can appreciate my feelings when I walked into that Kaufman jail and saw Bonnie behind the bars," Emma Parker asked readers to understand. "Death would have been much easier."[32]

Too poor to make bond for her daughter, Mrs. Parker received consolation from the jailer's wife, who told her "[Bonnie]'s not going to need it. They really haven't got a thing against her, and when the grand jury meets in June, they'll give her a no-bill."[33] That advice, using the legal jargon for evidence deemed insufficient for prosecution, proved prophetic. Over the sixty days it would take for the grand jury to reach its verdict, Bonnie bided her time, sticking to the "kidnapping" story Fults had concocted and otherwise keeping her mouth shut. Whatever she had to say, she confided to herself on paper, using old bank forms provided as stationery by the charitable jailer's wife.

Incarceration made Clyde Barrow a rattlesnake. It made Bonnie Parker a writer.

Bonnie cherished poetry and read it wherever she could find it. A copy of *The Most Wonderful Collection of Famous Recitations Ever Written*, a cheaply printed 1933 pamphlet that included William Shakespeare, Rudyard Kipling, and "Bard of the Yukon" Robert W. Service among its featured authors, was later discovered in one of Clyde and Bonnie's abandoned vehicles. Bonnie displayed a particular liking for the ballad form, with its regular rhythms and predictable rhyme schemes. While awaiting her fate in Kaufman, Bonnie composed her own "wonderful collection" of ten poems, which she titled "Poetry from Life's Other Side." Only one ever saw publication: "The Story of Suicide Sal."

Reworked several times by its author and rife with gangster slang, the poem tells of a country girl *"born on a ranch in Wyoming; / Not treated like Helen of Troy"* who falls for *"'the line' of a 'heat man,' / A 'professional killer' from 'Chi.'"* Abandoned by her lover during a robbery,

> "I took the 'rap' like a 'sportsman,'
> Not even one 'squawk' did I make.
> Jack 'dropped himself' on the 'promise'
> We'd make a 'sensational break.'"[34]

Sal gets word from "a gal in the 'joint'" that Jack has married a new "moll" and plans on "going straight." Now a "jilted gangster's gal," Sal exacts her revenge, leaving Jack and his moll dead "on the spot," only to fall victim to "a sub-gun" herself two days later. Hard not to read the poem as a form of self-help therapy working out Bonnie's complicated feeling for Clyde. But also hard not to sense her excitement for the life outside the law she has decided to embrace. Like Suicide Sal, Bonnie was ready to forgive Clyde for *"all this 'hell' he has caused me / And love him as long as I live."*[35]

Bonnie's poetry has been regularly dismissed as "doggerel." It's true that her cadences can be shaky, but while her verse may be no better than that of her models, it's certainly no worse. Whatever claims to style "Suicide Sal" may have had, they were lost on Bonnie's mother. "This bit of writing reminded me of a small child who learns certain grown-up words and says them over and over, often incorrectly and inappropriately, in order to prove to adults that [she] is getting on,"[36] Emma complained with a near-audible clucking of the tongue.

Mrs. Parker might have been horrified by some of the other poems in her daughter's collection, such as "The Girl with the Blue Velvet Band," the tale of a heroin addict, and the self-explanatory "The Prostitutes' Convention," for which Bonnie sought no maternal reviews. Whatever autobiographical tidbits those poems might contain (Jeff Guinn and others have suggested that Bonnie's introduction to the underworld may have predated her acquaintance with Clyde), "Suicide Sal" remained the one she most identified with, as evidenced by her continual reworking. When Joplin, Missouri, police, in a foiled raid less than a year later, uncovered its definitive draft along with a cache of revealing photographs, the poem helped fuel a press sensation.

Bonnie Parker's impulsive decision to forsake home and ride off with Clyde Barrow represents the first intersection between the real-life outlaws and their *Bonnie and Clyde* counterparts. Here as elsewhere, the filmmakers captured the story's essence while significantly altering the circumstances.

Screenplay and film alike open on Bonnie—specifically, a giant close-up of her mouth, bright with red lipstick. Still in a tight shot, the camera pans to a mirror, revealing Bonnie's full face. Penn reveals by degrees that Bonnie is stark naked in front of a full-length mirror, in a series of sharp cuts that creates a kinetic sense of restlessness. The camera frames Bonnie through the rails of a brass footboard as she lies in bed, a metaphorical cage against which she bangs the palms of her hands in barely contained frustration; a sudden fast push-in to her eyes makes her appear almost feral. Crossing to the window, Bonnie spies Clyde snooping around.

"Hey, boy! What you doin' with my mama's car?" she asks, a thin curtain barely concealing her nudity. ("A girl who would stand up in the window like that is a girl who is willing to do a lot to become famous,"[37] Penn observed of the staging.)

Hurriedly dressing, Bonnie races downstairs and bursts on to the front porch. "Four feet away from Clyde, she stops on a dime," the shooting script reads. "They stand there, looking at each other, smiling the same challenge. For a few seconds, no one speaks."[38] A pretty standard Hollywood meet-cute, and Penn shoots the couple's banter in a classic, unbroken tracking shot as Clyde persuades a willing Bonnie to join him for a stroll into town. What the script calls "a manner of mutual impudence"[39] pervades the exchange as the cocky, dapper Clyde attempts to guess his latest conquest's profession ("A movie star!—A lady mechanic?—A maid?—A waitress!") while Bonnie walks slightly ahead, looking back teasingly, purse swinging on her arm—a bit of business actress Faye Dunaway stole from Joanne Woodward in a similar moment in *The Long Hot Summer* (1958).

Newman and Benton reduce Clyde's backstory to a few lines of dialogue. "I was in state prison," he tells Bonnie, knowing it will impress her. "It was armed robbery." Walking the town's desolate main street, he ups the ante, offering to take off his shoe and show off his maimed foot (the writers get their facts wrong, placing the injury on Clyde's right foot instead of his left). There's more schoolboy than rattlesnake in Warren Beatty's performance in these early scenes, and the script makes no mention of bathroom rapes and prison tortures; this isn't *I Am a Fugitive from a Chain Gang*.

The promise of violence and sex—in that order—pervades the next sequence, where Clyde and Bonnie drink Cokes from a gas station cooler. Penn shoots the charged dialogue in tight, sensuous close-ups. "What's it like?" Bonnie asks suggestively. "What you mean, prison?" Clyde wonders. "No, armed robbery." "It ain't like anything," Clyde offers, prompting Bonnie to call him a "faker." Clyde surreptitiously pulls a .45 from his jacket. The gun receives its own loving close-up (specified in the script)[40]; Bonnie's fingers fondle the barrel.

Challenged to prove he has the "gumption" to use the weapon, Clyde ducks into the grocery store and emerges moments later with the .45 in one hand, a fistful of money in the other. "The moment is intense, as if a spark has jumped from one to the other," Benton and Newman indicate. "Their relationship, which began the minute Bonnie spotted [Clyde] in the driveway, has really begun. Clyde has shown his stuff and Bonnie is 'turned on.'"[41] Together they make their escape.

"Hey, what's your name, anyhow?" Bonnie remembers to ask as Clyde works the wires of a tan Ford coupe.

"Clyde Barrow," he says, slamming the hood.

"Hi. I'm Bonnie Parker. Pleased to meet you."

And with that, "VROOM! The car zooms off down the road, doing ninety. The fast country breakdown music starts up on the soundtrack, going just as fast as the car."[42]

Penn considered these opening moments of *Bonnie and Clyde* his favorite part of the film, and it's easy to see why. In the span of only eight-and-a-half minutes, the movie's first reel is a model of economical cinematic storytelling. The underpopulated Central Texas townscapes establish an atmosphere of deprivation and shriveled opportunities on a par with those of Depression-era films themselves, bone-dry backdrops against which Clyde and Bonnie's personalities spark like heat lightning. Does it matter that nothing of what transpires is accurate?

"I don't think the original Bonnie and Clyde are very important except insofar as they motivated the writing of a script and our making of the movie," Penn stated in 1967. "They were part of an event, they were there when it was happening.... They were the outlaws, they were the sports of nature, they were thrown off by the events of their day, and they did something about it.... [They] found themselves obliged to fulfill some kind of role which put them in the position of being folk heroes—violators of the status quo.... And, in that context, one finds oneself rooting for them and, unfortunately, we find ourselves confronted with the terrible irony that we root for somebody for a relatively good cause, who, in the course of that good cause, is called upon to commit acts of violence which repel us."[43]

At least one participant in the original events saw the story in the same way: Bonnie Parker herself.

Unlike Jesse James or Billy the Kid, Clyde and Bonnie did not have to wait for a John Newman Edwards or a Walter Noble Burns to become their posthumous Homer. Bonnie served as the lovers' enthusiastic balladeer, burnishing their legend even as they lived. "Suicide Sal" proved a warm-up exercise for the self-fulfilling epitaph "The End of the Line." Hammered out on a purloined typewriter in the back seats of stolen cars, burnished in the occasional motor court that offered refuge from dingy roadside camps, the poem became known by the title newspaper editors gave it, "The Story of Bonnie and Clyde."

After an opening stanza linking her and Clyde directly to Jesse James, Bonnie addresses the "fact" and "fiction" of their story:

> Now Bonnie and Clyde are the Barrow Gang.
> I'm sure you all have read
> How they rob and steal
> And those who squeal
> Are usually found dying or dead.
>
> There's lots of untruths to those write-ups;
> They're not so ruthless as that.
> Their nature is raw;
> They hate the law –
> The stool pigeons, spotters and rats.[44]

Bonnie sprinkles blackly humorous asides throughout the poem's sixteen stanzas. At one point, Clyde suggests they stop fighting the system and find work with the National Recovery Act, designed to put unemployed Americans back on their feet. At another, newsboys lament declining sales. *"I wish old Clyde would get jumped,"* says one. *"In these awful hard times / We'd make a few dimes / If five or six cops would get bumped."*[45]

The early ebullience gives way to a tone of dark inevitability—one that suggests Bonnie might well have approved of Newman and Benton's irreverent script.

> The road gets dimmer and dimmer;
> Sometimes you can hardly see;
> But it's fight, man to man,

And do all you can,
For they know they can never be free.[46]

* * * *

They don't think they're too smart or desperate,
They know that the law always wins;
They've been shot at before
But they do not ignore
That death is the wages of sin.[47]

Whatever her misgivings about Clyde's precipitous departure in that rain-soaked riverbed outside Kaufman, Bonnie showed no hesitation when Clyde sent for her after the fateful Stringtown shootout. The reunited couple endured an existence only hinted at in the fade-out to *I Was a Fugitive from a Chain Gang*. Through all the hardship to follow, there was this assurance: Clyde and Bonnie wouldn't be alone on their way to the end of the line.

They'd have plenty of guns to keep them company.

8

"INFRINGED!"

> The only thing that stops a bad guy with a gun
> is a good guy with a gun.
> —Wayne LaPierre, former executive vice president
> and chief executive of the National Rifle Association.

Even more than the average American gun owner, Clyde Barrow loved his firearms.

Really loved them.

Couldn't have too many of them, in fact.

In a twenty-five-page US Bureau of Investigation report dated August 17, 1933, detailing the Barrow Gang's most recent outrages, agent D. W. Brantley provided an inventory of weapons stolen a month before from a National Guard armory in Enid, Oklahoma—229 miles away from the gang's last known hideout in Joplin, Missouri. The arsenal included thirty-three Colt .45 semiautomatic pistols, two Remington .45s and three Browning automatic rifles (BARs), all marked "Property of the United States."[1] One of Clyde's confederates remembered him returning from the raid with "so many guns it looked like a gun factory."[2]

Clyde supplemented the Enid haul with repeated August thefts from the National Guard armory in Plattville, Illinois, adding another three BARs (along with nearly two dozen twenty-round magazines), ten Colt Model 1911 .45-caliber pistols, and two US Army Model 1903 .30-caliber rifles to his private collection; for good measure—or maybe just as keepsakes—he also snagged a couple of bayonets and their scabbards.[3] The brazen plundering of federal storehouses prompted one special agent to urge Bureau of Investigation director J. Edgar Hoover "that representations be made to the War Department that more careful steps [be] taken to protect armories from depredations by criminals, whereby such criminals become armed with government weapons." (Hoover deemed the recommendation "inappropriate" on jurisdictional grounds, but did call the matter to the attention of his superiors in the Department of Justice.)[4]

Always a stickler for style, Clyde understood that snazzy clothes alone didn't make the man: guns did, and the more the better. Like his heroes Jesse James and Billy the Kid, Clyde self-consciously embodied a classic Western archetype: The Man with a Gun. "The premier outlaws of the 1930s were well aware that they belonged to a tradition," noted one observer. "They were weaned on it and influenced by it; they paid obeisance to it in word and deed; and the trajectory of their brief, spectacular careers was ultimately defined by it."[5] As Bonnie's poetry and Clyde's actions demonstrated, for them "Robin Hood and Jesse James were alive and well and moving across the plains in automobiles."[6]

Clyde's real-life obsession with high-capacity firearms points to another uniquely national obsession, one fundamental to the outlaw ethos. In his seminal genre study *The Six-Gun Mystique*, John G. Cawelti posited that "American tradition has always emphasized individual masculine force; Americans love to see themselves as pioneers, men who have conquered a continent and sired on it a new society." This manufactured history of men against the wilderness "created the need for a means of symbolic expression of masculine potency in an unmistakable way."[7]

The gun.

American separation from the mother country was the direct result of an early act of gun control: British general Thomas Gage's attempt to seize the colonial arsenal at Concord, Massachusetts on April 19, 1775; Gage proved less adapt at gun-grabbing than Clyde Barrow. The myth persists in many quarters that colonists' facility with firearms constituted the key factor in

America's victory over the greatest military empire of the eighteenth century. "*Freedom from Great Britain was won not by supermen using superweapons,*" reads the official history of the National Rifle Association (NRA), driving the point home in italics. "*It was won by ordinary citizens whose will to fight for liberty was backed by an intimate knowledge of firearms gained through the use of personal weapons.*"[8]

What we now call "gun rights" are conspicuously absent from the debate that led to the US Constitution and the battle for ratification that followed. One searches James Madison's notes on the Constitutional Convention in 1787 and the eighty-five articles written in the Constitution's defense by Madison, Alexander Hamilton, and John Jay that collectively became known as *The Federalist Papers* for a single reference to firearms. "Where there was reference to guns in the founding era," notes Adam Winkler, professor of constitutional law at the University of California, Los Angeles, "it was almost exclusively in reference to armed militias that were necessary for the defense of the state and the nation."[9] That association was made explicit in the Bill of Rights, the ten amendments appended to the Constitution in December 1791 to assuage fears of a too-powerful central government. First priority was granted to freedom of religion, speech, and assembly. Guns came next, in the Second Amendment: "*A well-regulated Militia, being necessary to the security of a free State, the right of the people to keep and bear Arms, shall not be infringed.*"

Were it not for the vagaries of eighteenth-century syntax and punctuation, America today might be a less violent place.

"People ask: who is right? Did the Second Amendment protect militias, or an individual right to a gun?" notes Michael Waldman, president of the Brennan Center for Justice at New York University School of Law. "The answer: both and neither. It protected the individual right to a gun—to fulfill the duty to serve in a militia. To the Framers, even our *question* would make little sense. To us, today, their *answer* makes little sense."[10]

Lawyers and constitutional scholars have eagerly and often profitably stepped into the breach left by the resounding historical silence of the drafting and ratification of the Constitution. Does the preamble ("*A well-regulated militia*") limit the scope of the right that follows? What is the precise eighteenth-century meaning of the words "*bear*" and "*arms*"? And that's to name only two of the least arcane points of contention. Stephen Halbrook, the most influential advocate of the pro-individual rights position, states categorically "the American federal Bill of Rights was ratified, in part, as a formal recognition that private individuals would never be disarmed."[11]

In the words of Paul Andrew Hutton, "When you have something like owning a firearm enshrined in the Constitution of the United States, that says a lot about your society."[12]

For the better part of a century, popular and academic perceptions of America's westward expansion derived from the "frontier thesis" postulated by Frederick Jackson Turner in a paper delivered at the 1893 Chicago World Columbian Exposition. Little commented upon at the time, Turner's "The Significance of the Frontier in American History" exerted a disproportionate influence on generations of traditionalist American historians in its positioning of "the West" as the tipping point between "civilization" and "savagery," a social escape valve and equalizer that created the democratic American character. "For a moment, at the frontier, the bonds of custom are broken and unrestraint is triumphant," Turner maintained. "In spite of environment, and in spite of custom, [the frontier] furnishes a new field of opportunity, a gate of escape from the bondage of the past."[13]

For Turner, "democracy is action and will, and part of its spirit of adventure is a breezy defiance of the law. This was not history, but romantic nationalism,"[14] maintains cultural critic Dominic Erdozian in *One Nation Under Guns*. While Turner spoke to the American Historical Association, William "Buffalo Bill" Cody entertained capacity audiences just outside the fairground gates with his spectacular—and wholly fantastical—re-enactments of Custer's Last Stand and other "animated scenes and episodes, which had their existence in fact."[15] Many of these tableaux featured Annie Oakley, regarded as one of America's best marksmen.

By the time of *Bonnie and Clyde*'s release, the "frontier theory" was under heavy siege, the myth of Manifest Destiny superseded by a new narrative of brutal conquest inflected by contemporary events. "We all talk about the legacy of the frontier," Arthur Schlesinger Jr. raged in 1968. "No doubt the frontier has bequeathed us a set of romantic obsessions about six-shooters and gunfighters." He noted that "Canada and Australia were also frontier societies. Canadians and Australians too have robust, brawling traditions; they too like to strike virile poses. Indeed, the Australians exterminated their aborigines more efficiently than we did our Indians. But Canadians and Australians do not feel the need to prove themselves today by killing people."[16] The US homicide rate at the time exceeded that of both countries fourfold.

Drawing on popular reinterpretations of America's Western history, Richard Slotkin concluded that in the public imagination, "Extraordinary violence by privileged heroes, often acting in despite of law, has been the means of our national salvation."[17] Slotkin noted how "the outlaw becomes a hero who resists the forces of order, but in a way that reaffirms the basic values of American society.... [P]rogress is achieved, but traditional values and life-ways are preserved unharmed."[18]

No period has captured the attention of audiences more than that of the "Wild West," the relatively brief era between the end of the Civil War in 1865 and the height of the industrial Gilded Age at the turn of the twentieth century. Hundreds of thousands (millions?) of novels and short stories, histories and biographies, movies and TV shows have imprinted an unwavering image of the United States on a worldwide public; international news broadcasts in Europe and elsewhere routinely enhance their coverage of American stories with computer-generated gun graphics. "Truth be told, Americans have a real love of violence," Second Amendment scholar Winkler suggests. "One of the reasons the 'Wild West' became so popular was because of the role firearms played. It could be portrayed as very violent." *Portrayed* is the keyword. "We've completely mistaken the mythology of the 'Wild West' for what it was really like," Winkler reminds. "In fact, frontier towns had the strictest gun-control laws in the nation."[19]

Despite the assertion of classic historians like Ray Allen Billington that "seldom did a group of drovers leave [a cow town] without contributing to the population of 'boot hill,'"[20] Kansas trail-drive hubs like Abilene, Caldwell, Dodge City, Ellsworth, and Wichita saw very little fatal violence. Over a fifteen-year period from 1870 to 1885, the five towns *combined* registered a total of only forty-five homicides; annual gun murders never topped five in each city, and some witnessed no homicides at all. While firearms accounted for the principal cause of death, actual gunfights were practically non-existent: thirty-nine of the forty-five recorded victims died by bullet or buckshot, but fewer than a third managed to return fire; a good many were unarmed at the time of their demise.

Robert Dykstra, who compiled these numbers for his book *The Cattle Towns*, explained the reason for the low body count. "The problem for the cattle town people was not to rid themselves of visitors prone to violence, but to suppress the violence while retaining the visitors"[21] upon whom the town's businesses (both legitimate and otherwise) depended for their livelihoods. Regulations universally proscribed discharge of firearms within city limits, along with the possession of any weapons by persons other than law enforcement officers. "THE CARRYING OF FIREARMS STRICTLY PROHIBITED," a sign advised visitors to Dodge City. "LEAVE YOUR REVOLVER AT POLICE HEADQUARTERS" greeted newcomers to Wichita.

"It's easier today to carry a gun in Dallas, Texas, or Phoenix, Arizona than it was in Dodge City, Wichita or any other iconic cow town,"[22] observes Western novelist and historian Johnny D. Boggs. Town councils and county commissions took precautions against the carrying of concealed weapons; advocates of what is known today as "concealed carry" would have been immediately apprehended, disarmed, and jailed by sheriffs.

Arguably no armed encounter in the "Wild West" has become more lionized than "the Gunfight at the O.K. Corral," thirty seconds of mayhem that occurred on the afternoon of Wednesday, October 26, 1881, in a vacant lot adjoining a photography studio in Tombstone, Arizona. Celebrated in self-mythologizing films from *My Darling Clementine* (1946) to *Tombstone*

(1993) and re-enacted with numbing theme-park regularity today, the confrontation pitted Deputy US Marshall Virgil Earp, his brothers Wyatt and Morgan, and temporarily deputized John Henry "Doc" Holliday against brothers Ike and Billy Clanton and Tom and Frank McLaury. Both McLaurys and Billy Clanton died in the encounter, which left Virgil and Morgan Earp along with Holliday badly wounded; Wyatt suffered nary a scratch. The shootout contributed to Tombstone's most violent year with a whopping *five* total homicides (two of them of men named McLaury), making Tombstone barely worthy of the sobriquet "the Wickedest Town in the West."

For almost fifty years, Wyatt Earp and the encounter at the O.K. Corral remained virtually unknown to the American public. That changed with the 1931 publication of *Wyatt Earp: Frontier Marshall* by Stuart N. Lake. Written in the first person and purported to have been based on extensive interviews with the eighty-year-old lawman, who died before the book's release, *Frontier Marshall* became an immediate bestseller but has long since been exposed as an elaborate fabrication. A onetime professional wrestling promoter and aide to Theodore Roosevelt in the former president's failed 1912 third-party "Bull Moose" campaign, Lake admitted to exercising dramatic license in his portrayal of Earp as "an invincible champion with fists or gun, nerveless, lightning fast on the draw, a killer with a tender heart, a protector of the weak... in truth a Christ figure in cowboy boots wielding the thunderbolts of the Almighty."[23]

Lake's "biography" became the basis of all future iterations of the Earp story. Since the book's publication, George O'Brien, Randolph Scott, Henry Fonda, Burt Lancaster, James Garner, Kurt Russell, and Kevin Costner have all made the walk down Allen Street in nearly a dozen feature films, disparate in tone but all adhering to Lake's template. A fan-favorite episode of *Star Trek*, "The Specter of the Gun," aired on October 25, 1968, places Captain James T. Kirk, Mr. Spock and "Bones" McCoy in the O.K. Corral—on the losing side—as punishment for violating interplanetary protocol. The crew of the starship *Enterprise* survives thanks to a Vulcan mind-meld enabling them to believe that "the bullets are unreal, without body; they are illusions only" (an option not available in 1934 to Clyde Barrow and Bonnie Parker).

Lake earned a fortune from the ABC TV series *The Life and Legend of Wyatt Earp*, with Hugh O'Brian in the title role. The show preceded CBS's *Gunsmoke* on to the air in 1955 as television's first "adult" Western program, running for six seasons and spawning a host of merchandising tie-ins, including comic books, action figures, tableware, and mugs. Thanks to such promotion in the succeeding decades, the Gunfight at the O.K. Corral has become "so much a part of American folklore that scarcely a public confrontation of any kind can occur without someone evoking it."[24]

The brief episode, of no particular significance at the time, has nonetheless become a defining myth embraced by proponents of an armed society. Its reimaginings have "taught us that once there was a time when people settled their differences with guns, not lawsuits," Winkler writes in *Gun Fight: The Battle Over the Right to Bear Arms in America*, "when men were willing to risk their lives to defend their honor; when everyone was armed and gun violence was an accepted way of life. Like many myths, however . . . the lessons often taken from the Shootout at the O.K. Corral are profoundly misleading."[25]

Author Johnny Boggs agrees. "One way to look at the Gunfight at the O.K. Corral is as an arrest gone bad," he suggests. "And what most of the dead were meant to be arrested for was possession of a firearm."[26]

Tombstone's Ordinance No. 9 mandated against the carrying of deadly weapons, except for "persons immediately leaving or entering the city, who, with good faith, and within reasonable time are proceeding to deposit, or take from the place of deposit such deadly weapon." In court testimony, Virgil Earp insisted he meant only to disarm the Clantons and McLaurys, who had repeatedly refused to surrender their guns and had later been seen buying ammunition at the local dry goods store. No doubt Virgil dissembled—the bad blood between the two families encompassed more than Second Amendment issues. Regardless of underlying motives (a whole cottage industry of Tombstone lore continues to spew out conflicting interpretations), the victims were in clear violation of the law.

"The Shootout at the O.K. Corral, then, is not only a story about America's gun culture," Winkler states. "It is also a tale about America's gun control culture."[27]

It doesn't take a law degree to note that the words "well-regulated" and "right" occur in the text of the Second Amendment. For most of its history, the National Rifle Association endorsed that balanced philosophy. The organization demonized for its advocacy of unrestricted gun rights began its existence as a bastion for gun safety. "The Civil War ... demonstrated with bloody clarity that soldiers who couldn't shoot straight were of little value," wrote NRA cofounder George Wingate. Wingate experienced that horror firsthand, as a Union soldier in the Gettysburg campaign with the 22nd Regiment of the New York National Guard, where he earned the reputation of being a crack shot.

In the summer of 1869, Wingate met fellow New Yorker William Conant Church, a seasoned journalist who had embedded with the Army of the Potomac and later been made a brevet lieutenant colonel in charge of organizing the capitol's militia against a threatened Confederate attack. The two men shared a concern over the dismal marksmanship of Union riflemen and "sought to promote and encourage rifle shooting on a scientific basis."[28] European nations, they noted, had "long since instituted a thorough system of instruction of rifle practice."[29] In America, on the other hand, "the matter has been entirely neglected." With Union general and three-time Rhode Island governor Ambrose Burnside as its first celebrity figurehead, the NRA obtained a charter in November 1871 and opened up shop in Church's offices on 192 Broadway.

Over the course of its first few decades, the NRA relied almost entirely on state funding and other government handouts. All but extinct after 1892, the organization was rejuvenated in the new century, when the federal government in 1903 established the National Board for the Promotion of Rifle Practice and assigned the NRA to organize annual shooting competitions bringing together marksmen from both national armed services and state militias. The NRA's dedication to improving US military marksmanship took on new urgency in the lead-up to America's entry into World War I, when NRA shooting-match master Morton C. Mumma became commander of the army's Small Arms Firing School for the Instruction of Officers and Enlisted Men in Rifle and Pistol Shooting. In gratitude for the organization's services, the US government made $200,000 worth of decommissioned rifles available to NRA members at the war's end. (One can only imagine what Clyde Barrow might have thought at the sight of such lethal bounty.)

Second Amendment issues played no part in the NRA's post–World War I activities. But with the rise of organized crime that accompanied the onset of Prohibition, NRA leadership sought to draw a firm line between law-abiding members and the "criminal element." *Americans and Their Guns*, the NRA's first official history (published in 1967 while *Bonnie and Clyde* was in release), noted "under the conditions that prevailed in the 1920s and early 1930s, tighter regulations of the sale and use of firearms became inevitable."[30] To state it another way: the NRA recognized the need for a limited form of gun control. An editorial in the organization's in-house magazine, *American Rifleman*, written in the wake of the February 1929 St. Valentine's Day Massacre, advocated permits for the carrying of concealed handguns and the keeping of dealer records "so that police in recovering a weapon may trace its original purchaser."[31]

As gun violence continued and state laws proved unable to stop the bloodletting, President Franklin D. Roosevelt established the country's first nationwide anti-gun crime legislation. FDR's attorney general Homer Cummins made Clyde Barrow and Bonnie Parker the poster children for what the administration called a "New Deal for Crime." "Show me the man who doesn't want his gun registered," Cummins famously said, "and I will show you a man who shouldn't have a gun."[32] The National Firearm Act of 1934 imposed prohibitive taxes and registration requirements on automatic machine guns and short-barreled, sawed-off rifles and shotguns—weapons like Clyde's trademark "whippit" gun—and banned sound-suppressors (so-called silencers) outright. Subsequent legislation passed in 1938 added provisions requiring the licensing of all firearms sellers and made illegal the sale or transfer of guns to "prohibited persons" such as convicted felons. Its central provisions still remain in force.[33]

Behind the scenes, the NRA successfully lobbied to remove language that would have subjected handguns to the same registration requirements as other proscribed weapons (pistol owners accounted for a large part of the association's membership). "I think we should be careful in considering regulatory measures to make sure they do not hamstring the law-abiding citizen in his opposition to the crook,"[34] NRA president Karl Frederick cautioned; a membership letter-writing campaign flooded congressional offices and served as a precursor to the association's modern methods.

Testifying before the House Ways and Means Committee, Frederick lent his support to the bill in its final form. A conservationist at a time when gun ownership and recreation went hand in hand, Frederick had been awarded three gold medals for pistol shooting at the 1920 Olympic Games in Antwerp. Asked his opinion on any potential drawbacks to firearms restrictions, Frederick replied, "I do not believe in the general promiscuous toting of guns. I think it should be sharply restricted and only under licenses."[35]

Congressmen had another question for Frederick. Was the bill unconstitutional, or did it violate any constitutional provision?

In a reply that seems inconceivable in the twenty-first-century world of gun politics, Frederick said, "I have not given it any study from that point of view."[36] Protection for gun ownership, the NRA president insisted, "lies in an enlightened public sentiment and in intelligent legislative action. It is not to be found in the Constitution."[37] A subsequent editorial in *American Rifleman* urged readers who might take exception to that view to "keep your political interest and activity on a high plane of honest, frank discussion; and remember that there is neither rhyme nor reason in splitting open a good rifle club over a bum political argument."[38]

When a challenge arose to the National Firearms Act, it came not from the NRA, but a rather unexpected place: the US Department of Justice. Seeking a test case to circumvent future constitutional controversy, attorney general Cummins found his ideal client in the criminal underworld. Clyde Barrow and Bonnie Barker had been dead for three years when Jack Miller, a member of an Ozark crew known as the O'Malley Gang, turned state's evidence against his associates in exchange for freedom. Less than a year later, in April 1938, Arkansas cops busted Miller and a companion for crossing state lines with an unregistered sawed-off shotgun—a clear violation of the National Firearms Act. When the trial judge declared the legislation unconstitutional and ordered Miller released, Cummins sought an immediate appeal to the Supreme Court.

The case that became known as *United States v. Miller* (1939) marked the first time since the birth of the republic that America's highest tribunal agreed to address the Second Amendment directly. From the start, it was a one-sided argument: Miller went missing the moment he had been released; his bullet-riddled body turned up the month after oral argument, the result of an Oklahoma robbery gone sour. "UNABLE TO OBTAIN ANY MONEY FROM CLIENTS TO BE PRESENT AND ARGUE CASE,"[39] read the telegram to the court clerk from Miller's attorney, who advised the nine justices to decide the issue based on the government's presentation alone.

US Solicitor General Robert H. Jackson, himself destined for the Supreme Court after his blistering prosecution at the Nuremberg Trials (attended by a young Arthur Penn), argued that the Second Amendment right to keep and bear arms "is not one which may be utilized for private purposes but only one which exists where the arms are borne in the militia or some other military organization provided for by law and intended for the protection of the state." Citing numerous state and local edicts, Jackson reminded the justices that the weapons prohibited under the National Firearms Act "have no legitimate use in the hands of private individuals but, on the contrary, frequently constitute the arsenal of the gangster and the desperado."[40]

A unanimous Supreme Court agreed. "We construe the amendment as having relation to ... military service and we are unable to say that a sawed-off shotgun has relation to the militia,"[41] noted Justice James McReynolds in announcing the decision. The court established that Second Amendment protections extended only to weapons practical for militia use—and, more importantly, their actual use only in a "well-regulated militia." Latter-day gun-rights scholars, many funded by the NRA, have sought to cast doubt on the *Miller* decision. "Because the defendants made no appearance on appeal ... the court failed to benefit from hearing the adverse arguments which would have rendered balanced opinions more likely,"[42] Stephen Halbrook wrote.

Procedural improprieties notwithstanding, *Miller* went unchallenged for seventy years.[43] Its reading of the Second Amendment, together with the restrictions on gun ownership laid out in the 1934 National Firearms Act, would still be the law of the land three decades later, when a new, unprecedented wave of violence swept across America, one even more devastating than the lawless frontier of the 1930s, ultimately claiming the lives of a president, a crusading former attorney general, and the most prominent civil rights leader of his generation. "The successive shootings, in a short time, of three men who greatly embodied the idealism of American life suggest not so much a fortuitous set of aberrations as an emerging pattern of response in action," Arthur Schlesinger Jr. wrote, warning of "a spreading and ominous belief in the efficacy of violence and the politics of the deed."[44]

As before, events prompted a national reckoning on the troubling preponderance of firearms and people's willingness to back up their perceived liberties with lethal force. ("No one has ever attempted to assassinate a president with a bow and arrow,"[45] Schlesinger noted.) Once again, outrage would be followed by concrete action: the Gun Control Act of 1968. But the consequences would be very, very different.

By that time, Clyde Barrow and Bonnie Parker were long gone from the scene of the crime. But *Bonnie and Clyde* was on a cross-country rampage.

(*above*) Shot to pieces. Lawmen in Arcadia, Louisiana, converge on the shattered remains of Clyde Barrow and Bonnie Parker's last stolen Ford V-8. "I literally could not have heard thunder," one posse member said of the fatal barrage. Dallas Municipal Archives via University of North Texas Libraries, The Portal to Texas History.

(*below*) Dying over and over. Faye Dunaway replicated Bonnie Parker's death throes over eight takes and four grueling days of filming on a Warner Bros. ranch location far away from the real events. Warner Bros./Cinematic/Alamy Stock Photo.

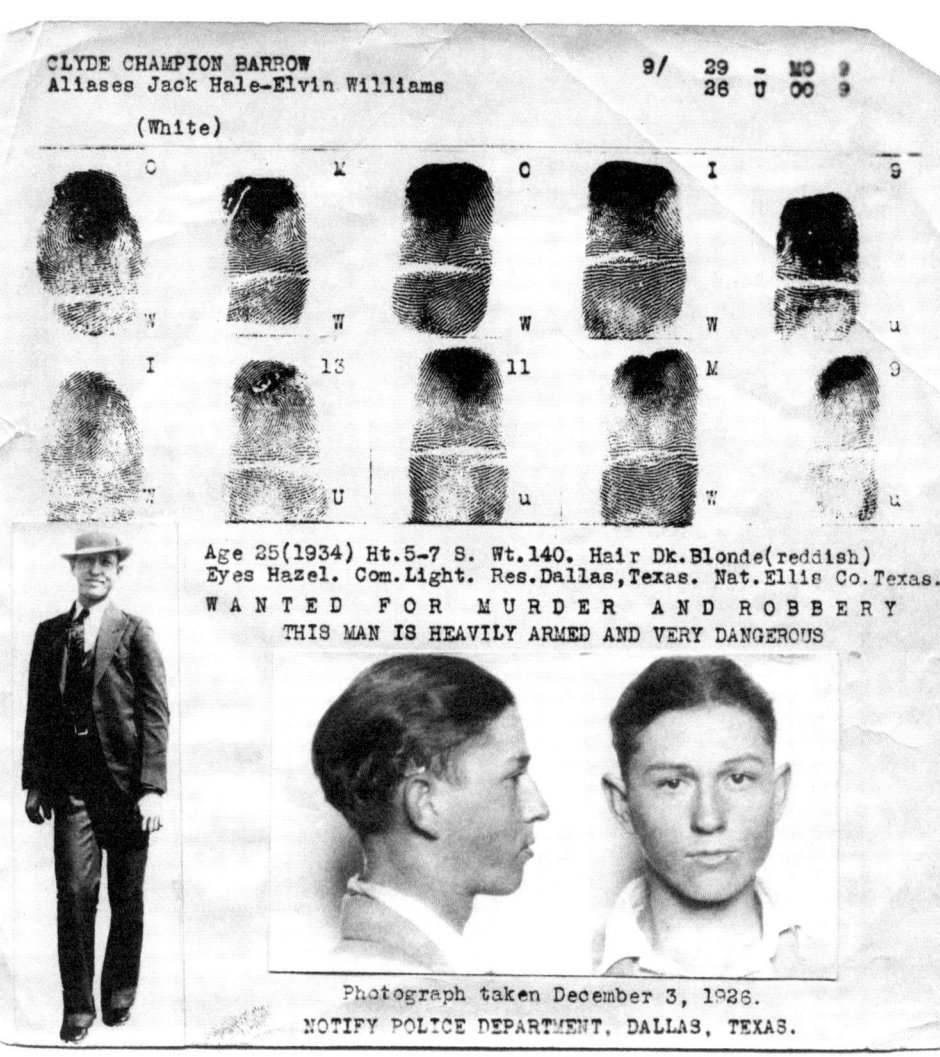

More "Our Gang" than gangster. One of Clyde Barrow's earliest mug shots remained on police and FBI files throughout his short career. Dallas Municipal Archives via University of North Texas Libraries, The Portal to Texas History.

(*opposite above*) "Mutt and Jeff." Screenwriters David Newman and Robert Benton, who brought their *Esquire* sensibility to the story of a couple of cheap hoods. Burton Berinsky/Courtesy of the Everett Collection.

(*opposite below*) Wish list. François Truffaut, the screenwriters' first choice to direct *Bonnie and Clyde*. The French director's *Jules and Jim* paved the way for a nouvelle vague treatment of the Barrow Gang story. Jack de Nijs for Anefo.

Born in gunfire. Paul Revere's "The Bloody Massacre" engraving, a wholly fanciful rendering of events that transpired on March 5, 1770. Courtesy of the Diplomatic Reception Rooms, US Department of State, Washington, DC.

(*opposite above*) Anything goes: Nils Asther and Barbara Stanwyck in Frank Capra's 1932 pre-Code interracial romance *The Bitter Tea of General Yen*. Columbia Pictures via Wikimedia Commons.

(*opposite below*) "I like violence." Director Arthur Penn, arguably cinema's keenest observer of a uniquely American obsession. His films of the late sixties and early seventies helped to define the New Hollywood. Courtesy of the Penn Family.

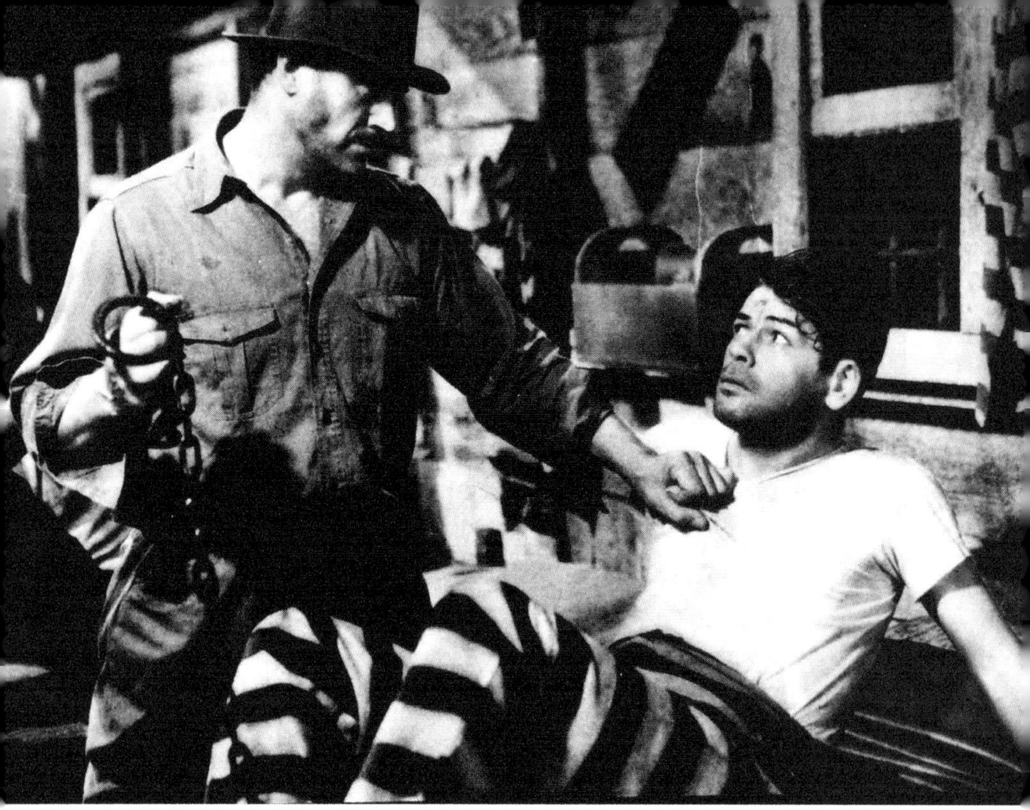

(*opposite above*) "I steal." Publicity still for Warner Bros.' *I Am a Fugitive from a Chain Gang* (1932), a classic of the pre-Code era and to this day one of the hardest-hitting films ever made. United Archives GmbH/Alamy Stock Photo.

(*opposite below*) Cashing in at the O.K. Corral. Hugh O'Brian in the title role of the long-running ABC series *The Life and Legend of Wyatt Earp*, which made a fortune for Earp huckster Stuart Lake.

Enough to make women's knees buckle. Warren Beatty at the height of his *Splendor in the Grass* stardom. He promised director Arthur Penn "an argument every night" and made good on his word. Moviestore Collections Ltd./Alamy Stock Photo.

(*above*) His initials on the water tower. Studio chief Jack Warner with Bette Davis and Joan Crawford. "Colonel Jack" considered his bladder an infallible barometer of a film's quality. Billy Rose Theater Division, New York Public Library.

(*below*) "Fadin' Away." *Bonnie and Clyde* marked the third of Faye Dunaway's films to be shot in 1966. Her punishing preparations for the role would have consequences in production. Courtesy of the Everett Collection.

Making their breakthrough. Estelle Parsons and Gene Hackman were the only actors ever considered for the supporting roles of Blanche and Buck Barrow. Warner Bros./Alamy Stock Photo.

Candid camera. One of the poses that made Clyde Barrow and Bonnie Parker a media sensation when published in the *Joplin Globe* two days after police discovered a camera in the gang's hastily fled garage apartment. FBI file photo.

MARVIN IVAN BARROW *ALIAS* BUCK BARROW
BLANCHE CALDWELL *ALIAS* MRS. BUCK BARROW

(*opposite above*) Art glamorizes life. Warren Beatty and Faye Dunaway re-create Clyde and Bonnie's Joplin photo for a moment not included in the final version of the film. Courtesy of Everett Collection.

(*opposite below*) "I did not look like that crying fat woman!" The real Blanche Barrow, fashionably dressed as always, poses with husband Buck in an undated doorstep photo. Dallas Municipal Archives via University of North Texas Libraries, The Portal to Texas History.

The scene of the crime. Warren Beatty (left) with Faye Dunaway and director Arthur Penn on location in Red Oak, Texas, for filming of *Bonnie and Clyde*'s pivotal murder sequence. A recently discovered cache of 8 mm film offers fascinating glimpses of the shoot. PictureLux/The Hollywood Archive/Alamy Stock Photo.

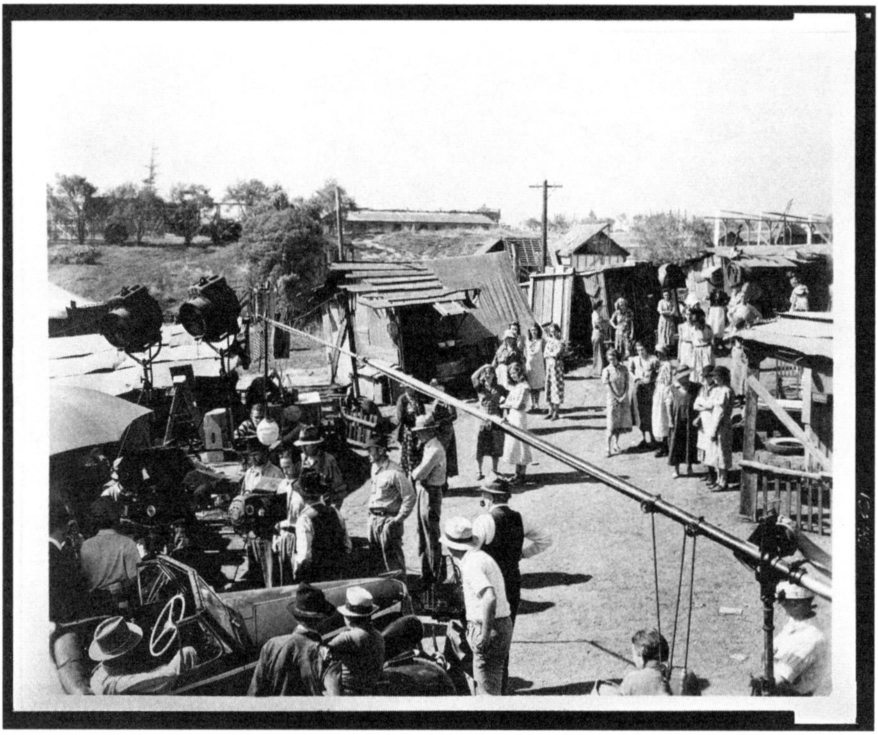

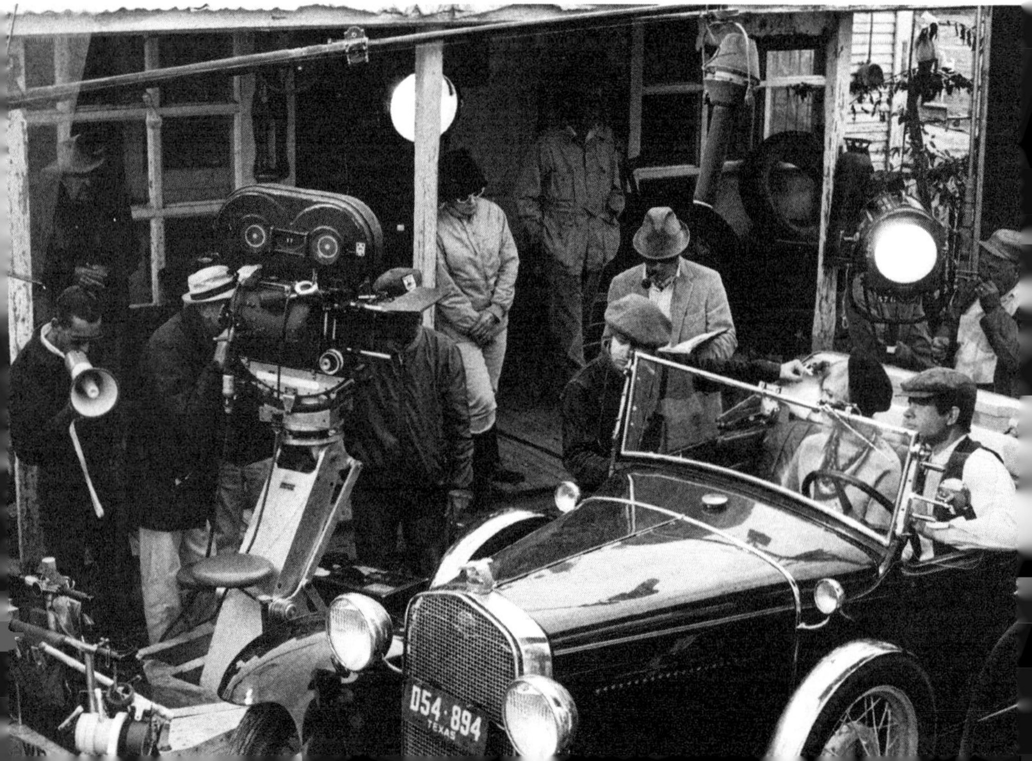
054·894
TEXAS

(*opposite above*) Small-town invasion. Location filming circumstances remained unaltered from the late 1930s to the late 1960s. Here, a recreated shantytown for John Ford's 1940 film of *The Grapes of Wrath*. Library of Congress.

(*opposite below*) On the streets of Midlothian, Texas, for the fall 1966 shoot of *Bonnie and Clyde*. Director Arthur Penn despaired of having to use the same bulky equipment as his predecessors. Picture Lux/The Hollywood Archive/Alamy Stock Photo.

"The best thing that happened to us." Dean Tavoularis (seen here on the set of *The Brinks Job* in 1978) made his debut as a production designer on *Bonnie and Clyde*. Barbara Alper/Getty Images, all rights reserved, 1978.

"Hip and young." Costume designer Theadora Van Runkle (right, with Faye Dunaway) was as stylish and attractive as the women and men she costumed. She saw the movie's potential from the first page of the script. Blue Robin Collectables/Alamy Stock Photo.

9

"AN ARGUMENT EVERY NIGHT"

What else is making a movie but attention to detail?
—Warren Beatty

My wife didn't speak to me for two weeks,"[1] Robert Benton remembered of the day Warren Beatty appeared on his Manhattan doorstep in June 1965.

The writer had only himself to blame. Beatty had cold-called Benton twenty minutes before. "I think he doubted me when I said who I was,"[2] Beatty later surmised (correctly). The actor mentioned he'd been having lunch with François Truffaut at Delmonico's and asked to see the latest draft of *Bonnie and Clyde*. "I said, 'yes, I'll bring it to you,' and he said, 'that's all right, I'll come by your apartment.'"[3] Benton told his wife, Sally, "Somebody's coming around to pick up the script." And then—there he was. Warren Beatty, in the flesh.

"That was when Warren was *really* Warren," Benton recalled. "I've seen women's knees buckle."[4] Knees like those of his wife, who answered the door. "She hadn't even had a chance to put on makeup."[5]

The heartthrob star of *Splendor in the Grass* (1961) and *Lilith* (1964) didn't stay long—and never said a word about having had a glance at the original treatment on the set of the still-unreleased *Mickey One*. Benton's phone rang a short while later. "I'm on page twenty-five and I want to do it," he announced. "Wait until you get to page forty-five," the writer advised. The phone rang again within the hour. "I'm on page forty-five and I know what you're talking about," Beatty said. "And I still want to do it."[6]

What Benton was talking about was the first appearance of the sexual triangle that caused consternation and offense in studio pitch rooms—so much so that Benton was convinced he and writing partner David Newman had tanked their movie careers before they'd even begun. The scene occurs earlier than Benton remembered, on page thirty-three of Beatty's copy of the undated screenplay. To put the moment in context: Bonnie and Clyde have just acquired a new accomplice, C. W. Moss (then called W. D.), a filling-station grease monkey impressed by their four-cylinder Ford coupe.

"A *stolen* Ford coupe," Bonnie corrects him, introducing herself and Clyde by name. "We . . . rob . . . banks."

When W. D. proves his aptitude for crime by snatching the gas station till, Clyde offers the new recruit the rumble seat. "For a moment we see them all sitting there, each smiling their little smile," this version of the script reads. "The moment is sexually charged as well—for Bonnie and Clyde the beginning of a *ménage à trois*."[7] As if that weren't direct enough, the next scene makes the implicit explicit:

Scene 23

EXT. MOTEL –NIGHT

We see the cabins, the lawn and the highway in front. The car pulls up, stops, and the trio emerge. They are high and laughing, their arms around each other, semi-staggering up the steps to their cabin-room. They go in. The door shuts. The CAMERA REMAINS where it was. Four beats of silence. Then W.D. comes out, still dressed. He is overwrought and disturbed, shaking his head back and forth. [...] The sexual proposition has just been put to him and he is reacting to it strongly negative.

W.D.
No sir! No ma'am! Nosiiir![8]

W. D. stalks to the shoulder of the highway, prepared to hitchhike. Bonnie and Clyde step out from inside the cabin and "just stand there silently, watching him. But they act as a magnet. They represent unswerving authority."[9] Left with no place to go back to because of his impetuous theft, W. D. relents and rejoins the couple inside. Scene 24 finds the threesome in bed together. Awakening with a start, W. D. suddenly "remembers what he did last night and his eyes open up as big as saucers and he leaps from the bed."[10] Newman and Benton intended the whole thing to be played for laughs, underlining the comedy with indications that "for all three of them the experience of the previous night has been really far out and wild."[11]

"I took discrete pains not to have an opinion"[12] on the *ménage*, Beatty claimed to filmmaker Laurent Bouzereau in a documentary accompanying the fortieth anniversary DVD release of *Bonnie and Clyde*. Benton's memory gibed with Beatty's. "[Warren] never said a word" about Clyde's bisexuality,"[13] the writer agreed. Director Arthur Penn would make the issue a moot point, but his involvement was still a year away, and Beatty wasn't exactly being candid in his opinions—not with Benton in June 1965, nor in his retrospective commentary. The Freudian nature of that original *Bonnie and Clyde* script "put me to sleep," Beatty admitted in a 1972 interview. "I've seen too much of that. I'm more interested in the relationship of the two of them to their society and the times. . . . The public's treatment of them. The love/hate that the public felt for them. The desperation for the little guy to get out of the crowd. That interests me. Clyde wanted to be somebody."[14]

The correlation between private individual and public persona—and the attempt to control one's media image—grounds Beatty's work as both actor and creator in films as diverse as *Bonnie and Clyde*, *Reds* (1981), *Bugsy* (1991), and *Bulworth* (1998). Beatty's biographer Suzanne Finstad observed that Beatty's own life "was defined by meticulous planning,"[15] an opinion shared by the actor's older sister, Shirley MacLaine. "He has to have control over everything," she said. "That was his ticket to survival."[16] (Clyde's sister Nell said much the same about her own brother.) It was inevitable that Beatty would someday play the ultimate control freak, Howard Hughes, as he did in his last released film to date, *Rules Don't Apply* (2016), the title itself an apt motto for its producer/director/writer/star.

Born March 1931 in Richmond, Virginia, Henry Warren Beaty (he added the extra "t" to his name), grew up in a family of Southern Baptist educators who "went to enormous lengths to maintain privacy," a family trait he "elevated to an art form,"[17] biographer Finstad noted. As a five-year-old, Beatty allowed himself to be corralled along with Shirley into his mother Kathlyn's little-theater forays. "[She] gave me a walk-on part in a play she was directing," Beatty remembered. "I walked across the stage, saying nothing, and that was it. She told me I was very good.... What made me want to try it in the first place? I don't know. I don't know. This probably has some ... embarrassing root."[18] Young Warren took refuge from his parents' incessant bickering and his father's alcoholism in books and music; like Clyde on the saxophone, Beatty became an accomplished piano player.

The movies offered escape: young Warren perfected imitations of gangster's gangster James Cagney and French matinee idol Charles Boyer; his mother laughed at Beatty pacing the floors saying, "Come wiz me to zee Casbah," Boyer's signature pickup line from his breakthrough American film, *Algiers* (1938). As a teen, Beatty developed a fascination with *Texaco Star Theater* headliner Milton Berle and made a specialty of mimicking "Uncle Miltie's" distinctive delivery. (Future collaborator Arthur Penn may have been holding the cue cards for these jokes as part of his entry-level experience in live television.) A liberal arts dropout at Northwestern University, Beatty moved to New York to study acting under Stella Adler, supporting himself with odd jobs including that of a "sandhog," digging tunnels for subways and sewers.

Beatty's early TV career offered no inkling of his eventual superstardom. His most prominent role, as rich jock Milton Armitage on the popular TV sitcom *The Many Loves of Dobie Gillis*, ended when Beatty quit the show midway through the first season. Titular star Darryl Hickman remembered Beatty as "very private, very hard to get to know, and kind of in another world—you could look at him and you'd think he was thinking of something else."[19] Added Bob Denver, who played Dobie's beatnik alter ego, Maynard G. Krebs: "We all thought [Beatty] was not long for episodic TV."[20] And he wasn't. A role in William Inge's *A Loss of Roses* earned Beatty a 1960 Tony Award nomination for Best Featured Actor in a Play and brought him to the attention of frequent Inge collaborator Elia Kazan, who cast Beatty opposite Natalie Wood in *Splendor in the Grass* (1961), his film of Inge's original script about sexual longing and societal repression in twenties-era Kansas.

Kazan, always gifted with actors, immediately divined Beatty's cinematic potential. "To be in love with Warren Beatty! What girl can run that fast?" the director asked in his autobiography. "Warren—it was obvious the first time I saw him—wanted it all and wanted it his way.... He had the energy, a very keen intelligence and more *chutzpah* than any Jew I've ever known.... [C]onfidence so great that he never had to advertise himself, even by hints."[21]

Beatty's confidence proved sometimes a blessing and mostly a curse when *Splendor in the Grass* turned the family Milton Berle impersonator into a generational icon. In the years immediately preceding the production of *Bonnie and Clyde*, Beatty found only frustration working inside the Hollywood system. His experience on *Lilith*, the final film of veteran director Robert Rossen, galvanized his determination to take a more controlling hand in his career. Beatty sleepwalks through the film as an occupational therapist at an elite mental institution, drawn to a schizophrenic patient played by French New Wave sensation Jean Seberg, who reminds him of his own mother. (It's that kind of film). Beatty found working with Rossen a comedown from the experience with Kazan and made no secret of his disappointment. "I saw [Rossen] wasn't making a good picture and told him so, which did not endear me to him."[22] The actor's unhappiness with his director—who in turn complained, "I had to hire this son of a bitch. He's driving me crazy"[23]—manifests itself in a performance that critic Judith Crist called "noteworthy for its non-acting and [Beatty's] apparent inability to deliver a line without counting to ten."[24]

For Beatty, the film marked a watershed. "An awful lot of people were saying to me, 'What the hell do you think you are? A producer?'"[25] he recalled. "It was clear to me I should get my act together and make my own pictures or it wouldn't be an enjoyable proposition for me. . . . I knew at that point that if I didn't control a film, and do it exactly the way I wanted to, that I would lose interest in movies completely."[26] Other actors had preceded him into the producing ranks: Kirk Douglas with Bryna Productions (*Paths of Glory* [1957], *Spartacus* [1960]), and Burt Lancaster with Hecht-Hill-Lancaster (*Marty* [1955], *Sweet Smell of Success* [1957]). Douglas and Lancaster were established stars, however, not twenty-eight-year-old upstarts, as Beatty was when he formed his own production company in early 1964. He christened the new enterprise Tatira, a conflation of his parents' names: Kathlyn (known as "Tat") and Ira. Its first production would be *Mickey One*, directed by Arthur Penn.

Despite Beatty's later insistence that Penn was the one and only director for *Bonnie and Clyde*, he certainly kept his options open. By the time he finally "bludgeoned Arthur to direct"[27] over salads at Dinty Moore's, the fledgling producer had shopped the script to old-guard stalwarts George Stevens and William Wyler, up-and-comers Sydney Pollack and Brian Hutton, as well as Karel Reisz and John Schlesinger, part of a new generation of British filmmakers currently enthralling audiences with their biting portraits of middle-class English life. A good thing for Beatty that François Truffaut had dropped out of the project: the director confided in a private letter that "Beatty and Marlon Brando and several others are on a little list I've classified in my head as, 'Better not to make films at all than to make films with these people.'"[28]

Always hypersensitive to other people's perceptions of him, Beatty may have suspected as much: "Truffaut was *utterly* bored by me," he admitted long after their initial meeting. "I think he did not like me for some reason of principle."[29] That principle, one that surely informed the cascade of "no's" his overtures to other filmmakers received, might have had something to do with the actor's penchant for challenging his directors at every turn. "He was arguing with them because he was generally right," maintained Robert Towne, then a screenwriter for low-budget exploitation horror flicks, whose crucial fine-tuning of the *Bonnie and Clyde* script led to a lifelong creative partnership with Beatty. "And nobody likes a smart-ass, particularly a pretty one, telling you you're fucking stupid and that you're wrong."[30]

Beatty took his role as a producer seriously—too seriously for some temperaments. "The great advantage I had getting famous when I was twenty-one was that I knew, very well, [legendary producers like] Sam Goldwyn, David Selznick, Sam Spiegel, Arthur Freed, Jerry Wald, Pancho Berman—so, as a producer, I felt, I'm responsible for the movie. I started it, I'm going to finish it, and if you're going to be a director on a movie I do, you better know you're gonna have to put up with that."[31] Beatty defined the process this way: "A healthy situation in movie making is when a certain amount of hostile intelligence can be directed at another hostile intelligence in an amiable atmosphere that doesn't deter either intelligence from functioning well."[32]

Beatty chose Penn to direct "not only because I knew him but because I could get into an argument with him. So when he said he wanted to make the movie, I said, 'I want to have one agreement: that if we make this movie, we will have an argument every night. If we don't have anything to argue about, I want to find something to argue about, because there's always something that can be better or can be thought about more.'"[33]

Which begs the question—knowing this, as he did, what persuaded Arthur Penn to abandon his reservations and agree to direct *Bonnie and Clyde*?

Penn had no illusions about what he might be getting himself into. "Warren isn't the easiest guy to work with," he said of their stormy relationship on *Mickey One*. "He's a very insistent and extremely intelligent guy who'll make you defend what you say until either you make it very clear to him or completely abandon your position."³⁴ Penn understood the process would entail far more than the threatened nightly argument and imposed one nonnegotiable demand. "We made an agreement to be frank with each other about what we were thinking, to say it very forcefully if necessary, and in the case of a complete disagreement, Warren would yield to what I wanted to do."³⁵ (It didn't always work out that way.)

Beatty called on all his formidable persuasive power in his meeting with equally willful studio boss Jack Warner. Even though Warner Bros.' release of *Splendor in the Grass* had launched Beatty's stardom, the studio hadn't been the actor/producer's first choice to make *Bonnie and Clyde*. He'd already tried his luck at 20th Century-Fox, where President Richard Zanuck, overwhelmed with preproduction on *Doctor Doolittle*, failed to see the script's potential. "That's one I kick myself in the ass for,"³⁶ Zanuck lamented (with good reason: *Doctor Doolittle* remains in the box office annals as one of the industry's costliest flops). When executives at United Artists, a company well-liked for the artistic freedom it granted to its filmmakers, dithered over a proposed budget, Beatty lost patience and headed over the Hollywood Hills to Burbank, where he sought to persuade one of Hollywood's most indomitable personalities to back his freshman producing effort.

By this time—the summer of 1966—seventy-three-year-old Jack L. Warner had already begun negotiations to sell the family studio for $184 million ($1.7 billion today) to Seven Arts, run by father-and-son investors Eliot and Kenneth Hyman. The Hymans had made a fortune syndicating the studio's collection of "Looney Tunes" and "Merrie Melodies" with Bugs Bunny, Daffy Duck, and Porky the Pig to television, along with Warner Bros.' 750-film pre-1950 library—including pre-Code classics like *I Am a Fugitive from a Chain Gang*—that became late-night TV staples. The sale to Seven Arts personally netted Warner $32 million ($295 million) and left him president of the studio. "The Colonel," as Warner liked to style himself based on his honorary World War II rank, didn't much like Beatty. He'd kicked him off the lot altogether for rejecting the lead role in the studio's film version of then-sitting President John F. Kennedy's wartime memoir, *PT 109* (1963), despite Kennedy's personal endorsement. True to form, Beatty had no regrets: "I told Kennedy I didn't think he should allow the movie to be made. I said I didn't think it was very good";[37] the role eventually went to Cliff Robertson.

At the time of the prodigal actor's visit, Warner was deeply immersed in preproduction on *Camelot*, the $15 million screen adaptation of the Broadway hit starring Richard Burton and Julie Andrews (neither of whom was destined to re-create their roles) to be directed by Joshua Logan—Penn's former Soldiers' Shows colleague from occupied Germany. Warner was so sure of the mega-budget film's success he intended to take personal producing credit, as he had for the first time on the multi-Oscar-winning version of another Alan Jay Lerner and Frederick Loewe musical, *My Fair Lady*, which revived the studio's sagging fortunes on its release in 1964.

Warner sought to establish the meeting's terms right at the outset.

"You have your opinion, kid, but do you know whose name is on that water tower?" he asked, pointing to the landmark outside his office that bore the distinctive "WB" shield.

"Well, it's got your name, but it's got my initials!"[38] Beatty responded, not missing a beat.

And then, as legend has it, he got down on his hands and knees—or lay down on the rug—or crawled across the floor to kiss "The Colonel's" feet—all the while begging, "You've got to let me make this picture."

All great stories. But, like most great stories ... they never happened.

"[Winston] Churchill said, 'History will be very kind to me because I intend to write it,'" Beatty quoted on the fortieth anniversary of *Bonnie and Clyde*. "So I think all this talk about—years after—when a movie was made, who knows what we remember or don't remember?"[39] What Beatty chose to remember—and it's borne out in the Warner Bros. files archived at the University of Southern California's Cinematic Arts Library—was that the decision to green-light *Bonnie and Clyde* came not from Warner personally, but at the urging of studio head of production, Walter MacEwen. Both MacEwen and advertising chief Richard Lederer had read the script and sensed its potential to tap into an emerging youth audience. Lederer remembered Warner Bros. in the mid-sixties as "a very conservative studio that put out one terrible movie after another. Nobody seemed to realize the audience was changing and we'd better change, too."[40]

A heavy internal lobbying effort finally broke down "The Colonel's" resistance. Beatty's deal called for him to receive $100,000 as actor and an equal amount as producer, the latter to be paid as a portion of the movie's gross receipts; Penn salary was set at $150,000, with another $100,000 deferred. Tatira, Beatty's production company, would be entitled to two-thirds of the first $300,000 in ticket sales after the studio recouped nearly three times its production cost, and 40 percent of profits thereafter—if there were any, and Warner doubted it. He had no intention of emptying studio coffers to satisfy Beatty's vanity. The preliminary budget of $1,655,137.50 was well below the studio average and amounted to a tenth of *Camelot*'s cost, testament to distribution head Ben Kalmenson's disregard for the whole enterprise.

Bonnie and Clyde would finally get made—but on a "B"-picture budget.[41]

By then, it was August 1966. Tatira's contract with Warner Bros. called for shooting to begin on October 4, with fifty-five days of principal photography and another six days of second-unit shooting (background and action shots not involving main cast members, often handled by a separate crew). The producer and director began casting in earnest, establishing their headquarters at Beatty's penthouse suite at the Beverly Wilshire Hotel. Dubbed "La Escondida"—The Hideaway—the command center consisted of "two rooms filled with a disorder of books, scripts, records, half-eaten sandwiches, and a slew of room service trays piled up against the door or buried amidst the debris of phone messages and crumpled typing paper."[42] There was also an AstroTurf terrace overlooking Rodeo Drive, a prime observation spot for Beatty to survey the parade of would-be starlets.

For a brief time at the outset of the project, Beatty had considered only producing, not starring in the film. He envisioned troubadour Bob Dylan as Clyde, with sister Shirley as Bonnie; one can only thank the movie gods for dictating otherwise. Once Beatty talked himself into the part, his thoughts turned to his *Splendor in the Grass* costar, Natalie Wood. Beatty and Wood had been more than colleagues on the Kazan film: they'd been lovers, flouting Wood's marriage to Robert Wagner, which ended in divorce a year later.[43] Her presence might have relieved producer Beatty of the worry of having actor Beatty shoulder an entire picture on his own, but Wood withstood his repeated overtures. Beatty also fielded the names of Ann-Margret, Sharon Tate, Sue Lyon, and Jane Fonda, who had costarred in Penn's *The Chase*. (Remembered Fonda: "Warren has an incredible way of making you *think* he's offering you a part... and then not using you—and you never feel rejected. That's a gift."[44])

Penn sat quietly through all his producer's musings. He'd already decided that a movie star would not play Bonnie. Only one actress ever received a formal offer: twenty-three-year-old Tuesday Weld, another member of the *Dobie Gillis* ensemble, whose passing resemblance to the real Bonnie Parker and wild-child screen persona—she'd been Stanley Kubrick's first choice to play *Lolita* (1962)—made her an ideal fit. The timing proved terrible. A new mother still breastfeeding her infant daughter, Weld didn't feel herself up to the task; she also found the script "really violent... I just thought it was a bit much."[45] Time was running out, and Beatty and Penn were short on options. "I was turned down by every living actress,"[46] Beatty marveled—clearly not a position in which he was used to finding himself.

Enter Faye Dunaway.

"I understood this role," the actress recounted in her autobiography. "I understood this kind of hunger, this kind of desperation, this kind of need."[47]

Dorothy Faye Dunaway grew up in Bascom, Florida, under circumstances Bonnie Parker might have recognized. "You could stand in the middle of the dirt road that ran in front of the house I was born in and look hard either way and see nothing but long rows of peanuts."[48] Her alcoholic father, John McDowell Dunaway, earned a meager living as a sharecropper, scraping by on ten dollars a month and housing his family in a sun-bleached, one-room frame house with an exterior pump and outhouse. Drafted into the US Army following the outbreak of World War II (reportedly at the written behest of Dunaway's mother, Grace, who made sure the monthly War Department allotment checks were sent directly to her), John Dunaway led his family on a peripatetic existence from base to base throughout Dorothy Faye's youth and adolescence, rarely lingering more than a few years in any one place.

Like Bonnie, young Dorothy Faye was "a yearning, edgy, ambitious southern girl" who "knew the only way to get what she wanted was through her own force of will. She was driven by her own desire. I know that territory—you do whatever it takes."[49]

Dunaway did just that.

Six days after arriving in New York City with a theater degree from Boston University, she landed a yearlong contract in the replacement cast for the Broadway production of Robert Bolt's *A Man for All Seasons* and simultaneously earned a coveted spot in the Lincoln Center Repertory Company training program run by Elia Kazan. Dunaway spent three years under Kazan's tutelage. Taken with the way she even then "walked around in a cloud of drama,"[50] the director cast Dunaway as understudy to his wife Barbara Loden in Arthur Miller's *After the Fall*, a thinly disguised account of the playwright's failed marriage to Marilyn Monroe. Dunaway's big break came as a discontented, hard-drinking young Boston Irish bride in the off-Broadway production of William Alfred's blank-verse period drama *Hogan's Goat*, a role that called for her to tumble down a flight of stairs to her death every night. An immediate hit, the production attracted a distinguished audience—including Arthur Penn. Had it not been for a casting director's prejudices, Dunaway might have landed a role in *The Chase*.

Best to stick with theater, she was told. "I wasn't pretty enough for the movies."[51]

Sam Spiegel, who happened to be producer of *The Chase*, along with *The African Queen* (1951), *On the Waterfront* (1954), *The Bridge on the River Kwai* (1957), and *Lawrence of Arabia* (1962), disagreed. Alerted to Dunaway by *his* casting director, Joyce Selznick, the niece of *Gone with the Wind* producer David O. Selznick, whose list of past discoveries included New York truck driver Bernie Schwartz (better known as Tony Curtis), Spiegel signed Dunaway to a non-exclusive five-picture contract. "[You're] star material," the producer told Dunaway after a screen test. "The kind of actress that could expect a thirty-year career."[52] Not to be outdone, producer/director Otto Preminger (*Laura* [1944], *Anatomy of a Murder* [1959], *Exodus* [1960]) then offered Dunaway a non-exclusive *six*-picture contract. (Both deals ran concurrently.)

"Like Dorothy in Kansas, I was picked up by the tornado, whirled around and finally spat out,"[53] the still-bruised actress mused in 1995.

Bonnie and Clyde was not the first but the *third* of Dunaway's films to be shot in 1966. First up came the Spiegel-produced *The Happening*, a trippy kidnapping romp headlining Anthony Quinn in what trailers described as "The Story of a Mobster, a Chick and Three Young Guys on a Wild $3,000,000 Caper!" Posters promised "It's . . . Like . . . Different!" Despite the pedigree of Quinn and director Elliot Silverstein, fresh off the success of *Cat Ballou* (1965), the movie more than lives down to its advertising. "My entire wardrobe consisted of less rather than more—miniskirts, minishirts and acres of bare midriff," Dunaway wrote. "My navel got almost as much exposure as my face."[54]

Preminger's *Hurry Sundown* was an altogether different experience. Dunaway coveted the lead female role of a wealthy socialite (eventually played by Jane Fonda) but instead played a white-trash dirt-farmer's wife clothed in distinctly unglamorous rags, a part she could identify with from her mother's and grandmother's experiences. The autocratic director browbeat Dunaway along with everyone else in his cast, which included Michael Caine, Robert Hooks, Burgess Meredith, and Diahann Carroll, in a turgid melodrama of

Southern race relations destined to be dated even as it was being made on location in Louisiana. "There are three kinds of directors," Dunaway said. "One who will help you, one who doesn't hurt you, and one who will drag you down. Otto was one of the ones who dragged me down."[55]

Fortunately for Dunaway, neither *The Happening* nor *Hurry Sundown* had yet been released by the time Beatty and Penn were casting *Bonnie and Clyde*. Unfortunately, both producer and director had seen cut footage from the Silverstein film, which made them unprepared for the actress who walked into La Escondida to read the script's opening scene with Beatty. The normally slight Dunaway—"not much more than skin and bones, 115 pounds on my 5'7" frame"[56]—had put on twenty-five pounds to play her role in *Hurry Sundown*. "She doesn't look like much,"[57] Beatty complained privately, also worried that Dunaway's high cheek-boned facial features—what he called her "bone structure"—might not be suited to the role of a small-town bandit. "Fuck, man. She looks like something you put on the prow of a ship," Beatty remembered thinking. "That face—looks like she could kill you by looking at you."[58]

Visibly nervous but encouraged by Penn's supportive presence, Dunaway managed to put her own insecurities aside and delivered a convincing reading. "In that moment," she recounted in her autobiography, "I was really ... home free."[59] Getting Beatty to sign off required a makeover at a Beverly Hills salon and a series of publicity photos shot at the behest of Dunaway's press agent by Curtis Hanson; the future Oscar-winning director of *L.A. Confidential* (1997) was then a freelance photographer-editor for *Cinema* magazine. "The way I shot her, backlit with her hair back, she looked softer and thinner,"[60] said Hanson, who took the developed slides along with a projector and an old king-size sheet with him to La Escondida to screen for Beatty.

Thanks in part to Hanson's photographs, *Bonnie and Clyde* at last found its Bonnie. Contracts on file at the Warner Bros. archives list Dunaway's salary at $30,000 for twelve weeks' work on the picture, with another two free weeks if needed. Indicative of Dunaway's newcomer status, internal Warner Bros.

communications consistently misspell the actress's name as "Fay." There was one unwritten stipulation: before shooting began, Dunaway needed to shed those excess twenty-five pounds, a task to which the actress applied herself with characteristic intensity. "I spent weeks walking around my apartment and working out wearing a twelve-pound weight belt," Dunaway wrote, "with smaller weights around my wrists to help me burn off the pounds faster. I only took the weights off to sleep and bathe."[61]

She did more than that: "[Faye] went on a starvation diet," Penn said. "I mean, not eating anything."[62] As would soon become apparent on location in Texas, Dunaway's regimen involved not only weights and abstinence, but a serious reliance on behavior-changing diet pills. The sacrifice wasn't only physical: "It cost me a lot of money not to work for Otto [Preminger] again,"[63] the actress admitted of the contractual dispute that erupted when her casting further poisoned the bad blood between her and the *Hurry Sundown* director. In the end, Dunaway could count herself lucky, whatever the expense. Had *Bonnie and Clyde* not come along, her next film might have been *Skidoo* (1968), Preminger's execrably awful attempt to cash in on the counterculture audience; Groucho Marx plays a mobster named "God," dressed in Hare Krishna robes.

Bonnie now secured, the other roles came together quickly, as Beatty and Penn turned to reliable colleagues from previous work. For the role of Buck Barrow, Clyde's ready-for-anything older brother, Beatty turned to Gene Hackman, who had appeared with him in *Lilith* and left a lasting impression. Their sole scene together in the Rossen film is the only one to lift Beatty's performance above the somnambulistic, something Beatty himself recognized. "I had to work like a demon to keep him from stealing that scene from me," Beatty conceded. "Hackman talks and he listens. And I thought, 'He makes me better in the scene.' It's wonderful playing opposite an actor like that."[64]

Hackman needed the work—and the $2,000 weekly salary with an eight-week guarantee—as much as Beatty needed a worthy sparring partner: since *Lilith*, he'd only managed one additional screen appearance, a small role as a doctor in the bloated screen adaptation of James Michener's *Hawaii* (1966). "I owe Warren my career," Hackman said candidly. "What if he hadn't remembered me from *Lilith*? Where would I be?"[65] (Not in *The Graduate*, which went into preproduction as *Bonnie and Clyde* wrapped. Director Mike Nichols fired Hackman three weeks into rehearsal for not learning his lines as cuckolded Mr. Robinson on that film, which made a star of Hackman's fellow Pasadena Playhouse graduate and onetime New York City roommate, Dustin Hoffman.)

For Buck's wife, Blanche, Penn insisted on Estelle Parsons, a gifted stage actress and onetime NBC *Today Show* reporter with no significant screen credits. "I was not having a good career at that moment,"[66] Parsons reflected. Grateful for the role, which came with a weekly $750, the lowest salary paid to the movie's principal actors, Parsons threw herself into research at New York City's 42nd Street Library. "I had a lot to contribute to the character ... because I knew more about [Blanche] than anybody in the movie wanted me or anybody else to know,"[67] Parsons said with visible pride years later, aware of the controversy her performance generated among Barrow Gang historians. Initially eager to meet the real Blanche Barrow, who alone of the movie's real-life counterparts remained alive to see it, Parsons lost her desire once she "broke in" the part, a decision she would later regret.

There remained the role of C. W. Moss, originally conceived as that "1931 version of a rock 'n' roll hood." It comes as no surprise that Dennis Hopper, the soon-to-be auteur of *Easy Rider* (1969), who had made an on- and off-screen specialty of rebellion, was Beatty's initial choice for the role. When Newman and Benton, at Penn's insistence, eliminated the ménage à trois and reconceived C. W. as a surrogate kid brother to Bonnie and Clyde, the part went instead to Michael J. Pollard in what became a career-defining performance. The twenty-seven-year-old actor was yet another *Dobie Gillis* alumnus, having substituted for Bob Denver as Maynard Krebs's loopy cousin when Denver was briefly drafted in mid-1959. The character of C. W. "came to me right before I walked through the door," Pollard said in a late-life interview. "Bob Dylan's album *Blonde vs. Blonde* had just been released, and

"I thought, 'That's kind of a nice voice [for C. W.] to have.'" Missing from Pollard's resume as a wheelman: he didn't know how to drive.

At the outset of preproduction, the screenwriters frequented La Escondida daily, attending casting meetings, working with Penn to further refine the script and accompanying Beatty and Penn to creative meetings with Warner Bros. production head MacEwen. "Warren said, 'He's going to say this, I'll say that, then Arthur will say that,'" Newman remembered. "We went in, and it went exactly the way Warren said it was going to happen. It was like *The Twilight Zone*."[68] As months shortened to weeks, Penn began to fear he'd exhausted the writers' imaginations, and worried that his own suggestions had "cut the guts"[69] out of their original material. "Arthur said to me at one point, 'Look, I like these guys a lot, but would I be letting you down terribly if I don't do the movie?'" Beatty claimed in an interview with Mark Harris. "This was in July of 1966, and . . . we started in October! So, rather than be graceful, I said 'Yes, you would be letting me down—what the hell are you talking about?'"[70]

Penn made no mention of such an existential moment in decades of interviews, and his silence on the matter convinces more than Beatty's manufactured crisis: directors on the cusp of filming frequently seek fresh input (when they don't replace the original writers altogether right at the outset), and Penn was no exception. Whatever the circumstances, Newman and Benton would not be accompanying the production to location in Texas. Beatty suggested Penn reconnect with Lillian Hellman, who had written *The Chase*, but disagreements on that production had ended Penn's working relationship with the playwright. Luckily, Beatty had a backup in mind—his pal Robert Towne.

Towne, who achieved lasting fame as the writer of Roman Polanski's *Chinatown* (1974), considered by many to be among the best original scripts in American film, had been an unofficial adviser to Beatty since their first encounter in the anteroom of their shared psychoanalyst (talk about a Hollywood meet-cute). According to Towne, he'd been the one to persuade Beatty to buy the rights to Newman and Benton's script in the first place.

"I saw the possibility of what eventually happened," he insisted to Beatty's biographer. "I was more vocal than anybody else around. I remember saying, 'Just do it. Do it.'"[71]

A Southern California native, born in working-class San Pedro but raised in affluent Palos Verdes and Brentwood, Towne early on cultivated the air of an all-knowledgeable Zen master, wearing his prematurely receding hair long and dispensing wisdom in page-long soliloquies. He was also a hypochondriac prone to imaginary allergies and given to extended periods of writer's block, incapable of delivering original material on deadline but adept at solving other writers' problems. He'd learned that skill in television, where he churned out episodes of *The Lloyd Bridges Show*, *The Outer Limits*, and *The Man from U.N.C.L.E.*, and perfected the art under the tutelage of exploitation film legend Roger Corman. For Corman, Towne wrote *The Tomb of Ligeia* (1964), the last and least of the prolific producer/director's Edgar Allan Poe adaptations starring Vincent Price.

Subsequent to their meeting on the way to and from the psychiatrist's couch, Towne and Beatty began exploring a modern update of seventeenth-century English playwright William Wycherley's *The Country Wife*. The story of a rake who feigns impotence to have sex with his best friends' wives appealed to Towne and Beatty's shared penchant for women and nightlife. Towne suggested reconceiving the character as "a guy everybody thinks he's gay, so he would be able to bang everybody."[72] It would take him only ten years to deliver the script, originally titled *Keith's My Name, Hair's My Game*, shortened to *Hair*, and finally made as *Shampoo* (1975).

Credited as a "special consultant" on *Bonnie and Clyde*, Towne became the retrospective recipient of significant praise. But his actual contribution to the script remains a subject of some controversy. According to Peter Biskind's gossipy, kaleidoscopic portrait *Easy Riders, Raging Bulls*, Towne bragged that he had "written" the movie, which launched his career as an uncredited major-studio script doctor.[73] That's one version. Asked point-blank in 1983, "Did Robert Towne help with the script?" Arthur Penn answered, "Not much."[74] The director also laid claim—rather, he gave credit to his wife,

Peggy—for one of the structural changes that fundamentally altered the movie's narrative trajectory.

In Newman and Benton's script, the gang's kidnapping of an undertaker and his girlfriend (itself based on the historical record) originally occurred after a reunion with Bonnie's family, just another moment in a rambling episodic structure. "I came back to New York for a last family visit before photography was to commence and brought the script with me for my wife to read," Penn recounted in 2000. "Without my raising the question of the family reunion scene, [she] unerringly pointed to the kidnapping scene. 'That has to precede the family reunion,' she said." Penn immediately saw his wife's reasoning. "[Bonnie] needed her family because death ... had forced itself into her consciousness. Clearly the line of the film would have a much stronger thrust with that change."[75]

Penn conveyed the sentiment to Towne, who rewrote the reunion scene accordingly, adding his most substantial contribution. As the reunion ends, Clyde assures Bonnie's mother that the couple plan to quit their life of crime and settle down not "more 'n three miles away. Now how do you like that, Mother Parker?" Towne's revision of Newman and Benton's script reads:

> *Bonnie's mother has undergone a funny sort of transformation during Clyde's speech – as if something had suddenly come into focus before the old woman's eyes.*
>
> MOTHER
> *I don't believe I would. I surely don't.*
> (*to Bonnie*)
> *You try to live three miles away from me and you won't live long, honey.*
> (*to Clyde*)
> *You'd best keep runnin', Clyde Barrow, and you know it.*[76]

Sometimes, a line of dialogue makes all the difference. "I don't know what would have happened if [the script] had been arbitrated,"[77] Towne mused in one of his many moments of self-reflection, referring to the Talmudic process by which the Writers Guild of America assigns screen credit. (Answer: He would have lost.) "Towne was a very important part of the process," said Benton, throughout his soft-spoken career the most chivalrous and diplomatic of writer-directors. "I honestly don't know who the *auteur* of *Bonnie and Clyde* was. I can't tell you that it was us, or Warren Beatty, or Arthur, or Towne."[78] That said, it's significant Benton never claimed Towne merited a writing credit, as he did for Penn.

Newman and Benton harbored no ill will. The screenwriting team had moved on. Since conceiving the idea for *Bonnie and Clyde*, they had contributed the book for a musical, *It's a Bird . . . It's a Plane . . . It's Superman!*, then in its Broadway debut; a box office disappointment, the show closed even before *Bonnie and Clyde* went into production, after only 129 performances. (Benton and Newman would contribute to the screenplay of *Superman* [1978].) Another script had found traction as well: *There Was a Crooked Man*, a misanthropic Western reworking of Jules Dassin's classic 1947 prison film *Brute Force*, whose uneasy mix of low comedy and violent action bore the writers' distinctive "New Sentimentality" signature. Kirk Douglas and Henry Fonda costarred in the 1970 film, directed by Joseph L. Mankiewicz.

Towne accomplished the necessary fixes to *Bonnie and Clyde* in a matter of weeks and continued to tinker with the script on location, pocketing $2,000 a week for "services to the company," according to studio files. Most of those tweaks concerned the fraught sexual relationship between Clyde and Bonnie. Benton and Newman had ditched the three-way shenanigans at Penn's request, making Clyde impotent rather than bisexual and emphasizing the contrast between Bonnie's sexual hunger and Clyde's fear of intimacy. "Anybody who sees this movie is going to know what's going to happen at the end—they're going to get killed," Towne reminded Penn. "There's no mystery in that. The only question you're going to have is *when* they're going to be killed . . .

and as a corollary, is there something that will need to be resolved between Clyde and Bonnie before that death that people are looking forward to?"[79]

There sure was: "C'mon, they've gotta do it *once!*"[80] Beatty urged his collaborators.

The couple consummate their relationship only a few short scenes before their violent death, in a field after they celebrate the newspaper publication of Bonnie's valedictory poem. "You made me somebody they're gonna remember," Clyde beams, and the lovemaking begins. Penn harbored conflicting thoughts. "I'm not entirely sure that was the right thing to do," he admitted in a 1969 interview. "But it seemed to me that a credible case could be made for a man who, having been terrified of women and sexual intimacy all his life, finally finds a woman who has completely severed all her connections with the world, including the one with her family and her mother [and] throws in her lot with him." The results, he acknowledged, are "open to quarrel."[81]

The frank sexuality of *Bonnie and Clyde* became as much a cause célèbre as its violence. Clyde and Bonnie's first attempt at lovemaking, on a bed full of guns in a seedy roadside motel room, ends in mutual frustration and recrimination when Bonnie's clearly indicated attempt at oral sex fails to arouse her would-be lover boy. Here, too, Penn knew exactly what taboos he was breaking. "In Hollywood pictures, the entire sexual level of existence is usually this: the actor finally makes it. It's always spectacular; it's always marvelous," the director said. "There are never any mistakes. There is never any anxiety. There's never any unhappiness associated with it. It's always perfect! I mean, if you can *once* get into bed with Doris Day, it's gravy from there on in—which is a *patent lie*. That was one of the things we wanted to address ourselves to in the film."[82]

By the time *Bonnie and Clyde* commenced principal photography on October 11, 1966, the once-formidable Production Code had begun to crumble.[83] In September of that year, Motion Picture Association of America president Jack Valenti unveiled a major revision of the 1934 guidelines. Where the prevailing code mandated that "no picture shall be produced which will lower the moral standards of those who see it," the new standards kept "in closer harmony with the mores, the culture and the moral sense and expectation of our society."[84] The battle over a Production Code Administration seal for Warner Bros.' rough-talking *Who's Afraid of Virginia Woolf?* (1966)—which "The Colonel" himself turned into a personal crusade—had been a catalyst for change. The long era of so-called compensating moral values was over. Anything and everything was now on the table—up to a point.

Still, old Hollywood morals die hard. Production Code head Geoffrey Shurlock fired off a three-page letter to Warner on October 13, lambasting the Towne-rewritten script for its "grossly animalistic" sex, "unacceptably brutal" violence, and lawless behavior that "goes entirely too far and would have to be kept within the bounds of common decency." Shurlock also objected to the "excessive" and "coarse" language, helpfully ticking off seventeen instances of "damn" or "damned," nine of "hell," and one each of "screwed," "son of a bitch," "dumb-ass stupid," and (the big one) "get into your pants."[85] An amusing note in production head MacEwen's handwriting in the Warner Bros. files, jotted down while on the phone with Shurlock, records that while there was "no objection to [Clyde's] being able to respond" to Bonnie's sexual overtures, steps must be taken to "eliminate the depiction of fellacio"—the misspelled word crossed out and then misspelled again two more times.[86]

By the time Shurlock's admonitory letter reached Beatty in Texas, production had been rolling for a week, with Jack Warner's personal blessing. "DEAR WARREN," read "The Colonel's" October 11, 1966, telegram. "HAPPY BONNIE AND CLYDE UNDER WAY. WISH YOU AND THE COMPANY GOOD LUCK AND A SUCCESSFUL FILM."[87]

One month later, Warner read the script for the first time.

"I can't understand where the entertainment value is in this story," he unloaded on MacEwen, who had pushed hard for the green light. "Who wants to see the rise and fall of a couple of rats? Am sorry I did not read the script before saying yes. I don't understand the thinking of Warren Beatty and Penn."[88] From that point on, producer and director would be routinely referred to in Warner's personal memos as "the geniuses." He didn't mean it as a compliment. Warner anticipated a total loss on the picture—one that could well negate any profits from other releases. "This era went out with Cagney,"[89] he groused.

Maybe gangster pictures *had* gone out with Cagney. But Clyde Barrow and Bonnie Parker were destined to become trendsetters—all over again.

10

"A COUPLE OF KIDS"

> Their whole image was one of glamour. Even if you
> did not approve of them, you would still have to envy
> them a little, to be so good-looking and
> rich and happy.
> —Jim Wright

For Barrow Gang biographer Jeff Guinn, "April 13, 1933, was the big day that America's love affair with criminals really blossomed into something."[1]

At approximately 4 p.m. that afternoon, a combined force of Joplin, Missouri police officers, and Missouri state highway patrolmen converged on a two-story garage apartment located at 3347-1/2 34th Street in the city's quiet Freeman Grove subdivision. Neighbors suspected a gang of bootleggers had been occupying the residence for the past several weeks; some heard stray gunshots, while others reported ever-changing V-8 sedans and roadsters being moved in and out of the garage. There was valid reason for neighbors' suspicions. Outlaws tended to congregate in Joplin for its location straddling the Missouri, Kansas, and Oklahoma state lines; under existing laws, a quick getaway rendered them immune from cross-border chases.

The five-man law enforcement crew, traveling in two cars, arrived at the apartment in time to see two of the alleged bootleggers pulling down the garage door on one of those suspicious roadsters. Caught by mutual surprise, cops and bootleggers engaged in a short volley of gunfire that left one lawman dead and another mortally wounded. The bootleggers managed to escape, but had been forced to abandon nearly all their possessions. In the garage, investigating officers found a stash of firearms including four rifles, a shotgun, a pistol, and one weapon so unfamiliar to ordinary cops that the official police report could only describe it as "an automatic rifle similar to a submachine gun."[2] FBI agents would later identify the weapon as a Browning automatic rifle.

In their haste to vacate the premises, the bootleggers had left a pot of beans burning on the stove, clothes soaking in the sink or half-packed into suitcases, a purse stuffed with incriminating documents, and scattered diamond jewelry linked to a recent robbery in nearby Neosho. Investigators also found a small sheaf of loose-leaf paper bearing the title "Suicide Sal" and a camera with a roll of undeveloped film still inside. Rushed to the photo department of the *Joplin Globe* for immediate processing, the images offered police their first candid looks at Clyde Barrow and Bonnie Parker.

Taken in late March, the photographs show the couple posed in front of a 1932 Ford B-400 freshly stolen from a Marshall, Texas, insurance salesman. Clyde and Bonnie took extra pains with their wardrobe that day to make the best possible impression. Clyde sits on the front fender, wearing a dark suit that nicely sets off the shiny BAR in his lap. Bonnie dazzles in a bolero jacket worn over a chevron-patterned sweater above a form-fitting long black skirt; a beret is set stylishly askew on her head. Police and public alike already knew Clyde's face via much-reprinted mug shots. Bonnie, however, was a relative unknown—until these pictures imprinted themselves on the popular imagination.

In one pose, Bonnie playfully "sticks up" Clyde, her right arm against his chest, left arm holding Clyde's own "whippit" gun. In another, Clyde effortlessly lifts Bonnie onto his shoulder. Even at nearly a century's distance, the affection between them remains electric; there's an unmistakable playfulness to the image. Of all the exposures on that single roll of film, it was Bonnie's solo portrait that became iconic, much to her own chagrin. Playing it tough, she leans against one of the Ford's headlights, left leg propped on the bumper, right hip outthrust, a service revolver held in her right hand. As a gag, Bonnie had snatched a cigar from a box found inside the car and clenched it between her teeth. *Click!* went the shutter—and the rest, as they say, is alternative history. Ever faithful to Bonnie's memory (despite his role in her execution), Dallas deputy Ted Hinton claimed that a Joplin newspaperman retouched the photograph as a joke, replacing the rose originally in Bonnie's mouth with a cigar, but his story fails to withstand even the most elementary scrutiny.[3]

The *Joplin Globe* published the photos on April 15, two days after their initial discovery, and placed them on its wire service, a new technology that allowed for instantaneous electronic reproduction. "This was really the first time that all over the country there [could be] pictures of these criminals," biographer Guinn continues. "And guess what? They're cute kids. Al Capone's a thug, Ma Barker's a chubby old lady, Pretty Boy Floyd's got a great name, but that's about it."[4] Plummeting newspaper subscriptions in Depression-era America forced editors to seek the most sensationalistic stories, and Clyde Barrow and Bonnie Parker more than filled the bill. "Here you've got a boy and a girl. They're obviously having plenty of weird sex because she smokes a cigar, and a girl who smokes a cigar will do anything,"[5] Guinn says laughingly.

Pre-Code cinema had its share of hard-boiled, cigarette-smoking dames—Kay Francis, Bette Davis, Barbara Stanwyck, Jean Harlow, Joan Blondell, and Glenda Farrell lit up whole packs on screen; Blondell even played a gangland boss in 1933's *Blondie Johnson*, released a scant two months before the Joplin shootout (tag line: "LOVE Made Her Beautiful ... WANT Made Her Daring ... MEN Made Her Ruthless!") But a cigar—not even Marlene Dietrich dared to break that taboo. From this point forward, newspapers would invariably refer to Bonnie as Clyde's "cigar-smoking moll." Mother Emma Parker lamented that it "made such lurid headlines, no paper would ever correct the story."[6]

That didn't stop Bonnie from trying. A month before their ambush by Frank Hamer's posse, the Barrow Gang apprehended Commerce, Oklahoma, police chief Percy Boyd after an attempted roadside arrest and subjected him to a nerve-racking daylong road trip into Kansas, depositing him in the countryside south of Fort Scott. As they parted ways, Boyd asked if the gang had any message to convey to the press. "Tell them I don't smoke cigars!" Bonnie instructed him. True to his word, Boyd duly passed on the correction, along with an account of his favorable treatment at the hands of the notorious cop killers. "It was in all the Oklahoma newspapers,"[7] a pleased Bonnie reported to her family.

By then, it didn't matter: the defiant, transgressive image had found purchase in the thirties American psyche. "That photo changed so much," says Guinn. "What's more newsworthy in a country with a Depression, farm foreclosures and everything else? Here's a sassy, pretty girl waving a gun and smoking a cigar, with all the Freudian implications. That took your mind off your financial problems for a while."[8] More than that: for an impoverished populace who regarded bankers and law enforcement as unsympathetic to their plight, "Clyde and Bonnie's criminal acts offered a vicarious sense of revenge. Somebody was sticking it to the rich and powerful."[9]

Despite Bonnie's complaints, she and Clyde reveled in their notoriety. Like certain actors, they kept clippings and made scrapbooks of their most memorable "reviews." Thumbed-through newspapers and magazines littered the seats and floorboards of stolen automobiles later recovered by police. Clyde and Bonnie "nurtured [their celebrity] because it was the greatest reward they were getting," says Guinn. "If you study their actual history, they were maybe the worst criminals, the most bungling bandits. They rarely knocked off anybody who had more than a few bucks; they mostly robbed gas stations and little general stores. But what they loved was that people knew who they were."[10] The Joplin profile exponentially increased the couple's national visibility. Reporters and photographers descended on the 34th Street hideout, documenting the apartment and its assorted debris and interviewing neighbors and police.

The media onslaught lifted Clyde and Bonnie from the realm of regional nuisances into that of national sensations: the biggest celebrities to come along in America since Thomas Edison and Henry Ford, according to Guinn.

Sex appeal played a huge part. Unlike the outlaws who had come before, Clyde and Bonnie were a couple, and their story resonated—indeed, still resonates—in a different way. Bonnie supplied "the extra oomph [Clyde] needed," Guinn explains. Without her, "Clyde is just some rough-and-tumble guy who commits some crimes. She made their story different; she made it more appealing to women. And then she ends up taking over the story. After they're dead, Bonnie becomes the star, Clyde's in the supporting cast. All the stories are about 'a diminutive bombshell in a tight sweater.'"[11]

No outlet specialized in such purple prose better than *True Detective*, which gave Clyde top billing in its May and December 1933 "Line Up" section, a monthly listing of prominent fugitives wanted for murder. The magazine's lurid coverage of the Barrow Gang's exploits laid the ground for the Bonnie and Clyde legend; author John Toland, whose *Dillinger Days* first inspired screenwriters David Newman and Robert Benton, largely recycled the pulp monthly's flights of speculation as "history." A rival publication, *Real Detective*, named Clyde one of "The New Bad Men of the Old Wild West," an exemplary outlaw who "lived up to the daring precedent" of Jesse James and Billy the Kid. Indicative of the couple's celebrity, Dallas police headquarters featured life-size cutouts of Clyde and Bonnie in its main hall to inform officers "what they looked like—and remember that they were still on the loose."[12]

For crime historian Claire Bond Potter, the romance that came to surround media coverage of the Barrow Gang "set the terms for the war on crime: producing themselves as celebrities and committing ordinary crimes in spectacular ways, they revived popular fascination with bandits."[13] For urban audiences especially, Clyde and Bonnie evoked nostalgia for a rural past that never really existed, much as the reimagined stories of bushwhacker Jesse James and cop killer Billy the Kid had done before them. "People like the mythology better," says Guinn, summing up the American obsession with outlaws. "Then you don't have a couple of grubby poor kids who just want desperately to be famous, and the way they chose was dangerous for everyone else—and fatal for them."[14]

Not only law enforcement took umbrage at the popular fascination with the Barrow Gang: other career criminals resented their ascending stardom. Just ask John Dillinger, destined to be named the FBI's Public Enemy No. 1—but only after Clyde and Bonnie's death in the Bienville Parish backwoods. "A couple of kids stealing grocery money,"[15] the Indiana-born, Midwestern-based thief observed dismissively of his Texas competition. Dillinger certainly earned bragging rights, knocking over twelve banks in four states over a one-year period from June 1933 to 1934 for a total haul of more than $300,000 ($7 million today). "Small timers get into the business, and ruin it for everyone," he quipped to reporters. At least one lawman failed to share the grudging admiration for Dillinger's prowess. According to former Texas Ranger Frank Hamer, Dillinger was no match for Clyde Barrow's "cleverness, desperation and reckless bravado."[16]

Much of Clyde's legend centered on his skill behind the wheel of a Ford V-8. "He drove like the devil, and he had the luck of one,"[17] Emma Parker said. Several factors aided and abetted that luck. The Federal Aid Highway Act of 1921 for the first time laid down more than 300,000 miles of macadam interstates, mostly in the South and upper Midwest, providing convenient escape routes for motorized criminals like Clyde, prone to driving a thousand miles at a stretch and able to outrun local police prohibited from crossing state lines. Clyde also benefited from Rand McNally's comprehensive atlases, first published in 1924 and updated every year. Thanks to McNally, Clyde came to know every road in a multistate radius that encompassed Texas, New Mexico, Oklahoma, Kansas, Nebraska, Arkansas, Missouri, Iowa, Illinois, Minnesota, and finally Louisiana.

"His mind was a photostatic copy of the intricate windings where he could rush in and hide, elude capture, fade into the landscape and become lost to sight,"[18] Mrs. Parker marveled.

Today, when interstate highways have long replaced and greatly shortened the routes once taken, it's astonishing to contemplate the thousand-mile treks Clyde was said to have accomplished and which contemporary accounts bear out. Few roads were paved. Most consisted of packed dirt that dissolved into a quagmire under even the slightest rain. A daylong drive at a speed limit of forty-five miles per hour might carry an average motorist three hundred miles. Clyde, of course, was no average motorist. Disregarding posted limits and able to man the wheel in marathon sessions, he achieved incredible distances—and achieved them while driving in his stocking feet, likely necessitated by nerve damage from the self-mutilation that rendered his left foot numb in shoes.

Newspapers and radio broadcasts made Clyde "a superman, gifted with super-human powers, beyond the reach of ordinary human beings,"[19] as his sister Nell put it, griping that after repeated high-speed pursuits, law enforcement considered Clyde "a sort of modern Fu Manchu, able to appear and disappear at will, leaving death behind."[20] One consequence of this reputation, endlessly propagated, was a rise in fatal and near-fatal attacks on other motorists. Crime historian Potter cited one typical, tragic example: that of a West Plains, Missouri, couple and their male companion, chased by a local posse on a tip from a gas station attendant. In a pursuit laced with vigilante gunfire, "the car skidded off the road, killing the driver."[21]

The real Clyde Barrow, meanwhile, regularly evaded surveillance when driving through populous towns and cities—disguised as a woman. According to Bonnie's mother Emma Parker, Bonnie would "paint [Clyde's] cheeks and rouge his lips and put one of her hats" on top of a store-bought blond wig. "'He made the cutest girl,'" Bonnie attested. "Our only trouble was that two blondes caused a commotion in traffic. When we'd stop for a red light, men would start giving us both the glad eye, so finally Clyde had to have the wig dyed black."[22] (Fabricated or not—what a scene that might have made in the early stretches of *Bonnie and Clyde*.)

Life in constant motion came to be the defining feature of the Barrow Gang. "Where y'all headed from here?" Bonnie's uncle asks in the family reunion scene from *Bonnie and Clyde*. "At this point, we ain't headed *to* anywhere," Clyde admits. "We're just runnin' *from*."[23]

For a time, the Barrow Gang were ubiquitous. "The newspapers figure, 'hey, anytime there's a robbery near us we can claim it was Bonnie and Clyde and run those pictures again,'"[24] Guinn explains. A jocular on-the-road scene in *Bonnie and Clyde* has Buck entertaining his driving companions with rumors gleaned from a newspaper lifted from a rural mailbox. "Law enforcement officers throughout the Southwest are frankly amazed at the way in which will-o'-the-wisp bandit Clyde Barrow and his yellow-haired companion, Bonnie Parker, continue to elude their would-be captors," he reads with glee. "The Barrow Gang has been reported as far west as White City, New Mexico, and as far north as Chicago," the unnamed paper claims, listing a string of bank and refinery robberies, as well as "two Piggly Wiggly stores in Texas and one A & P Store in Missouri."

As film scholar Richard B. Jewell observed of the film, "We watch Clyde and Bonnie become legends, blamed for every robbery and murder in a multi-state area. We watch as they contribute to their own mythology through Bonnie's poetry, through pictures of them and Texas Ranger Frank Hamer they send to the newspapers. We watch as authorities build them into superhuman outlaws to make their eventual capture/execution seem all the more momentous and heroic."[25] In real life, Clyde and Bonnie did their best to live out the legend. Like all legends, theirs was a lie. "There was nothing romantic at all about anything we did," onetime Barrow Gang member Ralph Fults told John Neal Philips. "Not for us—and certainly not for any of our victims."[26]

Before Joplin, Clyde and Bonnie lived an aimless existence through the late winter and early spring of 1932–1933, rarely staying more than a few nights in the same place and living off what they could steal, all the while sending coded postcards back to their families in Dallas pretending to be on an enjoyable holiday. Contrary to Dillinger's assessment (and the opinion of some modern observers), Clyde avoided higher-paying bank robberies not out of ineptitude but out of practicality. At this point, the Barrow Gang lacked the personnel to successfully execute more complicated heists. Their only confederate was W. D. Jones, a seventeen-year-old neighbor of the Barrow family who idolized Clyde.

Jones's initiation into the gang marked him for the death penalty when, in a panic amid the chaos of an aborted car theft, he shot a man off the running board of his own automobile—an incident that inspired one of *Bonnie and Clyde*'s most revolutionary moments. Rather than having to rely on the complicated choreography required to hold bank customers and tellers at bay, raid the safe, and manage a getaway, Clyde could hit small-town gas stations, cafés, and stores single-handedly. There was only one drawback: "small-time stickups ... needed to be repeated every few days. Takes of five or ten dollars didn't finance road expenses long, even in the Depression."[27]

On good days, Clyde, Bonnie, and W. D. might take advantage of one of the many roadside motor courts dotting the city limits of major highways. Celebrated in the novel and the film of *The Grapes of Wrath* and commemorated by a modern-day resurgence of Route 66 nostalgia, these tourist camps typically consisted of L-shaped rows of stucco or frame cabins arrayed around a filling station and diner; Clyde kept a lookout for those which also included attached garages able to conceal stolen cars with phony license plates. The motor courts' locations outside congested downtowns allowed for a fast departure, and the rooms benefited from clean beds and running water. To save on their limited resources, Clyde, Bonnie, and W. D. always shared a single cabin, giving birth to the salacious accounts of "perversion" that Benton and Newman would make an essential part of their original treatment and first-draft screenplay.

Most often, however, the gang lived in their car, day in, day out. According to her mother, "Bonnie said their best stunt was to drive into a town and run their car up on somebody's drive[way] for the night.... Cruising cops would deduce the car belonged there and leave them alone."[28] When no driveway presented itself in the long stretches of empty countryside, Clyde sought out a secluded campsite near a creek where "they would take turns standing in the icy water with a cake of soap, hastily scrubbing themselves of the accumulated grime of several days, returning to the car blue and shivering, and dressing while the winds whipped around them."[29] Close quarters and primitive conditions made for frayed tempers. Firsthand accounts of life with the Barrow Gang all mention Bonnie's finding refuge in bootleg liquor and Clyde's physical mistreatments; on the latter score, Bonnie gave as good as she got.

For the Barrow Gang, the nearly month-long idyll in Joplin represented a rare (it would in fact be the only) respite from this marginal daily routine. Clyde assured Bonnie their stay would be crime-free—a promise he mostly kept, aside from the occasional stolen car. They had visitors as well: Clyde's older brother Buck and his wife, Blanche. Marvin "Buck" Barrow had preceded Clyde into prison, arrested in the wake of a failed 1929 safe-cracking operation in Denton, Texas, after the driver—Clyde—cracked the axle and the hoodlums fled on foot. Clyde hid under a house; Buck fell to flesh wounds in both legs and earned a four-year stretch at the Texas state prison in Huntsville. Barely a month after his incarceration in January 1930, Buck walked out nonchalantly, exiting the door of the prison kitchen where he'd been assigned because of his injuries, commandeering a guard's unoccupied car, and driving straightaway to the family home in West Dallas, where he surprised sister Marie in the kitchen, still wearing his prison stripes.

Buck lost no time rekindling the two-day-old romance he'd begun before his apprehension with Blanche Caldwell Callaway, the eighteen-year-old daughter of an Oklahoma preacher; Blanche accepted his marriage proposal despite full knowledge of his criminal past and fugitive present, whatever both Barrow family lore and Blanche's own prison memoir have to say to the contrary. Like Bonnie, Blanche joined Buck in a string of petty crimes, but life on the road quickly lost its luster. Blanche urged Buck to surrender to Texas authorities and finish his sentence, which he did two days after Christmas 1931—much to the surprise of Huntsville prison authorities, who had inexplicably failed to find him missing in the first place. A model prisoner, Buck earned a full pardon in March 1932 thanks to persistent lobbying by both Blanche and his mother, Cumie.

For decades, the story persisted that Texas governor Miriam "Ma" Ferguson made Buck's pardon, one that wiped his criminal slate clean, contingent on his willingness and ability to persuade his brother Clyde to turn himself in. A clearly fabricated passage from *Fugitives*, the ghostwritten reminiscences of Emma Parker and Nell Barrow, has Buck waking in a sweat from dreams "that Clyde had been caught and brought to the death house... Something has got to be done to make Clyde straight with the law again."[30] Author Jan Fortune gives Nell a Robert Towne–worthy riposte to that one. "You fool around with Clyde," she tells Buck, "and you'll land back in the pen with a life sentence."[31] According to Blanche's equally unreliable memoir, Buck intended to forgo crime altogether and open a used-car lot, investing the fifty dollars he received with his parole in a couple of beat-up Model A Fords he planned to refurbish.

Whatever Buck's intentions, he put up virtually no resistance when Clyde invited him and Blanche to join the three-person Barrow Gang in Joplin. Screenwriters Newman and Benton imagine the moment in their preproduction script:

BUCK
Boy, are we gonna have us a good time.

CLYDE
We surely are!

BUCK
Yessir!
(a pause, then:)
What're we gonna do?

CLYDE
Well, how's this – I thought we'd all go to Missouri. They ain't lookin' for me there. We'll hole up someplace and have a regular vacation. All right?

BUCK
No trouble, now.

CLYDE
No trouble. I ain't lookin' to go back to prison.[32]

All accounts agree that Blanche made a brief show of resistance, replete with pleading and tears. But in the end, she resigned herself to the trip. Buck traded in the two Model As for a 1929 Marmon, and off they went. Blanche even brought along her dog, a white mutt named Snow Ball. She'd trained the dog to run to the car on command—just in case.

Estelle Parsons received a Best Supporting Actress Oscar for her portrayal of Blanche. Her performance left at least one viewer hugely unimpressed: Blanche Barrow. "They made me look like a screaming horse's ass,"[33] she protested to local reporters attending the Dallas premiere. To John Neal Phillips, who resurrected and edited her memoir, Blanche said quite a bit more. "That movie made me look like a goddamn crying idiot! I did not look like that fat crying woman!"[34] The film's notoriety "nearly caused my [second] husband to divorce me," she alleged. "Of course, my in-laws never liked me anyway."[35]

Parsons's performance is pitched at a high level of hysteria, but the interpretation derives in large part from Blanche's own recollections. Her memoir, begun in her cell in Camp 1 of the Missouri State Penitentiary in late 1933, overflows with scenes of sobbing and victimization. "I was an awful crybaby and must have been a burden to all of them,"[36] she writes at one point. Both the Barrow and Parker families took pains to minimize Blanche's involvement in the Barrow Gang's murderous exploits in an ultimately successful effort to secure her parole. "Newspapers have made Blanche out as a regular gangster's moll, but nothing was ever further from the truth," Nell Parker claimed. "She was a good country girl, timid, shy and rather quiet. I suspect if she'd known Buck was an escaped convict when she met him, she'd be running yet instead of serving time in a Missouri prison."[37] (She did know, and she didn't run.)

When in doubt, blame the screenwriters. Nevertheless, the character of Blanche Barrow represents a missed opportunity in *Bonnie and Clyde*. Far from the oblivious innocent rendered by Nell Barrow and depicted in the film, Blanche was a formidable personality—more than equal to Bonnie, and by all accounts considerably more attractive. "Blanche was what they called 'a real looker,'"[38] says Phillips, who knew her well in later years and could testify to her charisma. In photographs, with her wide-set eyes and round face, she bears more than a passing resemblance to fellow Oklahoman Kay Francis, Depression-era America's highest-paid female movie star, who specialized in roles of women brought low by bad choices.

Owing to Blanche's lack of a criminal record, Clyde assigned her to do the gang's shopping and miscellaneous errands. Not, perhaps, the best decision given Blanche's fashionable jodhpurs and designer sunglasses. "We didn't see many strangers, so you can imagine how this particular stranger—a rather good-looking gal dressed in a slinky riding habit—attracted considerable attention,"[39] remembered one mesmerized Missouri local. In her memoir, Blanche pleaded the excuse of being made to do everything under duress. But in an unguarded moment with Philips, she let slip the truth: "Clyde Barrow never held a gun to my head. I was there because I wanted to be there."[40]

Likewise, "Blanche Barrow" the character was there in the film because Warren Beatty wanted—absolutely *needed*—her to be there. In an effort to secure rights to her life story, Beatty paid a personal visit to Blanche at her country home in the Dallas suburb of Seagoville. As Blanche herself related the encounter: "One day I'm at home and there's a knock on my door. I open it, and it's the most beautiful man God ever made standing there. He says, 'My name's Warren. Can I come in and talk?' Well, I grabbed that boy's arm and dragged him right in!"[41] Beatty quickly noticed the piano in Blanche's parlor and began to improvise a tune. Smitten, Blanche proved more than amenable to the actor/producer's entreaties to use Blanche's real name in his upcoming film. The money he offered was equally tempting—enough for her and her husband to build a new fence around their property.

Beatty had one other enticement. "Before he left, this man who looked like an angel said, 'I've got some people who are already going to be in the movie.'"[42] At which point, Beatty whipped out a headshot of Faye Dunaway, conveniently forgetting to mention she'd been cast as Bonnie, not Blanche. No surprise, then, that Blanche erupted in fury upon seeing the finished film a year later. By then, the rights money had been spent, the fence had been built, and Blanche, like her screen counterpart, could only whine and complain. She wasn't alone: Clyde's fellow inmate Ralph Fults, who saw himself in the composite character of C. W. Moss, erupted, "You don't go up to a gas station and say your real name and then say, 'We rob banks.' They wouldn't have lasted two days!"[43]

Bonnie and Clyde compresses the Barrow Gang's stay in Joplin to an astonishingly compact six and a half minutes that neatly captures the ennui of those weeks in the 34th Street apartment. The sequence's first shot finds Buck paying off the landlord, as he and Blanche did under the alias "Callahan," handing over a whopping fifty dollars for a month's lease. "The apartment was nice enough for us," Blanche recorded. "There were two bedrooms, a living room, a kitchenette with built-in furniture, and a small bathroom."[44] (Self-serving portrait aside, her memoir abounds in the vivid detail of life on the road.) Blanche did most of the housekeeping. "Clyde and Bonnie's room was hardly ever cleaned, nor was the bed made," she took pains to note. "Bonnie seldom got up before twelve noon or one o'clock."[45] W. D. shared the lovers' room. "We used to laugh at him and tell him he was afraid to sleep alone,"[46] Blanche wrote. She entertained herself with jigsaw puzzles in between visits with Bonnie to Kress's department store and the occasional picture show. Mostly, everyone stayed in the house.

Buck's first instinct in the film is to pick up the phone and "order up a mess of groceries: three pounds of pork chops, four pounds of red beans, some Chase & Sanborn's coffee and about eight bottles of Dr. Pepper." That, too, derives from the historical record. "I usually ordered all our groceries by phone and had them delivered," Blanche said, adding that Buck sometimes picked them up personally. Even better: "After April 7th, when the sale of beer was legalized in Missouri, we bought a case of beer every day."[47] Blanche met the delivery boys downstairs, outside the apartment, but harbored grave misgivings. "I was sure one of them would get suspicious because they were not allowed to bring the packages upstairs."[48] That's how the film plays it, with Bonnie substituting for Blanche. Actual blame for the gang's discovery lay elsewhere.

Guns.

In a detail that's easy to miss on first viewing, Beatty's Clyde stumbles on the apartment threshold carrying a crate of firearms. It's a busy series of shots, linked by Buck's endless grocery order. Blanche inspects the kitchen and recoils at the decaying vegetables in the Frigidaire; Bonnie rocks in exasperation in the living room; Clyde deposits his .45 sidearm in the crate, and then we're on to a game of checkers and Bonnie reading stanzas from "Suicide Sal." Clyde carried more than a sidearm into the Joplin apartment. In sworn testimony to the FBI, Blanche tallied up "about fifteen guns, several Colt .45 [semi]automatics and three or four Brownie automatics,"[49] all stolen from a National Guard armory. While in Joplin, Clyde set about attempting to convert one of the BARs into a "whippit gun" even more lethal than the Remington Model 11 semiautomatic he'd previously transformed into a weapon of serious intimidation.

Clyde's affection for firearms transcended mere utility. Like the Jesse James described by hagiographer John Newman Edwards, he treated his weapons with fetishistic reverence. Clyde "loved his guns, named them all and spent hours cleaning and polishing them," his sister Nell worried, quick to add that "Buck had never owned one, and was, I'm inclined to believe, scared of them himself."[50] (Good luck persuading a jury of that one.) W. D. Jones recounted that Clyde "was never more than arm's reach from a gun." Clyde even prayed with guns, Jones said, "in bed or out of bed on the floor in the night, when he thought we was all asleep and couldn't see him kneeling there."[51] Preacher's daughter Blanche couldn't recall any such devotion, but did vouch for Clyde's mechanical experimentation, detailing how Clyde one night attempted to saw off the stock of a BAR to maximize its portability—only to have the gun loudly misfire. "The first [time he did that] he cut into the stock without realizing there was a [firing] mechanism inside there," continues historian Phillips. "And he was so pissed off at himself for not having explored [the weapon] first before he started whacking away at the thing. So the next one he did—it worked."[52] Success came at a cost. The wild gunshot alerted neighbors, who alerted local authorities, who called in state reinforcements—none of them realizing whom the "bootleggers" on 34th Street might be.

The raid on the Barrow Gang's Joplin apartment occupies a prominent place in Newman and Benton's script for *Bonnie and Clyde*. "The three major gun battles in this film, of which this is the first, each have a different emotional quality," the writers specify. "The quality for this Joplin battle is chaos, hysteria, extremely rapid movement and lots of noise. The audience should be assaulted."[53] They are. From the moment Beatty's Clyde first spies police cars pulling into the driveway ("The laws are outside! They're blocking the driveway!") until the gang's getaway less than a minute and a half later, the sequence is all noise, overlaid by Blanche's/Parson's ear-piercing scream. "The scream persists through the gunfire," the script dictates, "never lessening on the soundtrack. Its effect should be at first funny to the audience, then annoying, and finally terrifying."[54]

All those emotional beats come into play in the scene, which resonates with more than sixty gunshots. In fact, the "hail of gunfire" that accompanied the Barrow Gang's flight amounted to thirty shots or fewer, with Clyde's personal arsenal doing disproportionate damage. Constable Wes Harryman, there to serve a search warrant, fell to a sawed-off shotgun blast as he approached the garage door Clyde and W. D. Jones were hurriedly pulling down. A ten-pellet load of Clyde's buckshot caught Harryman in the right shoulder and neck, severing two arteries; he bled to death in the driveway. Joplin detective Harry McGinnis managed to get off three shots before another blast from the shotgun hit him in the face and nearly blew off his left arm.

"Clyde got as much thrill from shooting cops as the cops did shooting thieves or gangsters,"[55] Blanche remembered. "It comes so quickly and happens in an instant—you're there and they're there—they've got guns and you've got guns—you know it's going to be you or them and there's no time to think about anything else," Clyde allegedly told his sister Nell on one of his and Bonnie's periodic clandestine visits home. "It gets mixed up."[56]

In the film, the uneasy laughter provoked by Blanche's slapstick antics exists simultaneously with the sheer adrenaline rush of the getaway itself. As Blanche zigzags about, holding a spatula aloft in one hand, Buck blows away a policeman and releases the handbrake on the patrol car blocking their escape. Clyde explodes through the closed garage door behind the wheel of a V-8 sedan. Bonnie rides shotgun; C. W. Moss fires out the open rear window. Ramming the disabled police car back into a temporary roadblock, Clyde races down the street to retrieve the wildly running Blanche. "The back door is flung open and in almost the style of a cartoon, two hands reach out and lift her off her feet and pull her into the car," the script reads. "They speed away."[57]

Whatever its historical inaccuracies (and there are plenty of them, notably Bonnie taking an active part in the gunplay), it's a terrific set piece, exhilarating to watch and perfectly positioned just under the movie's halfway mark, when the earlier madcap thrills begin to give way to a prevailing sense of doom. To be fair to Parsons—and this is the sequence that likely secured her Oscar—Blanche herself confessed, "I think I might have gone insane for a few minutes."[58] Her prison manuscript does a screenplay-worthy job of painting the chaos and confusion of the Joplin raid in all its combined comedy and horror. At one point in the gunfight, her dog Snow Ball races out the swing door in the kitchen and heads downstairs into the street. Blanche instinctively follows the dog outside, where Clyde enlists her help in clearing the police car blocking the driveway.

Recoiling at the sight of the mortally wounded detective McGinnis, his left arm hanging by tendons from his shoulder, Blanche lets out a loud scream and starts running down the hill. "I don't know if I thought I could outrun the bullets whizzing by me or not. Anyway, I was trying to."[59] Hauled into the fleeing V-8 sedan, Blanche realizes she's still holding the pack of cards she'd been playing solitaire with in the moments before the raid. "Buck noticed them and almost broke my fingers trying to get them away from me," she remembered. "My hands were bloody and my dress looked like a red polka-dot print instead of plain blue."[60] As for Snow Ball: "That was the last time I saw our little white dog."[61]

"I don't think it's funny to see the policemen killed, although that doesn't mean there isn't a funny result visible in rather horrible things," Penn said at the 1967 Montreal Film Festival. "I went through a long war, which was rather horrible and funny. There is no question about it: the character of humor in violence is an immediate and constant correlative. They are there, and they are there in equal quantities—that was my personal experience."[62] To the horror of their postwar elders, youth audiences in 1967–1968 applauded and cheered these moments of anti-authoritarian revenge, surprising even Penn.

Clyde's overwhelming firepower was no screenwriter's invention. As evidenced by investigating officers' confusion over the BARs found at the 34th Street apartment, local police forces had no knowledge of—let alone access to—the kind of hardware Clyde wielded. "Poorly armed cops expected to confront small-timers whose firepower was equally limited," noted Jeff Guinn. "That gave Clyde and his cronies a tremendous advantage."[63] The failed Joplin raid convinced law enforcement the Barrow Gang was anything but a bunch of amateurs. "The Barrows ... are the toughest bunch of outlaws at large," Dallas FBI Special Agent in Charge F.J. Blake warned in a June 27, 1933, letter to George T. Corry, sheriff of Wellington, Texas, where an automobile mishap nearly ended Clyde and Bonnie's career. "It will be appreciated if you would kindly give us a resume of the affair, covering the kinds of guns they had."[64]

J. Edgar Hoover's G-men were taking no chances. "Unless peace officers are equipped with similar weapons and experienced in the use of them," one memo advised, "it is practically suicide for anyone to attempt to combat criminals who use Browning automatic rifles."[65] In Joplin, the Barrow Gang "had yet to experience a coordinated assault by well-prepared, well-armed officers aware of who they were up against."[66]

That would all change three months later.

11

"COLD, DEAD FINGERS"

> "One True Friend with Six Hearts in His Body
> Who Can Always Be Relied On."
> "The Gun That Won the West."
> "Consider Your Man Card Reissued."
>
> —Advertising slogans for, respectively, the Colt .45 revolver,
> the Winchester Model 1873, and the AR-15

One answer to the question 'Why do Americans love guns?' is, simply, that we were invited to do so,"[1] scholar Pamela Haag observes in her trenchant analysis *The Gunning of America: Business and the Making of American Gun Culture*. For all the constitutional rhetoric that overwhelms modern gun-rights debates, it must be remembered, "the Second Amendment did not design, invent, patent, mass-produce, advertise, sell, market and distribute guns."[2]

America's well-noted knack for ingenuity and innovation reached a pinnacle of achievement in the industrialized production of firearms, which transformed what was once the province of artisanal gunsmiths into a strictly commercial enterprise whose standardized methods anticipated the assembly lines of Henry Ford and his competitors by more than half a century. "The gunsmith would not have recognized a gun in the tessellation of industrial production," Haag writes of the fragmentation of the process. "The business ... moved from one man making one gun to more than 150 men each making one part of one gun."[3]

Despite the weapons bearing their names, America's nineteenth-century firearms barons could hardly be called gun enthusiasts. Oliver Winchester, a Baltimore clothier who made his first fortune in "men's furnishings" ("Suspenders, Gloves, Hosiery and READY-MADE LINEN,"[4] read one ad), owned precisely two guns, both antiques only for display. Eliphalet Remington, a deeply religious pacifist and closet poet (*"Hail sacred peace, thy gentle reign / Is now restored to us again,"*[5] he wrote in celebration of the end of the War of 1812), never fired a gun on Sunday. Samuel Colt, whose company did more than any to advance firearm technology and promote and entrench American gun culture, approached the manufacture of weapons much as he had the laughing-gas medicine shows he toured across the Northeast in the early 1830s: as a huckster's market to be created, then exploited.

"[The United States'] gun culture was forged in the image of commerce," Haag notes. "It was stamped, perhaps indelibly, by . . . the 'amorality of business.'"[6] For Senator Chris Murphy, writing in *The Violence Inside Us*, "there is no way to tell the story of American violence without placing much of the blame on the widespread marketing and ownership of these highly lethal weapons. . . . The grand heterogeneous experiment of America was going to be a tinderbox of violence no matter what; guns just set it on fire."[7]

In American popular culture, firearms have become synonymous with our national identity. "The firearms of the 'Wild West' are part of the story we tell ourselves about [our] history, even if that story's not entirely true,"[8] says Second Amendment scholar Adam Winkler. More than that, according to Richard Slotkin, "Since the Western offers itself as a myth on national origins, it implies that its violence is an essential and necessary part of the process through which American society was established and through which its democratic values are defended and enforced."[9]

In this evangelical vein, both Winchester and Remington dubbed their advance men "missionaries," stirring up demand for the salesmen to follow with entertaining displays of expert marksmanship. Eastern industry (both Colt's Patent Arms Manufacturing Company and the Winchester Repeating

Arms Company were based in Connecticut) did more than Western history itself to ingrain firearms into the American consciousness. "The legends that would become 'facts' about American gun culture made gun violence both more common and more coolly righteous than it was," Haag notes. "The violence of the lone gunman was not the violence we most had, but it was, apparently, the violence we most preferred."[10]

From the outset of American colonization, firearms served more than sheer subsistence purposes. "Euro American settlers had a long tradition of organized violence against unarmed civilian populations, their habitats and their food supplies,"[11] insists activist historian Roxanne Dunbar-Ortiz. Colonial American newspapers from Boston and Philadelphia were "awash in gun ads."[12] These promotional placements for exceptional craftsmanship ran alongside wanted notices for runaway indentured servants and slaves—many of whom had liberated a long gun or pistol before their departure. South Carolina's government took the unusual step of establishing a treaty with the Cherokee Nation agreeing to a bounty of "four blankets or two guns"[13] for the return of all escaped slaves, dead or alive.

Before the Civil War, however, while "firearms were commonplace, they were the subject of considerable regulation," says Winkler. "We were moving from a society that was rural to one that was becoming a little more urban, a little more civilized, and the idea that people would carry guns around with them all the time became a subject of controversy."[14] Before the outbreak of secessionist warfare at Fort Sumter in April 1861, firearms manufacture had in fact been a losing proposition for its pioneer industrialists. Samuel Colt obtained a patent for his revolutionary revolving cylinder on February 25, 1836. Legend has it that the inventor found inspiration in the turning of a ship's windlass while on a transatlantic voyage as a teenager; Colt publicity later claimed he'd fashioned a prototype pistol out of scrap wood he found on board. Ten years later, Colt was virtually bankrupt, having failed to secure a single long-term contract that could sustain his massive factory in Hartford, Connecticut.

"If America was born a gun culture, it was not reflected on Colt's bottom line,"[15] Haag wryly observes. US Army Ordnance Department director General James Ripley detested "Jim Crack" repeating firearms, calling them a "great evil" that wasted precious ammunition; Colt and his competitors regarded the general as a "fossil."[16] To sell guns on a full-time basis, it would be necessary to create a market, not only military, but also civilian. "The government may go to the devil," Colt decided. "I will go my own way"[17]

For Colt, opportunity came not in America, but Britain. On May 1, 1851, thirty-one-year-old Queen Victoria and her consort, Prince Albert, opened the Great Exhibition of the Works of Industry of All Nations in London's Hyde Park. This unprecedented display of multinational craftsmanship, numbering more than 100,000 man-made objects from around the world, was housed in a monumental, greenhouse-like structure known as the Crystal Palace; its architect, Joseph Paxton, had been a gardener. Spanning over eighteen acres and encompassing a thousand iron columns supporting 300,000 panes of glass, the Crystal Palace rose to a height that allowed the park's existing, centuries-old elm trees to grow undisturbed beneath its translucent canopy.[18]

America's contribution to the trade fair occupied a mere 40,000 square feet of an exhibition hall three times larger than St. Paul's Cathedral and consisted of only 536 objects, including Cyrus McCormick's mechanical reaper and a room fashioned entirely of "Vulcanite" by Charles Goodyear. In a classic display of British snobbery, *Punch* magazine suggested that "by packing up the American articles a little closer ... we shall concentrate all the treasures of American art and manufacture into a very few square feet, and beds may be made up to accommodate several hundred in the space claimed for, but not one-quarter filled by, the products of United States industry."[19]

One exhibit escaped this general derision: Samuel Colt's display of his latest revolvers. Colt supplied his London representative, Thomas Peard, with five hundred newly minted Navy 1851 pistols (so named for the martial engravings on the cylinder) and instructions to display them in "as showy and tasteful a manner as possible."[20] Peard chose to array the weapons in a circular formation, fanned-out like a deck of cards and mounted in an upright glass case. Even the eighty-two-year-old Duke of Wellington stopped by to admire Colt's handiwork. "It is with infinite satisfaction I inform you that the pistols command universal attention and praise," Peard informed his employer, adding that the display not only attracted "the most influential men in the country" but also "a large sprinkling of the fair sex."[21]

Colt arrived in London that August, bringing with him a pair of gold-inlaid Navy 1851 pistols for Prince Albert. The gun baron stepped up the lobbying effort, offering personal tutorials in the assembly and disassembly of his revolvers, and keeping a stash of cigars and premium brandy on hand for well-heeled patrons. Colt's pistols received only an honorable mention, but their manufacturer went on to become the first American ever to address London's Institution of Civil Engineers. His lecture, bearing the breathless title "On the Application of Machinery to the Manufacture of Breech-Loading Firearms," extolled the virtues of American industry while placing his invention squarely in the context of "the insulated experience of the enterprising pioneer, and his dependence, sometimes alone, on his personal ability to protect himself and his family" in a "most extensive frontier, still inhabited by hordes of aborigines."[22] Like Bonnie Parker, Colt was in the business of real-time brand-name crafting.

The British and European press response to Colt's Crystal Palace display solidified the perception of America as a place of unrestrained violence that continues to inform the international image of the United States. In the months leading up to the Great Exhibition of the Works of Industry of All Nations, British pacifists lost a war in the press to exclude "such weapons as were constructed only for the destruction of human life."[23] Colt's success fueled their outrage and fed the stereotype. "Caring little about the length of range, [Americans] are fond of something with which they can riddle a man's body in a second,"[24] protested one journalist. (Arthur Penn would make that point graphically in *Bonnie and Clyde*.) A French reporter praised Colt's pistols for their "most perfect uniformity of design" while damning their "murderous task."[25] A *London Times* editorial acknowledged "the virtues of this ingenious instrument" but expressed "suspicion that its principal effect has been hitherto to promote murder."[26]

The company's Crystal Palace publicity materials ballyhooed the efficiency of their product. Colt's revolvers, the advertising maintained, "had reached perfection in the art of destruction."[27]

For Colt, a customer was a customer; the color of the uniform didn't matter. Guns were merely merchandise to sell, and the faster the better. "Run the armory night and day with double sets of hands until we get 5,000 or 10,000 ahead of each kind [of weapon]," he wrote to his factory foreman shortly after South Carolina became the first state to secede from the Union in December 1860. "I had rather have an accumulation of our arms than to have money lying idle, and we cannot have too many [guns] on hand to meet the exigencies of the times. Make hay," he urged, "while the sun shines."[28] The *New York Times* exposed Colt as "A Revolving Patriot," accusing him of treason and charging that "if he could devise any safe way of more effectually aiding the rebellion, Mr. Colt would probably embrace it."[29] Following the attack on Fort Sumter in April 1861, Colt ceased (or claimed to cease) his sales operation in the newly formed Confederacy. "Patriotism at the eleventh hour," mocked the *Chicago Tribune*. "Better late than never."[30]

"Perhaps it is no more fair to blame a gun manufacturer for selling guns than it is to blame an umbrella manufacturer from profiting from rain," Colt biographer Jim Rasenberger writes (though he is quick to point out that "rain has no moral dimension, and war always does").[31] The same argument persists in Second Amendment discussions today. When it comes to firearms in America, commercial interests have always outweighed any scruples. "It would be a terrible state of affairs, if my conscience started to bother me now," wrote one Remington dealer during the 1934 congressional hearings that led to the National Firearms Act. "We certainly are in a hell of a business. A fellow has to wish for trouble to make a living, the only consolation being, however, if we don't get the business, someone else will."[32]

History and popular culture became the means by which to promulgate a carefully calibrated, firearm-friendly past. In Haag's estimation, "We wrote, staged, advertised, filmed, debated and televised our way into a gun culture more than we shot our way in."[33] Her observation is borne out by the sheer number of feature films and TV programs whose titles glorify weapons rather than characters: *Colt .45* (1950), *Springfield Rifle* (1952), and *The Gun That Won the West* (1955), to name just three among hundreds. Television audiences could choose from *Have Gun, Will Travel* (1957–1963), *The Rifleman* (1958–1963), and *Gunsmoke* (1955–1975), for a time the longest-running series in TV history. By the early 1960s, when *Bonnie and Clyde* began its long gestation, eight out of ten prime-time TV offerings were Westerns, dispensing firearm justice on a nightly basis. Arthur Schlesinger Jr. decried the "*Gunsmoke* ethos" he considered "not necessarily the best way to deal with human complexity" and "hardly compatible with any kind of humane or libertarian democracy."[34]

By the mid-twentieth century, "an image is promoted that if you are a real man, you own a firearm," says Adam Winkler. "Owning a firearm is not just a tool that you might have like a hammer or a screwdriver, but gets promoted as the kind of thing you have to have to prove you're American."[35] Advertising parlance terms this "cultivating a want" instead of a need. A mechanical device intended as a strictly utilitarian object—"a machine made to throw balls,"[36] as Oliver Winchester referred to a rifle—became over time a status symbol to be aspired to and treasured. "The gun was reoriented in two antithetical directions," Haag explains: "as a commodity of instinct, and as a luxury—and in both cases, an object of desire."[37] Like those of his fellow capitalists, Winchester's original aims were simple: "to put a gun within reach of every American and [urge] him to buy it."[38] Over a century of promotion and advertising that reshaped perceptions of firearms and enshrined their place in a manufactured history, this "unexceptional, agnostic prerogative of doing business"[39] evolved into the conscious creation of a market designed to fulfill Americans' individualistic self-image—a market that would later metastasize into proof of a particular political affinity.

Such slogans as "The Gun That Won the West," used to market the Winchester Repeating Arms Company's Model 73, did not originate on the late nineteenth-century frontier, but owe their resonance to marketing executives like Winchester's Edwin Pugsley, who coined the catch phrase for a 1919 magazine ad.[40] Two years later, and continuing until 1924, Winchester embarked on a "One in 1,000" campaign, promoting a subset of Model 73s as the best of the best and invoking their celebrity pedigree. Clyde Barrow's boyhood hero Billy the Kid allegedly owned one; estimated auction prices today range from $200,000–400,000. Pitchman Pugsley considered such campaigns "profitable malarkey," part of the "great deal of mystery and hokum still clinging to the gun business," though he admitted, "this is not good sales talk."[41]

A Fourth of July marksmanship challenge for one of these singular "One in 1,000" firearms provides the inciting incident for Anthony Mann's Western film noir, *Winchester '73*, released on the eightieth anniversary of the rifle's debut. Wyatt Earp presides over the Dodge City contest (Earp's mythographer, Stuart N. Lake, is credited with the story). James Stewart's Lin McAdam wins the prized rifle, only to be ambushed and robbed by his rival, setting McAdam on a trail of retribution; the rifle, meanwhile, passes from the thief to a corrupt trader to a Native American warrior to a young homesteader and a cocky gunslinger, all of whose stories end badly owing to their ownership of the weapon. The movie's final shot is a loving push-in to the rifle stock, engraved with a metal plaque commemorating McAdams's victory. "All these men running around to get their hands on this goddamn rifle instead of going after a beautiful blonde like me,"[42] complained costar Shelley Winters, whose character passes through almost as many hands as the titular firearm itself.

Masculinity lies at the heart of the American gun mystique. It isn't a new phenomenon. "The great advantage of this rifle over all others consists in the moral effect it has," Oliver Winchester wrote in promotion of the Model 73, "for if there is anything that will make a party of men, or one single man, stand up to fight to the last moment, it is the knowledge that he has a gun in his hands that will not fail to do its duty just when it is most wanted."[43] Early twentieth-century firearms advertising played on the outlaw notion, even then tapping into what one critic calls "the sense of decaying masculine potency which has long obsessed American culture."[44] Gunmakers targeted the preteen and teenage male demographic. A .22-caliber "would make a man of any boy,"[45] insisted one ad from the Winchester Repeating Arms Company. Winchester issued a direct-mail circular to its retailers, exhorting them to "send us a list of names of boys in your town, so we can send this illustrated letter under your own name."[46] The projected target: 3,363,537 youthful new customers.

Even more than its competitors, Winchester recognized the potential of moving pictures as the ideal delivery system. "Picture a red-headed boy in the front row of the movies," a letter asked retailers to imagine. "He's on the edge of his seat, eyes still popping out of his head as the end is written across a . . . film where Winchester rifles were the star speakers. Up flashes your 'ad' . . . What's the next thought in that boy's mind? What's he going to save his quarters for? A Winchester of course."[47] One of those wide-eyed kids might well have been a teenage Clyde Barrow. According to his sister Marie, Clyde's first gun was a .25–20 caliber lever-action Winchester 1892, purchased in the late 1920s, perhaps with some of those saved-up (or stolen) quarters.[48]

For its part, Colt's Patent Firearms Manufacturing Company utilized scare tactics to entice buyers in the fraught years after World War I. "We have made your home safe against the dangers of the Hun," company advertising boasted. "Now, keep it safe against the dangers of the unprotected. Get a Colt."[49] In paranoid language still echoed today, the manufacturer warned of a "threat at every curve, crossroad and hill." Automobile drivers were particularly at risk, Colt's claimed. "Suppose your car is held up by thugs tonight, in some lonesome country spot, how would you fare?"[50] its ads asked ominously. The company's answer: its .45 Colt semiautomatic, which always "Fires the First Shot First." Easy to use, too: "You don't have to tinker and fuss throwing off safety devices" because "when you *purposely* pull the trigger, you automatically press in the grip safety and the Colt shoots—instantly."[51] No gun, the ads promised, could be brought into action faster.

Clyde Barrow and Bonnie Parker certainly thought so: Clyde stole as many as he could carry from several armories; Bonnie had one on her lap when she was killed. In the wake of their side-by-side deaths, it was not only their real-life romance but also the allure of their firepower that attracted the public's attention. "Americans embrace outlaws more readily than other countries, and that's probably tied with guns,"[52] concedes historian Paul Andrew Hutton.

Bonnie and Clyde screenwriters Robert Benton and David Newman felt that attraction on a location scout of Clyde Barrow's grave at the Western Heights Cemetery in the former West Dallas. Visiting in the summer of 1964, they encountered the graveyard "abandoned" and "overgrown with weeds," but found the experience of "standing six feet over Clyde ... one of the strangest sensations we ever had."[53] More than sixty years later, the same, thrilling strangeness remains palpable. Though the cemetery encompasses memorials dating back to the region's founding, its only paved trail leads directly to the Barrow family plot, which includes Clyde's parents, Henry and Cumie, and his younger brother, L. C., known as "Flop" Barrow for "an unfortunate pair of ears."[54] "*Gone but not forgotten,*" reads the granite stone beneath which Clyde rests with his brother Marvin ("Buck"). Bright flowers—some real, others made of cloth—provide the only splash of color in the otherwise monotonous but well-tended green lawn.

As Bonnie Parker predicted, in death even more than in life the couple's story holds a powerful spell.

The conservative Catholic authors of the Motion Picture Production Code of 1930 understood this empathy all too well. "Criminals should not be made heroes, even if they are historical criminals," Daniel Lord and Martin J. Quigley insisted. Most of all, "methods of committing crime ... should not be so explicit as to teach the audience how crime can be committed."[55]

An addendum titled "Particular Applications of the Code and the Reasons Therefore" instructed that "the use of firearms should be restricted to essentials."[56] In practice, this meant that under no circumstances could a weapon be discharged and bullets strike a human target in the same shot; a cut must always intervene.

A gunshot fired on the moribund streets of a rural Texas town on October 22, 1966, changed that forever.

12

"WHAT'S WRONG WITH THESE GUYS?"

> Shooting a film is like a stagecoach ride in the Old West. When you start, you are hoping for a pleasant trip. By the halfway point, you just hope to survive.
>
> —François Truffaut, Jean-Louis Richard, and Suzanne Schiffman,
>
> screenplay for *La nuit americaine* (*Day for Night*, 1973)

American movie storytelling began with a bullet in the face. Edwin S. Porter's 1903 sensation, *The Great Train Robbery*, included a close-up shot of a mustachioed outlaw with a bandanna at his neck pointing his pistol—a Colt revolver, naturally—and firing it directly into the lens. Smoke issues from the revolver's barrel as the outlaw unblinkingly pulls the trigger one—two—three times.[1] "The resulting excitement is great," assured an exhibitors' catalog from distributor Edison Film Company, which helpfully recommended "this section of the film can be used either to begin the subject or end it, as the operator may choose."[2]

The Great Train Robbery packs a sensational amount of gun violence into its single reel (roughly ten minutes, depending at the time on the hand-crank speed of the projector operator). An express man is riddled with bullets in a duel over a strong box; a passenger is shot multiple times in the back attempting to escape; a tenderfoot is made to dance with the help of a volley of gunshots; a posse member is shot off his horse in the chase scene, and the surviving bandits meet their end in a vicious barrage of gunfire in a wooded remove not that much different from the landscape of *Bonnie and Clyde*'s ambush.

Edison's promotional materials touted the one-reel "headline attraction," shot in the New Jersey woods that served as the company backlot, as "posed and acted in faithful duplication of the genuine 'Hold Ups' made by various outlaw bands in the [F]ar West."[3] Porter's film was among the first cinematic efforts to employ editing to build tension. Western movie historians George Fenin and William K. Everson considered it "the first dramatically creative American film."[4] Edison's publicity promised "this sensational and highly tragic subject will make a decided 'hit' whenever shown."[5] *The Great Train Robbery* became the nascent industry's first blockbuster and laid the groundwork for virtually every Western to follow.

When it came time to shoot the pivotal scene in *Bonnie and Clyde* in which Clyde fires without a cut through an automobile window into the face of a bank official, the director knew the rules he would be breaking. "The gunshot in the same frame was very conscious," Penn told biographer Nat Segaloff, "his eyes twinkling with the mischief of achievement."[6] "I was going to do that," the director continued, "because all you're doing is sanitizing [the violence] if you have somebody shoot over here and you cut to somebody getting hit over there. That gap has changed everything."[7]

David Newman and Robert Benton had described the moment in a stand-alone stage direction in their script: "The man's face explodes in blood. Then he drops out sight,"[8] they wrote, conscious themselves of the taboo-defying action. (Jack Warner drew a circle around this text in his copy of the final shooting script, writing "NO!" on the margins in huge letters.[9]) "From that point on it's irreversible," Penn said of the killing's importance. "[Bonnie and Clyde] can never go back. Life is over for them at that moment. They change from being kids and bank robbers to killers. . . . For this reason, I think it's one of the best sequences in any of my films."[10]

What makes the outburst even more horrifying is its placement at the climax of an otherwise comedic, even slapstick sequence. After their earlier, amateur failures—including Clyde's hilarious "stickup" of a failed bank ("You git out here and tell my girl," he demands of the bemused lone teller, then shoots out the bank's windows in impotent frustration)—the couple pull off a flawlessly executed robbery, only to discover their newfound wheelman, C. W. Moss, has decided to park the car in their absence. The confusion allows enough time for the bank official to race into the street and mount the running board. "His screaming can barely be distinguished from all the noise,"[11] the stage directions indicate. That's when Clyde instinctively fires through the window, changing the trajectory of the film—and of American cinema.

The script locates the action in a small Kansas town, but filming took place in Red Oak, Texas. Now part of the seemingly endless Dallas-Fort Worth metroplex, Red Oak at the time was a hamlet of fewer than a thousand people on the northern edge of Ellis County, where the Barrow family once homesteaded and whose county seat, Waxahachie, marked Benton's birthplace. A recently discovered cache of eight-millimeter home movie film, shot by an unidentified Red Oak resident, provides an evocative behind-the-scenes record of the filming of *Bonnie and Clyde* in the fall of 1966.

Exhibiting the herky-jerky movement and sometimes murky exposures resulting from the era's wind-up amateur cameras, the footage nevertheless conveys a palpable sense of the excitement that inevitably results when a Hollywood production crew—even a low-budget one—descends on a flyspeck location. As might be expected, Warren Beatty dominates the coverage: glimpsed through the door of his trailer, reviewing his script in costume, feet propped on a shelf; signing autographs for a group of starstruck young girls; hoisting a baby; and most revealingly, flirting in full Clyde Barrow attire with a somewhat less-than-demure, bobbed-haired local woman clearly considering the possibilities.

A quarter-page photograph in the *Dallas Morning News* shows the actor squatting to be at eye-level with six-year-old Pamela Ann Mulkey between takes; a prop Colt .45 semiautomatic dangles from his hand.[12] "Any old time cop would have opened fire the moment Warren Beatty stepped out of the 1932 Durant sedan in the middle of Red Oak's Waller Street Saturday," noted Dallas reporter Kent Biffle, whose previous assignments included a search of the Texas School Book Depository with police officers on the hunt for President John F. Kennedy's assassin. "Actor Beatty was a faded photograph of Texas gunman Clyde Barrow," Biffle maintained. "The tough expression changed to a mild smile as Barrow touched his hat to a couple of passing farm wives and ambled on toward the bank."[13] Townspeople in Red Oak and elsewhere eagerly detailed their own experiences with the outlaw couple to Penn and his actors.

"For the people there, life hadn't changed that much since the real Bonnie and Clyde came through," said Gene Hackman, recalling how an elderly man approached him on a break from filming, pointed to the actor's hat and said, "Buck Barrow was my cousin, and he would never wear a hat like that."[14]

The Red Oak footage includes what appears to be three separate takes of the climactic killing, all beginning with the bank official falling to the ground as Clyde's '32 Durant sedan flees town pursued by a handful of policemen (played by actual Red Oak cops who eagerly volunteered for on-screen duty) blasting away with their service revolvers. A particularly gory home movie snapshot shows production manager Russ Saunders, who played the official, wiping stage blood off his face between setups. At least one resident found the historical re-enactment overwhelming. "Shooting Too Real for Man," reported a sidebar story in the Morning News. "An ambulance was summoned but the man was revived and went on his way."[15] The Dallas paper's headline deliberately conflated the industry term for production—"shooting"—with the real thing.[16]

In the years to follow, townspeople from Red Oak and other municipalities would recall cast and crew with fondness. "They were the swellest bunch of people you ever met,"[17] remembered one resident. The eight-millimeter footage, with its randomly caught images of Hollywood stars making faces for the camera and clearly thrilled locals mingling in costume between takes, inspires a sense of collaborative synergy—everyone involved working in perfect harmony. In some cases, location shooting can engender a terrific spirit of creative camaraderie. Thrown together in an unfamiliar setting, frequently in places with limited after-hours entertainment, cast and crew bond into a temporary family, akin to that of circus performers. A team spirit prevails: People devote all their energies to the betterment of the project, aware that their contribution may result in something that lifts the picture out of the ordinary—and maybe, just maybe, renders it something special.

Bonnie and Clyde was not one of those productions.

"Film making in a capricious climate is a little like making love to a woman whose husband is known to have a violent temper," Robert Towne reflected when the experience was over. "At least the same question must be asked—considering the risk, is it going to be all that much better?"[18] As Mark Harris recounted in *Pictures at a Revolution*, Beatty "had assembled a creative team with nothing to lose, but also little reason for optimism."[19] In Towne's view, "Warren's attitude very often was, 'Get somebody who's really talented at a point when they're going to be more pliant or malleable than they might otherwise be.' And very often that's after a shaky or bad experience."[20]

"Now that I think of it," said Beatty in 2007, "almost everyone connected with that movie felt just a little bit insulted by the movie business before they came to [*Bonnie and Clyde*]. Everybody had something they knew they could do better and they all showed up and did it."[21] Estelle Parsons remembered things the same way: "My impression was that people were down on their luck. It was like doing an independent movie."[22]

That's because—it *was* an independent movie. Of sorts. Up to a point.

"Why aren't [Penn and Beatty] on the lot?" "Colonel" Jack Warner demanded of studio production chief Walter MacEwen. "Why do they have to be in Texas? Mike Curtiz could shoot on the lot!" Warner bellowed about the studio's most accomplished craftsman, who had made *Casablanca* (1942), among countless other films, entirely on Warner Bros. sound stages. "What's wrong with these guys?"[23] Nothing, from Penn and Beatty's point of view: they'd insisted on location shooting to give themselves a measure of freedom from studio interference, as Warner well knew.

That independence came at a cost. "It will be necessary for many of the crew members to double up,"[24] read a memo from assistant director Jack Reddish apologizing for skimpy production lodgings at the North Park

Inn located at 9300 N. Central Expressway in Dallas (today the site of a big-box strip mall), which served as command central for *Bonnie and Clyde*'s production. While not exactly a shoestring, the movie's "final" $1.8 million budget allowed for few extravagances in any department.

For Robert Benton, "it was very important ... that the people who were from Texas, when they saw the film, it would have felt real for them—it would have felt true."[25] Towne also saw the advantages of the hamlets that lay "like dusty dominoes on the oppressive, table-flat lands surrounding Big D[allas]." He remembered especially the "high-tension wires and telephone poles [that] never seem to show up on back lots, but ... make things real."[26] For Beatty, "without things like crab grass, telephone poles ... poorly patched asphalt in the streets—you've got a back lot and you've already begun to lose your battle with all the artificial elements you fight against in trying to make what appears on film look real, or credible."[27]

"We weren't out to make a historical reconstruction of the thirties," Penn told an interviewer in 1977, explaining the decision to shoot *Bonnie and Clyde* in color rather than black and white.[28] "We wanted to make a film that would conjure up the spirit and atmosphere of those times through the modern sensibility of the sixties."[29] To achieve that, the production "stripped away almost all the extraneous details we could," Penn said. "The visual essence of the picture is what it leaves out, for the most part.... We were creating the world as two narcissistic, mutually involved kids might view it: as a series of targets.... The movie is, in that sense, an abstraction rather than a genuine reportage."[30] *Bonnie and Clyde*'s minimalistic approach to period remains one of its greatest artistic strengths, suggesting much with the barest detail. In Clyde and Bonnie's get-to-know-you stroll through "West Dallas" (shot in Venus, a suburb of Midlothian), a handful of FDR posters, a trio of period cars and some peeling coming-attractions advertisements outside a boarded-up movie theater serve to establish time and place. "And that was *it*,"[31] Penn said.

Then and afterward, the director unfailingly gave all the credit to first-time art director Dean Tavoularis. The thirty-four-year-old's work, Penn insisted, was "the best thing that happened to *Bonnie and Clyde*."[32]

A gifted draftsman, Tavoularis had begun his industry career in the animation department at Walt Disney Studios, where he worked as an "in-betweener," filling the gaps left by principal animators on the thousands of frame-by-frame drawings for such films as *Lady and the Tramp* (1955). "My job [on that one] was to draw the teeth of a crocodile as it opened and closed its mouth," Tavoularis remembered, "and it drove me nuts....It was a detail of a detail of a detail."[33] Tavoularis participated in the production of the studio's first full live-action feature, *20,000 Leagues Under the Sea* (1954) and graduated to assistant art director on *Pollyanna* (1960) and *The Parent Trap* (1961), working under veteran art director Robert Clatsworthy, whose decidedly not-family friendly pre-Disney credits included Orson Welles's *Touch of Evil* (1958) and Alfred Hitchcock's *Psycho* (1960). When Clatsworthy left the "Mouse House" for Columbia Pictures, Tavoularis went with him, assisting on a series of Stanley Kramer films including *Ship of Fools* (1965) and *Guess Who's Coming to Dinner* (1967)—the latter of which would compete with *Bonnie and Clyde* for that year's Best Picture Oscar.

While working with Clatsworthy on the caustic Hollywood exposé *Inside Daisy Clover* (1965), Tavoularis befriended hair stylist Jean Burt ("J.R.") Reilly. Reilly's clients included the movie's star, Natalie Wood, already under serious consideration to play Bonnie Parker. "J.R. called me up one day and said, 'Have you ever heard of Bonnie and Clyde?'" Tavoularis remembered. "He said [Warren Beatty and Arthur Penn] wanted a new look for the movie, and he mentioned me as a promising art director that they should meet."[34] After two sessions with the producer and director at Beatty's Beverly Wilshire hideaway, Tavoularis was hired. By his own recollection, Penn and Beatty were swayed not by any specific ideas Tavoularis may have pitched, but by his dislike for the whole big-studio system, which mirrored their own.

"I was very dissatisfied with art direction back then ... I often cringed at the stuff I would see," he confided. "I remember when I was starting out as an assistant, I asked an art director why the décor on movie sets was so beefed up—why everything was so big and fake." Told that "if you put a real molding up on the ceiling, it would be too small and the camera wouldn't pick it up," Tavoularis thought, "[that's] one-hundred percent bullshit. It's just a little detail, but it explains the whole mentality in Hollywood back then."[35]

Bonnie and Clyde's design costs didn't provide for moldings—or much of anything else, for that matter. A preliminary budget dated June 29, 1966, allotted $35,867 for art direction, $144,533 for set construction, and an additional $52,460 for on-site setup. A revised October 6 budget reduced art direction costs to $15,028—less than half of the original estimate—and slashed set building expenses to $58,065.[36] Tavoularis made an asset of the need to shoot on existing—what are called "practical"—locations. "I was very happy to see that Texas had not progressed very much out of the Depression," he said. "You had all these beautiful streets with wooden sidewalks and businesses that were mostly shut but perfectly preserved."[37] In atrophied towns bearing such names as Ponder, Pilot Point, Lavon, Maypearl, and Crandall as well as Red Oak, Tavoularis experienced a sense of suspended time ideally suited to *Bonnie and Clyde*'s "one foot in each decade"[38] approach. "I would go into shops down there, like a men's clothing store, and they still had boxes with men's shirts in them from the 1930s, like they'd just locked up the place and left."[39]

Filming on practical locations, some of them the very streets frequented by Clyde and Bonnie, did more than establish the picture's spare, distinctive look. The elegiac atmosphere itself—that part of Texas in the fall is redolent with faded autumnal hues and ominous skies—exerted a profound influence on cast and crew alike. "Life was shaping art," Towne wrote in an essay after the movie's release. "Warren and Faye were not working on Bonnie and Clyde; Bonnie and Clyde were working on them. They were seeping into the actors, with them always, a pervasive and subtle part of the location . . . as continuing and inescapable as the weather."[40]

Tavoularis built sets in a former automotive garage in central Dallas, taking care to make them interchangeable for budget reasons. "I tried to make them look real—and that's another thing I hated about the Hollywood sets back then: the walls would go all the way up and you'd never see the ceiling because that's where they'd put the lights." Instead, Tavoularis "deliberately made the ceilings low because I wanted to give the feeling that the characters were more and more trapped."[41] (Only upon close inspection after many repeat viewings of the film does the repurposing of the artificial walls become apparent; the gang's Joplin City apartment, for instance, bears notable similarities to the rundown flophouse they retreat to after the bank official's murder.) For exteriors, the art director's biggest issue was automobiles. The production traveled with a retinue of some twenty period Fords, Chevys, and Dodges, "acquired on the location site for several hundred dollars, refurbished with tuned-up motors and after their 'acting chores' were completed . . . sold at a profit to vintage vehicle fanciers."[42]

The Red Oak eight-millimeter footage abounds in lovingly shot images of mint-condition Model A Fords, De Sotos, and Pierce Arrows being maneuvered into position, some rented at prices ranging from $400 to $1,500, others lent gratis to the production. *Dallas Morning News* reporter Kent Biffle recorded a moment where "Tommy Pitman of Dallas, owner of the classic Pierce, threw himself bodily" between the 1932 Durant sedan being driven by actor Michael J. Pollard as C. W. Moss and the car he links bumpers with in the slapstick getaway attempt. "My heart picked up a few beats," sighed Pittman. "In New York you don't need a car," Pollard muttered, to which his wife responded, "He's been practicing driving for a week. You should have seen him before."[43]

Cars and clothes can make or break a period picture. Tavoularis provided the cars. The clothes came from Penn and Beatty's other untested talent, costume designer Theadora Van Runkle.

"I did not know how to do a movie or anything," Van Runkle remembered of the moment when her mentor, designer Dorothy Jeakins, recommended her to create the wardrobe sketches for what Jeakins called "a little cowboy movie that won't be much good"[44]—meaning *Bonnie and Clyde*, still regarded within the industry as a thirties-era Western. "I knew exactly what I'd do when I read the first page [of the script]," Van Runkle said. "I knew that it would be a huge hit, and I knew I would be nominated for an Oscar."[45] (She was right on the first count.) The former catalog illustrator, then a thirty-eight-year-old widow with two children and few prospects, brought her sketches to the "La Escondida" hideaway, where she found Beatty in the midst of "all these beautiful golden girls walking around in little pleated skirts and bare golden legs, and they were all almost identical and all just irresistible."[46]

Despite such distractions, her ideas resonated with Penn. "If our movie can be as great as these drawings," the director told Van Runkle, "we'll have a hit."[47] The aspiring costume designer had perfectly caught Penn's sense of clothing "meant to reflect the period without being period costumes."[48] There was only one problem with Van Runkle's employment: she wasn't an enrolled member of the Costume Designers Guild. "Sorry, kid, you can't do the movie . . . you're not in the union,"[49] Beatty told her; he'd be forced to hire someone older. "So I did something uncharacteristic," Van Runkle confessed. "I leapt across the room and grabbed him by his shirt collar, and I said, 'You've got to give me this job!'" Never one to deny a woman's entreaties, Beatty went head-to-head with the guild's president, "a southern woman who swore a lot, and they swore at each other for about five minutes, and when [Warren] hung up, he said, 'You got the job.'"[50]

Photographs and documentary footage of Van Runkle from the *Bonnie and Clyde* era reveal her to be even more stylish and attractive than many of the men and women she costumed. "Theadora was hip and young when costume designers weren't hip and young," says David LeVay, who became Van Runkle's assistant in later years. "She was quite tall and quite elegant. I can imagine people tripping over themselves to work with her."[51] Former Costume Designers Guild president Deborah Nadoolman Landis remembers Van Runkle "had this incredible Glinda the Good Witch persona that made everyone feel they were the most important people in the room when she was talking to them."[52] Beyond sheer personality, "Theadora was the best artist I ever met, and she had her own style,"[53] La Vay says. Costume sketches in his possession evince Van Runkle's exquisite draftsmanship as well as her ability to capture the essence of a particular period or trend without relying on slavish reproduction.

Taking her cue from the photographs uncovered in the Joplin raid, Van Runkle outfitted Faye Dunaway in close-fitting skirts and tight sweaters complemented by matching scarves and a beret, a nod to period authenticity but one perfectly suited to the French New Wave. Warren Beatty sported double-breasted jackets, vests, and tank-top undershirts, an ensemble its creator called at once "puritanical *and* pure sex."[54] Van Runkle lost the battle with both stars over their hairstyles. "What I wanted was for Faye to wear a marcel wave, and I wanted Warren's hair to be parted in the middle, and then shaved [as Clyde's was]. I thought he was going to faint."[55] Instead, Dunaway wears her hair straight, while Beatty's coiffure looks... well, much as it does in nearly every Warren Beatty film. Van Runkle conceded, "a lot of designers have criticized the hair in the movie, but the fact of the matter is it really goes with the clothes and makes [them] look divine."[56]

The costume designer had even fewer resources to work with than art director Tavoularis: $12,573 for men's wardrobe, a dollar more for women's clothing, according to the October 6, 1966, budget, with another $15,646 for makeup and hair. At least Tavoularis had the opportunity to see the movie through shooting. Van Runkle never made it to location, relying instead on her wardrobe mistress, Norma Brown, responsible for on-set costuming, who "followed my instructions to the slightest drapery."[57] Beyond the trendsetting wardrobe for Clyde and Bonnie, Van Runkle had to make do with stock costumes available in Warner Bros.' extensive warehouse. As Blanche Barrow, Estelle Parsons recalled she "wore Barbara Stanwyck's jodhpurs and Dorothy Malone's skirts, whatever was left over from other movies."[58] The designer found herself flummoxed by the need for multiple versions of a single outfit required by the movie's many violent action sequences.

"I made all kinds of mistakes," Van Runkle acknowledged decades later. "I didn't know anything about continuity. I didn't know how to break down a script. I just stumbled through."[59]

"Stumbling through": as good an epigraph as any for *Bonnie and Clyde*'s Texas odyssey.

Penn described his directorial technique as a "search for controlled accidents. By that I mean we set up the scene quite clearly but then try to introduce elements that might perhaps throw the actors off and catch them in an unguarded moment."[60] Penn attributed the technique to his days in live television, "where there was no possibility of storyboarding and everything was shot right on the spot—on the air, as we say—at the moment we were transmitting."[61] Unlike many modern directors, Penn didn't plan the day's shots in advance, and considered the whole process of storyboarding—the sketching-out of every angle—"pretty lousy. I prefer to be open to what the actors do, how they interact to a given situation."[62] The director recognized that "on the occasions when I have been too meticulously prepared a kind of rigidity appears in my work which I don't really like."[63]

Small chance of that happening on the *Bonnie and Clyde* set. "What we would do is shoot during the day, then at night get together in the motel and rehearse the next day's scenes,"[64] Penn recounted. "We would sit around and talk but often we got our best rehearsal in the motel the night before we shot a given scene." It helped that Penn loved actors. "I enjoy pushing them as far as they can go."[65] Gene Hackman, for one, appreciated the trust. "[Arthur] didn't have—or at least he didn't project—a preconceived idea about the way a scene was supposed to go, which is a great knack of some directors to make an actor feel as if everything is his idea."[66]

Penn achieved this not through autocratic instruction and specific line readings, but by "setting a problem in motion which will result in what I want rather than telling them how to achieve the final result."[67] The affinity between director and performer is on powerful display in Buck Barrow's death scene following an encounter with a mob of armed vigilantes. Already suffering from a mortal head wound, Hackman's Buck finally succumbs to his injuries as the vigilantes close ranks and a blinded Blanche screams, "Don't die, Daddy! Don't die!"

"What do you want me to do here?" Hackman asked of his final on-screen moments.

"Have you ever seen a bullfight?" Penn responded. Hackman admitted he had. "You know, after the sword is in, what does the bull do?" Penn hinted. "Gene paused, then said, 'I got it.'"[68]

On screen, Hackman staggers on all fours toward his killers, then collapses sideways to the ground with the same deadening arc as the ritually slaughtered bull. Penn's camera mercilessly cranes down to a close-up of Buck's bloodied hand; the fingers twitch momentarily, then fall still. "You watch the life go out of a body instead of a movie 'die,'" Penn said. "It was just something I liked."[69]

"I don't know if I have ever worked with a director who knew more about what an actor needed—to be pushed, nudged, guided or given an image,"[70] a grateful Hackman said of Penn.

Faye Dunaway agreed. "A great director helps you do better than you ever thought you could, and Arthur is a great director,"[71] she wrote, comparing him favorably to Elia Kazan. Dunaway considered Penn "as much philosopher as artist." She wrote of watching her director from a distance "as he surveyed the landscape—a cigar perpetually in hand, horn-rimmed glasses perched on his nose, soaking everything in."[72] (Towne remembered that ever-present cigar as well: "[Arthur] waved it over the entire production like a magic wand.")[73] Even the hard-to-please Beatty responded favorably to Penn's emphasis on what he called "kinetic behavior." The actor took to wearing his shoulder-holstered Colt .45 full-time throughout the production. "He never played a scene without it, never, because he felt it was so much a part of his character," Penn said. "And it *did* make his suit fit a certain way; it made him stand a certain way. I think these things have peripheral benefits that we may not be conscious of, but they do help convey character."[74]

Despite Beatty's celebrity, attested to by eight-millimeter footage of autograph signings and reports in the *Dallas Morning News* that "if any of you gals want to catch up with Warren—here's a tip: wait in front of the Majestic Theater [in Dallas, where] he goes to the screening room every night,"[75] the first-time producer felt himself on trial by his own crew. "They were appalled that this snot-nosed pretty boy was making a movie when it was clear he had no idea that everything he was doing was completely wrong,"[76] Penn sympathized. Nothing could have been further from the truth. "As it turned out," Hackman told Beatty's biographer Suzanne Finstad, "[Warren] was a lot better at his job than they were at theirs."[77]

One sixteen-year-old Texas extra named Patsy Ann McClenny took inspiration from watching "a young, beautiful, elegant man be the one in power."[78] The lithe teenage blond had graduated from day player to serve as Bonnie's driving double; those are her hands in close-up shots on the stick shift, which Dunaway couldn't operate. She spent the on-set downtime listening to Beatty's conversations with Penn. "I hung on every word,"[79] McClenny remembered, vowing to pursue her own movie career. (She achieved her goal as actress Morgan Fairchild.)

Beatty demonstrated astonishing discipline throughout the filming. "If you let your energy level fall, if you get drunk or stay up all night and come in the next morning and have no energy, you are letting down the people with the money,"[80] he insisted—a rigorous aesthetic utterly unappreciated by Jack Warner. "From the first day of shooting, I felt there was one thing I could never run away from in this film," Beatty told a reporter for *Life* magazine. "No matter what was wrong with it, I was gonna step up and take the complete blame. For a change, there wouldn't be any cop-outs."[81]

To the astonishment of all involved, Beatty's commitment extended to his off-set celibacy. "Warren never fucked around with *anybody*," Towne remembered. "I mean, not with a soul."[82] "He was acting and he was producing, that was what he had his mind on,"[83] confirmed art director Tavoularis. The proscription extended to costar Dunaway. Mark Harris recorded a moment during a rehearsal at the North Park Motor Inn when Beatty, "as if checking off items on a list," said to Dunaway, "'we need to talk about the before-fuck and the after-fuck [for the characters].' That was about as romantic as things got." (Dunaway's version: "We had a tacit understanding that we'd simply remain friends.")[84]

Hackman called the filming of *Bonnie and Clyde* "as good an experience as I've ever had. I remember just sitting there in the car, the five principal actors, all of us there filming, and thinking to myself, 'Man, isn't making movies great?'"[85] Almost no one else associated with the film remembers it that way. "Was it tense?" script supervisor John Dutton parroted back an interviewer's question. "Are you kidding? It was excruciating!"[86] Most if not all that tension arose from the daily battles Beatty waged with Penn. "Conflict equals drama, drama equals story, and you need a story every day," Beatty told *Los Angeles Times* staff writer Geoff Boucher. "There have to be problems because that makes it interesting."[87]

Two tantalizingly brief shots in the Red Oak eight-millimeter footage provide visual evidence of the ongoing "discussions" between producer and director. In the first, Beatty ascends the camera platform where Penn is framing the climactic chase. In the next, he and Penn are seen engaged in an apparent disagreement over the chosen angle; Penn points one way, Beatty another. Art director Tavoularis noted that Beatty "was always at Arthur Penn's ear about everything. The wardrobe, a dolly shot, when to change a set-up. He was hands-on, a very active producer. But I would never describe it as unfriendly."[88] Dunaway had the same impression. "They were very good partners," she said of Beatty and Penn. "I think Warren trusted [Arthur], and I think he understood what the dramatic material needed to work for an audience."[89]

"Certainly there were differences—*certainly!*" Penn acknowledged. "But they didn't result in being obstacles to the work going on."[90] (According to the director's son, Matthew, Penn preferred to characterize the disputes as "vigorous, passionate exchanges."[91])

Newcomers to the set would nonetheless be disconcerted by the protracted shooting delays caused by the producer and director hashing out their differences in public view. "What's happening? Is this movie going to get made?" a distressed Gene Wilder asked Estelle Parsons on his first day of shooting. (Wilder made a memorable screen debut in *Bonnie and Clyde* as an undertaker brought along with his fiancée on a Barrow Gang joyride.) "Oh, don't worry," Parsons reassured him. "This happens every day."[92]

"Among sane people, who have the same end in sight, there shouldn't be a battle for control,"[93] Beatty explained to Curtis Hanson, who became the production's unofficial stills photographer. The producer preferred to regard the daily "arguments" as "discussions." Still, Beatty realized "I can be obnoxious. And I knew that I would be hard to take in a one-on-one dialectic with Arthur, that finally he would say, 'I just can't take it anymore.'"[94] Early in their collaboration on *Bonnie and Clyde*, producer/star and director had been riding in the same car when, Beatty remembered, "we pulled onto Sunset [Blvd.] and I said, 'Let's have an argument! What do you think the biggest casting problem in the movie is?' And he said, 'You.' He told me to stop thinking about the production and start thinking about playing the part. And he was right."[95]

To prevent the arguments/discussions from getting too personal, Beatty called in a referee. Robert Towne had presumed that his role on location in Texas would be to polish the occasional scene (that and pretending to work on the script that eventually became *Shampoo*). Instead, he discovered his job "was to listen to Beatty and Penn fight."[96] As Beatty put it, "Three heads are better than two, because if two people disagree, it's more possible for it to become personal. You need someone to say, 'Hey, schmuck!' So Robert was really helpful when we were kicking around things."[97] Script supervisor John Dutton recalled multiple occasions where arguments had to be put on hold to salvage a shooting day, only to resume at dinner or back at the North Park Inn, where Towne would be summoned to take notes. "My overall impression was feeling like a fool,"[98] the writer admitted to Penn's biographer.

When not being forced to act as intermediary, Towne struggled to address Penn's notes on specific page revisions. "I was in a hotel room working on scenes every day, and I would be told, 'Try it this way.' . . . I thought, 'Jeez, I must be terrible, because Arthur Penn kept asking me to do it again and again. Then I realized Arthur was really using me the way a good director uses an actor: 'Try the scene this way. Try the scene that way.' It was very intelligent of him."[99] Penn particularly worried over an upcoming scene in which Texas Ranger Frank Hamer happens on the Barrow Gang alongside a rural road. The confrontation results in Hamer being apprehended by the gang and forced to submit to a series of compromising photographs.

As things turned out, Penn had ample reason to feel uncomfortable. But at the moment, he and Beatty had more pressing concerns.

One in front of the camera, the other behind it.

13

"WE'RE IN THE MONEY"

> The cards were just stacked against us, that's all.
> —Clyde Barrow

For Clyde Barrow and Bonnie Parker, the end of the line came almost three months to the day after their narrow escape from Joplin, Missouri, police.

Following that violent encounter, which resulted in the deaths of two law enforcement officers, Clyde and Bonnie had temporarily parted ways with Buck and Blanche, with a plan to rendezvous in southwestern Oklahoma across the border from the arid Texas Panhandle. Saturday night, June 10, 1933, found Clyde at the wheel of yet another stolen Ford V-8, heading east along Texas Highway 203 outside Wellington, one of two parallel roads with bridges spanning the Salt Fork of the Red River; Bonnie rode shotgun, while W. D. Jones slept in the back seat. Rand McNally's trusty atlas likely directed Clyde over the newly paved highway rather than the older hard-packed dirt road. Traveling at over seventy miles per hour, headlights darkened or dimmed, Clyde zoomed past a detour sign warning of a washed-out bridge.

The ravine came up suddenly.

The V-8 went airborne, then plummeted thirty feet into the dry riverbed, rolling over twice before coming to a landing in the sandy bottom. The impact threw Clyde clear of the car but left him unhurt. Neighboring farmers alerted by the crash helped him pull W. D. out of the wreckage, but Bonnie remained unconscious in the overturned passenger seat, one leg caught in the crumpled door. The accident split the engine block and ruptured the gas tank. Everyone could smell the fumes. Accounts differ as to whether the V-8 then burst into flames or battery acid seeped into the Ford's cab.

For Bonnie, the results were horrific. W. D. Jones remembered, "the hide on her right leg was gone, from her hip down to the ankle. I could see the bone at places."[1] Bonnie's "stockings began melting into her legs," according to another version, causing her to "[scream] for Clyde to kill her."[2] With the Good Samaritans' help, Clyde and W. D. managed to extricate Bonnie from the wreckage and carry her up the slope to the nearby Pritchard family farmhouse, where Sally Pritchard did her best to treat the wounds with a remedy of baking soda and yellow Cloverine salve.

"She needs a doctor," Mrs. Pritchard insisted.

"No," Clyde and Bonnie answered in unison.

"We can't afford that,"[3] Clyde added cannily.

At this point in the story, Clyde did something inexplicable—as he had that moment back in 1932 when he left Bonnie and Ralph Fults to their own fates in a rain-soaked creek bed outside Kaufman, Texas, while he high-tailed it to safety. Forced to choose between Bonnie and the guns left behind in the totaled Ford, Clyde chose the guns.

"If she dies, she'll just have to die," Clyde told farmer Jack Pritchard, according to biographer Jeff Guinn, who records the story in *Go Down Together*, with the caveat that "if, in those first terrible moments in the Pritchard house, he did say something so callous, it was probably because [Clyde had] also been battered up in the wreck."[4] Extenuating circumstances aside, the fact remains that Clyde abandoned Bonnie to retrieve his share of the Barrow Gang's cache of weapons, which numbered several Browning automatic rifles, many of them liberated from National Guard armories whose losses had begun to attract FBI attention.

Clyde's absence allowed for one of the gang's rescuers, the Pritchards' neighbor Lonzo Cartwright, to slip away and alert local authorities. When Collingsworth County sheriff George Corry and Wellington town marshal

Tom Hardy finally arrived, Clyde promptly took the lawmen into custody, commandeering Corry's Chevrolet as an ambulance. Bonnie lay stretched out on the back seat between the two kidnapped lawmen, who by this time had realized the accident victims were something more than "local kids who'd been out drinking, and who maybe carried a gun or two for a thrill."[5]

"You coppers ever hear about the two Barrow brothers?" Clyde asked on the drive to the Oklahoma border, unable to resist the temptation to print the legend.

"Can't say that I have," Marshal Hardy responded disingenuously, prompting Bonnie to whisper, "Don't you mugs ever read the papers?"[6]

Incredibly—even miraculously, given the circumstances—Clyde managed to make the planned rendezvous with Buck and Blanche in southwestern Oklahoma. Blanche remembered that "Clyde's nose was broken and his face was all cut up" and that "W.D.'s face wasn't much better." Bonnie's condition left her aghast. "[She] was a mass of burns and cuts. . . . Her chin was cut to the bone. Her chest was caved in. . . . She was screaming and moaning like she was dying and appeared to be unconscious. All of us thought she would die before daybreak."[7] In the moment, Clyde and Buck's principal concern was what to do with the lawmen Clyde had brought along for the ride.

"Want 'em tended to?"[8] Buck asked.

Moved by the way Corry and Hardy had cared for Bonnie on the cross-state journey, Clyde opted for clemency. He instructed Buck to tie the lawmen to a tree. Buck complied—using a string of barbed wire. By the time the officers managed to free themselves thirty minutes later, the Barrow Gang's trail had gone cold.

The near-fatal crash outside Wellington—one of the most foundational episodes in the story of Clyde Barrow and Bonnie Parker—plays no part whatsoever in *Bonnie and Clyde*. The accident left Bonnie crippled for life, unable to walk without assistance and often reduced to having Clyde carry her from place to place; her injuries made Bonnie virtually incapable of having committed the crimes later attributed to her. To render Bonnie Parker incapacitated would have been box office anathema in 1960s Hollywood (even in an industry on the verge of transition) and would have been out-of-synch with the filmmakers' expressed intention to coalesce two distinct decades and present their protagonists as "people whose style set them apart from their time and place so that they seemed odd and aberrant to the general run of society."[9]

Right up until the end, Warren Beatty and Faye Dunaway simply look *better* than everyone else in the film. The concluding ambush scene derives its considerable power in part from the shock of seeing such beauty violently defiled. The director's envisioning of Newman and Benton's script emphasizes Clyde's and Bonnie's youthful rebellion. "They really set out to level things a bit," Penn explained. "The banks had the money; they didn't have the money. That just didn't seem right to them. So, they decided to get a little bit of it.... They were more thieves than murderers. They killed accidentally and they continued to kill accidentally."[10]

The real Clyde Barrow had no compunction about killing—and almost never killed "accidentally." To his family, Clyde often professed that he hadn't pulled the trigger in his many fatal encounters. Raymond Hamilton had. Or W. D. Jones. Or Henry Methvin, or any other in a list of part-time henchmen. Sometimes he merely made excuses: "The cards were just stacked against us, that's all."[11] Bonnie's mother saw through the lies—or at least claimed to, after the fact. "Since [Clyde] later killed so many men and admitted the killings to us,"[12] Emma Parker wrote, she came to know when to doubt newspaper and radio accounts of murders attributed to Clyde and Bonnie when they were nowhere near the scene of the crime. "They just hung it on us for luck," Clyde said, even then feeling the weight of celebrity. "They've got to hang it on somebody, you know."[13]

In *Bonnie and Clyde*, on the other hand, Warren Beatty is invariably the hapless victim of other people's aggression. The pattern establishes itself in an early grocery store robbery. "Let's see now . . . A loaf of bread, a dozen eggs, quart of milk, four fried pies," Clyde inventories, holding a grocery bag in one hand and training his gun on the gray-haired, bespectacled clerk with the other. "Come on now—you sure you ain't got no peach pies?" he asks with a dazzling smile. "I don't believe— . . ." A beefy, no-necked butcher intrudes into the frame horror-film style and proceeds to drive a meat cleaver into the counter, narrowly missing Clyde's back. The two men grapple in a bear hug and topple over a merchandise case. Waiting outside behind the wheel of the getaway car, Bonnie hears a shot.

The action cuts back inside, where Clyde manages to extricate himself from the butcher's grasp, only to be tackled again on the doorstep, where he pistol-whips the butcher unconscious. "Why'd he try to kill me? I didn't want to hurt him," Clyde wonders as Bonnie drives. "Try to get something to eat around here and some son-of-a-bitch comes up on you with a meat cleaver. I ain't against him," Clyde protests. "I ain't against him." Beatty plays the scene with an expression of pained amazement—that of a child who's just woken up to a world of adult consequences—and his delivery makes Clyde's protestations sound sincere, as the real Clyde Barrow's excuses must have sounded to his family.

The scene originally scripted by David Newman and Robert Benton, however—which Penn shot as written—carried a different thrust. In that version, Clyde's gunshot occurs not off-camera, but in the scene. Finding his gun arm pinned in the butcher's bear hug, "CLYDE tries to raise the barrel at an upward angle to shoot; finally he is able to do so. He fires. The bullet enters the BUTCHER'S stomach. The BUTCHER screams, but reacts like a wounded animal, more furious than ever."[14] As in the film, the sequence concludes with the pistol-whipping and Clyde's expression of self-defense. "Damn him, that big son-of-a-bitch. . . . I didn't want to hurt him. It wasn't a real robbery. Some food and a little bit of dough," he says, "panting; trying to get control of himself."[15]

In their final assembly of the film, Penn and editor Dede Allen removed the shooting altogether, resulting in an abrupt jump cut to disguise the wound in the butcher's stomach. The butcher's bloody apron helps to sell the illusion, but there's still a noticeable visual stutter between the two men falling into a shelf of merchandise and the butcher's recovery just after Clyde exits the frame. Director and editor likely realized that the shooting could damage the impact of the key moment in their story: Clyde's later running-board killing of the bank official —that all-in-one frame meant to shatter not only the automobile window and the clerk's glasses, but also the Motion Picture Production Code.

Yet even here, when "Clyde fires through the window" and "the face of the man explodes in blood,"[16] the shooting is reflexive, unpremeditated, and immediately followed up by Clyde's expressions of remorse. The Barrow Gang takes refuge in a small-town movie house, where the opening scene of Warner Bros.' *Gold Diggers of 1933* heralds:

> We're in the money!
> We're in the money!
> Old Man Depression
> You are through
> You've done us wrong.

Bonnie sits enraptured, arms around her knees, watching chorines dressed as enormous stacks of coins while Clyde berates C. W. Moss two rows back for *his* responsibility in the bank clerk's murder.

"You ain't got a brain in your skull," he fumes of Moss's bone-headed decision to parallel park the gang's car during a robbery. "On account of you, I killed a man," he whines. "Do another dumb-ass thing like that, again, boy, I'm gonna kill you," Clyde threatens, grabbing C. W. by the collar.

"Sshh!" Bonnie protests, losing patience. "If you boys wanna talk, why don't you all go on outside?" She turns back and leans forward, drawn toward the screen as the chorus girls celebrate how "*We never see a headline about a breadline today / And when we see the landlord, we can look that guy right in the eye.*"

The moment feels authentic to the Bonnie Parker revealed in her teenage diary, caught up in the Hollywood romances that offered escape from her unpromising circumstances. Newman and Benton purposefully wrote *Gold Diggers of 1933* and its sunny theme song into their original script, but the clips used eliminate close-ups of costar Ginger Rogers, who refused permission for use of her image despite Penn's repeated requests. (Given Rogers's staunch conservative Republican leanings—she had supported Barry Goldwater in the 1964 presidential election—one can only surmise the film's subject matter may have played a role in her decision.)

Bonnie and Clyde's sixties-era enshrinement of thirties-era Clyde Barrow and Bonnie Parker as "accidental" killers hounded by the establishment reaches a high point midway through the film, in an extraordinary extended sequence that tracks the Barrow Gang's escape from well-armed cops in Platte City, Missouri, and their subsequent ambush by vigilantes in Dexfield Park, Iowa. Running nearly ten minutes with minimal dialogue, the combined scenes represent a high point in American action filmmaking, its considerable firepower to be imitated and exceeded in succeeding years but never surpassed (though Sam Peckinpah tried). What goes little remarked-upon in aesthetic discussions of Penn's artistry is how accurately the sequence reflects the historical record.

In the three months following the raid in Joplin, Missouri, the Barrow gang had wandered the Midwest, committing a series of petty holdups. Tensions between Clyde and Bonnie and Buck and Blanche had reached a breaking point. "Clyde was too much of a dirty rat. His own brother couldn't stay with him or get along with him without fighting two-thirds of the time," Blanche wrote in her prison recollections. "Take all your guns away from you and you would throw up your hands and beg like a baby because you can't make it unless you have enough guns behind you to supply a whole army,"[17] Buck taunted his brother; at the time, the Barrow boys had just raided the Enid, Oklahoma, National Guard armory.

By the time the gang reached the Red Crown Motor Court six miles south of Platte City, Blanche and Buck had decided to break away at the next opportunity. For the time being, however, the four were bound together by mutual necessity. As the only Barrow Gang member whose picture hadn't appeared in any papers, Blanche served as front woman for all public transactions: renting rooms, buying meals, and fetching medicines and salves for the crippled Bonnie. Not trusting ointments, Clyde purloined a doctor's bag packed with Amytal and syringes from an Enid, Oklahoma, hospital parking lot; later seized as evidence by Missouri authorities, the bag spawned tabloid-ready rumors of the outlaws' degenerate drug addiction.

Clyde liked the look of the Red Crown's tourist cabins: sturdy brick construction, a private garage. What he didn't know was that the motor court and its adjacent tavern also served as an informal command central for Platte City police and the Missouri Highway Patrol. "Two-way radios were still nonexistent for most lawmen in the region, so officers and supervisors would often meet somewhere at mealtimes to exchange messages and receive orders," biographer Jeff Guinn explained in Go Down Together. "The Red Crown was a favorite spot because the food was so good."[18]

According to FBI files, the Barrow Gang checked into the motor court on July 18, 1933, at approximately 10 p.m. Wearing her attention-getting jodhpurs, Blanche rented two cabins for a party of three, paying four dollars in loose change "undoubtedly looted earlier in the day from the cash registers and gum machines at the three service stations in Fort Dodge"[19] the gang had raided on the way. Observing from behind the counter of Slim's Castle, the quick-stop filling station across the way from the Red Crown, proprietor Kermit Crawford considered the new arrivals "school kids taking a couple days off to shack up and have a good time."[20] Motor-court owner/operator N. D. Houser took note of how the driver of the Ford V-8 bearing Oklahoma plates backed his automobile into the garage; Houser's suspicions deepened when his new guests began to obscure their windows with newspaper.

The Barrow Gang's stay at the Red Crown lasted barely a day.

Moments after checking in, Clyde dispatched Blanche to buy chicken dinners and beer from the tavern. "They ordered so much food I told them the owner would know there were more than three of us," Blanche protested. "Oh, they won't think anything," Clyde said dismissively. "Just get the food"[21] The movie employs a cinematic cheat to motivate the ensuing action. Retrieving the chicken dinners, Blanche asks C. W. for the cash, allowing a deputy at the counter to spy the pistol tucked into the waistband of C. W.'s jeans (a quick zoom-in underscores the point).

Determined not to make the fatal blunders of their counterparts in Joplin, Platte City, authorities descended on the Red Crown at 11:30 p.m. on July 19, reinforced with bulletproof vests, handheld iron shields, .45-caliber Thompson submachine guns—and an armored car, "an ordinary sedan whose sides had been reinforced with extra metal."[22] Platte County sheriff Holt Coffey approached Blanche and Buck's cabin with Missouri Highway Patrol captain William Baxter. Coffey knocked on the door.

"The sheriff—open up!"

From that point onward, eyewitness accounts collapse into a morass of conflicting agendas. Blanche later claimed that Buck told her to say, "The men are in the other cabin." In Guinn's account, it's Clyde who responds from the adjoining room. "Just a minute," he says, "and then the Barrow Gang started shooting . . . blasting their bullets at the lawmen right through the doors and windows."[23] Toland's purple-prose version in *Dillinger Days* opens the barrage with Clyde's command to "Let the bastards have it!"[24]

The lawmen's armaments proved ineffective almost from the first few seconds, when blasts from Clyde's BAR perforated the armored car, striking its driver in both legs and shattering the steering wheel; the horn continued to blare throughout the firefight. "It was shot up like a sieve,"[25] a later FBI report confirmed. *Bonnie and Clyde* shows the Barrow Gang wielding Tommy guns and at one point deploying grenades, neither of which factored into their defense. (Despite Clyde's avowed distaste for them, the Tommy gun's appeal as the movie gangster's weapon of choice informs every version of the story, to the chagrin of historians and on-set advisers.)

Lawmen raked the front of the cabins indiscriminately, pockmarking the stones. Clyde, Buck and W. D. blasted back through doors and windows with their BARs. One eyewitness stood transfixed as "long shafts of flame spewed through the shades as lawmen in all directions dove for cover."[26] Sheriff Coffee's sixteen-year-old son Clarence saw his father "pushed ... back like he was hit by a high-pressure hose"[27] when a high-caliber slug impacted his shield. Lethal stray rounds from the fusillade reached across the highway as far as the tavern, causing staff and patrons to scramble for cover.

Young Coffee took refuge in the kitchen behind a cast-iron stove; an armor-piercing shell penetrated both the building's brick wall and the stove itself, breaking his arm. Astonishingly, while many were seriously wounded, no law enforcement officers were killed in the Platte City standoff. But policemen die in *Bonnie and Clyde*: six of them, to be precise, one murdered at shockingly close range from a moving car, while another's already prone body is repeatedly raked by semiautomatic fire. It speaks to the volatility of the late sixties that such moments resulted in eruptions of applause and cheers from inner-city audiences.

Buck Barrow was less fortunate than his assailants.

While Clyde, Bonnie, and W. D. Jones had access to the garage from an interior door, Buck and Blanche were forced to exit their cabin. In their flight to join the others, Buck took a .45 slug in the left temple. Buck crumpled to the ground, his BAR firing skyward. "They've killed Buck!"[28] Blanche shouted. But they hadn't. The bullet exited "clean" from Buck's forehead and left him dazed but still conscious, a gaping hole exposing his brain. *Dillinger Days*' thoroughly mixed-up account of Platte City includes the detail of Blanche and Bonnie (who couldn't walk at the time) shielding Buck with mattresses as he "burst from the building, two pistols cracking."[29] Patently ridiculous—but catnip to screenwriters Newman and Benton, who incorporated the detail into one of *Bonnie and Clyde*'s most memorable moments, when Buck and Blanche make a break holding a mattress between them.[30]

For all her later self-professed ineptitude and insecurity, Blanche showed incredible fortitude in Buck's extremity. "Skinny and scared as she was, Blanche still helped Clyde drag Buck into the car while W. D. provided covering fire."[31] Saving the man wasn't enough. Clyde also had to save the gun, suffering a painful burn on his right hand when he grabbed Buck's fallen BAR by the barrel. Blanche crouched protectively over her husband in the back seat. "I was holding his head as close to my breast as I could, and had both my arms wrapped around him, trying to protect him should the officers shoot into the car."[32] Which one did, shattering the back window. Shards of glass flew everywhere. Splinters caught Blanche in both eyes. "I can't see!"[33] she screamed. The V-8 flew through a cloud of stinking teargas smoke and evaporated into the night.

"For the first time, the police had the initiative, knew who they were dealing with and had time to develop a plan of attack," twenty-first-century Barrow Gang enthusiasts James R. Knight and Jonathan Davis note. "In spite of all this, the Barrows escaped again.... There was nothing to do but keep driving."[34] The script for *Bonnie and Clyde* evokes the sheer desperation of the Barrow Gang's escape in a passage of stage direction rarely equaled in American screenwriting. "Packed inside this car right now is more sheer human misery and horror than could be believed," Newman and Benton wrote. "It is hell in there, hell and suffering and pain."[35]

Penn conveys the sensation in two deliberately disorienting shots: the first a jumble of the Barrow Gang shouting and tumbling over one another in the fast-moving V-8 that is equal parts early German expressionism and the stateroom scene from the Marx Bros.' *Night at the Opera* (1935), followed by a sustained close-up of an unblinking Clyde focused on the road ahead, sweat beading his face.

Gruesome as the scene becomes, Blanche painted an even darker picture in her prison memoir. "The floorboard of the car was so soaked we could hear the blood gush under our feet," she wrote. Partially blinded by the glass shards in her eyes, Blanche struggled with Buck to keep him from "tear[ing] the bandage off his head and start digging into the wound with his fingernails."[36]

Stopping only long enough for C. W. Moss to hot-wire a second car, *Bonnie and Clyde*'s outlaws finally come to rest in a wide meadow. Though the script indicates ("in a long shot that takes in everything") that the meadow is "surrounded by a ring of trees,"[37] Penn stages the scene in almost utter darkness, the only illumination provided by the automobiles' headlights. Per the script, the gang spills out of the cars "in horrible shape . . . half-dressed . . . bloody, dirty, in tatters." [38] The tenderness of what follows—parallel moments of empathy in the most appalling of circumstances—ranks among Penn's greatest achievements as a director.

When the glare of the headlights prompts an outcry of pain from Estelle Parson's Blanche ("My eyes, the light hurts so bad!"), Faye Dunaway's Bonnie comforts her with a pair of sunglasses purloined from a bank guard in a long-ago robbery. "Here, hon'. Here," Dunaway says softly. Overlapping this, Gene Hackman's Buck grows delirious in the arms of Warren Beatty's Clyde. "I believe I lost my shoes, Clyde," he blurts out. "I think the dog got 'em." (Another of Robert Towne's North Dallas Motor Inn eureka moments.)

The scene falls silent, punctuated only by Buck's labored breathing and the monotonous chatter of crickets. In individual close-ups, backlit by headlights, the characters are blood-spattered, miserable, hopeless—and finally insignificant. The sequence concludes on a despairing wide shot of the two getaway cars in a black void, their headlights tiny, flickering stars. Not until *The Godfather* (1972) would another major studio film dare to approach such chiaroscuro audacity.

After a night of circuitous driving, the Barrow Gang had come to rest on the outskirts of Dexter, Iowa—two hundred miles from Platte City—on the site of a derelict amusement complex known as Dexfield Park. *Bonnie and Clyde* abbreviates the Barrow Gang's four-day stay there to a single night and day, achieved with a brilliant match dissolve from night to dawn. (This is the scene for which screenwriters Benton and Newman invoked "a certain *Seventh Seal* quality for just the first moment," where the Barrow Gang "look[s] like a troupe of traveling actors, living out of their caravan, pursued by death.")[39] As autumnal morning light seeps into the blackened image and the transition resolves itself, Clyde and Bonnie can be made out resting against the wheel and running board of the V-8. Blanche and Buck sleep beside them while C. W. busies himself inside a second car, stolen during their flight. A man in a white shirt steps out of heavy tree cover in the middle distance and stands center-frame.

"Surrender!" he shouts.

"The man lingers there for a moment," the script indicates. "He looks strange, white, luminous, like an apparition—and then he vanishes into the woods." His disappearance is followed by "silence, long enough to make you think it was perhaps an illusion." (In the film, this occupies an anxious seven seconds.) "Then there is a volley of gunfire—a noise so large as to be an almost impossible sound—coming from the woods, all around, everywhere."[40] The ensuing battle has come to be known as the "ring of fire," so-called for the gang's encirclement by lawmen and vigilantes converging on them from the surrounding woods.

Penn and Beatty both recognized the sequence as a narrative and cultural touchstone—which made the ring of fire a recurring centerpiece in their daily discussions. The future Morgan Fairchild, doubling for Faye Dunaway in Midlothian in the early days of the production, recalled director and producer arguing about the "ring of fire, ring of fire, ring of fire. I didn't know what it was until I found out they were trying to figure out how to do the scene in which [Bonnie and Clyde] wake up and [they're] surrounded by cops. They talked about how to edit it, frame it, put it together," she said. "I hung on every word."[41] The "discussion" persisted until nearly the end of production. According to call sheets in the Warner Bros. archives at the University of Southern California Cinematic Arts Library, filming of the "ring of fire" sequence occurred on December 2, 1966, on a private preserve south of Dallas known as Lemmon Lake.[42]

In its broad outlines, the ring of fire essentially adheres to the events that unfolded shortly after 5 a.m. on Monday, July 24, 1933. Tipped off by reports of squatting vagrants and the finding of bloody bandages along the roadside—not to mention "a short, limping stranger in Dexter who was driving a car full of bullet holes"⁴³ poorly camouflaged with mud—Sheriff Clint Knee suspected that Clyde Barrow had rolled into his jurisdiction. Reports of a handsome outsider ordering takeout meals replete with plates and silverware from a local meat market confirmed those suspicions; with Blanche blinded and both Bonnie and Buck incapacitated, Clyde had no choice than to risk exposure. Knee began to assemble a posse of fellow law enforcement officers, including two Polk County officers and six additional policemen from Des Moines.

Word spread quickly. Enticed by rumors that the feared cop killers were camping nearby, vigilantes "gathered . . . along with dozens of thrill seekers, who wanted a front seat at the confrontation. More than a few had been drinking and some even showed up with dates."⁴⁴ "There wasn't too much excitement around in 1933 in July," recalled Dexter resident Kirt Piper, then a teenager. "All these people were within two hundred yards of where [Clyde and Bonnie] were camped. We just stood there and waited."⁴⁵ Night marshal John Love considered most of the citizen volunteers unfit for duty. They "acted like it was a hayride or something. We had to take guns off three of them who weren't safe to have them."⁴⁶

A slew of firearms came into play when the posse started shooting. Return fire from Clyde and W. D. Jones's BARs "convinced most of the amateurs that shootouts were more serious than hayrides."⁴⁷ The Barrow Gang managed to crawl their way into the V-8 sedan. Clyde attempted to drive through the posse, but a bullet caught him in the left arm, causing him to lose control and run the sedan aground on a tree stump. The gang tumbled out the doors. Seeing them make a desperate dash for the second car, lawmen and vigilantes trained their fire on the vehicle, blasting it with "a wall of lead. Sixty-four slugs found their mark, cracking the engine block, blowing out the windows and destroying the tires."⁴⁸

In the subsequent confusion, Clyde, Bonnie, and W. D. Jones became separated from Buck and Blanche, who were left to fend for themselves while the others sought escape in a brush-covered riverbank. Carried on W.

D. Jones's back, Bonnie took a vigilante's shotgun blast in the shoulder but somehow kept moving. "We left bloody ripples behind us as we swam,"[49] she told her mother. Clyde bolted over the opposite bank in search of a vehicle. During the long interim, Bonnie allegedly contemplated suicide. She told W. D. Jones she wished for a gun.

"You couldn't do any good with it," W. D. responded.

"I could do all the good I wanted to with it,"[50] she replied. Clyde returned moments after, having secured a vehicle at gunpoint from a local farming family.

A similar scene played out simultaneously with Buck and Blanche, trapped behind a log as the posse closed the circle. "At times . . . it seemed as if the log in front of us was being cut with saws instead of bullets from machine guns, rifles and shotguns,"[51] Blanche recorded. Despite the gaping hole in his skull, Buck continued to resist capture, shielding Blanche from harm as he fired into the advancing vigilantes. According to Blanche, Buck was hit six times before he could be persuaded to surrender.

"Make him raise his hands," one deputy ordered Blanche.

"He can't," she moaned. "You've killed him."[52]

A Des Moines photographer who accompanied police to the scene snapped an image of Blanche as deputies placed her into custody. Dressed in jodhpurs and wearing the protective sunglasses, she struggles to wrench free, her anguished face turned straight at the lens. "All [Blanche] could see was a shadowy figure aiming something at her," wrote Barrow Gang biographer Jeff Guinn. "She thought it was a gun, and that she and Buck were about to be summarily executed."[53] Contrary to the film, Buck Barrow did not die in Dexfield Park, but lingered for nearly a week in a Perry, Iowa, hospital, where his head wound "gave off such an offensive odor that it was with the utmost difficulty that one could remain within several feet of him."[54] Asked by FBI agents "why he and his companions so ruthlessly took human life," Buck responded, "Well, I had to see that I did not get hurt."[55]

In their original conception of the sequence, screenwriters Newman and Benton opted for an impressionistic approach. Dexfield Park is the last of the story's three major action sequences (after the shootouts in Joplin and Platte City), and the first-time scenarists intended the scene to land very differently from its predecessors. After the initial volley of gunfire, the script instructs that "from this point on, the sound of guns is unnaturally muffled on the soundtrack. We hardly hear them at all . . . it is like a dream."[56] The track is meant to fall *completely* silent once the Barrow Gang attempts its escape. "The car performs its eccentric dance, all in utter silence (no sound of the motor, nothing). The film should have the feeling of slow motion, as the car swerves and loops along the edge of the woods."[57]

Newman and Benton go full French New Wave in the moment when the V-8 smashes into a tree stump. "The picture stops, freezes for three beats," the script specifies, deliberately recycling a technique employed by François Truffaut throughout his career. "We hold the image of the moment of the crash, with pieces of metal crumpling and flying into the air, suspended there by the stop-film [*sic*]."[58]

To his everlasting credit, director Arthur Penn dispensed with such pretense.

Far from allowing the ring of fire to play out in slow motion, Penn instead enhances its velocity, at times even speeding up the action through a process known as "under cranking," achieved in postproduction by printing the filmed image at an advanced rate. Rather than silence, the director underscores the scene with an unceasing barrage of gunfire and the posse's primal shouts. The sequence is at once a fantastic adrenaline rush and a terrifying indictment of an armed society. Filtered through the distorting lens of Charles Whitman's University of Texas tower rampage and released to theaters in a season of rage and assassination, *Bonnie and Clyde*'s ring of fire sequence encapsulated Penn's corrosive perspective on American violence.

The director interrupts the action just long enough to find a deputy in the brush firing a high-powered rifle. Clyde's upper left arm explodes in a profusion of blood courtesy of a well-loaded—even overloaded—squib. The posse's ritualistic demolition of the gang's second getaway vehicle plays out with savage, uncontrollable fury. "Shoot it!" "Knock the hell out of it!" off-screen vigilantes shout. And for the next minute, "we see the car die in front of our eyes."[59]

The vehicle rocks on its axles as bullets shatter the windows, pierce the tires, and blow off the silver-rimmed headlights, and then bursts into flames to a chorus of war whoops. As Newman and Benton intended, in Penn's staging "the death of the car is as painful to watch as the death of a human being."[60] It is, in fact, a precursor to the even more graphic deaths of Bonnie and Clyde two reels later—a premonition of mortality only made apparent in repeated viewings.

When death came for Clyde Barrow and Bonnie Parker, it came not at the hands of liquored-up vigilantes. It came at the hands of a legally assembled posse of Texas and Louisiana lawmen given lethal authority by a Texas governor. Of the seven men duly sworn in to carry out the sentence, one would ultimately claim principal credit—and suffer lasting consequences.

His name was Frank Hamer.

Exquisite draftsmanship. Four original costume sketches for *Bonnie and Clyde* by Theadora Van Runkle. Leonard Stanley collection, Margaret Herrick Library, Academy of Motion Picture Arts and Sciences.

(*opposite above*) "As much a philosopher as an artist." Faye Dunaway and Arthur Penn in a moment of off-set affinity. Despite their differences, she considered him "a great director." Warner Bros./Courtesy of Everett Collection.

(*opposite below*) "I can be obnoxious." Warren Beatty on location in Texas behind a massive 1930s-era Mitchell camera, double-checking Arthur Penn's framing. Warner Bros./Courtesy of Everett Collection.

"She thought it was a gun." Blanche Barrow reacts to a photographer's flash in Dexfield Park, Iowa. Note the trademark jodhpurs. In the film, Estelle Parsons wore Barbara Stanwyck's recycled costumes. Des Moines Register via Wikimedia Commons.

Someone might take offense. This scene between Faye Dunaway (as Bonnie) and Denver Pyle (as Frank Hamer) prompted a lawsuit and a corrective Netflix film. Warner Bros./RGR Collection/Alamy Stock Photo.

(*opposite above*) Straight out of central casting. No less an expert than Tom Mix told Frank Hamer that he had "the looks and the athletic ability to become a great cowboy star." Courtesy of Texas Ranger Hall of Fame and Museum, Waco, Texas.

(*opposite below*) A man and his gun. Frank Hamer's preferred weapon became an advertisement for the lethal power of Colt firearms. The Texas Ranger once knocked a reporter to the pavement using only the barrel. *Arms Gazette,* March 1978.

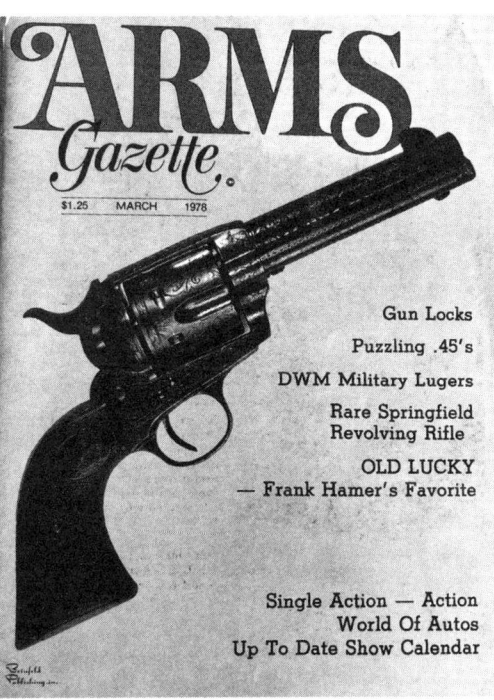

(*above*) *La Matanza*. This image of Texas Rangers (one of whom might be Frank Hamer) posed over the bodies of "Mexican Bandits" became a popular postcard on the Texas borderlands. Courtesy of Bullock, Texas State History Museum.

(*below*) A cornfield on the outskirts of Midlothian, Texas provided the location for one of *Bonnie and Clyde*'s most memorable scenes, but also became ground zero for a major creative crisis. Warner Bros./courtesy of Everett Collection.

(*above*) Stepping out of a Dorothea Lange photograph. Red Oak, Texas, schoolteacher Mabel Cavitt memorably played Bonnie's mother in a reunion scene that foreshadows the tragic ending. Warner Bros./Shutterstock.

(*below*) Black people with guns. Black Panther Party cofounders Bobby Seale (left) and Huey Newton (right) challenged prevailing views of the Second Amendment. Collection of the Smithsonian National Museum of African-American History and Culture.

"Wild, mean and ornery." Nevada rancher Cliven Bundy's decade-long feud with the Bureau of Land Management over grazing rights earned him outlaw status and sparked a movement that continues to roil the modern West. Greg Skidmore/Alamy Stock Photo.

"Like Woodstock for patriots." A militiaman stands watch over an arid ravine in the hours before what will become known as the "Battle of Bunkerville." Will Seberger/ZUMAPRESS.com/Alamy Live News Stock Photo.

Martyr to the cause. La Voy Finicum in his role as self-appointed spokesman for the January 2016 occupation of the Malheur National Wildlife Refuge. Unlike Cliven Bundy's, Finicum's outlaw trail ended in death. Jeffrey Schwilk/Alamy Stock Photo.

"We see things in a similar way." Editor Dede Allen created the tempo for *Bonnie and Clyde* and went on to a six-film collaboration with director Arthur Penn. Stock photo via Cinemontage.

Truth in advertising. *Bonnie and Clyde*'s initial release was confined to handful of second-rate theatres and drive-ins. Credit for the now-legendary tagline belongs to Warner Bros. head of advertising Richard Lederer. Warner Bros.

Cast publicity photo. The rifles held by Gene Hackman and Michael J. Pollard pass muster, but Clyde Barrow would never have approved of Warren Beatty and Faye Dunaway's tommy guns. Warner Bros./Courtesy of Everett Collection.

"Worst foot forward." *New York Times* film critic Bosley Crowther set the tone for the early negative reviews of *Bonnie and Clyde*—and paid a stiff price for his continued disparagement. Billy Rose Theatre Division, New York Public Library.

(*below*) Sex sells. Twenty-thousand people attended the funeral of "the worst woman bandit since Belle Starr." Bonnie's attendance figures were double those of Clyde's. Dallas Municipal Archives via University of North Texas Libraries, The Portal to Texas.

"Killer in Skirts." Poster for *The Bonnie Parker Story* (1958), produced and distributed by grindhouse American International Pictures. Reynold Brown via Wikimedia Commons.

"Shooting is what I'm good at." *Gun Crazy* (1950) anticipated *Bonnie and Clyde's* transgressive approach by nearly sixteen years. Its brazen violence and twisted sexuality remain startling. Distributed by United Artists.

That certain je ne sais quoi. Warren Beatty and Faye Dunaway at the Paris premiere. The marquee behind them reads "They're young . . . they're in love . . . and they live dangerously." Jean-Claude Deutsch/Paris Match Archive/Getty Images.

"Why not?" Director Sam Peckinpah screened a print of *Bonnie and Clyde* before outdoing its concluding violence in the "Battle of Bloody Porch" that climaxes his originally X-rated *The Wild Bunch*. Warner Bros./still courtesy of W.K. Stratton.

14

"A .45 SLUG IN THE GUT"

> I've always been able to sleep a
> good sleep every night.
> —Frank Hamer

Frank Hamer never appears in David Newman and Robert Benton's original draft of *Bonnie and Clyde*.

Instead, the character is named Frank Bryce, described as "tall, strong, contemptuous of almost everyone and particularly women and criminals; some hidden evil in him sometimes shows in his face."[1] Bryce is first introduced when he discovers the Barrow Gang's stolen Ford V-8 idling on a country road where Clyde has stopped to take a piss. The sheriff pulls a revolver and stealthily approaches the car from the rear, unaware of Clyde emerging from the surrounding woods, tugging at his zipper, gun tucked into his pants.

"The following scene is played exactly like a classic fast-draw in an heroic Western," the script specifies. "BRYCE spins around. Both men fire simultaneously, but CLYDE has the draw on him, and the aim. The gun goes flying from the sheriff's hand. A really razzle-dazzle display of grandstand marksmanship from Clyde."[2] (In a previous century, Benton and Newman would have made terrific dime novelists.) At that point, "the gang leaps from the car and surrounds [Bryce], guns drawn.

C.W.
Boy! What a shot, Clyde!
BUCK
Sweet Jesus, I never seen shootin' like that![3]

Towne's North Dallas Inn revision elides this dialogue to Buck's "I never seen such shootin'!"[4] but otherwise leaves the action intact. Bryce is trussed up with his own handcuffs and pinned against the fender of the V-8 while the Barrow Gang contemplates his future. Clyde snatches away Bryce's credentials. "Now you ain't hardly doin' your duty, Texas Ranger," he scolds. "You oughta be at home looking after the right of poor folks, not chasin' after us."[5] (The finished film bears minor alterations in this dialogue.)

"Take his picture!" Bonnie shouts.

Out comes Blanche's camera, with Buck posing the shot. "BRYCE is obviously not pleased with this turn of events," the script notes. When Bonnie "plants a big kiss on him while still ogling [the] camera," Bryce, "whose simmering hostility we should be more sensitive to than the gang is,"[6] spits on Bonnie. In an on-screen eruption still startling for its ferocity, Clyde "pulls Bryce off the fender by the handcuffs, spinning him around crazily like a lasso." Bryce is "literally ricocheted off the car by the force and ...plummets down the embankment to the edge of the water below."[7] The near drowning that follows ends with the still-handcuffed Bryce being set adrift in a rickety skiff, with Clyde shouting after him:

CLYDE
WE GOT YOU... HEAR?...
REMEMBER... YOU... YOUR FACE...
WE GOT IT... WE GOT YOU... WE GOT YOU![8]

"As you know, I am asked to police scripts with a view to anticipating, if possible, any lawsuits predicated on violation of somebody's right of privacy or libel, etc." Warner Bros. attorney Carl Milliken wrote to Arthur Penn on

September 12, 1966, by which time the Bryce character had been officially rechristened Frank Hamer. "It is with this responsibility in mind that I have reviewed your script."[9] Milliken's interoffice communication took pains to point out that "FRANK HAMER is a real individual, still living, as far as we know" (he wasn't) and underlined the possibility that he might "take exception to the demeaning characterization utilized in the kidnapping sequence."[10] Milliken had given the studio fair warning. Hamer's widow and his heirs took understandable offense, filing an injunction against Warner Bros. from "publishing any motion picture using or portraying Frank Hammer [sic] in any manner without the express permission of all said clients."[11] (The plaintiffs' own attorney consistently misspelled the family name in his filings.) Fearful of repercussions, the studio hastily settled for $20,000, "a significant sum at the time," according to one law enforcement historian. "But the damage had been done. History would recall Frank Hamer as the bad guy who killed the romantic outlaw duo."[12]

Frank Hamer "did not run down Bonnie and Clyde,"[13] scholar Robert M. Utley states plainly in *Lone Star Lawmen*, the second in his two-volume account of the Texas Rangers, attributing much of the legwork to Bienville Parish, Louisiana sheriff Henderson Jordan. For biographer John Boessenecker, on the other hand, Hamer was "the greatest lawman of the twentieth century."[14] When the ex-Ranger died of a heart attack in 1955 at age seventy-one, headlines across the country heralded him as the man who "captured" Bonnie and Clyde. The *Texas Ranger Dispatch*, the official publication of the Texas Ranger Museum in Waco, declared Hamer to be "the man that many believe to be the greatest Ranger of the first half of the twentieth century."[15]

Speaking from the troubled perspective of *Bonnie and Clyde*'s release in 1968, which found America consumed in social and racial upheaval, Arthur Penn said, "I'd be hard-pressed at this point to make any choices between Sheriff Hamer and Bonnie and Clyde. I think I'd choose Bonnie and Clyde."[16] Barrow Gang chronicler Jeff Guinn agrees with that assessment. "Frank Hamer in his own way was a greater thug than most of the outlaws he chased. If you want to talk about somebody who polished his own image, Hamer was far better at it than Bonnie and Clyde. He used to brag that he could hear sounds miles away no one else could, and that his eyesight was so good he could see a bullet in flight."[17]

Francis Augustus Hamer stood six foot three and weighed 230 pounds. An admiring article in *American Gun* magazine written five years after his death described Hamer as "the real character all TV casting directors are striving for . . . big, strong and silent . . . able to communicate his dislike while doffing his hat and saying, 'Yes, ma'am.'"[18] (The *Dallas Morning News* maintained that Hamer was "as talkative as an oyster."[19]) No less an expert on motion picture appeal than Tom Mix recognized Hamer's screen potential early on. When the young lawman visited Universal City in 1918, Mix told Hamer that he "had the looks, the bearing and the athletic ability to become a great cowboy star."[20] Hamer resisted the overture; he joked that Mix had seen too many of his own movies.

At the time, Hamer had made a reputation for himself as the city marshal of Navasota, Texas, where at age twenty-four (like a mythic frontier lawman) he'd single-handedly rid the cotton boomtown of its troublesome elements, despite pushback from city fathers who decried his overzealous methods. "Frank had no help; his backup was his hands and feet,"[21] writes Boessenecker. Though he carried a pistol, Hamer unholstered it only in extreme circumstances, relying on brute physical force. "When he boxed a man alongside the head, it reminded me of a grizzly bear cuffing a steer," remembered one colleague. "Hamer's open palm always took the fight out of the hardiest ruffian."[22]

This being Texas, whenever fists proved ineffective, firearms came into play.

"All boys in rural Texas were expected to know how to load, shoot and clean guns," Boessenecker recounts of Hamer's early years—a description that applies equally to Clyde Barrow. "In the Hamer household, even the girls learned to use firearms. Frank's sister Pat carried a toy pistol as a child, wore a real one on her hip as a young woman, and in old age kept a handgun in her purse."[23] As a young man, Hamer was steeped in the honor code that pervaded Southern culture in the decades following the Confederacy's defeat. "I was born and raised not to take an insult," he said. "Any time a man insults me he has to back it up."[24] In Texas, this ethos evolved into what has come to be known as the "stand your ground" defense. Under state law, even nondeadly threats could be met with withering force and juries turned a blind eye to asymmetrical killings. (In Texas today, the carrying of firearms in public places remains unrestricted.[25])

In his post–Barrow Gang celebrity, Hamer often boasted of his prowess with firearms, claiming that he had been in fifty-three gunfights, suffering seventeen wounds. "We're here to enforce the law," he said, "and the best way is a .45 slug in the gut."[26] "How many men have you killed?" a journalist once asked, estimating the number at twenty-three, "not counting Mexicans." "I won't talk about that," Hamer replied. "All my killings were in the line of duty. It was an unpleasant duty."

REPORTER
Does your conscience bother you?

HAMER
Not a bit.[27]

Hamer's chosen weapon was a specially engraved Colt .45 revolver he nicknamed "Old Lucky," presented to him by county attorney C. M. Spann in appreciation for services rendered. Luck played no role in Hamer's marksmanship: he could be equally deadly with a Colt pistol or a Remington rifle, and frequently engaged in sharpshooting exhibitions where, it was said, Hamer "called the shots *before they hit.*"[28] Other public displays proved more dubious. Responding to an unflattering article in the *Houston Press*, Hamer confronted the reporter outside the Houston Press Club. "I notified [your] paper some time ago that if it ever wrote anything against me I would fix somebody," Hamer announced. "The next one of you fellows I see on the street, I am going to smoke him off the earth,"[29] he promised—then proceeded to knock the newsman to the pavement with the barrel of "Old Lucky."

In Brownsville a few years later, Hamer accosted Texas state representative J. T. Canales, said to be compiling a dossier of Ranger atrocities along the Texas-Mexico border. "I am going to tell you if you don't stop that you are going to get hurt," Hamer warned. Canales appealed for protection to the local sheriff, who advised him, "Take a double-barreled shotgun and I will give you a man and you go over there and kill [Hamer]. No jury would ever convict you for that."[30] (Canales wisely declined.)

What historian Doug J. Swanson calls a "Cult of Glory" has surrounded the Texas Rangers from their inception in 1835, when Stephen F. Austin's provisional government, on the verge of separation from Mexico, established three companies of citizen-soldiers charged to patrol ("range") the territory against marauders—understood to mean indigenous people and Mexicans. "The Rangers had for years and years a network of enablers and a fable industry who promoted this image," Swanson said in a 2024 interview with the *Washington Post*. "That's what Hollywood wanted and the newspapers of the day wanted, so that's what survived."[31]

Both the Rangers and Samuel Colt can be said to have established their reputations on the same day: June 8, 1844, when a fifteen-man Ranger force under the command of twenty-three-year-old Jack "Coffee" Hays on patrol in the central Texas hill country came under attack from a Comanche war party that outnumbered the interlopers by four to one. In the past, the Rangers' flintlock rifles, which required laborious loading and reloading, proved no match for the Comanches' deadly facility with bow and arrow. This time, Hays's men came to the fight armed with new Patterson Colt handguns, equipped with a five-chambered revolving cylinder.

The weapon was far from foolproof. For one thing, it was too heavy, earning it the unflattering nickname "hand cannon." For another, reloading required replacement of the entire cylinder with another, already fully loaded—difficult to choreograph in the heat of mounted battle. Still, "the [Patterson Colt] had two enormous advantages: it could be fired from the saddle, and it could be fired five times in fairly rapid succession."[32] Each Ranger carried two guns, which meant up to ten shots could be fired in less than forty seconds.[33]

The withering firepower stunned the attacking Comanche war party. The three-mile-long running engagement resulted in the death of thirty-two attackers, leaving only one Ranger dead, and another, Samuel Walker, pinned to the ground with a lance, gravely but not mortally wounded. "I will never again fight Jack Hays, who has a shot for every finger on the hand,"[34] one Comanche chief reportedly said of the engagement, known as "Hays' Big Fight" or "The Battle of Walker's Creek." In his after-action report, Hays heaped credit on Colt's invention. "I cannot praise these arms too highly," he wrote. "Had it not been for them, I doubt what the consequences had been."[35]

Recovered from his wounds, Walker wrote to Colt personally. "Without your pistols we would not have had the confidence to have undertaken such daring adventures," he rhapsodized. "With improvements, I think [the revolver] can be rendered the most perfect weapon in the world for light mounted troops, which [are] the only efficient troops that can be placed upon our extensive frontier to keep the various warlike tribes of Indians & marauding Mexicans in subjection."[36]

Thus the "six-shooter" was born.

With the outbreak of the Mexican-American War in 1846, Hays, Walker, and the Texas Rangers found themselves on the front lines in Monterey serving under General Zachary Taylor. After the successful siege and subsequent sacking of the city, now-Captain Walker traveled to Washington, DC, in November 1847 seeking support for his regiment of US Army mounted riflemen. After the celebration and lobbying concluded, Walker headed to New York to meet with Samuel Colt in person. "No man ever rode more gallantly to another's rescue,"[37] observes firearms historian Jim Rasenberger. Despite the testimonials from the Battle of Walker's Creek, Colt had failed to secure a government contract for his firearms and was once again on the brink of bankruptcy. The inventor's deference to his client's suggestions resulted in what has been described "one of the largest and most powerful pistols ever produced."[38]

The Colt Walker, as it came to be known, was fifteen and a half inches long with a nine-inch barrel, equipped with a six-shot cylinder carrying .44-caliber ammunition, made of steel heavy enough to render unconscious anyone not worth shooting. It was destined "to kill more men than any handgun ever made."[39]

The weapon found favor in the War Department, which contracted for an order of a thousand pistols priced at twenty-eight dollars each. By the time the revolvers came into production, however, Walker was dead, killed in a cavalry charge in the Mexican village of Huamantla, and the Texas Rangers' conduct had received considerable criticism. "On the day of battle, I am glad to have Texas soldiers with me for they are brave and gallant," General Taylor attested, "but I never want to see them before or afterward, for they are too hard to control… There is scarcely a form of crime that has not been reported to me as committed by them," he set down in a written report. "The mounted men from Texas have scarcely made one expedition without unwarrantably killing a Mexican." Based on the "constant recurrence of such atrocities," Taylor requested "no more troops may be sent to this column from the State of Texas."[40]

By the time an eighteen-year-old Frank Hamer joined the Texas Rangers in 1906, this tendency toward extreme violence—a natural outgrowth of what Robert Utley terms a "six-shooter mindset"[41]—had become even more commonplace. "Low pay, relaxed standards, and harsh conditions attracted Rangers who confused derring-do with a license to lay waste," writes Swanson. "Many of [the recruits] had killed men in the past, which in some circles was required for appointment to the border corps."[42] Raised on a ranch in San Saba County, Hamer lacked such homicidal credentials but demonstrated law enforcement potential by single-handedly apprehending a horse thief. "Who the hell are you?" the local sheriff demanded to know. "I'm Frank Hamer!"[43] the amateur man hunter declared—the first utterance of what became (according to his own legend) Hamer's signature introduction to miscreants.

As a Ranger, Hamer served under Captain John H. Rogers, a devout, teetotaling Presbyterian who carried a Bible in his saddlebag and armed himself with a curved-stock rifle specially crafted to accommodate a shooting arm left crippled in multiple gunfights. Later to be enshrined as one of the Texas Rangers' greatest leaders, Rogers "instilled in [Hamer] a deep conviction for justice and a strong notion that his duty as an officer was to protect the weak from the strong."[44]

None of those principles mattered on the Texas-Mexico border. Hamer's early years of service with the Rangers coincided with most anarchic period of the Mexican Revolution, rife with gunrunning and cross-border raids. Texans refer to this period from 1915 to 1919 as the "Bandit Wars." Mexicans more accurately refer to it as "La Matanza"—"The Killing Time," a period of what would now be called state-sanctioned ethnic cleansing. When Texas-based Mexican seditionists in the lower Rio Grande Valley responded to a call for a general Southwestern uprising known as the Plan of San Diego, Governor James Ferguson ordered the Rangers to "go down there and clean it up if [you] have to kill every damn man connected with it." Ferguson assured Texas Ranger commander Henry Lee Ransom that "I have the pardoning power and we will stand by [your] men."[45]

A former Houston sheriff dismissed for "violent and unlawful tactics"[46] (as well as a string of questionable homicides in "self-defense," including the murder of two African American brothers), Ransom had participated in the US Army's scorched-earth suppression of the Philippine Insurrection and had perfected the required methods. Frequently disguising their operations as efforts to suppress bootlegging—the combined Mexican Revolution and Prohibition providing perfect cover—Ransom's death squads laid waste to entire villages. Such "evaporations" earned the Rangers the reputation of "los diablos Tejanos."

A damning photo exists of Hamer and another Ranger posed on horseback over the corpses of men later identified as Jesus Garcia, Mario Garcia, and Amado Munoz, above a caption reading "Mexican Bandits Killed at Norias." Hamer and his partner hold lariats outstretched between them, in preparation to drag the dead bodies over the prairie. The photograph became a popular postcard, sold at drugstores and tobacconists across the

Texas borderlands, what one Hispanic critic has called an "effective method of racial intimidation."[47] Biographer John Boessenecker concedes, "Hamer's judgment in posing with the dead bodies was extremely poor,"[48] but alleges the Rangers in question only stumbled across the bodies after an assault by local law enforcement.

"If Hamer participated, it would have been the blackest episode in his career and a damning indictment,"[49] Boessenecker says, while willing to give his subject the benefit of the doubt. Regardless of responsibility, such outrages eventually led to US Army intervention, prompting Governor Ferguson to issue official orders for the Rangers to desist from "the summary execution of Mexicans."[50] A US Senate investigation in 1920 would conclude that "during the bandit troubles between August 4, 1915, and June 17, 1916, one hundred Mexicans have been executed by the Texas Rangers . . . without due process of law." The Senate report acknowledged that the figure might be "as high as three hundred" and added that, according to the Rangers' own dubious data, "most of these executions . . . implicat[ed] the particular Mexicans in the raids."[51]

Throughout his law enforcement career, Hamer drifted in and out of the Rangers, accepting jobs as marshal for Grimes, Texas; deputy sheriff and livestock theft investigator for Kimble County; special ranger for the Texas and Southwestern Cattle Raisers Association; and most memorably as a federal Prohibition agent. In that capacity, often utilizing "cold-blooded" tactics of "questionable legality,"[52] Hamer led raids on some of Texas's most lawless oil towns, including Mexia, where a guitar-playing, preteen Clyde Barrow had once entertained roughnecks for tips. Hamer rejoined the Texas Rangers in 1922 as a senior captain, his appointment coinciding with the rise of the Ku Klux Klan, a Reconstruction-era racist organization that had recently found new life in large part due to D. W. Griffith's *The Birth of a Nation* (1915).

The Rangers' crusade against Klan outrages lacked a certain enthusiasm. Modern historians agree that those Rangers who weren't active KKK members quietly endorsed the organization's ends, if not its means. "With the Klan trumpeting its dedication to law enforcement and [Governor Pat Neff] making it a prime objective of his administration, the movement held appeal,"[53] noted Robert Utley. Moreover, as Hamer's biographer admits, "Frank Hamer surely was, like many white Americans of the time, especially those living in Texas, a white supremacist."[54]

Before his pursuit and murder of Clyde Barrow and Bonnie Parker, Hamer achieved notoriety as "the first and only Texas Ranger to lose a prisoner to a lynch mob."[55] The incident in question occurred in Sherman, Texas, on May 9, 1930, when the rape trial of a black suspect named George Hughes descended into apocalyptic violence. Hamer had previously managed to prevent lynchings on a dozen prior occasions. But this time, he and three fellow Rangers, along with the town sheriff and four deputies, proved unequal to the mob that descended on the county courthouse, screaming, "We'll get the nigger!"

"Any time you feel lucky, come on." Hamer challenged, blockading the entrance to the courtroom. "But when you start up the stairway once more, there [are] going to be a lot of funerals."[56]

Hamer personally fired a load of buckshot into the legs of the ringleaders. Despite the brave front, when rioters broke the windows, threw in a five-gallon can of gas and lit a match, Hamer and his men retreated to the astonishment of visiting reporters and the delight of the vigilantes. "Bidding goodbye to the mob," wrote one newspaperman, "[the Rangers] left the city, going toward Dallas"[57]—leaving prisoner Hughes behind, confined in the courthouse vault for his own protection.

Hamer later claimed he had abandoned the scene to request backup from Texas governor Dan Moody on a private telephone line, a search that took him thirty-five miles away. By the time those reinforcements arrived, in the form of Sergeant Manuel "Lone Wolf" Gonzaullas, the courthouse was reduced to cinders and Hughes hung from a cottonwood tree, his penis stuffed into his mouth while the lynch mob sang "Happy Days Are Here Again." The city's black district had been thoroughly ransacked; its residents fled. A detachment of National Guard troops finally restored order. Despite

Hamer's and the Rangers' atrocious dereliction of duty, "many editorials in Texas newspapers said that Hamer and his crew had performed their best under difficult circumstances. Some even blamed the lynched man for inciting the riot."[58] It was left to Hamer's own Ranger colleague to offer the most definitive verdict. Hamer should have "shot the hell out of the mob"[59] and then called for assistance, said "Lone Wolf" Gonzaullas.[60]

The collapse from order into savagery at Sherman inflicted a blow to the Texas Rangers' reputation from which they took over a decade to recover. "Not just one Ranger, but several, constituted the force at Sherman and proved all but helpless against the mob," the *Wichita Falls Times* noted. "The stock of the Rangers has taken a terrific tumble as a result," the paper continued, editorializing that the organization's national standing among law enforcement agencies "has been badly fractured, if not shattered."[61] On her inauguration day, January 18, 1933, incoming Texas governor Miriam "Ma" Ferguson (wife of the same Jim Ferguson who had instructed the Rangers to "kill every man" in the so-called "Bandit Wars") sacked the entire forty-four-man Ranger force. Her motives weren't entirely altruistic: the Rangers, in an egregious breach of protocol, had actively campaigned for her opponent—and lost their bet. The Texas legislature added insult to injury, approving Ma's slate of "cronies and hacks,"[62] reducing the overall force to thirty-two men, gutting the Ranger budget by 45 percent and docking officers' salaries on every level.

Frank Hamer had already resigned as a Texas Ranger. His last few assignments following the Sherman catastrophe had proved less than illustrious: monitoring communist parades in Austin (where he confiscated a sign reading "Equality for the Negro Masses") and warning of non-existent Marxist plots to blow up Texas oil fields. His efforts to lobby the newly installed administration of Franklin D. Roosevelt for the position of US Marshall also came to nothing. "I was offered a position . . . at $800 per month and unlimited expenses, a car and a chauffeur," he wrote bitterly—and untruthfully—in a letter two decades later. "I politely informed them that I would not work for the Roosevelt regime for $800 an hour."[63]

In fact, Frank Hamer was unemployed—and, it seemed, unemployable. Had it not been for a couple of Texas crooks named Clyde Barrow and Bonnie Parker, history might not have accorded Hamer much attention.

On January 16, 1934, Clyde realized his long-held ambition to exact revenge on the Texas prison system. Exercising his usual careful planning, Clyde arranged for a pair of Colt .45 semiautomatic pistols to be cached under a bridge outside the Eastham Prison farm grounds the night before. That morning, he and Bonnie staged a diversion, allowing five inmates—including Clyde's old associate Raymond Hamilton and soon-to-be new sidekick Henry Methvin—to recover the guns and escape from a work detail; one guard was fatally shot and another wounded in the breakout. *Time* magazine headlined the escape on its newly instituted crime page, taking pains to note that Clyde's "paramour, the cigar-smoking Bonnie ('Suicide Sal') Parker,"[64] sat honking the horn in the getaway car. Embarrassed by the brazen flouting of authority, Texas prisons general manager Lee Simmons persuaded "Ma" Ferguson to authorize a "Special Escape Investigator for the Texas Prison System." Despite her well-publicized dispute with Hamer, the governor acceded to Simmons's recommendation of the ex-Texas Ranger for the job.

For all the charges of "defamation" and "character assassination" that would be leveled against *Bonnie and Clyde*, Penn's film did more to embellish Hamer's involvement in their demise than the facts themselves. While it's true that Simmons persuaded "Ma" Ferguson to sign on to Hamer's appointment, the ex-Ranger followed a trail already well laid out by Dallas deputy sheriff and onetime Bonnie Parker suitor Ted Hinton, his partner Bob Alcorn, and especially Bienville Parish, Louisiana, sheriff Henderson Jordan. That backwoods lawman, "an easygoing, sunburned fellow in a fawn-colored Stetson,"[65] had already tracked the criminal couple to a farm in Gibsland owned by the parents of Henry Methvin (another of C. W. Moss's real-life inspirations).

Hamer and Jordan got along well, "but they strongly disagreed about whether to give the outlaws a chance to surrender. . . . 'We agreed to take Barrow and the woman alive if we could,'"[66] Hamer insisted, unconvincingly.

Printing the legend, Hamer's largely fanciful biography, *"I'm Frank Hamer!"* published the year *Bonnie and Clyde* won Oscars, prefaces its climactic moment with its hero stepping out of the woods to shout "Stick 'em up!"[67]—a command his prey fatally disobey.

Whatever the actual circumstances, Hamer's participation in the death of Bonnie and Clyde served to restore the Rangers' reputation. "[His] widely publicized fame . . . recalled the past glories of the Texas Rangers and restored them to the affections of Texans," wrote Robert Utley, and "helped lay the groundwork for significant reforms."[68] In May 1935, the Texas Rangers were formally incorporated into the Texas Department of Public Safety (DPS), which established strict mental and physical standards. (Today's Texas Rangers remain under DPS aegis.) Walter Prescott Webb concluded his glowing panoramic history of the Texas Rangers with a portrait of Hamer as a transformational figure who "covered that period of transition in Texas from frontier simplicity and directness to modern complexity."[69]

To consecrate their resurrection, the newly reorganized Rangers enthusiastically promoted Paramount's *The Texas Rangers* (1936), ostensibly based on Webb's glorification of the force. Directed by Texas native King Vidor, the film premiered in Dallas on the state's August 21 centennial celebration. Fred MacMurray and Jack Oakie star as a pair of stagecoach robbers converted from law breaking to law enforcement by the life-saving actions of a Texas Ranger. Joining the force for their own larcenous purposes, they ultimately help to defeat crime boss "Polka Dot" McGee in a storyline that would have mystified author Webb, who received an $11,000 check for his original material. Eastern critics, whose judgment remained uninformed by personal visits west of the Mississippi River, heaped praise on the movie as a historically accurate production that outlined "the work of the band of fearless men who brought order to the Lone Star State."[70] This even though Vidor filmed his celebration of Texas Ranger fortitude not in his home territory, but in neighboring New Mexico.

Eighty-five years after he put an end to Clyde Barrow and Bonnie Parker, Frank Hamer finally earned a movie in his own right.

The 2019 Netflix film *The Highwaymen*, written by John Fusco and directed by John Lee Hancock, casts Kevin Costner as the former Texas Ranger, past his prime and dissatisfied with civilian life. "Hey, mister—were you really Frank Hamer?" a child asks after witnessing a less-than-impressive Coke-bottle shooting practice with "Old Lucky." "Goddamn, I'm an old man," Hamer grumbles. Fusco and Hancock structure the narrative as a redemption drama for Hamer and partner Maney Gault (played by Woody Harrelson), inaccurately depicted as a down-at-heels drunk living in a foreclosed shack. Overcorrecting for the 1967 film's glamor, Clyde and Bonnie are glimpsed only in fragmentary images—Clyde's spats, Bonnie's face in a dirty pocket mirror.

One memorable scene, however, depicts in darkly comic fashion the ready availability of American firearms. Preparing for the hunt after the Barrow Gang, Hamer and Gault step into a small-town dry goods store, where Hamer asks to inspect a Thompson submachine gun, a Colt Monitor automatic rifle, a Colt .45 semiautomatic pistol, a 1917 Smith & Wesson handgun, a Browning automatic rifle, a Remington Model 11 with a twelve-inch barrel, and a Winchester .30-.30 rifle, along with a dozen magazines, two cylindrical drums for the BAR, and a half-moon magazine for the Smith & Wesson.

"That'll do it," Hamer says.

"What'll do it?" asks the perplexed storeowner.

"All of 'em," Hamer clarifies, requesting an additional "four cases of .45 lead for good measure." As Hamer and Gault exit the store, the proprietor and his son lugging their arsenal behind them, the camera lingers on the entrance, where gold lettering reads NO GUNS SOLD TO MINORS.

The climactic ambush scene adheres to the sequence of events given by Hamer at the time and recounted in the family-authorized biography *I'm Frank Hamer: The Life of a Texas Police Officer*. Ordering his posse to "stay behind the blind," while he "presents himself," Costner's Hamer steps out on to the highway and shouts "Stick 'em up!" Time hangs suspended. For the first time, we see Clyde and Bonnie (played by glorified extras) in close-up. Then a devastating barrage riddles the outlaws' V-8.

Unlike the perspective in *Bonnie and Clyde*, the action unfolds almost entirely from the posse's point of view: shot after shot of automatic and semiautomatic firepower being directed at the rolling death car. The closing credits play over Hinton's sixteen-millimeter footage of the aftermath. A title card notes that Hamer "returned [home] and to retirement," conveniently leaving out his post–Barrow Gang career as a for-hire strikebreaker.

In the end, it was all too little, too late. *Bonnie and Clyde* got there first. Just barely.

15

"FADIN' AWAY"

> This is one film that can never be called "pretty."
> —Burnett Guffey

A cornfield on the outskirts of Midlothian, Texas, nearly spelled the end for *Bonnie and Clyde*. Not once, but twice.

At the end of the first week's filming, Arthur Penn assembled his cast and crew at Dallas's Majestic Theatre to screen the production's first set of rushes (also known as dailies), raw footage presented in take after take after endless take, from every angle. A once-magnificent 1921 movie palace, boasting twin marble staircases, crystal chandeliers, brass mirrors, and a lobby fountain, the Majestic had hosted the regional premieres of Warner Bros.' *The Public Enemy* and *I Am a Fugitive from a Chain Gang* in its Depression-era heyday. The *Bonnie and Clyde* company took their seats in slightly tattered woven cane chairs beneath a projected sky of floating clouds and twinkling stars. Massive Corinthian columns flanked the stage, where Harry Houdini, Mae West, and Bob Hope had once performed live. In today's era of dailies via encoded streaming with a personal password, it's inspiring to conjure up the nervous anticipation that prevailed among the select audience.

The lights dimmed.

The curtains opened.

The rushes began.

And Faye Dunaway almost vomited.

"I sat in the aging theatre that reeked from years of popcorn, my feet on carpet whose design had long ago lost the battle to soft drinks and crushed candy, and tried not to throw up as the images flickered by on the screen,"[1] the actress wrote in her autobiography.

While Dunaway had made two movies before *Bonnie and Clyde* (neither yet in release), she had never seen herself on screen—and when she finally did, she hated the young woman she saw there. "When I saw these early rushes and how I looked, right away I was gone. Right away I was a dead woman," Dunaway wrote. "It was like, 'God, do I really look like that?'"[2] The actress's memoir abruptly cuts to Dunaway in that Midlothian cornfield, hugging her knees to her chest, trying hard to "make myself somehow smaller," while hay bales "are drying to a golden brown in the Texas sun." For three days afterward, she "would come to the field and sit there, cut off from everyone," feeling "silent, sullen [and] morose."[3]

At the time, Dunaway focused her resentment on Penn. "It wasn't his fault, the way I looked on film, but boy, did I blame him,"[4] she said. (The same way she would later blame Roman Polanski for his allegedly excessive control over her appearance in *Chinatown* [1974].) From the director's point of view, he'd learned a painful lesson. "After that, I sort of closed the dailies," Penn said. "Actors can't look at themselves—all they see is flaws. I have never done it again."[5]

Accounts differ as to whether Dunaway experienced a momentary failure of nerve or a full-on nervous breakdown. "Remember, she was next to Warren, who was terribly pretty himself," said costume designer Theadora Van Runkle. "It wasn't easy for her."[6] Stimulants didn't help matters. In her autobiography, Dunaway makes mention of "one of the half-dozen Cokes I would drink each day to keep from wilting."[7] Van Runkle blamed the actress's erratic behavior instead on the appetite suppressors she ingested on a daily basis. "Once I took one of [Faye's] diet pills, and I stayed awake for *days*,"[8] Van Runkle said. The dependency took such a toll on Dunaway's figure that the designer's crew had to resew Bonnie's original costumes to account for the additional weight loss. Male crew members mocked the actress behind her back as "Fadin' Away." "Don't get me started on being a woman in a situation like that,"[9] Estelle Parsons sympathized in retrospect. (Parsons channeled her personal irritations with her costar into the on-screen resentment between Blanche Barrow and Bonnie Parker.)

As so often happens on film sets, life bled into art. Dunaway's insecurities enrich her performance as Bonnie; her unpredictable, erratic behavior becomes of a piece with the script's iconoclastic tone and the picture's abrupt editing rhythms. "There was a real kind of fierceness in Bonnie that I recognized in myself as well," she wrote. "Bonnie was Tennessee Williams, *Cat on a Hot Tin Roof* time."[10] "It was a terribly sad thing that this 'way out'—this new freedom [Bonnie] hoped for—turned out to be the greatest prison of all," she told *Dallas Morning News* reporter Kent Biffle. (True to Bonnie's spirit, Dunaway also felt compelled to mention "that was a gag when she posed for the pictures with the cigar," adding, "I've got it in my contract that I only have to smoke one cigar a day."[11])

Dunaway features prominently in the Red Oak eight-millimeter footage: making eyes at the camera over lunch, writing Bonnie Parker–like in a private journal, at one point even goofing around with Beatty between takes of the bank robbery scene. By this time, nearly two weeks' distance from that catastrophic dailies screening, Dunaway had "accepted who I was and that's how I looked, and it was okay, and I went on."[12] Still, the insecurities lingered. "We'd be ready to do a shot, and Faye would need the make-up woman," Parsons sighed. "We'd be all set to roll, and, oops, Faye would need to have her hair combed. That was the way she kept herself going."[13]

For a time, Dunaway's only real friend on the production was Michael J. Pollard—who kept his own on-set sanity intact with nightly doses of acid. The two shared an affection for Lenny Bruce (Dunaway had been the late comic's lover) and entertained themselves with imitations of classic Bruce routines and the nonstop playing of Bob Dylan's *Blonde on Blonde* album, no doubt to the annoyance of double-bedded neighbors at the thin-walled

North Dallas Motor Inn. "It all worked somehow, you know?" Pollard said. "Like the Yankees work somehow."[14]

Tensions remained, especially with Dunaway's costar/producer. "There are many ways in which [Warren] and I are alike," Dunaway admitted with thirty years' hindsight, "some that worked to help us through the filming of *Bonnie and Clyde*, others that made it harder."[15] Like Beatty, Dunaway considered herself a perfectionist. "We want to get it right and neither of us is quick to compromise for anything less. Just where and how one finds perfection in a performance, however, is a point we diverged on."[16] For Dunaway, the best performance came on the third or fourth takes. "I can go to the thirtieth take," she insisted, "but I find I get pretty stale after the fifth or sixth." On the other hand, "Warren will do thirty takes without thinking about it twice."[17]

Beatty's willingness to subject himself—and the entire crew—to endless repetitions of the same scene was already well established by the time he came to produce *Bonnie and Clyde*, and only grew more legendary when he became a director himself. As an example of Beatty's compulsiveness, Dunaway cited the scene early in the film where a sexually excited Bonnie mounts Clyde in the driver's seat of their stolen car. "Take it easy!" Clyde protests, worried that she's crumpling his hat. Pulling off the road, Clyde ejects himself from the car while Bonnie fumbles for a cigarette. (Both characters, the script notes, are "unbuttoned and unglued.")[18]

"All right now. Look here," Clyde upbraids Bonnie. "I might as well tell you right off. I ain't no lover boy."

"Your advertising is just dandy," Bonnie retorts. "Folks 'd never guess you've got nothing to sell."

"Ain't nothin' wrong with me! I don't like boys!" Clyde protests, smashing the back of his head against the doorframe in his hurry to escape from the conversation.

"We did thirty-eight takes of that particular scene," Dunaway remembered. "Each time [Warren's] head hit the door with an audible smack on the way out. By the time Arthur yelled 'Cut!' for the . . . final time, I'm not sure which of us was in more pain—but Warren thrives on going the limit."[19]

One of Dunaway's most unforgettable moments in *Bonnie and Clyde* occurs in the same cornfield where she took refuge after first seeing her onscreen avatar. Learning that the gang's latest enforced guest, Eugene Grizzard (Gene Wilder in that debut role), is an undertaker, Bonnie orders him and his fiancée ejected from the car. Newman and Benton's script indicates that Bonnie has "felt the cold hand of death" and that "from this point on, the audience should realize that death is inevitable for the Barrow gang, that it follows them always, that it waits anywhere . . . It is no longer a question of whether death will come, but when it will."[20]

The next scene picks up with the gang searching for Bonnie, who's gone missing after the encounter. Running alongside the car, Clyde spots Bonnie, "her yellow hair unmistakable even at this distance . . . carrying a brown paper bag that has split, from which she has occasionally lost clothing."[21] (Not a screenwriters' invention, the incident derives from historical accounts of one of the couple's many feuds.) Clyde chases after her, "so exhausted from the run that he has real trouble cornering her as they maneuver up and down the rows of corn."[22] Whatever the prevailing on-set animosities, Dunaway and Beatty play the couple's reunion with desperate intensity.

"Please, honey, don't ever leave me without saying nothing," Clyde pleads.

"I wanna see my mama," Bonnie tells him. "She's getting so old, and I—I wanna see her." They remain clasped together, Clyde's ever-present shoulder holster pressing into Bonnie's chest as they embrace.

In a film simultaneously heralded and condemned for its violence, the crane shot where Clyde chases Bonnie through the cornfield remains one of the most evocative pastoral images not only in *Bonnie and Clyde*, but in all of American cinema. As Clyde races through the trail of stalks left in the wake of Bonnie's flight, passing clouds darken the ever-changeable Texas landscape—one of those happy accidents that director Penn depended upon—manifesting in light and shadow that harbinger of death Newman and Benton could only attempt to conjure in words. Capturing the moment, however, precipitated *Bonnie and Clyde*'s second and more serious existential crisis, prompting cameraman Burnett Guffey to succumb to a heart attack—or, as Beatty recalled it, "an I-can't-do-it attack."[23]

Given the independent spirit that pervaded *Bonnie and Clyde*'s production, it's difficult to understand how someone of Guffey's generation and temperament came to serve as director of photography in the first place.

An Oscar winner for Fred Zinnemann's *From Here to Eternity* (1953), Guffey's career dated back to 1924, when he served as an eighteen-year-old camera assistant on John Ford's Western epic *The Iron Horse* (if you're looking to find the origin of Western movie clichés, this is the place to find them). Graduating to camera operator on Ford's *The Informer* (1935), Alfred Hitchcock's *Foreign Correspondent* (1940), and Charles Vidor's *Cover Girl* (1944), Guffey went on to become Columbia Pictures' premier director of photography on such canonical films as Robert Rossen's *All the King's Men* (1949) and Nicholas Ray's *In a Lonely Place* (1950), the latter one of the nearly twenty gritty film noirs Guffey made his specialty. After his Academy Award for the Zinnemann film, Guffey burnished his credentials with a one-year term as president of the American Society of Cinematographers from 1957 to 1958, where he successfully lobbied for a six-day week for his members.

Penn had already weathered battles with cameramen like *The Left Handed Gun*'s J. Peverell Marley ("I got one-a-them TV guys") and Joseph La Shelle, who had taken hours on end to garishly overlight every scene in *The Chase*, indoors and outdoors. Why hire Guffey, then? Penn never said, and the extant Warner Bros. files housed at the University of Southern California provide no enlightenment. At a 1970 American Film Institute seminar, Penn derided "this 'We've Never Done It Like This Before' way of working. Directors in America have to deal with this notion of 'we have thirty years of experience doing it. We do it better than anybody in the world.' And that, in one sense, is absolutely true," he conceded. "But they also do it more impersonally than anybody in the world."[24]

At the height of the Hollywood factory era, Penn explained, "you went to work at the studios as a director . . . but in point of fact the movie was really in the hands of the technicians. . . . If a cloud goes over a shot . . . then it's not going to cut with the next shot,"[25] went the prevailing wisdom. In the cornfield scene, Penn remembered, "I said, 'Let's go,' and one of the [camera] guys said, 'cloud coming.' I said, well for Christ's sake, let's shoot with the cloud coming.' And he looks around and says, 'Right. He wants to shoot with the cloud coming.'" Penn credited Beatty, who sided with him in the dispute, for providing "that last kick in the ass to get over wanting to be a nice guy with the technicians."[26]

Problems with Guffey manifested themselves early in preproduction. Dean Tavoularis, who made the miscalculation of designing low-ceilinged sets before the cameraman came aboard, was the first to feel Guffey's displeasure. "When [Bernie] arrived in Texas, he went on his own to visit the stage, then left and sent me a message to come and see him that night," the art director said. "I showed up at his hotel room, and he came to the door wearing a robe, holding a scotch and soda." Pouring a drink, Guffey mentioned, "'I was out on the stage and looked at the sets' . . . So right away I started explaining my reasons for these choices—that I had not done it out of ignorance, but because I was trying to find the visual equivalent of the theme and story . . . He shook my hand and we never discussed any of that again."[27] Tavoularis realized Guffey was "sizing [me] up, waiting to hear if I knew what I was doing. It was very clear—I was just a little chick, and he was a veteran."[28]

Guffey had sound technical reasons for disliking Tavoularis's sets, as well as many of the practical locations. The cramped spaces left precious little room for the standard complement of lighting and equipment to which he had become accustomed after decades in the studio system. *Bonnie and Clyde* was photographed with the same bulky, unwieldy Mitchell cameras that had been used on the Warner Bros. pre-Code classics whose archetypes Penn & Co. were now dismantling, an irony not lost on the director. "I can't think of another industry in which the essential tool was designed in 1932 and has remained exactly that way," Penn said. "Not the telephone, not the aviation industry, not anything."[29]

His style of shooting required a camera that was "lightweight, vital, fast, mobile. Really at the service of the scene, rather than scene at the service of the camera."[30] The director made no secret on set of his dislike of what he called "the pristine nature of traditional [American] cinema."[31] "This nonsense of the actors having to hit marks and so forth because the man who is operating the camera cannot see through the camera, and the man who is changing focus cannot see what is happening, but has to relate to where the actors stand on the floor, is absolutely absurd. Just absurd."[32]

Beatty, Benton, Tavoularis, and Towne all attested that the fundamental disagreement between Penn and Guffey arose from the director's insistence on the use of what is known as "source" lighting—illumination provided only by what can be seen in the frame, rather than artificially enhanced. Guffey "hated the way Arthur was shooting the movie and he would bitch and grouse to anybody who was around,"[33] Towne remembered. Guffey pushed back against this naturalistic approach. The location interiors in *Bonnie and Clyde*, particularly those shot early in the schedule, display the same flat, undifferentiated lighting that mars virtually every 1960s studio film.

Take the scene where Clyde treats Bonnie to dinner at a roadside café following his impetuous, impress-the-girl-with-the-gun holdup of a grocery score. Tavoularis painstakingly converted a former bank in the tiny town of Lavon to suit the occasion,[34] but the setting might as well have been a *Pillow Talk* soundstage. Guffey's lighting is unattractively garish, and the choice of angles renders most of Tavoularis's work irrelevant; the scene plays out primarily in close-ups without any sense of the atmosphere so redolent in later sequences.

In his defense, the cameraman had real-world issues to consider. "Bernie was of the school that said, you've got to put a lot of light on the faces, because a lot of the revenue came from drive-in theaters,"[35] Beatty acknowledged. Industry oracle *Variety* in its weekly box office reports distinguished grosses in "open-air" and "hard-top" theaters, recognizing the bifurcation of the marketplace. By 1958, the year that saw the release of Penn's debut Billy the Kid film, *The Left Handed Gun*, drive-ins accounted for nearly one-third of American screens and regularly out-grossed traditional theaters in suburban areas.[36] Modern 4K restorations of films from this transitional era only serve to magnify the faults necessitated by screening environments where movies had to compete with the headlights of the carloads of viewers. As Beatty recalled, whenever Penn insisted on reduced lighting, Guffey always responded, "You'll never see it in the drive-ins!"[37]

It was enough to give any veteran studio cinematographer a "heart attack."

Exit Burnett Guffey. Enter, briefly, Ellsworth Fredericks —incredibly, yet another veteran studio cameraman a generation removed from *Bonnie and Clyde*'s principal creators. Again, the Warner Bros. archives offer no clue to the sixty-two-year-old Fredericks's hiring. Fredericks spent extensive time in television on such shows as *Alfred Hitchcock Presents*, while also serving as director of photography on feature films as varied as Don Siegel's *Invasion of the Body Snatchers* (1956), William Wyler's *Friendly Persuasion* (1956), Elia Kazan's *Wild River* (1960), and John Frankenheimer's *Seven Days in May* (1964). "It was impossible," Estelle Parsons said. "The shots were so conventional that it became like a typical Hollywood movie. The guy would set up a shot, and Arthur would throw up his hands."[38] (Which specific shots and scenes Fredericks supervised remain lost to cinema history; call sheets in the studio archives consistently list Guffey as cameraman.)

In less than a week, Guffey was back on set, and a new détente prevailed. "Penn had new respect for how hard [Bernie] had been struggling to take the look of the film in the direction he wanted,"[39] Harris recounted. For the pivotal reunion scene with Bonnie's family (staged in a disused stone quarry on the outskirts of Red Oak, Texas), Guffey's expertise proved crucial in helping Penn achieve the otherworldly quality he sought. Newman and

Benton's first-draft screenplay describes "a magic, isolated landscape seen from a distance, lit by a bright sun,"[40] an image they drew deliberately from the films of Ingmar Bergman. "It had to be a scene that was both happening [in the moment] and already belonged to the future," Penn elaborated. "I said to Bernie, 'I'd like this to look like an old sepia photograph.'"[41] When the image through the viewfinder proved "too brilliant" with light, Guffey said "Give me a minute" and dispatched a gaffer to the nearest hardware store to fetch a section of window screen.

Inserted between the camera lens and the aperture, the crosshatched metallic threads "broke down the sharpness just enough to have that quality of a dream,"[42] Penn marveled. Guffey's five-and-dime innovation lends the sequence an ethereal timelessness. Sun-burnished amber images, many posed in conscious imitation of John Ford Westerns, set solitary characters against the dreary, hopeless landscape, and position family groups in carefully arranged assemblies: a picnic, a prayer. In one shot, a young boy playing cops and robbers rolls down a sand dune in slightly slowed motion; his carefree gestures will be tragically mirrored in Clyde's death throes.

Beyond the store-bought window screens, Guffey's work in *Bonnie and Clyde* abounds in on-the-fly inspirations brought about by production circumstances. To balance the light between interior and exterior in the movie's many driving scenes, Guffey employed a commercially available "Sun Gun," a portable spotlight which allowed enough illumination to be cast on the passengers' faces to prevent under- or overexposure; the appliance later became a must-have accessory for amateur eight-millimeter photographers.

To accommodate Penn's demands, Guffey also brought into play an unprecedented number of lenses, ranging in focal lengths from extreme wide-angle 9.8 millimeter to extreme telephoto 400 millimeter. Penn took a liking to the telephoto lens and deployed it in a shot remarkable for the time and still striking today: a long, panning take of a small-town storefront that eventually finds wheelman C. W. Moss's father through the window of an ice-cream parlor, in the act of betraying Bonnie and Clyde to former Texas Ranger Frank Hamer.[43]

"A 400 mm shot! It'll shake and nothing's going to have any depth of field," Penn enthused. "All the while I kept saying, 'Yeah, tell me more, tell me more.' And, by God, it came out looking just the right way. Of course. It's *sensational* dramatically."[44] The visual treatment rendered unnecessary the page and a half of dialogue screenwriters Newman and Benton had provided in the script.

"We did some things that might be regarded as wrong photographically, but they created the atmosphere of realism that was wanted,"[45] Guffey admitted to a reporter for *American Cinematographer* magazine, which featured *Bonnie and Clyde* on the cover of its April 1967 issue, above the headline "Raw Cinematic Realism." Having made his peace with the director, Guffey told the American Society of Cinematographers' in-house publication that Arthur Penn and Warren Beatty "were out to get stark realism on celluloid. Nothing was to be beautiful. Everything was to be, you might say, *harsh*."[46] Adjusting the facts to fit the interview, Guffey maintained, "we had agreed in advance that there would be no 'slick' Hollywood photography." In a nod to Dunaway's ordeal during production, Guffey acknowledged that he shot the actress "with no diffusion whatsoever. She was not so hard to photograph because she had a good face."[47]

With films like *From Here to Eternity* and *Birdman of Alcatraz*, Guffey had established a reputation for black-and-white realism; for him, *Bonnie and Clyde* marked an experimental foray into color. "Color in itself sometimes detracts from realism because it comes out pretty whether you want it to or not," he told *American Cinematographer*. "Arthur Penn attempted to use color without pointing it up . . . or glamorizing it in any way, because he felt this would create a more convincing effect of realism. I think he succeeded because this is one film that can never be called 'pretty.'"[48]

"Pretty" or not, *Bonnie and Clyde*'s dailies made a favorable impression. Not on Faye Dunaway, perhaps. But back in Burbank, Warner Bros. production chief Walter MacEwen, who had championed the film over "Colonel" Jack Warner's strenuous objections, sensed vindication for his advocacy. "I have been seeing every foot of film shot to date," he wrote to Beatty at the North Park Motor Inn in Dallas. "To say we are pleased with it is an understatement. Stay as sweet as you are, complete the goddamn show on schedule, and let's put it together as fast as we can without any loss of quality."[49]

It wouldn't be quite that easy.

16

"TRAIL'S END"

> Nobody ever asks, "Whatever happened
> to Jesse James?"
>
> —Eric Hobsbawm

The thing that makes the most famous outlaws compelling," says historian Mark Lee Gardner, "is the audaciousness of their crimes." For Billy the Kid, that means "it can't be some kind of simple heist. It's got to be this incredible escape from Lincoln County jail. Two guards murdered with their own guns—maybe the greatest escape in Old West history." For Jesse James, in the aftermath of the Northfield, Minnesota, raid that ended his outlaw career, "even the Northfield papers wrote in awe of Jesse's escape. They thought it was amazing he and his brother Frank were able to elude a posse that numbered more than a thousand men."[1]

Billy the Kid certainly relished the attention he received in Eastern newspapers. Gardner, who traced Sheriff Pat Garrett's pursuit of the Kid in *To Hell on a Fast Horse*, insists that young William Bonney "read newspapers whenever he could get his hands on them."[2] Making the cover of the faraway *Boston Police Gazette* as the "Boy Chief of New Mexico Outlaws" had to be "surreal for him." Especially the magazine cover depicting him "rescuing some Mexican damsel, which was of course completely invented."[3] In 1873, Billy posed for a traveling tintype photographer in Fort Sumner, New Mexico, dressed in rumpled trail clothes and holding a Model 1873 Winchester by the muzzle; a six-gun protrudes from the cartridge belt around his waist.

The sole surviving image of one of the West's most notorious outlaws "is anything but a flattering photograph," Gardner concedes "His mouth is partially open, exposing his buckteeth, and his eyelids appear to be drooping, snake-eyed." Though the camera rarely lies, Gardner nonetheless hypothesizes that it is as if Billy the Kid "was just too big—or too elusive—to be captured in a tintype that would fit in the palm of one's hand."[4]

The Barrow Gang's infamous Joplin, Missouri, photographs transformed Clyde and Bonnie—especially Bonnie—into the equivalent of today's Instagram influencers, people famous for being famous. Screenwriters David Newman and Robert Benton, creators of the "New Sentimentality" that valued style above content, consciously made this element an essential part of their story fabric. "By the time their careers ended, [Bonnie and Clyde] had achieved an almost supernatural status in the eyes of many newspaper readers," Benton wrote. "How could a little blonde girl and her man escape so many lawmen, time and time again? They were folk heroes, and though their defeat was wished (that was, after all, a part of American lore—that the bad guys be as fascinating and marvelous as could be for a while, but that ultimately the good guys must win) their career was followed by millions."[5]

A wonderfully entertaining bank robbery sequence occurring almost exactly halfway through *Bonnie and Clyde*'s two-hour running time equates crime and celebrity and serves as the movie's comedic high point. Set in an unidentified Midwestern town, the sequence begins with Clyde, Bonnie, and Buck entering a Farmers and Merchants Bank. (The facade and square in Pilot Point, Texas, where the scene was shot, remains unchanged today). "Good afternoon. This is the Barrow Gang," Clyde announces. "Now, if everyone will take it easy, nobody will get hurt." Buck leaps over the cage with feline agility while Bonnie stares down a female teller. A scarecrow of a farmer in overalls quakes with raised hands.

"That your money, or the bank's?" Clyde asks.

"Mine," the farmer says.

When a guard attempts to reach for his gun, Clyde blows off his cap. "Next time, I'll aim a little lower," he warns, then turns back to the farmer. "All right, you keep it then." (As with many such incidents in *Bonnie and Clyde*, the moment has real-life antecedents.) On their way out the door, Buck pauses to pull the sunglasses off the face of a wizened guard. "Take a good look, pop," he encourages. "I'm Buck Barrow. We're the Barrow boys." An alarm rings deafeningly. The gang makes its escape into the V-8 where Blanche and C. W. await.

Flatt and Scruggs's "Foggy Mountain Breakdown" accompanies the getaway, a raucous piece of filmmaking that crosscuts the Barrow Gang's escape (they race past art director Dean Tavoularis's period-perfect Burma Shave highway signs while reloading their semiautomatic weapons) with scenes of the bank's guards and managers posing for press photographs. "There I was, staring square into the face of death," proclaims the capless guard, while the fortunate farmer declares, "All I can say is, they did right by me, and I'm bringin' me a mess o' flowers to their funeral." Exploding flashbulbs bridge the back-and-forth. Further blurring the line between reality and fiction, the movie's one-line walk-on roles were all played by Texas locals, selected by Dallas casting director Peter Maloney. Pilot Point resident Joe Spratt, who claimed to have witnessed an actual Barrow Gang robbery, earned one hundred dollars for his day's work on the film as the lucky farmer. (Whether he laid flowers in gratitude on Clyde's and Bonnie's graves remains unknown.)

Bonnie and Clyde's B-picture budget may have necessitated the casting of nonprofessionals rather than experienced actors, but their appearance on the fringes of (and, from time to time, at the very heart) of scenes lends the action a tangible sense of verisimilitude. Past and present coexist in the appearance of these townspeople, many of them children or young adults when the Barrow Gang paid their communities a different kind of visit. "In many of the towns we shot in, the set would become a sort of Bonnie and Clyde reunion; people would pack a lunch, round up the kids, and come for the day," Dunaway recalled. "It was as if we had stepped into a tide pool of memories. Old stories were dredged up and told again, rumors were rehashed, scrap books were pulled out ... and we were all slipping away in time."[6] The sentiment ran both ways. "Pilot Point Is Proud to Have Been Selected to Participate in 'Bonnie and Clyde,'" one local newspaper ad celebrated, though town fathers included a then-contemporary photo of the main square to "reassure readers that it was now 'peaceful.'"[7]

For many viewers, the film's most memorable face belongs not to one of its stars, but to Mabel Cavitt, plucked from a crowd of onlookers to play Bonnie's mother in the reunion scene. Penn reportedly cast the silver-haired, sixty-six-year-old Red Oak, Texas schoolteacher on the spot owing to her "extraordinary resemblance to Faye."[8] A still taken on the set that day affirms Penn's judgment. Drably dressed in earth colors by costume designer Theadora Van Runkle's team and wearing no makeup, Cavitt appears to have stepped out of a Dorothea Lange photograph straight on to location, especially as filtered through cameraman Burnett Guffey's window-screen-diffused lens. She and Dunaway share an affinity that's even more convincing given the spontaneity of the circumstances.

"In point of fact, I think the effectiveness of [Mabel's] scene ... is not so much in what she did, but in the way the two professional actors [Beatty and Dunaway] responded to it and dealt with it," Penn said. "*They* converted a relatively primitive piece of acting into a complicated and sophisticated piece of acting. . . . Now, had they been three people without technique, I think it would have been deadly."[9] Cavitt lived to see *Bonnie and Clyde's* twentieth anniversary, passing away on her birthday in 1988. Though her simple grave in the Red Oak cemetery records only dates, both her obituary—and her listing on the International Movie Data Base (IMDB)—fittingly accord her the title of "actress"—one of the movie's many instances of life imitating art imitating life.

For the residents of those small Texas towns in the autumn of 1966, Clyde Barrow and Bonnie Parker had achieved the status of folk heroes.

In life, however, their renown came at a price. Like every celebrity before them, Clyde and Bonnie discovered that after a certain point they no longer controlled their own story. The public did, and its expectations demanded fidelity to a preconceived image. "Public opinion and the heroes we raise up almost inevitably peak, and then it's all downhill,"[10] observes Jeff Guinn.

The turning point came on Easter Sunday, April 1, 1934.

Arriving early for a prearranged rendezvous with their families off Texas Highway 114 near Grapevine, twenty-five miles northwest of Dallas, the couple took advantage of the glorious spring day to enjoy some much-needed rest. With them was Henry Methvin, recently sprung from the Eastham Prison Farm, who had replaced W. D. Jones as their constant companion. A hulking, none-too-bright twenty-two-year-old brute, Methvin served as the original basis for C. W. Moss, in Newman and Benton's conception of the character as "a 1931 version of a rock 'n' roll hood."[11] While Clyde napped in the back seat of the gang's latest stolen Ford V-8 and Henry paced outside smoking, Bonnie played with the gift she'd brought along for her mother: a white rabbit named Sonny Boy.

At approximately 3:30 p.m., Bonnie sighted three Texas Highway Patrol officers cruising the highway on motorcycles. Attracted by the flashy black automobile with yellow-wire rims perhaps in need of roadside assistance, two of the patrolmen broke formation and headed toward the gang's hillside. Both were in their mid-twenties. E. B. Wheeler had four years of experience, but H. D. Murphy was marking his first day on the job. Bonnie alerted Clyde to the "laws'" approach.

"Let's take 'em," Clyde told Methvin—his code for kidnapping. Misunderstanding the cue, Methvin opened fire with his BAR, blasting Wheeler off his motorcycle. Rookie Murphy fumbled to load his shotgun. Clyde beat him to the draw. Passing motorists Mr. and Mrs. Fred Giggal, out for a leisurely Sunday drive, got more than they bargained for when they saw Methvin emptying his weapon into the fallen patrolmen; their bodies jerked spastically. "I screamed at my husband to hurry—they knew we had seen the shooting and would kill us,"[12] Mrs. Giggal said in sworn testimony. But Clyde was already making tracks in the opposite direction.

Neither of the Giggals remembered seeing a woman at the scene—an inconvenient fact for Texas prison administrator Lee Simmons, already embarrassed by the Eastham Prison Farm breakout and now doubly compromised by the fact that one of its escapees had just killed a Texas highway patrolman. Fortunately for Simmons, a nearsighted farmer named William Schaeffer who lived four hundred yards from the murder conveniently swore he saw a woman approach the downed officers and shoot Murphy repeatedly, giggling at how his head "bounced like a rubber ball."[13] The *Fort Worth Star-Telegram* duly informed its readers that "a cigar butt bearing small teeth marks, such as might have been made by a woman" was found on the scene. "The cigar, if it even existed, would have had nothing to do with Bonnie,"[14] Guinn points out. But the Easter Sunday shootings resulted in a turnaround in Clyde and Bonnie's media profile.

"Now all of a sudden Bonnie's a killer," Guinn continues. "She's the one egging on Clyde. He's not the dangerous one—*she* is—which is even more colorful than her as a promiscuous girl Friday."[15] Worse for Bonnie, rookie patrolman Murphy's fiancée, Maree Tullis, proved even more adept at optics, wearing her wedding dress to Murphy's funeral, her virginal image prominent in local newsreels. Once the "sexy companion of a criminal kingpin," Bonnie transformed overnight into "a kill-crazy floozy who laughed as she finished off an innocent rookie patrolman and simultaneously ruined the life of a sweet young girl who'd been about to marry him."[16] A difficult-to-find stone obelisk, erected in 1996, marks the place where patrolmen Murphy and Wheeler fell. "I want the world to know what vicious killers and murderers [Clyde and Bonnie] are,"[17] Wheeler's widow said at the dedication, the wound still festering a half century later.

After Grapevine, only one thing could redeem Bonnie and Clyde's reputation.

Their deaths.

Premonitions of their own mortality haunt accounts of the Barrow Gang's brief two-year crime spree. Bonnie, always the more theatrical of the pair, frequently expressed herself in fatalistic terms. "Life's not worth living without you,"[18] she wrote to Clyde in the Denton County jail as early as February 1930, two years *before* they embarked on a collective life of crime. Both Clyde and Bonnie spoke of death openly to their families. On one visit to West Dallas after the assault in Dexfield Park, Iowa, Clyde took time out to select the headstone underneath which he would lie with his brother Buck. Bonnie's morbidity surpassed her lover's. "Don't let them keep me at the undertaker's," she pleaded with her mother on their last meeting. "Bring me home to die—it's been so long since I was home."[19]

Like Clyde, Bonnie had preplanned the scene. "I want to lie in the front room with you and [my family] sitting beside me. A long, cool, peaceful night before I leave you. That will be nice—and restful."[20] An "influencer" to the end, Bonnie had even selected the photograph she wanted placed on her corpse: the joyous image, made famous in the aftermath of the Joplin raid, of Clyde holding her apparently weightless body in his arms. Not a cigar in sight.

One of the most intriguing imponderables of *Bonnie and Clyde* involves a scene where the lovers enact their own funeral in a tawdry Platte City motor-court room a few hours before "the laws" descend. The ghoulish interlude does not appear in Newman and Benton's original script. Robert Towne, hacking away at the North Dallas Motor Inn, wrote it during production at director Arthur Penn's insistence—under protest. "I thought—to my chagrin as I say it now—that Bonnie might have wanted to perform her own death, something that grew out of the romantic idea she had about herself, a kind of overembellished funeral with a movie star look, and that was what I kept pressing for," Penn said in self-defense. "It was a colorful idea, but too elaborate. Warren didn't like it at all, and neither did Towne."[21]

That's putting it mildly.

"Warren came to me and said, 'You can't write that fuckin' scene, 'cause it's a fuckin' pretentious piece of shit,'" Towne remembered. "I thought, well,

I'll try to make it work; it's only paper. I kept trying . . . and it never looked particularly good, and Warren kept yelling at me about it. 'We can't pamper him! How can you do this?'"[22]

Though some sources claim the scene was shot and later cut from the film, the funeral pageant does not appear among the deleted scenes on the movie's comprehensive fortieth anniversary DVD extras, suggesting Penn abandoned the idea before it could occupy valuable and fast-disappearing shooting days. Nonetheless, the mock funeral offers a fascinating insight into the essential fatalism of the outlaw mystique that Penn sought to capture for the film.[23] Seen in a mirror,

> BONNIE lies stiff as a statue on the white mattress, impeccably dressed for her funeral. Candelabras made of beer bottles lie at her head and feet. BONNIE's hands and face are powdered and painted a waxen white. She wears a garish silk bow in her hair which is, for this occasion, curled like a little girl's.

"A little unsure of the whole thing," Clyde lies down beside Bonnie, beer bottle in one hand, Tommy gun in the other, cigar clamped in his teeth. Unsatisfied with his tie ("You can't wear polka dots on an occasion like this!"), an inebriated Bonnie "weaves her way over to the dresser" to select a replacement. "Lie down before you fall down," Clyde tells Bonnie, who "reaches up like a zombie"—credit Towne, whatever his objections to the assignment, for knowing the exact word to choose—to snatch a flower from a hat on the dresser. Together, she and Clyde look into the mirror. "Tickled" despite himself, Clyde joins Bonnie as she begins to serenade their mirror images "like some hoydenish vaudevillian." They sing to the tune of Frederic Chopin's funeral march:

BONNIE/CLYDE
Did you ever think when a hearse went by,
That someday you may die?
They'll wrap you up in a big white sheet
And bury you down just about six feet.

Together they lie down on the bed. "All right, shut your eyes now," Bonnie tells Clyde. They alternate a countdown.

"One for the money."

"Two for the show."

"Three to get ready."

"Four to go!" the couple says in unison.

"As they approach four," Towne writes, "we should feel that somehow when they shut their eyes, they really will die. They shut them on GO, and the screen goes black."[24]

Beatty and Towne were right to protest the scene's inclusion. Penn stuck to the script—and delivered the movie's most heartfelt scene. Left alone in their cabin while their confederates fetch chicken dinners, Faye Dunaway's Bonnie and Warren Beatty's Clyde experience their first moment of real emotional intimacy. "Oh, baby, I've got the blues so bad," Bonnie says, lying on the bed in a floral-embroidered pink nightgown as Clyde sits beside her. Her mother's foreboding words at the family reunion have left their mark. "I don't have no mama—no family either," she grieves. "Hey, I'm you're family," Clyde tells her. Bonnie curls up on Clyde's lap, arms wrapped around his waist.

"You know, when we started out, I thought we was really goin' somewhere," she says. "But this is it. We're just goin', huh?"

The shooting script, which hews closely to Newman and Benton's original version, makes clear "there is nothing rhetorical about it—it is a real question."[25] Clyde doesn't answer for a long moment. Then he says, haltingly:

CLYDE
I—I love you.

Penn follows this with one of *Bonnie and Clyde*'s most empathetic images: an extreme close-up of a beaming, reassured Bonnie drawing Clyde's hand to her face and holding it there. Dunaway considered the scene her best moment in the film (she's right—and Beatty's not bad, either), one that "touched the core of my being" and penetrated to the heart of what she saw as the character's "tragic irony. [Bonnie] got out only to see that she was heading nowhere and that the end was death."[26] The quiet exchange, shot simply in extended takes with a minimum of cutting, conveys the sense of mortality far more effectively than Penn's mock funeral might have—with none of the artifice.

The director lost the argument over the funeral interlude, but as the shoot progressed, "the violence and morbidity of *Bonnie and Clyde* became, more than ever, the focus of Penn's attention."[27] He concentrated his energies on the final ambush. All published versions of the film's screenplay—along with all original copies that remain in the Warner Bros. archives at the University of Southern California—retain Newman and Benton's conception that at "no point in the gunfight do we see BONNIE and CLYDE in motion." Instead, the script interpolated two photographs: "one of Clyde, half out of the car, taking careful dead aim with his gun," and another of Bonnie, "in terror, a pack of cigarettes clutched tight, looking as fragile and beautiful as she can be."[28]

Penn had something very different in mind.

"The final scene was a paradoxical sequence that was going to make this film into something mythic,"[29] he said in 2008. "The ending was so clear to me," he claimed elsewhere. "In fact it was the only thing which was clear."[30] Stylistically, Penn wanted to "launch the outlaw couple into legend," and "having seen enough Kurosawa by that point, I knew how to do it."[31] The Japanese master's *Seven Samurai* was not the sole inspiration for the unprecedented, trendsetting violence that concludes *Bonnie and Clyde*. When the film went into production in the fall of 1966, American troop levels in

Vietnam approached the half-million mark; a resultant increase in nationwide protests led to the opening of a House Un-American Activities Committee investigation targeting demonstrators as alleged Communists.

"I would be the last person to suggest that I wasn't reordering history in order to fit my needs in telling my version of Bonnie and Clyde's story," Penn freely admitted in an interview. "You use history and social situations for insight, and also to say, 'This is the way I understand the background and foreground of a given situation dramatically.'"[32] One critic would later herald the ambush scene as "an image of blind violence on the part of organized society, a violence far surpassing that which it is supposed to be putting down."[33]

"Remember, this was [also] the time of Marshall McLuhan," Penn instructed interviewer Peter Biskind, citing the Canadian philosopher whose groundbreaking 1964 study *Understanding Media: The Extensions of Man* famously declared, "the medium is the message." "The idea was to use the medium as a narrative device. I wanted to take the film away from the relatively squalid quality of the story into something a little more balletic."[34]

Somewhat disingenuously, Penn claimed, "it didn't even occur to me, particularly, that [*Bonnie and Clyde*] was a violent film. Not given the times in which we were living, because every night on the news we saw kids in Vietnam being airlifted out in body bags, with blood all over the place."[35] Whatever his statements during production and in later reminiscences, the ever-present specter of American violence consumed Penn during the making of *Bonnie and Clyde* and continued to inform his work throughout the Seventies. "The causes are unclear but little by little the word 'violence' has taken on a particular connotation without real meaning," the director offered in 1971. "These past few years everyone has said that by definition violence is bad ... I don't believe that right now the word simply evokes good or bad, just or unjust. It has lost its moral dimensions."[36]

When the time came to re-create Clyde and Bonnie's deaths, the company had been ordered back to the Warner Bros. lot in Burbank. As far as the studio was concerned, Penn and Beatty had overstayed their Texas welcome.

"There was always a sense of something between a request and a threat about our need to come back to the studio,"[37] Dean Tavoularis confirmed. The waning days of December found the production "weeks over schedule and well over budget,"[38] said script supervisor John Dutton. "Time is of the essence," Jack Warner wrote to production chief Walter MacEwen. "It won't be long before I should be leaving [Warner Bros.], but I will be fooling around waiting for geniuses to make up their minds, which I am not going to do. If [Penn and Beatty] had to finance just ten percent of the picture they would not be so thoughtless."[39]

Halfway out the office door, with production not yet wrapped, the "Colonel" fretted that *Bonnie and Clyde* would be beaten to theaters by 20th Century-Fox's *The St. Valentine's Day Massacre*, nearing completion at the helm of Roger Corman, given his first major-studio opportunity—and a reported $2.5 million budget that dwarfed Penn's. With the final scene set for filming on the studio's Albertson Ranch in Triunfo, California, and a handful of driving shots and retakes of location interiors (known as "pickup shots") to be completed on studio soundstages, Warner and MacEwen could better ride herd over their resident "geniuses." Even back on the lot, the production ran over schedule. The sheer logistics required to bring off the ambush scene all but guaranteed delays. Penn's "balletic" vision of Clyde and Bonnie's final moments was something unprecedented.

As the actual history unfolded on the morning of May 23, 1934, the lovers paused at the sight of a disabled Ford Model A logging truck sticking out into the right shoulder of Louisiana Highway 154. Clyde knew the truck well. It belonged to Iverson "Ivy" Methvin, Henry Methvin's father. Clyde had bought the truck himself, in recompense for the Methvin family sheltering him and Bonnie in the wake of the Grapevine killings. What Clyde didn't know was that the Methvins had struck a deal, brokered by Frank Hamer and Lee Simmons, granting their son Henry amnesty in exchange for putting Clyde and Bonnie in the lawmen's gun sights.

"[The Methvin family] were real crude and rude and felt the best way to get what they wanted was through violence," Gibsland, Louisiana,[40] resident H. M. Parnell said of his neighbors with visible disdain in a later documentary. Henry's betrayal of his patrons won him a governor's reprieve from the certain death sentence he would have suffered had his role in the killing of Texas highway patrolman H. D. Murphy ever come to light. No idiot, Texas governor "Ma" Ferguson knew that Henry was also wanted for a related murder in Oklahoma and would pay the price there. (Which he did.)

According to posse member Ted Hinton, Ivy Methvin rebelled at being used as a decoy. "The truth is, Methvin protested stoutly and to no avail," Hinton wrote. Hamer ordered his informant be handcuffed to a tree, where "he could stand or he could sit. But he wasn't about to go anywhere until we allowed him to go." Even by 1934 standards, Hinton avowed, "Methvin's civil rights were violated.... But none of the six of us who were intent on capturing or stopping Clyde and Bonnie were thinking at that moment about whether we were justified in doing what we were doing."[41] Said Hamer, never one to worry about repercussions: "I told [Methvin] that if he didn't get back into his truck and do what he was told to do, Bonnie and Clyde would not get the chance to kill him because I would."[42]

The ambushers' vantage point allowed for a full view of the roadway in both directions. From the driver's perspective, ascending a gradual rise, the dense tree cover presented an impenetrable screen. The approach of Clyde and Bonnie's V-8 coincided with that of a logging truck traveling in the opposite direction. As one historian laid out the scene, "There was no way the logging truck, Ivy Methvin's truck and the V-8 sedan were all going to fit on the same section of the narrow road."[43] When Clyde came to a full stop, the hellfire erupted. "The first two shots hit Barrow in the head," according to John Neal Phillips. "Twenty to twenty-seven other slugs hacked through Barrow's body," causing his stockinged left foot to slip off the clutch and the car to "wobble uncontrollably down the road."[44]

While there is no way to be certain whose bullet killed Bonnie, Hamer followed the car with his Colt Monitor machine rifle, taking no chances. After unloading a blast through the rear windshield, he calmly walked to the front of the Ford and fired repeatedly into Bonnie's lifeless body. "I gritted my teeth and pulled the trigger as quickly as I could—pulled it again and again," the ex-Texas Ranger told reporters. "If you are an officer sworn to do your duty you can't afford to feel mercy for such murdering rats, whether they are male or female."[45] The noise of the onslaught was so overpowering that railroad tree-cutting crews a mile away were convinced someone had been using dynamite to clear the roadbed.

In their last moments, Clyde Barrow and Bonnie Parker were denied a final moment of closure. The gunfire hit them without warning, shredding their bodies in sixteen seconds. *Bonnie and Clyde* tailors the scene to fit the legend in the making.

Returning from a grocery-shopping trip to town, the couple encounter C. W. Moss's father Malcolm waving them down on the highway shoulder. Clyde pulls off the road and comes to a stop. He emerges from the car munching on a pear. (According to Dunaway, she and Beatty were meant to nibble on a more symbolic peach, but none could be had in the California winter.)[46] Bonnie watches through the windshield as Clyde approaches Malcolm.

"What you got there?" Clyde asks.

"Got a flat tire. Ain't got no spare," says Malcolm, played with memorable cornpone duplicity by character actor Dub Taylor—like Denver Pyle as Frank Hamer, a living nod to the movie's Western forerunners. The sound of a motor calls both men's attention to a chicken truck approaching from the opposite direction. Then —

EXTERIOR—NEW ANGLE

A flock of birds flies out from the trees. The sound of their wing-beats is a little like gunfire.[47]

No birds feature in Newman and Benton's original script. There the ambush begins when Hamer sees the chicken truck "from a long way away and realizes he cannot afford to let anything pass between him and his quarry. He decides the time is now." Hamer leaps from the tree cover. "Barrow!" he shouts. The point of view shifts to the men in the cab of the chicken truck, who "see ahead of them an incredible shooting match." In terror, "they jam on the brakes and leap out of the truck [and] run as fast as they can into the meadow, away from the trouble."[48]

Towne didn't dream up the birds, nor were they part of Penn's ecstatic, Kurosawa-inspired vision. The notion came instead from art director Dean Tavoularis. "As a prelude for the audience, I thought we could have all these birds fly out, like a premonition," he related to Jordan Mintzer for the Cinematheque Francaise. "I didn't tell Arthur about it, I told Warren. He liked it very much, and I was with him when he went up to Arthur and said: 'Dean has this idea with the birds coming out...'" Tavoularis remembered the director being unenthusiastic until Beatty improvised, "It's Russian—it's a very Russian kind of thing, like a Russian cinema touch.' I thought: *bravo to him*. And so Arthur said, 'Yeah, OK, let's do that.'"[49]

The art director's dramatic instincts resulted in one of *Bonnie and Clyde*'s most legend-making moments. Clyde and Bonnie turn to marvel at the flight of the birds, then, seeing a telltale rustling in the brush, turn back to each other for one last, passionate, agonizing look. Having sold the idea, Tavoularis immediately wondered, "*How the fuck am I going to do this?* . . . So I reached out to the prop department and told them to get me any kinds of birds—sparrows, finches, whatever." The effect would require several wire cages, each housing a dozen birds and concealed amid the brush, along with "a bunch of handlers to open them on cue because they all had to fly out at the same time." Tavoularis made sure to have enough birds, cages, and handlers available "for at least two takes, since something can always go wrong."[50]

Something did go wrong—nearly everything, in fact. And the birds proved to be the least of the problems.

Penn hadn't made things easier on himself by insisting that the makeup department rig Beatty with a detachable scalp piece that could be ripped away at the onset of the gunfire to duplicate the Zapruder footage of John F. Kennedy's assassination in Dallas. On the first take, the use of high-speed synchronized cameras in widely spaced positions made it impossible to properly "slate" the footage using the traditional striped clapper board essential to synchronize picture and sound in the editing room. "So I would signal Warren and he would squeeze the pear [in his hand] and that was the signal for the special effects guys to start firing.... We spent the whole first morning rigging it. And we get ready and it's tense, it's really tense around the set."[51]

Tavoularis's birds erupted on cue.

But Beatty froze.

"He squeezes the pear but he stands there watching all this happening around him," Penn said of the moment. "Faye is dying the death of the damned and everything was going on, and Warren hasn't moved. So that whole morning was gone."[52] The flub could only have worsened the costars' already fraying professional relationship. Beatty much later threw the blame on to the makeup department, claiming that the scalp piece had failed to tear off, spoiling the take. And so it went, day after excruciating day, two takes each day, from December 29, 1966, until January 3, 1967, mercifully interrupted by the New Year's holiday. Finally, after eight takes constituting thirty-two separate camera angles, Penn deemed himself satisfied.[53]

All that remained were the driving interiors. "If the movie had been shot just a couple of years later [with more portable equipment], there would have been no need of rear projection," Penn said of the process, long a Hollywood staple, in which a prop car, shaken by invisible stagehands, appears to move against a pre-filmed background. "But the terrain of the road was just too rough for those cameras and sound equipment."[54] Making a virtue out of necessity, Penn and cameraman Burnett Guffey gave these process shots a deliberately throwback look that reinforces the film's intertwining of old and new.

Jack Warner hadn't bothered to read the script of *Bonnie and Clyde* until it was too late. But on the film's last day of production, he made a display of his once-invincible authority. "There had been a long tradition at Warner Bros, with their B movies, that Jack Warner would give them a time frame and then come down to the set, no matter how far along they were, and say, 'Your picture wraps tonight,'" Penn recounted. "That became sort of legendary."[55] Penn discovered how alive the legend remained. "We finished *Bonnie and Clyde* on a Friday and were having a wrap party, but the photographs that open the movie—the stills —we were gonna do without the crew, in a studio off the lot. And we kept the costumes for them."[56]

Then Warner crashed the party.

"You wrap the movie tonight," he announced without prelude. "We thought he was kidding," Penn wrote. "Not at all. This was a last hurrah. 'You wrap the movie tonight.' We pointed out that meant the whole crew would still be on the clock, to be paid while they ate and drank. '*You wrap the movie tonight!*' the "Colonel" insisted. Production chief Walter MacEwen stood behind his boss, wearing what Penn called a chagrined "What can I do?" expression on his face. Faced with such intransigence, "That's what we did. It was beyond reason. We took the stills [with the whole crew hanging around]!" Penn said. "The cost was preposterous. The movie wrapped on that note of mordant tantrum."[57]

Bonnie and Clyde's production ordeal was over. But its problems were just beginning.

17

"MARTYRS"

> Political power grows out of the barrel of a gun.
> —Mao Zedong

Americans love their folk heroes. Especially folk heroes with guns. Nothing beats a good David and Goliath story. Scrappy individuals who rebel against an unjust system, often resorting to methods deemed illegal by corrupt authorities. Men (they are almost invariably men) "who are unwilling to accept the meek and passive role of the subject peasant," as Eric Hobsbawm writes in *Bandits*. "The stiff-necked and recalcitrant, the individual rebels ... the men who make themselves respected."[1] Such men are outsiders, men who refuse "to accept the normal roles of poverty, and [establish their] freedom by means of the only resources within reach of the poor—strength, bravery, cunning and determination."[2]

"Clyde Barrow and Bonnie Parker did not fight the state in any purposeful or direct sense, but one could imagine that they did as they survived each violent conflict with authority," noted crime historian Claire Bond Potter. Even when the press and eastern popular opinion turned against them after the killings of two highway patrolmen in Grapevine, Texas, "the murder of police officers was probably received ambivalently by the urban poor," Potter surmised, "since these were men who enforced evictions, arrested the jobless and homeless, and sent loved ones off to long prison terms for petty crimes."[3] *Bonnie and Clyde* makes this notion explicit in a scene immediately following the bloodshed in Dexfield Park, when a badly wounded Clyde, Bonnie, and C. W. Moss find shelter and sympathy in an Okie shantytown.

At first, the squatters are reticent to the point of hostility at the arrival of a gleaming white Ford V-8 pulling into their encampment. They relax their guard once it becomes clear who these strangers in their midst might be. As more and more people begin to circle the car, every wide-angle, deep-focus frame is meticulously composed to evoke memories of John Ford's adaptation of *The Grapes of Wrath*. A teenage girl in sackcloth presses her face against the V-8's rear window; a man in overalls reaches tentatively into the back seat to touch Clyde's hand; children gather curiously at the door ("Is that really Bonnie Parker?"); a woman at a campfire pours a tin of soup and hands it to C. W. while a bearded grandfather passes along a coat and blankets. "The people push in a bit closer for a last look,"[4] the script indicates. The V-8 glides out of the camp, dust blowing across the panorama of displaced people.

"In such a catastrophic economic situation like that of the Thirties . . . seeing young people like Bonnie and Clyde doing these kinds of things makes us feel sympathetic despite the violence," Penn said. "The film doesn't pass judgment on what they did, it only shows what happened at a certain moment in time when these two young people took initiative."[5] Clyde Barrow and Bonnie Parker accelerated the transition of horse-riding nineteenth-century outlaws into twentieth-century gangsters speeding across newly asphalted roads. Their spiritual heirs in the sixties made the David and Goliath story a weapon for societal and political upheaval, often upending the archetype.

Bonnie and Clyde's production and release coincided with the rise of the Black Panther Party of Self-Defense founded by Oakland, California, college students Huey Newton and Bobby Seale in October 1966—the same month that saw Penn's cast and crew in Red Oak, Texas, filming the code-breaking murder of a bank official. Inspired by the teachings of militant civil rights leader Malcolm X (assassinated in February 1965), Newton and Seale's express purpose was to combat law enforcement abuse of Oakland's poor and black population by any means necessary. In the preceding months, Bay Area police had been responsible for the fatal shootings of three black men in petty crime incidents; one had been shot seven times in the back for trespassing. White grand juries ruled such outrages to be justifiable homicides. "As one Panther said, 'It didn't make sense to report the police to the police.'"[6]

Instead, the Black Panthers chose to exercise their Second Amendment rights as American citizens. Utilizing the proceeds from on-campus sales of Chairman Mao Zedong's *Little Red Book* to "those leftists in Berkeley" ("Get your *Red Book!*" Seale hollered on the quad like a carnival barker), the founding Panthers began to amass an arsenal of legal weapons. "If you ever had a 'Freedom Now' feeling, you would have sure got it if you saw how we took off to buy some shotguns,"[7] Seale recorded in *Seize the Time*, his memoir of that era. Not just shotguns: .45-caliber and 9 mm pistols, a .357 Magnum, and a supply of M-1 semiautomatic rifles (precursor to today's shooter preference, the AR-15). "We bought up guns like a son of a bitch," Seale recalled with satisfaction. "The Party was in motion. Dollars for books to be able to get more guns."[8] For Huey Newton, firearms were "the only things the pigs will understand. The gun is the only thing that will free us—gain us our liberation."[9]

Weapons in hand, the Panthers began to shadow neighborhood patrols by Oakland police. At the time, California statutes carried no restrictions against the open carrying of loaded firearms provided they were legally purchased and visible. Confronted by rattled cops in February 1967 who demanded, "What are you going to do with [those guns]," Newton fired back, "What are you going to do with *your* gun?" Newton asserted his legal right to bear weapons and warned one officer, "If you draw that gun, I'll shoot back and blow your brains out." "You're—you're just turning the Constitution around,"[10] the officer stammered. "[Huey] is the baddest motherfucker in the world!"[11] Seale thought. "With weapons in our hand," Newton told him, "we were no longer their subject but their equals."[12]

Such defiance—which only a few months later would erupt into lethal armed confrontations—earned the Black Panthers a reputation as "the latest incarnation of the Depression-era gangsters and desperadoes who were misusing firearms to undermine order and stability in society,"[13] in the words of Second Amendment scholar Adam Winkler. The threat posed by the Panthers resulted in major shifts in firearms legislation on both the state and federal level—laws passed, as one historian noted, "not to control guns but to control blacks."[14]

The turnaround came on May 2, 1967, when Seale and other Panthers upstaged California governor Ronald Reagan's fried chicken lunch with visiting eighth graders on the west lawn of the Sacramento statehouse. "There were thirty brothers and sisters," Seale recounted. "Twenty of the brothers were armed."[15] To the gap-mouthed amazement of the students, the fully armed Panthers exited their cars and marched up the capitol steps, intending to disrupt a debate over a bill to prohibit the open carrying of weapons.

"What are you, a gun club?" one bystander asked.

"No, we're the Black Panther Party," Seale responded. "We're black people with guns. What about it?"[16]

News crews on the scene to cover Reagan's photo-op "saw the better story developing and rushed to follow the heavily armed Panthers."[17] The assault on the California Assembly unfolded in chaotic, even comical fashion. "Where in the hell's the Assembly? Anybody in here know where you go in and observe [them] making these laws?" Seale shouted. "Nobody said anything. Then somebody hollered out, 'It's upstairs on the next floor.'"[18] Incredible as it seems now, statehouse security made no effort to restrain the Panthers' advance—they'd been scrupulous in adhering to the letter of the existing law. Seale and his comrades proceeded as far as the assembly gallery before Democratic speaker Jesse Unruh ordered the entourage out, not on account of their weapons, but because of the trailing retinue of cameramen.

"Get [them] out of here, they're not supposed to be in here,"[19] Unruh shouted, more discombobulated by the media onslaught than the sight of

Eldridge Cleaver wearing a .357 Magnum sidearm. In their scrambling to follow the breaking story, reporters and TV news crews had completely missed Seale's manifesto on the capitol steps and asked him to repeat it for their evening editions. "Oakland's Black Panthers Wear Guns, Talk Revolution," the next day's *San Francisco Examiner* bannered, adding the alarming sub-headline, "It's All Legal!"[20] Outraged editorials across the state and country excoriated what they termed the "Sacramento Invasion." "Even the National Rifle Association, the most militant defender of the right to possess arms, should agree that [such] incidents . . . cannot be tolerated in modern society,"[21] bewailed the *Los Angeles Times*. The paper's law-and-order stance had enabled the reign of Los Angeles Police Department chief William Parker, whose administration became notorious for its open racism and brutality.

As it happened, the NRA *did* agree with the editorials—at least, it claimed to. So did Ronald Reagan. "There's no reason why on the street today a citizen should be carrying loaded weapons,"[22] the governor said at the signing ceremony for California Assembly Bill 1591 (known as the Mulford Act for the Republican assemblyman who introduced it), which prohibited the open carrying of a firearm without a permit. The bill became law just over a month after the Black Panthers' defiant demonstration in Sacramento. Guns, Reagan said, were "a ridiculous way to solve problems that have to be solved among people of good will."[23] (As president of the United States fifteen years later, Reagan adopted very different rhetoric. "It does my spirit good to be with people who never lose faith in America," he said in an address at the National Rifle Association's 1983 annual meeting in Phoenix, Arizona. The former actor earned a sustained standing ovation when he declared, "Guns don't make hard-core criminals. Hard core criminals use guns, and locking [them] up and throwing away the key is the best gun-control law we could ever have."[24])

The NRA appeared to adopt a conciliatory position in its qualified endorsement of the Gun Control Act of 1968, the first major piece of congressional firearms legislation since the 1934 National Firearms Act that the crimes of Clyde Barrow and Bonnie Parker had helped to establish. The association did "not necessarily approve of everything that goes 'Bang!'"[25] the NRA's *American Rifleman* informed its readers, referring specifically to the "Saturday Night Special" .38-caliber weapons targeted in the legislation— handguns responsible for what it called "urban crime," a dog whistle for minority violence. In its member mailings, the NRA laid out its agenda in Manichean terms. The Second Amendment was not the issue at hand. "The real issue over gun control," one pamphlet asserted, using language all the more chilling for its modern relevance, "is whether or not White Americans will be able to defend themselves against an uncontrollable, well-armed Black army as soon as the summer riots turn into all-out race war."[26]

As it did in 1934, the lobbying organization worked assiduously behind the scenes to gut the Gun Control Act of provisions it deemed unacceptable. President Lyndon B. Johnson had ascended to high office in the wake of an assassination carried out with a used 6.5 × 52 mm Carcano rifle advertised in the pages of *American Sportsman* and purchased for $19.95 (plus $1.50 for shipping). Johnson had two primary goals in seeking the legislation: a federal firearms registry and a universal licensing requirement for gun owners. The NRA found strong advocates in South Carolina Republican senator Strom Thurmond and Michigan Democratic representative John Dingell, whose efforts doomed both measures. Dingell served as an NRA board member and went so far as to equate the Gun Control Act with confiscations of firearms held by Jews and dissidents carried out by Adolf Hitler in the early delays of his chancellorship. Johnson signed but ultimately decried the watered-down measure, venting his anger at "the voices of a powerful lobby . . . that has prevailed for the moment in an election year."[27] Political scientist Robert Spitzer noted that while the 1968 act was "the most sweeping gun regulation enacted up to this time . . . its scope was modest and, as a consequence, its impact was minimal."[28]

In later interviews, Arthur Penn acknowledged that the Black Panthers were very much on his mind during the making of *Bonnie and Clyde*. "I personally believe that it's a worthwhile organization," he told interviewers from the French magazine *Positif* in 1971. "Unfortunately the press and the government have continually claimed the Black Power movement is made up of irresponsible and vicious people who want to take back from whites what they rightfully feel is theirs." The resulting backlash, Penn said, "gave the police the opportunity to commit real acts of violence."[29] The director noted how black audiences enthusiastically embraced the story of a couple of good-looking white outlaws.

"This is the way; that's the way to go, baby. Those cats [Clyde and Bonnie] were all right,"[30] a group of black viewers told Penn after one screening. "They really understood, because in a certain sense [they] have the same kind of attitude of 'I have nothing to lose' that was true during the Depression for Bonnie and Clyde. . . . It's rebellion, not riot."[31] Quoting educator and civil rights activist Robert Parris Moses, an early leader in the Student Non-Violent Coordinating Committee, Penn asked, "When the law becomes an outlaw and the law[man] is a criminal, who then decides what constitutes legality?"[32]

For an influential and growing group of senior law enforcement officers in the American West, the answer became simple. "The COUNTY SHERIFF is our nation's LAST LINE OF DEFENSE for the preservation [of] and return to fundamental and individual liberty," wrote former Graham County, Arizona sheriff Richard Mack, founder of the Constitutional Sheriffs and Peace Officers Association (CPSOA). Constitutional sheriffs—also known as "sagebrush" sheriffs—take their inspiration from the Reconstruction-era Posse Comitatus Act of 1878, a sop to the former Confederacy that prohibited federal authorities from the use of military intervention in local matters, essentially enabling the rise of Jim Crow laws. Because a county sheriff is elected rather than appointed and therefore not answerable to any federal agency, the reasoning goes, that officer has no obligation to enforce any law he may deem unjust. Had there been a constitutional sheriff in 1955 Montgomery, Alabama, Mack liked to claim, segregationist policies there may never have been enforced. "Today, that constitutional sheriff does the same for Rosa Parks the gun owner," he explained.[33]

Gun rights—more than that, the equation of firearms with American identity itself—became the Sagebrush Sheriffs' rallying cry. The Paonia, Colorado-based *High Country News* noted in February 2016 that "a majority of the region's three hundred rural sheriffs, Republicans and Democrats alike," shared Mack's "constitutionalist" views, signing on to protest any restrictions on firearms ownership—even in the wake of the horrific December 2012 Sandy Hook Elementary School shooting in Newtown, Connecticut, which left twenty children and six adults dead. "Sheriffs who did not join the charge were added to a list of 'red coats' on the CSPOA website," the magazine noted, "and risked the wrath of their gun-loving constituents."[34]

As Graham Country sheriff, Mack sued the administration of President Bill Clinton in 1994 over a provision in the Brady Act, passed one year earlier, that required local law enforcement to execute background checks on gun sales. Four years later, in a 5–4 ruling, the William Rehnquist Supreme Court sided with the sheriffs, agreeing that the measure was unconstitutional. Mack's defiance gained him Frank Hamer–like celebrity, making him "a folk hero to the then-burgeoning Patriot movement, which is centered [on] the belief that the federal government is taking away individual liberties."[35] In the printed legend of American history, guns and freedom have become synonymous. "The reason the 2nd Amendment exists is not for self-protection," instructs Paul Andrew Hutton, adding his own constitutionalist gloss on the scholarship. "It exists so that an armed populace can overthrow a tyrannical government—because [the founders had] just done it."[36]

"When guns are outlawed, I become an outlaw,"[37] declared one twenty-five-year-old Gulf War veteran outraged by the passage of the 1994 Public Safety and Recreational Firearms Use Protection Act (popularly known as the Federal Assault Weapons Ban), which narrowly restricted the possession and use of certain military-grade semiautomatic weapons. Timothy McVeigh went on: "The government is afraid of the guns people have, because they have to have control of the people all the time,'"[38] he maintained, stating his determination to "take pro-active steps to prevent the loss of all I hold dear."[39] McVeigh was later executed for perpetrating what remains the deadliest act of domestic terrorism on American soil: the April 19, 1995, bombing of the Alfred P. Murrah Federal Building in Oklahoma City, which claimed the lives of 168 people (nineteen of them children) and injured 680. "Once you take away the guns, you can do anything with the people."[40]

McVeigh made his remarks to a student reporter for Southern Methodist University's *Daily Campus*, who encountered him in April 1993 on the grounds of the Branch Davidian complex in Waco, Texas, where the US Department of Alcohol, Tobacco and Firearms (ATF) mounted a siege against millenarian cult leader David Koresh and his followers. News reports had drawn McVeigh as an observer to the site, where he set up a makeshift stand on the hood of his car selling bumper stickers reading FEAR THE GOVERNMENT THAT FEARS YOUR GUN and A MAN WITHOUT A GUN IS NOT A CITIZEN. McVeigh "regarded guns as instruments of freedom, and any attempt to regulate them, especially by the federal government, as a form of oppression,"[41] journalist Jeffrey Toobin writes in his book *Homegrown*.

Following weeks of unproductive negotiations, Koresh's pasteboard Mount Carmel complex fell to the combined forces of the ATF and the FBI in fiery circumstances that remain disputed but ended in the deaths of four federal agents and eight-two Branch Davidians, including twenty-eight children. McVeigh carried out his revenge bombing on the catastrophe's second anniversary, which grimly coincided with the bicentennial of the skirmish between American minutemen and British regulars on the commons in Lexington, Massachusetts, the "shot heard 'round the world" that set the American Revolution into motion.

Today, the confrontation between the forces of tyranny and liberty plays out across that most fabled of American landscapes:

The West.

"To understand the West is to understand America," says Montana author Betsy Gaines Quammen. "The myths are so foundational to the whole country."⁴² Chief among these is the iconic notion of the "cowboy." Often wrapped into the character of a gunslinger, the cowboy represents the individual unbound by authority and not beholden to the reigning social mores—a free spirit first, last and always. "It's ridiculous," Quammen scoffs. "The cowboy was a guy who lived paycheck to paycheck, he was probably drinking a lot, and he had to check his guns at the city limits. Yet something about being a cowboy is so important to Westerners and to Americans."⁴³

For Richard Slotkin, the dime-novel version of the outlaw/cowboy "becomes a hero who resists the forces of order, but in a way that affirms the basic values of American society."⁴⁴ Whatever the individual circumstances, the hero's proficiency with a pistol plays an outsize role. "Since the western offers itself as a myth of American origins," Slotkin wrote in *Gunfighter Nation*, "it implies that violence is an essential and necessary part of the process through which American society was established."⁴⁵

In April 2014, the deeply intertwined American preoccupations with liberty, outlaws, cowboys and guns found embodiment in a single, ready-for-his-close-up individual:

Cliven Bundy.

Dressed for media appearances in jeans, bolo tie, and broad-brimmed Stetson hat, Bundy spoke with pride in a slow, country drawl of his ancestors, part of the "Dixie Mission" of the Church of Jesus Christ of Latter-Day Saints dispatched by Mormon leader Brigham Young to plant cotton in the Great Basin region encompassing parts of today's Nevada, Arizona, and Utah. The effort proved a dismal failure, but with true Mormon grit the family held on despite the odds. Occupying a particularly godforsaken corner of the Mojave Desert outside present-day Mesquite, Nevada, Cliven made his living as a casaba melon farmer, utilizing seeds that had "been passed down through the family for over a hundred and forty years."⁴⁶ (To date, only one film has ever been made about a heroic melon farmer: 1974's *Mr. Majestyk*, written by no less than Elmore Leonard, starring Charles Bronson as an independent operator beset by the rhinestone-cowboy enforcers of a commercial conglomerate.)

The Bundys also grazed hundreds of heads of cattle on public lands under the administration of the federal Bureau of Land Management (BLM). Cliven's cows were part Hereford, part Angus, part Brahman, essentially "mutts, a mix bred to range the harsh Mojave without much assistance from humans."[47] Later court documents described the herd as "wild, mean and ornery,"[48] an apt description for Cliven himself. After accumulating more than one million dollars in unpaid grazing fees and associated fines—the result of thirteen years of federal negligence to reclaim the debt—in 2011 Bundy received a cease-and-desist order from the BLM with a notice of intent to confiscate his cows. He then issued a "Range War Emergency Notice and Demand for Protection" to Clark County sheriff Douglas Gillespie, invoking the Posse Comitatus Act.

Unfortunately for Cliven Bundy, he had appealed to the one local law enforcement officer *not* part of the Sagebrush Sheriffs movement—a "red coat." Forced to take his appeal to the courts, Bundy suffered another setback when the US District Court of Nevada declared him in violation of the law and allotted him forty-five days to remove his estimated thousand head of mean and ornery cattle from BLM land. An FBI safety assessment "determined that Bundy wasn't a threat."[49] That proved to be a dangerous—and potentially fatal—miscalculation. Mainstream media coverage of these "scofflaw would-be ranchers"[50] failed to recall the symbolic precedent set by the Bundys' outlaw antecedents. Like the depredations of Jesse James and Billy the Kid (and, yes, Clyde Barrow and Bonnie Parker), Bundy's intransigent defiance of federal authorities served to symbolize a final stand by rural America against an existential assault on a traditional American way of life.

The defining image of what came to be known as the "Battle of Bunkerville" on April 12, 2014, depicts a lone sniper lying prone on a Nevada Interstate 15 overpass, sighting down the barrel of his Saiga .223 semiautomatic rifle (a variant of the AR-15) toward BLM agents prepared to seize Bundy livestock herded through the arid wash below. The prospective shooter is Eric Parker, a member of the militia movement Idaho III%; the percentage derives from the erroneous notion that only 3 percent of American colonists took arms against Britain in the American Revolution. Parker had plenty of company that day. Stonewalled by Clark County sheriff Gillespie, Cliven Bundy and his sons Ryan and Ammon issued a call to arms over social media, resulting in what one firsthand observer called "Woodstock or Selma for 'Patriots'.... And like Woodstock, it was a badge of honor, especially if you got there early."[51] A notice posted outside the Bundy compound, clearly visible in YouTube footage of the standoff, reads "MILITIA SIGHN IN [sic]."

And they did. The Three-Percenters, the Praetorian Guard, the White Mountain Militia, and many others. "This is a protest by rural Americans, so dress accordingly," advised Oath Keepers founder Stewart Rhodes, destined to play a major role in an even more disruptive protest against presumed federal overreach.[52] Rhodes drew his followers from among the ranks of "that lonely guy . . . who all of a sudden could become a gangster or an outlaw, who could find community in being part of a militia," according to his estranged wife, Tasha Adams. Recruits were "prone to a hyper-masculinity. . . . The only value they see is providing and protecting." When "you can't cowboy your life," Adams said, "you're apt to be enticed by the myths Rhodes offered."[53]

At Bunkerville, Rhodes attempted to dissuade his coreligionists from the overt display of weapons but encouraged them to "BRING CAMERAS."[54] Constitutional sheriff spokesman Richard Mack advocated a considerably less guarded approach. "We were actually strategizing to put all the women up front," he told Fox News. "If [the BLM] were going to start shooting, it's going to be women that are going to be televised across the world getting shot by these rogue federal officers." Unlike Frank Hamer, Mack clearly had no qualms about someone "busting a cap into a woman."

"I would have put my own wife and daughters there, and I would have been screaming bloody murder to watch them die," Mack said, adding with proper Western chivalry, "I would've gone next."[55]

Thankfully, there were no martyrs in the shot-free two-hour standoff, which ended with the BLM rescinding the round up and retreating with state law enforcement. Chastened by Waco, federal authorities evinced no taste for gunfire, disappointing at least some of the assembled militia. "We locked [the feds] down," bridge sniper Ryan Payne maintained to the *Missoula Independent*. "We had counter sniper positions on their sniper positions.... So, it was a complete tactical superiority. If they made one wrong move, every single BLM agent in that camp would've died."[56] Bundy supporters cheered as confiscated cattle were released back on to public lands, led by a man on horseback brandishing a large American flag, a much-shared piece of viral video that recalls the jingoistic opening of John Ford's cavalry romance, *She Wore a Yellow Ribbon* (1949).

"If Cliven wasn't a rancher and [his stand was taken] for other things, I don't think he'd have nearly the following he did," says Betsy Gaines Quammen. "He is so appealing in terms of what resonates with the American psyche and what it means to be an American.... There is an enthusiasm for the Bundys that comes about because people feel they were taking back what they were entitled to. We see this recycled over and over again. It seduces people, whether they know they're being seduced or not."[57] As example, Quammen points to the success of the Taylor Sheridan–created neo-Western TV series *Yellowstone* (2018–2024), featuring Kevin Costner as the patriarch of a rapacious Montana ranching family violently fending off attempts to uproot their way of life.

The program became the most-watched new cable series in its debut season, averaging 5.1 million viewers per episode; by the end of *Yellowstone*'s five-season run, that number had swelled to more than twelve million and spurred a modern-day land rush. "People were sitting at home [during COVID-19] seeing these wide-open spaces and these cowboy narratives, and they were, like, 'I'm going there!' That goddamned show has really screwed up my state,"[58] Quammen says, recounting stories of people who bought property sight unseen as a result, inflating the real-estate market beyond the means of most locals.

Like all good movie-ready stories, Bunkerville inspired a sequel.

In January 2016, Cliven's son Ammon Bundy led an armed occupation of the BLM-maintained Malheur National Wildlife Refuge in Harney County, Oregon, outside the town of Burns—a federal preserve established by Theodore Roosevelt. The ostensible cause had been provided by the recent sentencing of father-and-son ranchers Dwight and Steven Hammond for two counts of arson on federal land. The Hammonds, who claimed they started the fires to prevent the encroachment of invasive plants on their property (but which other witnesses testified had been cover for illegal poaching of deer), had not requested any assistance. In fact, both father and son had waived their appeal and agreed to serve their mandatory five-year terms.

Mainstream news outlets derided the Malheur occupiers as "Y'all Qaeda," "Vanilla ISIS," "TaliBundy," "YeeHawdists" and "Yokel Haram," among other colorful nicknames. Occupiers styled themselves the Harney County Committee of Safety, "a governmental body established by the people in the absence of the ability of the existing government to provide for the needs of civilized society,"[59] spiritual descendants of the eighteenth-century American colonial Committees of Safety responsible for fomenting resistance to British oppression. Individual militia members patrolled the compound perimeter and frequently harassed Burns, Oregon, law enforcement; Harney County sheriff David Ward was yet another "red coat."

When one freelance reporter asked an anonymous participant "whether the protesters were endangering the Second Amendment by brandishing AR-15s," the answer was that "an occupation like this was the entire purpose of the Second Amendment."[60] Nevertheless, Stewart Rhodes and the Oath Keepers declined an invitation to participate. "We oppose what you have chosen to do," Rhodes politely informed Ammon Bundy, "because it is not in direct defense of anyone."[61]

In retrospect, "there was a tendency on the part of those watching Malheur that it was somewhat clownish," says Quammen. "There was a feeling of condescension: 'what a bunch of bozos.' Then when you looked at the aftermath to see what they had actually been up to...all of a sudden it doesn't feel so clownish."[62] Viewed as farce, the Malheur occupation was elevated to the level of tragedy when one of its most vocal adherents, fifty-four-year-old small-time Arizona rancher Robert LaVoy Finicum, was shot in a snow bank attempting to outrun an FBI roadblock en route to seek assistance for the occupation from Sagebrush Sheriff authorities in a neighboring county.

Finicum had been only an observer at Bunkerville two years before, but the experience of riding horseback in the wash transformed him. Formerly prompt in paying his minimal grazing fees, Finicum cut off all correspondence with the BLM and embarked on an outlaw trail; he called his ensuing website "One Cowboy's Stand for Freedom." At Malheur, Finicum secured the role of self-appointed spokesman for the occupation. "Do not worry how big Goliath is," he reassured one group of local ranchers. "You must be willing to put everything on the table—for freedom. If you are not willing to put everything on the table for freedom, are you worthy to have freedom?"[63] Finicum was regularly photographed on sentry duty at Malheur, sitting in a rocking chair, rifle on his lap. He projected an avuncular cowboy presence and spoke in quiet, measured terms. "I have no intention of spending any of my days in a concrete box,"[64] Finicum replied when asked what might happen to him should the confrontation turn violent.

But...

Before his participation in Malheur, Finicum self-published a novel, *Only by Blood and Suffering* (subtitle: *Regaining Lost Freedom*). A fiendishly entertaining survival yarn, obsessively footnoted with firearms forensics, the book tells the story of a Utah ranching family who close ranks in the wake of a devastating attack by unidentified foreign powers that reduces America to a state of anarchy and eventual totalitarian takeover. It reads like an average episode of *Yellowstone*—if that series' Dutton family were working-class ranchers confronted with dystopian disruption. "Atrocities greater than what is written in this book"—which includes incidents of cannibalism, rape, and lynching—"were personally experienced by my own family members,"

Finicum insisted in his introductory warning. "It would be unwise to cling to the belief that 'it won't ever get that bad.'"[65]

The story climaxes with its outgunned hero making his last stand against the federal agents who have been stalking him and his family. "My right wrist flicked and with a blur, my hand palmed the rosewood grips of my .44–40," Finicum wrote in the first-person narrative. "In a flash, the old pistol cleared the leather holster with the hammer eared back. By reflex, I pulled the trigger, the hammer fell, and the gun bucked in my hand."[66] Three bullets later, the federal agents lie dead. But Finicum's alter ego has been mortally wounded, and the novel ends in a dying man's fantasy of his old life restored.

LaVoy Finicum's real life ended on a remote stretch of Oregon State Highway 395 on January 26, 2016. "You back down or you kill me now," he shouted to federal agents through the window of his white pickup truck while attempting to evade a county-line roadblock. "Go ahead, put a bullet through me! I don't care! You want blood on your hands, get it done!"[67] Viewing FBI drone footage of the incident, along with cell phone video taken inside the truck, it's difficult not to conclude that Finicum had already chosen "death by cop." Unlike the cathartic ending of *Bonnie and Clyde*, his demise seems to occur in suspended time: cold, clinical, silent. Finicum, outside the car, reaches into his heavy jacket for a loaded 9 mm Ruger SR. Three shots from Oregon state police and FBI officers rip into the rancher's body. He collapses snow angel-like into the embankment. Stray shots shatter the pickup truck's back window.[68]

In death, LaVoy Finicum attained the cowboy folk hero status he sought but which had eluded him in life.

He had written his own legend.

18
"A SQUALID SHOOT-'EM-UP"

> It's a piece of shit.
> —Ben Kalmenson, Warner Bros. head of distribution

If I have to get up and pee during this, you'll know the movie stinks,"[1] Jack Warner notified Arthur Penn and Warren Beatty.

"The Colonel" made the pronouncement in his luxurious private screening room, right before taking a seat to view "the geniuses'" rough cut of *Bonnie and Clyde* in early June 1967. Original oil paintings by Renoir and Monet hung on one wall. Floor-to-ceiling bookshelves housed gray-green leather-clad scripts of every film ever made by Warner Bros. "We were still in first of the ten reels that constituted the movie when Jack arose and left the room," Penn remembered. He and Beatty shared a look, "uncertain whether or not to stop the projection." They didn't. "Jack returned to his seat. The [story] began to gain velocity, and we thought we had him." They didn't. "He was up again, peed, returned, watched, peed, returned, peed and the longest, most diuretic film in human memory came to an end."[2]

"How long was that movie?" Warner asked one of the retinue of minions who joined him for the screening.

"Two hours and fifteen minutes." Came the reply.

"Well, that's the longest fucking two hours and fifteen minutes I've ever spent,"[3] "The Colonel" grumbled about the four-piss picture.

"What the hell *was* that?" Warner demanded to know.

Silence ensued.

"... the hell was that?" he asked again.

At which point, Beatty launched into a spiel about the classic tradition of pre-Code Warner Bros. gangster films.

"So you see, Jack, this is, in a sense, an *homage* to those great films," Beatty concluded.

Another, longer silence. Then:

"[What] the fuck is an *homage?*"[4]

"It was the beginning of a very dark time," Penn recounted with a shudder. "Warner took in *Bonnie and Clyde* with the eyes, the ears, and the taste of an angry, cut-off man and hated everything about it."[5]

In part, Warner's verdict had been predetermined by that of his distribution chief, Ben Kalmenson, who attended a prior New York screening the director and producer had arranged for the studio's marketing team. One former colleague described Kalmenson as "a crotchety, opinionated guy, a real old distribution hand, basically a jumped-up film salesman."[6] Head of advertising Richard Lederer, an early champion of the script, thought the movie more than measured up to its early promise, "All of us most particularly impressed, particularly with the film's exciting style," he wrote in an interoffice memo. "Very fresh and original."[7] Kalmenson felt otherwise. "It's a piece of shit," he told Penn, an "infallible judgment" that "brought little pleasure to our hearts."[8] Kalmenson thought so little of the film "that when he handed out a schedule of Warner Bros.' summer releases to his distribution team, [*Bonnie and Clyde*] wasn't even listed."[9]

Tensions between the filmmakers and the studio had already reached a breaking point earlier that spring. What particularly galled Warner was Penn's insistence on cutting the picture in New York rather than in Los Angeles, out of view of old-guard editing department minder Rudy Fehr. "If Arthur Penn is going to sit around and take his time cutting this picture, it will go on and on for an indefinite period,"[10] Warner feared. Using head of production Walter MacEwen as an enforcer, "The Colonel" tried to circumvent the problem while the movie was still on location. "I know Arthur has been accustomed to painstakingly editing his pictures far from Hollywood," MacEwen wrote to Beatty at Dallas's North Park Motor Inn. "I do not necessarily disagree with this method from an artistic POV," he added, choosing his language carefully. "I do, however, feel that if [Arthur] tried it once in the healthy professional atmosphere which I believe exists in Burbank, he would prefer it."[11]

Penn had already experienced that "healthy professional atmosphere" on *The Left Handed Gun* and *The Chase*, and held his ground. In April 1967, as postproduction ground on, an exasperated MacEwen, again acting on Warner's orders, telegrammed Beatty at the Delmonico Hotel in New York to advise that the studio would no longer foot the bill for the cost of off-lot editing rooms. Studio lawyers also reminded the producer that, by contract, Warner Bros. retained the right to take over the film if a final version were not delivered by April 28, a deadline the picture seemed almost certain to miss. Beatty stood by his director, with good reason.

For the first time in his studio career, Arthur Penn had found an editor willing to work as a collaborator, not an adversary. Someone who shared his creative sensibility and willingness to break boundaries. A woman who would help Penn to refine his vision in an artistic partnership destined to endure across six films spanning more than a decade.

"I'm a gut editor,"[12] Dede Allen said of her approach. "You have to be able to figure out what a director wants, and very often they're not clear themselves, or they don't say it."[13]

Allen learned the craft under the generous tutelage of Robert Wise, who had cut Orson Welles's *Citizen Kane* (1941), among many credits in his own distinguished editorial career. With only a handful of industrial films in her résumé, at age thirty-five Allen earned her first feature editing credit on Wise's bracing, angry heist film *Odds Against Tomorrow* (1959). The director provided Allen with the most valuable lesson of her career. After assembling a sequence to Wise's precise instructions, she found herself taken aback by his "horrified" reaction.

"Let me tell you something, Dede," Wise counseled her. "I don't care what I tell you. If it's not working and it's not playing, don't show me, no matter what I told you. It's your job to make it work and play. Otherwise you're wasting my time and yours."[14]

Allen applied that knowledge to *America, America* (1963), Elia Kazan's sprawling, semi-autobiographical three-hour immigrant saga. Plagued by creative and production problems, the film emerged as Kazan's most daring and personal film, due in no small part to Allen's ability to find the narrative heart of a story. When Arthur Penn, unable to secure the services of *Miracle Worker* editor Aram Avakian, sought advice, Kazan unhesitatingly recommended Allen.

The director's rapport with his new editor took time to develop. "I'm basically as inarticulate as Arthur is articulate," Allen told Penn biographer Nat Segaloff. "He absolutely intimidated me."[15] They found common ground in their enthusiasm for the nonlinear techniques of the French New Wave and an understanding of actors. "We see things in a similar way," Penn said, adding, "Dede has characteristics I don't have. She's dogged and will stay with something until it's right."[16] He considered Allen "so much more than an editor. She's an artist who's an absolutely essential part of the creative process."[17]

"He really trusted Dede," says the director's son, Matthew. "He admired her artistry, he admired her intellect, he admired her ability."[18] By her own account, Allen visited the Texas location to assist Penn in the staging of the gun battles "because, logistically, the size of them was fairly big and [Arthur] wanted to make sure he didn't miss anything,"[19] but mostly remained in the confines of her East Coast cutting room, working long hours to assure that a first assembly would be ready a few weeks after the conclusion of principal photography. Typical of nearly all directors, "After filming I'm completely exhausted and wonder whether what I have in my hands is any good," Penn said. "I always slip away for a couple weeks to rest. The first thing I do when I get back is look at what [the editor] has done."[20]

In the past, Penn had found that "the first, put-together version [of a movie] is like a suicide note. It has no rhythm, it's flaccid, it's excessive—there *are* no 'emerging qualities.'"[21] Not so with Allen: "She'll put together a very careful first assembly and unlike most other editors is able to give some real coherence to the footage."[22] Penn observed that "unlike the people who edited *The Left Handed Gun* and *The Chase* . . . Dede always chooses the best takes."[23] It helped that Allen had a phenomenal visual memory for dailies and a talent for reading a director's body language. "I used to tell my assistants that if Arthur does something like clench his jaw in a certain way, just note what line that was on."[24]

There was certainly no shortage of footage to select from. "I shoot at a very high ratio—almost indecently high,"[25] Penn told the American Film Institute. "[Arthur] shoots a lot to give himself options in editing,"[26] Allen said approvingly. "I like to be able to develop the internal rhythms of a picture in the cutting room," Penn confirmed. "That's where I think it truly happens. In fact, the [film stock] is the cheapest part."[27]

Jack Warner disagreed. Warren Beatty recalled with chagrin how "The Colonel" had appeared unannounced in the studio screening room when he and Penn were viewing retakes of Clyde and Buck's reunion scene. "We did some over-the-shoulder shots.... We had about 125,000 takes ... and this was the one day, of all the god dammed days, that Jack Warner picked to come and see the rushes," Beatty said. "Hey, kid, Bogart wouldn't do that," Warner chided. "You think Errol Flynn would put up with that many takes? For Christ's sake, kid!"[28]

Penn's insistence on leaving himself options had gotten him unceremoniously fired by producer/star Burt Lancaster and replaced by John Frankenheimer back in 1963 on the World War II art heist action drama *The Train*, but the director made no apologies for his methods.[29] "What you feel on the set that given day in August is not at all what you're going to feel when you deposit that scene in the continuum of the narrative of the film on some day in September in a cutting room three thousand miles away," he said. "To assume that the rhythm you maintain on the set will carry over suggests that you have superb musicianship, or, as in my case, a recognition that you have a tin ear and had better get a lot of material."[30]

In cutting *Bonnie and Clyde*, Penn gave Allen one overarching note: "Arthur kept encouraging me, 'Let's go faster!'"[31] In retrospective tributes, virtually everyone involved in *Bonnie and Clyde*'s production—including

Penn—credited her with finding the visual equivalent to the script's staccato irreverence. "Dede created the tempo of this movie," co-screenwriter Robert Benton insisted. "The whole point of being Bonnie and Clyde was [that] they didn't know what was going to happen the next day. They didn't know if they were going to get away with it, get killed, thrown in jail, get rich—they didn't know. [Dede] captured that nervous energy."[32] Allen achieved this quality through a deliberately disruptive cutting style that emphasized momentum over continuity, the seamless shot-to-shot transitions that came to define the Hollywood Style. Penn had no interest in "continuity of action. I was interested in the idea of appetite . . . [Bonnie's] appetite for anything that would replace the tedium of her life. . . . And that set the tone for the whole film. . . . It was a metaphoric visual style."[33]

Allen and Penn establish their approach right from the outset, with the jarring opening close-up of Bonnie's mouth, followed by the restless series of shots that precede her first encounter with Clyde. Throughout the film, the editing creates a sense of uncertainty and nervous expectation—anticipation that, in the movie's final third, approaches dread. Sequences end in abrupt cuts to black. The action lurches from place to place minus the usual transitional niceties. While the Barrow Gang's actual odyssey lasted just under two years, events in the film appear to unfold in a matter of months—possibly weeks, even a few days. Like the characters themselves, the viewer is given little opportunity to think and reflect on their actions—only to *experience* them.

"*Bonnie and Clyde* had a pace and tempo that could never go the opposite way. It carried you along at such a pitch that you were never let down, even for a generation that [had been] raised in another tempo," Allen explained. Though her credits already included *The Hustler* (1961) and would go on to number *Slaughterhouse Five* (1972), *Dog Day Afternoon* (1975), and Warren Beatty's *Reds* (1981), she considered *Bonnie and Clyde* "the most finely honed picture I ever worked on."[34]

Most discussions of the picture's editing naturally focus on the concluding ambush. From the moment art director Dean Tavoularis's covey of birds take flight until the sustained, all-but-silent image of Frank Hamer and his posse approaching the bullet-riddled windshield, the sequence incorporates fifty-one separate shots in fifty-four seconds. "We ended up with so much good footage that we could have made a film about the massacre alone,"[35] Penn joked of the miles of film shot during the four-day marathon of violence. "It's been so over-written [about],"[36] mused Allen, who in fact left the cutting of that sequence to her assistant, Jerry Greenberg.

"I was appalled, I was just appalled," Penn confided to his biographer of his viewing of the first version of the massacre. "It crashed in flames. But then Dede—she's tremendous—at that point she says, 'Okay, now let's go to work. We know what to do.'"[37] Allen refuted Penn's claims entirely. "I made some slight changes," she said, emphasizing *slight*, "but basically Jerry edited it, and didn't get credit. They wouldn't give assistants credit [in those days] at Warner Bros."[38] (Greenberg soon became an acclaimed editor in his own right, most notably for his Oscar-winning work on William Friedkin's *The French Connection* [1970] and his collaboration on Francis Ford Coppola's *Apocalypse Now* [1979].)

When Penn and Allen finally emerged from the cutting room, the film's running time had been shaved from two hours and fifteen minutes to an hour and fifty-one minutes. Producer Beatty remained a constant presence throughout postproduction; his always-obsessive focus now shifted from the movie's look to its sound. "It [came] down to the speed of the motor . . . making sure [those old cars] would look like they'd go fast," recalled Allen, who considered Beatty "the best producer I ever had."[39] Beatty devoted special attention to the film's gun battles. Penn and Allen pulled many of the ballistic sound effects from George Stevens's *Shane* (1952), whose realistic violence shocked mid-century audiences. Like Stevens, Penn and Beatty insisted the gunshots be mixed and played at exceptionally high volume. A studio memo dispatched to exhibitors attempted to enforce adherence to the filmmakers' wishes, but projectionists routinely disregarded the instructions. At the movie's London premiere, the gunshots barely registered as "pops," prompting an alarmed Beatty to race "up eight flights of steps" to the projectionist's booth.

"I said, 'Hello. Is something wrong with the sound?' and he said proudly, 'Oh, no, no, I fixed it! I haven't had a picture this badly mixed since *Shane*.'"[40]

As specified in the script, Lester Flatt and Earl Scruggs's 1949 recording of "Foggy Mountain Breakdown" became *Bonnie and Clyde*'s signature theme music. The propulsive melody with its distinctive twang would become associated with the Depression, but Earl Scruggs didn't compose it until more than a decade after Clyde and Bonnie's deaths. Rural Texas listeners at the time tuned into the music of Bob Wills, Milton Brown, and other Western Swing artists. For incidental underscore, Warner Bros.' music department recommended "'pros' of the caliber of Alfred Newman, Alex North...Bronislau Kaper and Fred Steiner,"[41] but Penn and Beatty rejected the notion of a full orchestral score and instead selected *Bye, Bye Birdie*'s Charles Strouse, whose simply arranged, unobtrusive melodies in the film's intimate moments convey a sense of longing and loss.

None of this painstaking craftsmanship mattered to Jack Warner, and even less to distribution chief Ben Kalmenson. The picture's fate had already been written—or written off.

In Dede Allen's opinion, "I think that *Bonnie and Clyde* struck [Jack] Warner as slightly un-American. He wanted to be a good boy very badly. He wanted to prove he was the most American [mogul].[42] (Five years after the film's release, Warner's conduct on another film would validate Allen's assessment, when "The Colonel" ordered two numbers cut from the screen adaptation of the musical *1776* at the express request of President Richard M. Nixon.) For Kalmenson, patriotism had nothing to do with it. "He wanted to bury [the movie], and he did,"[43] one associate said. When advertising president Richard Lederer campaigned for a red-carpet premiere in one of Manhattan's most lucrative cinema districts, Kalmenson instead consigned the film to a couple of second-rate theaters in Times Square and Murray Hill, with the remainder of the film's cost to be recouped from Southern drive-ins.

"They figured the redneck kids would like the guns,"[44] Penn surmised.

Beatty then offered to buy back his movie from the studio at cost. "Well, that really perked up Warner's interest," he chuckled years later. "He wouldn't sell it to me, but they got a little more interested in it."⁴⁵ For the first time since the start of production, the producer reached out to screenwriters Newman and Benton, asking the former *Esquire* editors to fashion an advertising strategy with Lederer. Out of that came *Bonnie and Clyde*'s immortal tagline, entirely Lederer's invention:

THEY'RE YOUNG.

THEY'RE IN LOVE.

AND THEY KILL PEOPLE.

Beatty was bluffing. He had balls, but he didn't have the money to buy back his picture. In the end, he didn't have to. Something else saved *Bonnie and Clyde* from drive-in death.

War in the Middle East.

On June 5, 1967—only a few days after Penn and Beatty's disastrous screening in Jack Warner's private home theater—Israel launched a preemptive strike against the combined forces of Egypt, Syria, and Jordan, which had been amassing for a planned invasion. What became known as the Six-Day War ended on June 10 in a lopsided Israeli victory, expanding the barely twenty-year-old country's borders into the Sinai Peninsula, the West Bank of the Jordan river, and the Golan Heights, placing over one million Arabs under direct Israeli control and, for a time, securing the future of the Jewish state. Just as his studio in its thirties heyday had enthusiastically championed the New Deal and stood up to the Nazi menace in Europe by shuttering its German operations before any of its competitors, Jack Warner embraced the Israeli cause as a personal crusade.

"He raised more money for Israel than anyone else in town,"⁴⁶ Beatty told *Los Angeles Times* reporter Patrick Goldstein. With the Seven Arts takeover of the studio nearing completion, the soon-to-be-ex-mogul found reason to display some of his legendary combativeness, insisting that the studio retain the family name (it still does, despite the countless takeovers since) and summoning employees to a soundstage celebration of the Israeli victory. "In a defiant mood, the pugnacious old man wasn't about to sell off anything," wrote Mark Harris. "Even a movie he suspected was worthless."[47]

Warner Bros. scheduled *Bonnie and Clyde* for an August 13, 1967, opening—a Sunday, traditionally one of the slowest days at the box office and an indicator of the studio's lack of confidence in the film. The producer and director hoped to better their odds with an advance premiere at the Montreal Film Festival, being held in conjunction with the well-publicized Expo '67 world's fair. They showed an early cut to *TV Guide* and *Today Show* critic Judith Crist, who had served as chair of the 1966 Montreal international jury. Crist had been the only American reviewer to admit to liking Penn and Beatty's previous venture, *Mickey One* ("In fact, I loved it,"[48] she professed in her introduction to Beatty's biography). With *Bonnie and Clyde*, "it was passionate love at first sight."[49] Crist recommended the film to Montreal festival director Rock Demers, who proclaimed himself "absolutely astonished" and slotted the film for the festival's opening night on August 4. Demers remembered that when he told an unnamed Warner Bros. executive of his plans to "really create an event" out of the film, "the studio began to show more interest."[50]

Before consenting to the Montreal screening, Warner Bros. thought best to test the waters with a sneak preview of *Bonnie and Clyde* at the Village Theatre in Westwood, an upscale neighborhood adjacent to the University of California Los Angeles campus. Robert Towne was there. "When Warren's name came on the screen as producer, there was audible tittering and laughter in the audience, and then, 'Yeah, right,'" he remembered. "Not jeering, but a certain amount of incredulity at seeing his name as producer."[51] (Towne had already seen the film in a private screening, and confidently predicted it would gross $30 million.) No one was laughing at the film's conclusion. "It got applause, and people *screaming!*" vouched Michael J. Pollard, seeing

Bonnie and Clyde for the first time. "I never heard of that in a movie! It was phenomenal from the beginning."[52]

A second, private screening at the Directors Guild of America went even better. The invitees included George Stevens and William Wyler, both of whom Beatty had approached to direct the film, as well as Billy Wilder, Frank Sinatra, and onetime Bonnie contender Natalie Wood. "I had invited a lot of those people who I thought were my betters when I started in the movies," said Beatty, who treasured the three-minute standing ovation as his "best memory" of the film. "It was like watching the basketball go through the net the first time."[53] Penn sat out the screening at home in New York. "Wish you could have been [there] to take the bows to which you are entitled for a remarkable film," studio production chief MacEwen cabled. "The good word has spread all over town."[54]

Arthur Penn, Warren Beatty, and Faye Dunaway rode into the Montreal world premiere of *Bonnie and Clyde* in a fleet of vintage thirties-era automobiles. Two hours later, they basked in the glory of what festival director Demers claimed was a twenty-minute standing ovation. "I remember shaking hands with a very happy Warren at the beginning, and a very, *very* happy Warren at the end," he told biographer Suzanne Finstad. "It was a never-ending ovation."[55] At the next day's press conference, Penn took the opportunity to place the film in contemporary context. Assailed by questions about the picture's atonality, Penn fired back: "There is no question about it—the character of humor in violence is an immediate and constant correlative. . . . The killings get less impersonal and, consequently, less funny." Calling himself "a coward," Penn intimated that his "pacifist character or nature perhaps makes me more acutely aware of violence as practiced among human beings, and it somehow interests me more. I find myself drawn to demonstrating it—to dealing with it."[56]

As the press conference wore on, Penn dug even deeper into the theme. "We were trying to distinguish between the rigid morality which could very well render someone impotent at the private level," he maintained, "while at the same time he could exceed all limits of external morality and still feel at one with himself."[57] Guns made all the difference. "It seems to me not too uncharacteristic of things that are visible in ... the United States today: a churchgoing, highly moralistic, highly puritanical society, which has integrated and made a part of itself a kind of violence against other human beings which, viewed from the outside, seems absolutely intolerable."[58]

At least one person at the press conference took umbrage—not only at Penn's remarks, but at everything *Bonnie and Clyde* represented. "Hollywood moviemakers seem to have a knack of putting the worst foot forward at international film festivals," New York Times film critic Bosley Crowther wrote in an August 5 dispatch. "Now they've done it again."[59]

As (bad) luck would have it, the venerable Crowther—the éminence grise of New York film critics, thus by extension of *all* American critics—was the only US film journalist present in Montreal. Warner Bros. had embargoed any reviews until the film's official American opening the following week, but Crowther's ire could not be contained. Calling *Bonnie and Clyde* a "slap-happy color film charade" that "whips through the saga of the cheapjack bandits as though it were funny instead of sordid and grim," he noted that "some more sober visitors from the United States were wagging their heads in dismay that so callous and callow a film should represent their country in these critical times."[60]

"*This was during the Vietnam war!*" Penn raged a half century later. "What's the excess? Oh, in the *movies* you shouldn't; but at *home* you can live with it! Out on the street you can live with it, but at home we don't talk about the war! It was crazy."[61]

Crowther's outrage extended beyond the film and its makers to those brazen enough to find the film enjoyable. As one observer later reflected, Crowther didn't just pan the film—he panned the *audience*. "Was the ... reaction a true expression of appreciation for the film or ... a sort of rocking along with a form of camp?"[62] he fulminated. In his official August 14 *New York Times* review, Crowther denounced *Bonnie and Clyde* as a "ridiculous, camp-tinctured travest[y] of the kind of people these desperados were" that "might be passed off as candidly commercial movie comedy, nothing more, if the film weren't reddened with blotches of violence of the most grisly sort.... It leaves an astonished critic wondering just what purpose Mr. Penn and Mr. Beatty think they serve with this antique, sentimental claptrap."[63]

Despite his opposition to censorship, advocacy for socially conscious cinema, and early embrace of Italian neo-realists Roberto Rossellini and Vittorio De Sica as well as the work of Ingmar Berman, Crowther remained a deeply conservative moralist of the kind Penn called out in Montreal. His displeasure at on-screen violence dated back to the forties, with tongue-clucking reviews of *The Killers* (1946) and *White Heat* (1949), among the films he thought would provoke "unhealthy stimulation"[64] in moviegoers. Before seeing *Bonnie and Clyde*, Crowther decried Robert Aldrich's *The Dirty Dozen*, a counterculture-tinged World War II action drama whose cast included Donald Sutherland as a proto-hippie in GI uniform, calling it "a studied indulgence of sadism that is morbid and disgusting beyond words."[65]

The critic included *Dirty Dozen* on his list of "Movies to Kill People By," calling them "as socially decadent and dangerous as LSD."[66] (Also on the list: Roger Corman's *The St. Valentine's Day Massacre*, which had in the end preceded Penn's film into theaters, along with the first two entries in Sergio Leone's "Dollars" trilogy of Clint Eastwood Westerns, *A Fistful of Dollars* [1964] and *For a Few Dollars More* [1965], which United Artists had released in tandem to phenomenal success in the early spring of 1967.) "Something is happening in movies that has me alarmed and disturbed," the July 7 column began. "Moviemakers and moviegoers are agreeing that killing is fun."[67] Penn's provocative comments at *Bonnie and Clyde*'s press conference only hardened the critic's opinion.

"He sort of warned me that he was going to attack it," Penn said, "and I thought, well, here it comes."[68] The director also thought: "It was the best advertising we could have had."[69]

Except—it wasn't.

Far from being encouraged by the rapturous Montreal reception of *Bonnie and Clyde*, Warner Bros. instead retrenched in the wake of Crowther's *New York Times* review. According to one account, Kalmenson (who likely found validation for his own dismissive opinion) went so far as to consider pulling the film's New York booking altogether and cutting the studio's losses. Beatty made a successful pitch for use of the revamped "They Kill People" ad campaign, and the release—such as it was—proceeded as planned. *Bonnie and Clyde* opened as scheduled on Sunday, August 13, 1967, at the Forum and Murray Hill theaters in New York City; a third screen, the B-circuit Vogue Theater in Los Angeles, followed a week later. Defying Warner Bros.' low expectations, by October the film would rank as the third-highest grossing film in America.

Bonnie and Clyde "was actually making pretty good money," Dunaway wrote in her autobiography, but "still, Warner [Bros.] was putting almost no money into publicizing it."[70] Already at work with Steve McQueen on her next film, *The Thomas Crown Affair*—a role she had landed because of Penn and Allen's sharing of cut footage with her new director Norman Jewison—Dunaway missed the one and only scheduled red-carpet event: the movie's southwest premiere on September 13—at the Campus Theater in Denton, Texas.

As reported by the *Pilot Point Post-Signal*, a "gigantic and luxurious red carpet"[71] was laid down in front of the theater, whose box office bore mock bullet holes and the words "BONNIE AND CLYDE WAS HERE" in garish red lettering. A photograph of the preliminaries finds a decidedly disgruntled Beatty, dressed in black pants and jacket with an open-necked white shirt, standing in a Holiday Inn parking lot with Estelle Parsons, Michael J. Pollard, and hotel manager Jim Poteet and his wife (identified in the caption as "Mrs. Jim Poteet"). Manifesting Beatty's mood, the sky behind them is overcast, the pavement glistens with recent rain. Pollard wears a gray turtleneck sweater and cap along with black sunglasses, looking as though he's about to rob the hotel cash register.

The stars embarked on a school bus tour of "the scenes of their crimes" in the surrounding townships, where students dismissed from classes for "Bonnie and Clyde Day" plied them with doughnuts and coffee and the local chamber of commerce handed out special-edition newspapers and "Bonnie Parker Cigars." Celebrities and citizens alike posed with Tommy gun-wielding Barrow Gang mannequins. The *Denton Record Chronicle* reported that a Warner Bros. executive who accompanied the cast "climbed on a horse and showed . . . residents that New Yorkers can ride, too!"[72] (Sadly, no footage is known to exist.) Beatty spoke at a "drama seminar" and struggled to discuss the controversy surrounding the movie's glamorization of criminals. "Violence is a matter within an individual," he told the assembled students. "The Depression brought on Bonnie and Clyde's spree. They had an excuse to strike out at the Establishment and they grabbed it." When the school bell rang mid-seminar, the auditorium emptied out. "Was it something I said?"[73] Beatty joked.

Thirteen hundred people, including many who appeared as extras in the film, attended the screening, preceded by a parade and a down-home, $2.50-a-plate Texas barbecue. The Denton audience erupted in whoops, cheers, and thunderous applause at the sight of familiar places and faces, with particular acclaim reserved for Pilot Point resident Joe Spratt, the farmer who promises to lay flowers on Bonnie and Clyde's grave. For all the hometown enthusiasm, a "subdued audience" filed out of the Campus Theater that night, wrote Keith Shelton in the *Denton Record Chronicle*. "Most [viewers] were in agreement that it was not your ordinary crime movie."

Unlike his East Coast counterparts, Shelton credited *Bonnie and Clyde* as "real violence and death . . . not 'bang, bang, you're dead.'"[74] University of North Texas *Campus Chat* critic Pat Bryan celebrated the film as "real, human and true-to-life, unlike other modern Hollywood productions."[75] *Bonnie and Clyde* played five sold-out shows a day in Denton (at 1:05, 3:15, 5:20, 7:30, and 9:30 p.m.) but Warner Bros. booked it for only two weeks. "*Dr. Zhivago* Coming Next" read the studio's local newspaper ads, heralding the road-show engagement of a two-year-old film that represented a last-gasp pinnacle of the classic Hollywood filmmaking Penn and Beatty were rebelling against.

Back in New York, younger audiences had begun to discover the film. "The kids knew from each other . . . that there was this movie," Penn told biographer Segaloff. "And they began to line up. Then the exhibitors began to say, 'Hey, gimme back that movie that you guys took out of here after three days.'"[76] For Ben Kalmenson and Warner Bros.' distribution team, however, the continuing onslaught of negative press proved decisive.

If anything, *Newsweek* critic Joseph Morgenstern outdid Bosley Crowther in his outrage. "In *Bonnie and Clyde*," he wrote, "some of the most gruesome carnage since Verdun is accompanied by some of the most gleeful fiddling since the Grand Old Opry. The effect is ear-catching, to say the least. For those who find killing less than hilarious, the effect is almost stomach-churning."[77] It probably didn't help Morgenstern's temperament that Beatty sat behind him in Warner Bros.' Fifth Avenue screening room, attempting to peer over his notes. "Try to imagine *In Cold Blood* being played as a William Inge comedy, including an attempt at lyricism consisting of a slow-motion sequence in which the inert bodies of Bonnie and Clyde, being perforated by the law's lead, rise and fall and pitch and turn with something of the same grace that Vittorio Mussolini must have seen in Ethiopia when he compared bomb bursts to rose petals."[78]

See it again, insisted Morgenstern's wife, the actress Piper Laurie.

With an audience.

"Last week this magazine said that *Bonnie and Clyde* . . . turns into a 'squalid shoot-'em-up for the moron' trade because it does not know what to make of its own violence," Morgenstern wrote in the next edition of *Newsweek*. "I am sorry to say I consider that review grossly unfair and regrettably inaccurate. I am sorrier to say I wrote it."[79] Seeing the film a second time, with a paying audience whose reaction left him scrambling for a pen with "this cold sweat on the back of my neck,"[80] Morgenstern realized "I had become so surfeited and preoccupied by violence in daily life that my reaction was as excessive as the stimulus." Precisely because "*Bonnie and Clyde* combines gratuitous crudities with scene after scene of dazzling artistry . . . it is an ideal laboratory for the study of violence, a subject in which we are all matriculating these days."[81]

"I got it wrong," Morgenstern later said of his initial pan. "I was not ready for the violence and kind of shrank from it."[82]

"Can you picture it? The guy's honest enough to change his mind," Beatty queried Roger Ebert, then beginning his career as a film critic for the *Chicago Sun-Times*. Ebert's had been one of the relatively few voices raised in support of *Bonnie and Clyde*, which he declared "a masterpiece." A handful of Cassandras had joined Ebert in their contrary opinions: Judith Crist, who had been responsible for the Montreal premiere, in *Vogue*; Penelope Gilliatt in the *New Yorker*; Gene Shalit in *Ladies' Home Journal*; and William Wolf in *Cue* had also been strong advocates. So had, of all places, the *National Catholic Reporter*, which turned the general outrage back on itself, writing, "There is a grim irony in hearing critics scream bloody murder when finally presented with an approximation of the genuine article. . . . Where were their outcries when a whole society was being marinated in violence?"[83]

Business for *Bonnie and Clyde* remained steady in the few cities and theaters where the film was actually playing. "Lines began to appear at the box office [in New York]," Penn told Mark Harris for *Pictures at a Revolution*. "All these wonderful-looking kids of what was beginning to be the 1960s, probably smoking dope while they were waiting to get in."[84]

Gradually, grudgingly, Warner Bros. began to add other single-screen runs in Chicago, Denver, Baltimore, and Washington, DC, where results mirrored those of New York and Los Angeles. But the studio resisted Penn and Beatty's exhortations to embark on a general US release. Kalmenson had convinced himself the movie had no "legs," and proved it in a self-fulfilling saturation run in the Midwest. The distributor booked *Bonnie and Clyde* into thirty-five theaters in Kansas City, Omaha, and surrounding areas, but provided no promotional support. When the inevitably lackluster returns came in, Kalmenson found the justification he needed to ensure the film would not be seen in wide release outside New York. On October 10, 1967—barely three months into its initial release—Warner Bros. stopped booking *Bonnie and Clyde* altogether.

Lamented Penn: "It started out—and it was dead."[85]

19

"HE'S NOTHING BUT A LITTLE-BITTY FART"

> They're dead now. They should let 'em rest.
> But they don't.
> —Marie Barrow

Death did wonders to restore Clyde Barrow and Bonnie Parker's reputation.

"I've met people who have gotten married on the site where [Clyde and Bonnie] were ambushed and killed," says Barrow Gang historian John Neal Phillips, shaking his head. "People who go to the graves and leave long involved letters—as if Bonnie and Clyde are going to read them. People who leave toy guns and poker hands and spent cartridges. I often wonder what somebody like Clyde Barrow would say if he was standing off to side of the ambush site watching people exchange vows 'until death do us part.'"[1]

"There is no explaining it, but curiosity to see a famous desperado laid out makes people crazy as loons,"[2] wrote Dallas deputy Ted Hinton in his account of the ambush and its aftermath. Moments following the fatal encounter, Hinton set down his BAR and picked up a sixteen-millimeter movie camera to record the first images of the couple's bullet-riddled bodies inside what soon came to be known as the "Death Car." Off-camera, lawmen hunted for souvenirs. Texas prisons general manager Lee Simmons had given Frank Hamer his pick of any booty. Hamer claimed the formidable arsenal of weapons and ammunition, along with a box of fishing tackle. Hinton's partner Bob Alcorn snatched up Clyde's saxophone (which he later returned to the Barrow family), while Bienville Parish sheriff Henderson Jordan allegedly absconded with a suitcase full of cash that went unrecorded in the official inventory.[3]

Hamer detailed Alcorn and ex-Texas Ranger Maney Gault to stand guard over the car and corpses while he and the others drove to a filling station in Gibsland, the nearest town, to make their official reports.

"Well, we got them," Hamer informed Simmons with characteristic loquaciousness. He added: "They died with guns in their hands."

The posse's calls were overheard by the party-line telephone operator, as well as a handful of Coca-Cola-drinking Gibsland loafers, who piled into their automobiles and trailed the lawmen back to the ambush site along Highway 154. By the time a tow truck arrived carrying Bienville Parish coroner J. L. Wade, "a great crowd was already gathered," Hinton remembered. "People were on their hands and knees gathering up spent shell casings and digging with pocketknives to retrieve bullets embedded in trees. It was getting to be a strange kind of carnival atmosphere."[4] The atmosphere only grew more macabre as curiosity seekers descended in droves.

People milled around the death car. Someone threw open the door on Bonnie's side. "Shut that door!" one officer shouted. The man complied—"accidentally slamming the door on Bonnie's already mutilated right hand. The latch failed to hold, causing the man to slam the door again and again." Finally, another onlooker "stepped over to the car and lifted Bonnie's [mangled] wrist into her lap."[5] One man had to be physically restrained from cutting off Clyde's ear with a pair of scissors. Others got away with locks of Bonnie's hair.

What was later estimated to be a two-hundred-car convoy accompanied the posse and tow truck to the parish seat of Acadia, where coroner Wade could conduct a more detailed autopsy. (His preliminary findings: "gunshot wounds."[6]) As the entourage passed through Gibsland, the tow truck either broke down or was deliberately stopped by Sheriff Jordan outside the town's public school, whose pupils happened to be in recess. "The sheriff wanted to show the gathering students what ultimately becomes of legendary outlaws like Clyde Barrow and Bonnie Parker,"[7] former Barrow Gang member Ralph

Fults insisted to John Neal Phillips. Then twelve-year-old Polly Palmer remembered how she hopped onto the running board of the car and peered through the passenger window. "I wish I had never gone out to that car," she shuddered. Clyde's body had been covered by what local press referred to as an "Indian blanket," but Bonnie's remained exposed. Gunfire had nearly severed her upper lip from her mouth. "It still bothers me,"[8] Palmer said sixty years after the event.

Normally a town of three thousand residents, Arcadia had swelled to a population of sixteen thousand by the time the delayed procession arrived outside Conger's Furniture Store, whose storeroom doubled as a funeral parlor. Undertaker "Boots" Bailey and his assistants were hard-pressed to fight the crowd as they struggled to load Clyde's and Bonnie's bodies onto gurneys. "God damn!" one onlooker exclaimed. "He's nothing but a little-bitty fart!"[9] The crowd broke the furniture store's windows and demolished its stock in its attempt to gain access to the autopsy. Bonnie's mother lamented that "the undertaker said he had not been able to embalm the bodies properly" and was only able to "keep [the crowd] back by squirting embalming fluid on them." She also noted "officers of the law offered no aid in controlling the mobs."[10] (One tantalizing account suggests that the mortician in question was none other than Dillard Darby, kidnapped by Clyde and Bonnie a year before and immortalized by Gene Wilder in *Bonnie and Clyde*.[11])

Allowed into the coroner's inquest, local photographer King Murphy captured graphic images of the couple's shot-up naked bodies with their executioners looming large behind them in coats and ties. Murphy and his wife turned their bathtub into a developing tank to keep up with the escalating demand. Prints sold at five dollars to individuals—and fifty dollars to the press, whose ranks swelled as news of Clyde's and Bonnie's "capture" spread. Hysteria overtook Arcadia's main street, its fury palpable in photographs and newsreels taken at the time. One visiting reporter recounted that "it was impossible to purchase a cold drink... and storekeepers and stand operators were calling frantically on neighboring towns to send supplies to meet the unprecedented demand." Beer prices shot up from fifteen to twenty-five cents a bottle, cigarettes to twenty cents a package, while "it was almost impossible to get a sandwich, two slices of bread and a small piece of ham, at any price."[12]

Both Cumie Barrow and Emma Parker learned of their children's death via telephone calls from reporters. Neither could bear to make the journey to Louisiana. Instead, Clyde's father Henry and Bonnie's brother Buster arrived to claim the bodies. "Bonnie and Clyde had been dead thirteen hours, yet the dried blood had never been washed from their bodies," Emma later said, "and they still lay, unclothed, in the undertaker's parlor."[13] Buster found what was left of Conger's Furniture Store looking "as if a herd of cattle had stampeded through it. . . . [C]igarette butts were ground into the rugs."[14] Ghouls lurked everywhere. Even before Clyde's badly embalmed body made its way back to West Dallas, an unnamed showman had offered the Barrow family fifty thousand dollars for their son's corpse, intending to "mummify the body and put it on tour with a traveling tent show."[15] The Barrows never condescended to respond.

In her final poem, "The End of the Line," Bonnie had written that she and Clyde would "go down together; they'll bury them side by side." But her wish was not to be. "[Clyde] had her for two years. Look what it's got her," Emma Parker reportedly said. "He's not going to have her anymore. She's mine now."[16] With an attention to appearances her daughter would have appreciated, Emma had Bonnie dressed in "the loveliest blue silk negligee that money could buy. It matched her blue eyes."[17] Bonnie's hair was marcelled (as the movie's costume designer Theadora Van Runkle had originally desired for Faye Dunaway) and her nails polished to a fine sheen. Lilacs from an anonymous admirer were placed in her hands, and a white veil was drawn over her face to mask her facial disfigurement.

"I didn't look at Bonnie till she was in her casket," Emma said, "and even then, it was a terrible shock because of what the bullets had done to her little red mouth."[18]

For his interment, Clyde's family chose a "crisp, light grey suit and matching tie."[19] The Barrows had wished to bury their son wearing his cherished wristwatch and diamond stick pin, both recovered by the Arcadia undertaker but missing from the personal belongings Henry Barrow finally received after hours of waiting; a pearl stickpin served instead. If anything, the outlaw couple's viewings at cross-town funeral parlors and separate funerals outdid the sorry spectacle of Arcadia. "It was a Roman holiday," one observer said in disgust. "Hot dog stands were set up; soda pop vendors arrived to serve those who waited to view all that was left of the south[west]'s most noted desperadoes."[20]

Ten thousand people crowded outside the Sparkman-Holtz-Brand Funeral Home to attend what one moralistic newsreel narrator called "the homecoming of Clyde Barrow." Film footage shows an orderly crowd, dressed in their best Sunday clothes on a Thursday afternoon, making their way along a heavily policed, roped-off line "for a fleeting glimpse of the boy who had wrought such death and destruction. Everyone wanted to see how such a bad boy looked in death."[21] More than a few smiled for the camera in genuine excitement. The collective mood deteriorated as the day went on. Historian John Neal Phillips painted a vivid picture of a mob "tearing shrubs out of the ground and heaving them through the air" and the "hoots and catcalls" of the people moving past "an indignant Henry Barrow and the inexpensive broadcloth-lined casket containing his infamous son."

"I'm glad he's dead!" exclaimed one drunk, prompting Clyde's father to clear the room and order the doors closed. "The remaining lines grudgingly dispersed and trudged homeward," Phillips wrote, "urged on by a growing number of police sentries."[22]

Onlookers were more well-behaved at the McKamy-Campbell Funeral Home three miles away, where an estimated twenty thousand people—twice the number to attend Clyde's viewing—filed past the bier of what the same newsreel narrator eulogized as "the worst woman bandit since Belle Starr."[23] Bonnie's funeral two days later was more chaotic. "The presence of newsreel cameramen and still photographers prompted the immediate family to witness the graveside ceremony from the sanctuary of the limousine,"[24] according to Phillips. Dallas newsboys contributed an enormous floral wreath in appreciation of the half-million papers they'd sold in the wake of her death. Clyde, too, had been bequeathed a send-off bouquet at his funeral, this one dropped from a private plane by local Dallas kingpin Benny Binion, destined to become a Las Vegas legend. Spectators tore the wreath to shreds as they fell over one another fighting for keepsakes.

Less than a week after they had been lowered into their final resting places, a two-reel short titled *The Retribution of Clyde Barrow and Bonnie Parker* opened at Dallas's Majestic Theatre (three decades later to be the site of *Bonnie and Clyde*'s one and only dailies screening). A fly-by-night outfit billing itself the Jamieson Film Co. obtained the rights to Hinton's sixteen-millimeter death car footage and made it the centerpiece of a "comprehensive" account of the couple's criminal career. Hastily staged scenes depict a nattily dressed, just-pardoned Clyde emerging from his cell in the Huntsville prison; his meeting with Bonnie outside a Dallas café, and their (discredited) joint gunning down of highway patrolmen E. B. Wheeler and H. D. Murphy outside Grapevine, Texas; Bonnie's double is shown racing to Wheeler's prone body, rolling him over with her foot, and firing into his head with a semiautomatic rifle. Hinton and Alcorn play themselves in a re-created prelude to the ambush, standing in for the full seven-man posse. "Let him have it!" Alcorn shouts as he and Hinton rise out of the brush and fire their rifles.

"Clyde Barrow's mania—his guns!" the narrator exclaims over the staggering inventory of firearms found inside the car. "At night he would clean, oil and polish them, and for each one of them he had a pet name." (All true.) As lawmen's hands finger the couple's personal effects, including "many of the feminine aids to beauty," the tone shifts. "Vanity, thy name is woman!" the narrator intones. "Really a pretty girl, Bonnie was found at the time of her death to have had a new permanent wave. Her fingernails were clean and prettily manicured, as were Clyde's, which was probably due to Bonnie's influence. This would indicate," the narration suggests, "that aside from her association with Clyde during their murderous moments, she was a perfectly normal girl in many respects." Following an account of the couple's funerals, the film concludes with the obvious message: "Truly, crime does not pay."[25]

"The Most Sensational Film Ever Made!" the ads promised. At least one moviegoer agreed: Clyde's mother, Cumie Barrow. "You can't do that to my boy!" she shouted in mid-screening that opening week, charging down the main aisle toward the screen. Theatre staff removed her from the auditorium, but Cumie's tirade continued in the lobby, where she ripped away posters and a display photograph of Clyde and Bonnie. Taken to police headquarters, Cumie offered a grudging apology and was released. The following day, she teamed up with Bonnie's mother Emma to file an injunction against the Jamieson Film Company to prevent future showings of the film. The suit alleged *The Retribution of Clyde Barrow and Bonnie Parker* caused "humiliation and embarrassment to family members who had never been in trouble."[26] The movie's brief run ended shortly thereafter.

Next came *True Detective Mysteries*. The pulp magazine, noted for its lurid cover illustrations and eye-popping headlines, launched a six-part serial titled "The Inside Story of 'Bonnie' Parker and the Bloody Barrows" in its June 1934 issue. Ostensibly the work of Joplin, Missouri chief of detectives Ed Portley "as told to C.F. Waers," with a final chapter credited to none other than Bienville Parish sheriff Henderson Jordan, the serial had been in the works for some time but was held back from publication until news of Clyde and Bonnie's capture or death could ensure big sales numbers. Over six installments from June through November, insatiable readers thrilled to a story of depredation and deviancy designed to reflect the nation's shifting attitudes in the wake of FDR's "New Deal for Crime." The serial wasted no words of sympathy for its subjects. "Clyde with his small size, his weak chin, his soft hazel eyes and wavy brown hair seemed effeminate," Waers wrote. "In contrast, [Bonnie] liked to wear masculine clothes, her mouth was hard, her hair a striking yellow, and she habitually smoked big black cigars."[27]

The *True Detective* articles set the template of the Barrow Gang as trigger-happy degenerates that would persist for the next thirty years. In his 1963 book *Dillinger Days*—read by *Bonnie and Clyde* screenwriters David Newman and Robert Benton—John Toland recycled the pulp-magazine narrative, lifting virtually unchanged character descriptions and even whole purple-prose accounts of the gang's run-ins with law enforcement. Clyde and Bonnie were a "strange pair," Toland maintained. As in the *True Detective* series, Clyde's "weak chin" and "soft hazel eyes" again contribute to his "effeminate appearance" (as do the "pixie ears"), while Bonnie's "striking yellow hair" sets off her "hard, determined mouth." Stating outright what *True Detective* left its readers to suspect for themselves, Clyde harbors "homosexual tendencies" to match Bonnie's "sexual aberrations."[28]

Long before Benton and Newman embarked on their revisionism, the Barrow and Parker families sought to establish a counternarrative. Bonnie, of course, had been the original mythmaker, with her "End of the Line" ballad, reprinted in newspapers across America as "The Story of Bonnie and Clyde." According to crime historian Claire Bond Potter, shortly before her death Bonnie may have been at work on a longer prose account intended as a "plea for public sympathy and understanding."[29] Fragments of the typed manuscript were found in a stolen car abandoned in Kansas. "For the few people who have sons and daughters to go astray or be unjustly accused, I can add that the 'law' can be mistaken," Bonnie began. From there the manuscript fragments. "In this story, I do not propose . . . anyone. I believe we are innocent. . . . Intend to tell . . . sordid facts . . . guilty of lots . . . and yet there are petty and . . . thieves all over the country."[30] Wire services broadcast the discovery coast-to-coast on April 7, 1934. Bonnie's death just over a month later preempted the tell-all's completion.

Fed up with the portrayal of their children as mad-dog killers, Emma Parker and Clyde's sister Nell collaborated with reporter and sometime playwright Jan Fortune on what they hoped would be a corrective. In August 1934, three months after the Bienville Paris ambush and with the *True Detective* exposé still hitting newsstands, Dallas-based Ranger Press issued *Fugitives: The Story of Clyde Barrow and Bonnie Parker, As Told by Bonnie's Mother (Mrs. Emma Parker) and Clyde's Sister (Nell Barrow Cowan).* The book's foreword promised, "There is nothing in these pages which would attract any normal person to the life of an outlaw," but the account nonetheless sought to put human faces on two young people who "never knew the happiness of safety and security" and "had no home and rarely enough money."[31] Ghostwriter Fortune pitched her tale as "a thrilling story of the exciting and hectic experiences of two youths who were misfits in society."[32]

Both Emma Parker and Nell Barrow disavowed much of the contents of Fortune's book, claiming that they did not recollect saying the things attributed to them. A 2013 reprint acknowledged that the author "may have taken some journalistic liberties."[33] Clyde's younger sister Marie Barrow, who had not been consulted, took particular exception to Fortune's version of the story and late in life worked with another Dallas author to write a corrective to the corrective; in the end, she refused to have the memoir published because even it failed to portray the Barrow family "in a sufficiently positive light."[34] While for years historians have regarded *Fugitives* as untrustworthy, recent research "has also shown that the book is more accurate—in some places—than previously believed." More importantly, the anecdotal remembrance was "the first attempt to tell the story from the family point of view" and "the beginning of the legend of Bonnie and Clyde."[35]

Incongruous as it seems, given their protest of *The Retribution of Clyde Barrow and Bonnie Parker* and the ongoing controversy over *Fugitives*, both Cumie Barrow and Emma Parker signed on in March 1935 as part of a road show led by "Crime Doctor" Charles Stanley that featured the Death Car as its main attraction. Stanley had obtained rental rights to the vehicle from its original owner, one Ruth Warren of Topeka, Kansas, who had reported the deluxe model four-door V-8 sedan stolen from her driveway a month before Clyde and Bonnie's final ride and insisted it be returned whatever its condition. (Mrs. Warren's request frustrated the moneymaking ambitions of Sheriff Jordan, who considered the car his rightful gain and was holding it for safekeeping in the Arcadia, Louisiana, impound lot.) Stanley barnstormed the country with the Ford loaded on a flatbed truck, an irresistible enticement to his fire-breathing anti-crime lectures. Cumie and Emma were joined on the tour by Clyde's father Henry and sister Marie. Also part of the entourage: John Dillinger's father, John Sr. Times were tough, the Barrow family's fortunes had plummeted since Clyde's and Bonnie's deaths, and the prospect of steady income likely outweighed any moral reservations.

A 1968 LP recording, released to cash in on *Bonnie and Clyde*'s box office success (and "correct its mistakes") provides a vivid inkling of Stanley's spiel. "There is no romance in living a hand-to-mouth existence," he thunders Walter Winchell–like, "always a-go in a dirty car, always hiding, fearing to stop among decent people, fearing to sleep for fear of awakening in manacles. There is no joy in such an existence, and there is no glory in a dying body riddled by the bullets of society's protectors and avengers." Stanley accompanied the brimstone with a gory slide show, following which the Barrows, Emma, and Dillinger Sr. fielded questions about their murderous offspring. The "Crime Doctor" routinely played to capacity audiences, but whatever the financial advantage, "after a few weeks the combined toll of strenuous travel and reliving painful memories proved too much for Cumie and Emma."[36] Together with Henry and Marie, they bid farewell to the tour and returned to Dallas.

The Barrows and Emma left in the nick of time. When Frank Hamer caught up with Stanley's act at an automobile showroom in Austin, he leaped onto the dais, announced (as always) "I'm Frank Hamer!" and slapped Stanley so hard across the face it knocked him down. "Don't ever use my name again in public!"[37] he bellowed before confiscating the showman's slides and stalking out. The ex-Texas Ranger had become infuriated by the morbid enjoyment Stanley took in Clyde and Bonnie's ambush and his entirely correct allegations that "the desperadoes had been set up . . . and executed without mercy."[38] "I slapped that guy clean across the room and told him if he ever showed those pictures again, I would crawl on my hands and knees to South America to kill him,"[39] Hamer told Austin reporters. One Hamer biography claims that Stanley "was not heard from again until after Hamer's death some twenty years later,"[40] but in fact the "Crime Doctor" continued to tour until 1952—though "he never came back to Austin."[41]

Leave it to J. Edgar Hoover to set the record straight.

"I'm going to tell the truth about these rats," the director of the now full-fledged Federal Bureau of Investigation announced at the outset of his 1938 book *Persons in Hiding*. "I'm going to tell the truth about their dirty, filthy diseased women."[42] Having won the "war on crime," Hoover was determined to put an end to gangster hero worship by exposing not only Clyde and Bonnie but also Dillinger, Machine Gun Kelly, Pretty Boy Floyd, Baby Face Nelson, and the "Ma" Barker Gang and their confederates as a sorry bunch of yellow-bellied cowards, the product of "a widespread deterioration in family values, of parents who did not teach their children right from wrong."[43] Hoover engaged publicist Courtney Ryley Cooper, a former circus clown whose clients included both "Buffalo Bill" Cody's Wild West Show and the Ringling Bros. and Barnum & Bailey Circus to write the official history; the printed legend would serve as "fact" until the release of FBI files in the late 1980s.[44]

A nationwide bestseller, Hoover's book became a hot Hollywood property. Paramount's eponymous 1939 version, with a script cowritten by *They Shoot Horses, Don't They?* author Horace McCoy, casts Patricia Morrison as Dorothy "Dot" Bronson (Bonnie) and J. Carrol Naish as Freddie "Gunner" Martin (Clyde). In this telling, which prefigures postwar film noir, Dot/Bonnie is a coldly calculating dominatrix, a beautician with a taste for furs and expensive perfume branded *Tantalizing*. "I'm sick of riding in an old jalopy that smells of old tires and greasy overalls," she complains to a soon-to-be-discarded boyfriend in an early scene. "And I'm sick of hamburgers and dancing in two-bit roadside joints." "You talk big, don't you?" says Freddie/Clyde, who conveniently rids Dot of her troublesome suitor in a bungled but fatal beauty parlor robbery. "I think big—and that's the way I want to live—big!" she replies.

Fade out and up to target practice in a farmer's field, where Dot proves herself the superior shot. "You keep saying to yourself, 'I'm a big guy behind this gun. Nothing can stop me,'" she reassures Freddie.

Throughout the film, Dot serves as both the brains and balls of the two-person criminal outfit. When she spies a headline reading UNKNOWN BANDITS HOLD UP FEDERAL RESERVE TRUCK during a filling-station robbery, Dot scoffs that "nobody ever got anyplace being unknown," then picks up the phone, calls the newspaper, and passes on an anonymous tip naming Freddie as the mastermind. "I'm gonna give you a reputation," she tells her reluctant companion. Does she ever: FBI PSYCHIATRIST ASSERTS "GUNNER" MARTIN PUPPET IN WIFE'S HANDS, a later headline mocks. Actor Naish, who made a specialty of weaselly lowlifes given to profuse facial sweating, is in his element as the humiliations mount up. "Freddy 'll do the cooking. He loves it," Dot tells her parents on an unannounced visit. "Ain't no natural man likes cookin'," her mother retorts. "All the boys know Dottie does the shooting for you," G-man Pete Griswold (played woodenly by top-billed Lynne Overman) taunts Freddy in a climactic scene that sets in motion the Production Code–required final act of retribution. At the fade-out, Dot and Freddy inform on each other, rats to the end.

In 1945, Poverty Row studio Producers Releasing Corporation attempted to win Production Code approval for *Wanted for Murder*, whose script cast aside fictional aliases and named Clyde and Bonnie as its protagonists. A synopsis on file in the Production Code Administration Records at the Academy of Motion Picture Arts and Sciences' Margaret Herrick Library reveals that while the (sadly unnamed) screenwriters evinced only glancing allegiance to facts, their story included many incidents left out of previous and future versions of the story; Clyde's self-mutilation and Bonnie's horrific automobile accident injuries are both featured. Production Code staffer

C. R. Metzger deemed the script an "unacceptable cavalcade of crime and gangster activities . . . that violate 10 of the 12 special regulations re: Crime in Motion Pictures."[45]

In his accompanying two-page cover letter, Joseph Breen took pains to enumerate every single violation, including "the participation of a 17-year-old boy [an earlier incarnation of the character who became C. W. Moss] actively engaged in crime and committing murder and some scenes of excessive brutality and possible gruesomeness." (The same nouns and adjectives would be wielded against David Newman and Robert Benton's script.) Breen took particular offense that "there is no definite condemnation of any of these acts, in fact a slight condonation [sic] of them comes through at times." In Breen's "considered opinion . . . such a story definitely could not be approved by us."[46] (*Wanted for Murder* was never made.)

Cut to 1958. *The Bonnie Parker Story*, made by legendary exploitation film producer Samuel Z. Arkoff and his American International Pictures, took inspiration from a recently published article in the men's magazine *Argosy*. "Killer in Skirts" described Bonnie as "blonde and stacked and ninety pounds straight out of hell—tommy-gunning, stogy-smoking Bonnie Parker, America's deadliest sweetheart."[47] The movie's poster included the tagline "She Lived Like a Woman and Killed Like an Animal!" Pulchritudinous Dorothy Provine perfectly fits the bill, first glimpsed in a voyeuristic title sequence while changing into a waitress uniform; rockabilly music twangs on the soundtrack as a single bare light bulb swings overhead, emphasizing Provine's curves. When a diner customer gets too grabby, Bonnie hurls a pan of hot grease into his face. "Maybe I'm too hot for you to handle!" she warns. Another patron, would-be bandit Guy Darrow, enjoys the spectacle.

"Team up with me and we'll just take what we want," he tells Bonnie back in her apartment. "Otherwise, you'll wind up on a street corner—and you won't be selling newspapers." The tables turn quickly. Tired of Guy's small-time ambitions, Bonnie takes charge. "You think you can just sit on your rear and play it safe?" she challenges. "We been doin' what you want, now we're gonna start doin' what *I* want. We're gonna get some kicks—some *real* kicks, in big-city style."

Able to subvert certain Production Code restrictions owing to its zero-grade status, *The Bonnie Parker Story* gets away with murder, along with copious amounts of sexual innuendo. The couple's first filling-station robbery is preceded by enthusiastic necking (hot enough to cause the attendant to remove his cap and wipe off the sweat as he sneaks looks through the windshield) and culminates with Bonnie shooting up the pump. "*KISS ME!*" she orders Guy when an orgasmic fireball erupts. The moment sets off a behind-the-steering-wheel bout of lovemaking nearly equal to Faye Dunaway's insatiable pawing of Warren Beatty in the first reel of *Bonnie and Clyde*. Interrupted by a pursuing patrolman, Bonnie coldly guns the officer down from behind the passenger door, a moment of savagery meant to recall the actual Bonnie's apocryphal murder of highway patrolman H. D. Murphy in Grapevine, Texas.

Prolific B-movie director William Witney (whose Quentin Tarantino–inspired cult reputation far exceeds his actual ability) deploys most of his threadbare resources in the unexpectedly gripping final ambush. Lawmen take up positions outside a dilapidated roadhouse strategically located at a bend in the highway. "They're a mighty tricky pair," the movie's Frank Hamer surrogate, played by TV Western character actor Douglas Kennedy, advises his posse. "No matter how dead they look, don't stop firing until I tell you!" Bonnie, not Clyde, is behind the wheel as they approach the roadhouse. Too late, Clyde spots the crouching posse and frantically grabs the wheel. Gunfire rakes the car, which plunges down an embankment and rolls on to its side. The final shot holds on the image of a smoking tire spinning on its axle. Bonnie's voice rises on the soundtrack, reprising an earlier line. "We got ourselves a one-way ticket. There's nothing you can do once you get on but ride right to the end of the line."

Of the several films derived from or inspired by the Barrow Gang story—including Fritz Lang's *You Only Live Once* (1937) and Nicholas

Ray's *They Live By Night* (1948)—Joseph H. Lewis's *Gun Crazy* (1950) is *Bonnie and Clyde*'s most direct cinematic antecedent. Rightly acclaimed for its bravura action sequences and Production Code–bending depiction of adoring sweethearts who also happen to be psychopathic criminals, the low-budget crime drama was a particular favorite of François Truffaut, who arranged a private showing of the film for screenwriters David Newman and Robert Benton during their initial New York meeting. *Gun Crazy*'s influence on *Bonnie and Clyde* is readily apparent in a shared amoral approach to the subject and characters, as well as in incidental details: Peggy Cummins's Bonnie character (called Annie Laurie Starr in a deliberate reference to both Annie Oakley and Belle Starr) sports a tight sweater and stylish black beret in several scenes; Theadora Van Runkle's later, trendsetting designs for Faye Dunaway were likely no coincidence.

Most striking is *Gun Crazy*'s singular focus on firearms. The prologue opens with the teenaged Clyde character (here named Bart Tare and played by a very young Russ Tamblyn) throwing a rock through a hardware store window to steal an ivory-handled Colt pistol. A subsequent juvenile court trial scene establishes Bart's peculiar obsession. "He absolutely had to have [a gun]," a worried teacher recalls on the stand, "just as other boys have to have jackknives, or harmonicas, or baseball bats." "Shooting is what I'm good at," Bart explains to the judge. "It's the only thing I like. It's what I want to do when I grow up." Pressed on the matter, the boy admits, "I like shooting [guns]. I don't know why but I like shooting them. I feel awful good inside, like I'm somebody."

Next seen as an adult (John Dall in his best screen role), with the reformatory and a stint in the army behind him, Bart contemplates "getting a job with Remington or one of those outfits." Instead, a trip to a traveling carnival introduces Bart to trick sharpshooter Laurie, who makes a blazing low-angled appearance in fringed buckskin and cowboy hat, firing her pistol straight at the camera à la *The Great Train Robbery*. Bart is immediately hooked. An impromptu marksmanship contest seals their destined-to-be-fatal attraction.

As with all iterations of the Clyde and Bonnie story, Laurie's prevailing sense of boredom provides the impetus for larceny. "I want action!" she exclaims at one point, in a line that could have been lifted from the pages of Bonnie's diary.

Gun Crazy's most celebrated sequence is a brazen daylight robbery of a small-town savings and loan. Conceived by original writer Mackinlay Kantor (who noted on the margins of his script, "*I believe that this scene can be a triumph of suspense*"),[48] the set piece plays out in an unbroken three-and-half-minute shot from the back seat of a car, captured in one take by Lewis and his crew—without permits—on the main street of Montrose, California. Dressed in cowboy carny attire, Laurie and Bart, with Laurie at the wheel, cruise through a small Midwestern town and pull up to the curb outside a savings and loan. Bart ducks out the passenger seat and heads through the front door. Seconds tick past. A cop (crime-movie fixture Robert Osterloh) saunters on to the corner. Laurie buys time. She distracts the officer with her fancy costume and offers up her "prop" pistol for him to admire—seductively asking if she might have a look at his weapon in return.

Bart bursts out the savings and loan doors moments later. Laurie retrieves her pistol and clobbers the cop on the head. She and Bart pile back into the car and speed away with alarm bells and sirens blaring behind them. (According to director Lewis, the unrehearsed action was so believable that bystanders began screaming, "They're robbing the bank!"[49]) Still without a cut, Bart steers through opposing traffic. "Is anybody behind us?" he asks. Laurie turns to view the unseen mayhem behind them. In one of the genre's most iconic push-in close-ups, the look on Cummins's face is borderline pornographic.

"Suddenly we realize that there is something deeply disturbed and dangerously exciting about Annie Laurie Starr," film noir archivist Eddie Muller writes in his definitive account of the film's making. "In that thrilling moment, Peggy Cummins and Joe Lewis immortalized her forever as film noir's most ferocious femme fatale."[50]

As for Bart: In a foreshadowing of Clyde's impotence in *Bonnie and Clyde*, his expert marksmanship is severely compromised by his inability to fire on a living target. After a later robbery, during which Laurie viciously guns down two bystanders and a security guard, Bart's psychosis nearly results in the couple's capture until he summons up the guts to shoot out the pursuing cruiser's tires. Dalton Trumbo's final production rewrite of Kantor's original script resolves the issue in a dark denouement. Bart finally does become a killer—shooting Laurie point-blank in a fog-ridden swamp to prevent her from gunning down Bart's childhood friends, now part of a posse bent on their capture. Eternally bonded by their firearms fixation ("We go together like guns and ammunition go together," Bart tells Laurie moments before their demise), the lovers die side by side.

"In *Gun Crazy* . . . [t]he action has a life of its own, and the characters often do not have time to fully contemplate or understand why they are its victims," Paul Schrader wrote in a reappraisal of the film that could just as readily apply to Arthur Penn's treatment of the same material. "It is an exhilarating tribute to reckless love and non-stop action. There are no excuses given for the gun craziness—it is just crazy."[51]

By the spring of 1968, when *Bonnie and Clyde* finally found its audience, all of America had gone gun crazy.

20

"OPENING THE BLOODGATES"

> We were churning in a sea of rage.
> —Todd Gitlin

Troubled times made *Bonnie and Clyde* a blockbuster.
What was to become the most violent year in an already bloody decade began with the Tet Offensive, a devastating surprise attack launched by North Vietnamese forces in the early morning hours of January 30, 1968, the Vietnamese New Year, that struck over thirty-six provincial capitals and five cities including Saigon. Images of dead and wounded American soldiers in the country's first televised war became a numbing nightly backdrop. Middle Americans at their dinner tables witnessed the execution of a bound Viet Cong prisoner, shot point-blank in the head by South Vietnamese police general Nguyen Ngoc Loan. "When so many movie critics complain about violence on film," one industry spokesman observed, "I don't think they realize the impact of thirty minutes on the [NBC] Huntley-Brinkley newscast—and that's real violence."[1]

Closer to home, the assassinations of Martin Luther King Jr. and Robert F. Kennedy in the late spring and early summer of that year precipitated a season of turmoil that culminated in the Democratic National Convention in Chicago, Illinois, when on August 28 violent clashes between police officers and anti-war protesters played out in real time across the country on live television. "Having stepped into the aura of violence, many of the middle-class young were stunned into a tolerance, a fascination, even a taste for it," wrote cultural critic Todd Gitlin, who lived through and participated in many of the decade's seminal events. "I doubt that [revolutionary] movement cadres grew up any more—or less—rageful than an equivalent population of law-school students," Gitlin added, "[or] more 'violence-prone' than ROTC cadets or bombing pilots."[2]

Faced with unprecedented unrest, Americans armed themselves in unprecedented numbers. According to one report, gun homicides over the decade from 1958 to 1968 increased by 51 percent; assaults committed with a firearm escalated 84 percent. Such was the demand for guns that American arms manufacturers faced overseas competition for the first time since the establishment of the republic. In 1955, weapons made by Austria's Glock and other foreign factories accounted for a paltry 67,000 imported firearms; by 1968, that number exceeded one million. "Violence is necessary and it's as American as cherry pie,"[3] proclaimed Black Panther "minister of justice" H. Rap Brown, prompting gun-culture critic Richard Hofstadter to note, "presumably he did not expect his listeners to be so uncritically patriotic as to think that violence must be good because Americans have so often used it."[4]

It was thus inevitable that the makers of *Bonnie and Clyde* would find themselves both credited for exposing the malevolent heart of American society and blamed for ushering in a new era of screen permissiveness.

"That was the period when nobody in Long Island understood [*Bonnie and Clyde*] because it was violent," recalled editor Dede Allen. "All my friends who were left-wingers would say, 'How could you work on a film like that?' They didn't understand the film. Their kids understood it, but they didn't. They didn't understand that we were a country of assassins. . . . A complete disconnect."[5] At the film's Montreal premiere press conference that so enraged *New York Times* critic Bosley Crowther, Arthur Penn maintained that "we have a violent society. It's not Greece, it's not Athens, it's not the Renaissance—it is the American society, and I would have to personify it by saying that it is a violent one. So why not make films about it?"[6] The director took pride in the fact that younger viewers accounted for the bulk of the movie's gross receipts. "After seeing the film, sometimes three or four times, they leave the theater and realize what's happening in the streets isn't very different."[7]

"THE NEW CINEMA: VIOLENCE ... SEX ... ART ..." screamed the December 8, 1967, cover of *Time* over a collage of *Bonnie and Clyde* images created by artist Robert Rauschenberg. Renouncing the magazine's initial critique of the film as a "Low-Down Hoe-Down" and a "strange and purposeless mingling of fact and claptrap,"[8] the accompanying five-thousand-word text heralded the film as "not only the sleeper hit of the decade but also, to a growing consensus of audiences and critics, the best movie of the year ... a watershed picture, the kind that signals a new style, a new trend." Writer Stefan Kanter predicted (accurately) that "in the wake of *Bonnie and Clyde*, "there is an almost euphoric sense in Hollywood that more such movies can and will be made."[9]

As Mark Harris noted with admirable understatement, "twenty-seven weeks after it opened, *Bonnie and Clyde* had become a phenomenon without ever becoming an actual hit."[10]

Since being unceremoniously pulled from US theaters by Warner Bros. distribution chief Benny Kalmenson in October 1967, the film had mesmerized audiences in London and Paris. "As far as I can see there are people," Faye Dunaway remembered of the Champs-Elysees premiere, where she, Warren Beatty, and Arthur Penn, along with screenwriters David Newman and Robert Benton and their wives, were driven to the cinema in vintage thirties automobiles. "Many are young girls, teenagers; all are wearing berets, their hair styled in variations on the loose pageboys of Bonnie Parker and wearing knockoffs of the ... clothes Theadora Van Runkle designed for me to wear."

On both sides of the channel, the film inspired musical tributes. British rhythm and blues singer Georgie Fame scored a No. 1 hit with "The Ballad of Bonnie and Clyde," whose opening lyrics declared "*Bonnie and Clyde were pretty-looking people / But I can tell you people they were the devil's children.*" Fame's promotional materials and onstage performances leaned heavily on the movie's visual aesthetic. So, too, did Brigitte Bardot, who appeared dressed in Bonnie attire on a live French TV special alongside her "Clyde," composer and singer Serge Gainsbourg. Dunaway reported that the small factory outside Lourdes where traditional French berets were manufactured had increased production from five thousand to twelve thousand berets *per week* to keep up with increasing demand. "All this I knew," Dunaway reported, "but I wasn't prepared."[11]

Neither was Warner Bros.

Thanks to the studio's utter lack of confidence in the movie's prospects, *Bonnie and Clyde* had, as a self-fulfilling prophecy, returned a mere $2.5 million in rentals (profits to the studio after subtracting distribution costs) in its initial limited release. Then came the Oscar nominations on February 20, 1968, when Warner Bros.' "little cowboy movie that won't be much good" received ten citations, tying with *Guess Who's Coming to Dinner?* as most-nominated film. "This time, the public was ready," Harris reported in his definitive account of that year's Oscars race. "Many of the same theaters that had knocked the picture off their screens after a week or two in the fall of 1967 now reported grosses for the re-release that were five and six times what the film had taken in originally."[12]

Penn and Beatty, who had partnered as producers and endured the death of a thousand salary cuts in exchange for a share of the profits to keep their vision intact, now reaped the benefits of their sacrifice. By the time *Bonnie and Clyde* finished its second, blockbuster run, it had grossed $50.7 million in the United States and $70 million worldwide. Beatty's profit participation earned him over $6 million, while Penn's exceeded $2 million. "*Bonnie and Clyde*'s sudden and immense box office success," Harris wrote, "flabbergasted Warner Bros., made Warren Beatty [and Arthur Penn] wealthy beyond [their] wildest hopes, and turned the movie into the narrow front-runner for Best Picture."[13]

Exit Bosley Crowther, whose personal crusade against the film had earned him a new assignment. "At the *New York Times*, they never fire you—they feel too guilty," remembered former culture editor Arthur Gelb. "They just put you on a different path and give you more money to soothe their guilt."[14] The quarter-century-long dean of American critics remained an industry reporter at large but would never write another review; twenty-six-year-old Renata Adler became the paper's first-string critic. Engaging in a natural cycle of corruption endemic to movie journalists, Crowther retired from the *Times* in September 1968 to become an executive consultant to Columbia Pictures. He offered his last assessment of *Bonnie and Clyde* in a 1978 compendium of the century's greatest movies. "No film turned out in the 1960s was more clever in registering the amoral restlessness of youth in those years,"[15] he wrote—a decade too late.

"Warren got Bosley Crowther fired,"[16] Robert Towne told Beatty's biographer with considerable satisfaction. Few of Crowther's youthful colleagues, who considered him an outdated bully, were sorry to see him go. His enforced departure paved the way for one of the new guard to establish her own reputation as a force to be reckoned with.

"How do you make a good movie in this country without being jumped on?"[17] Pauline Kael asked in the opening line of her seven-thousand-word review of *Bonnie and Clyde* in the October 21, 1967, issue of the *New Yorker*. "When an American movie reaches people, when it makes them react, some think there must be something the matter with it—maybe a law should be passed against it."[18]

The Bay Area native, a professional contrarian then known mainly for her regular thrashings of mainstream studio films in the pages of *McCall's* and the *New Republic*, regarded *Bonnie and Clyde* as "the most exciting American movie since *The Manchurian Candidate* [1962]," director John Frankenheimer and writer George Axelrod's mordant conspiracy thriller of brainwashing and political assassination. Kael's impassioned essay (originally written for and rejected by the *New Republic*) displayed the sardonic wit, all-knowing tone and unapologetic subjectivity that would characterize her reign as the *New Yorker*'s most prominent film critic and spawn a generation of acolytes known as "Paulettes."

Read today in a different context, Kael's review of *Bonnie and Clyde* is more interesting for what it has to say about the undercurrent of violence in American culture than its observations on the film itself. "*Bonnie and Clyde* needs violence; violence is its meaning,"[19] she wrote. "Our best movies have always made entertainment out of the anti-heroism of American life.... [T]hey bring to the surface what, in its newest forms and fashions, is always just below the surface." Like "many of our other famous outlaws and gangsters, the real Bonnie and Clyde seemed to others to be acting out forbidden roles and to relish [them]." Outlaws, she went on, "capture the public imagination, because they take chances, and because, often, they enjoy dramatizing their lives."

Kael refuted the notion of "historical accuracy" entirely. "Why the protests about *Bonnie and Clyde*, in which the criminals *are* criminals?" she asked—then in trademark fashion answered her own question. "I would suggest that when a movie clearly conceived as a new version of a legend is attacked as historically inaccurate, it's because it shakes people a little.... [P]art of what makes a legend for Americans is viewing anything that happened in the past as much simpler than anything we are involved in now."[20] Nearly alone among her contemporaries, Kael recognized *Bonnie and Clyde* as a spiritual descendant of the pre-Code movies from which the filmmakers took their inspiration. "Structurally, [the film] is a story of love on the run, like the old Clark Gable-Claudette Colbert *It Happened One Night* [1934], but turned inside out," she noted.

Kael, who regularly blurred the line between reviewer and subject, had met for lunch with Benton and Newman before publication to probe their original intentions, and took the opportunity amid her seven thousand words to express her skepticism about the prevailing auteur theory. While praising Arthur Penn for his "gift for violence" (even ranking him alongside Sergei Eisenstein and Luis Bunuel in that regard), elsewhere she faulted the director for being "a little too clumsy and rather too fancy ... too much interested in being cinematically creative and artistic to know when to trust the script."

Even though "Penn can't redeem bad material, nor ... does he necessarily know when it's bad ... [he] can be a remarkable director when he has something to work with."[21] Citing the final massacre scene as "the best editing in an American movie in a long time ... a horror that seems to go on for eternity, and yet doesn't last a second beyond what it should," Kael conceded that "one may assume Penn deserves credit for it along with the editor, Dede Allen."[22]

"I was outraged," Penn complained to an American Film Institute audience in 1970, still feeling the sting three years later. "It was one of the worst pieces of reportage inside of a great piece of criticism I've ever read. She suggested that whoever made this film was pretty good, but I was not very good. Now, I don't know who else made this film. ... [Pauline] had the sense that the script had sprung full-blown from nowhere and that we had gotten it onto the screen through the marvelous presence of Warren Beatty and Faye Dunaway and a terrific cameraman ... and gotten it into theaters. Well, that's a lot of crap. And it's also irresponsible. She called my office to check out certain things and there were many things she could have informed herself about had she been disposed to doing so."[23]

Penn opted to skip the 1968 Academy Awards ceremony, originally scheduled for Monday, April 8, at the Santa Monica Civic Auditorium but postponed for two days in the wake of Martin Luther King Jr.'s funeral. *Bonnie and Clyde* entered the race neck and neck with *The Graduate*, but in the end claimed only two trophies: for Estelle Parsons as Best Supporting Actress and Burnett Guffey for Best Cinematography; the recalcitrant cameraman thanked "everyone who helped me do it" in a one-line speech before walking offstage. Mike Nichols claimed the Best Director Oscar for *The Graduate* (the picture's only win in seven categories), while *Guess Who's Coming to Dinner?* author William Rose bested Newman and Benton for Original Screenplay, prompting one of the ceremony's most memorable on-screen gaffes.

"All of our friends kept saying, 'You're gonna win, you're gonna win!'" Benton recounted. "It never occurred to [David and me] that all of the nominees had friends who were saying to them that *they* were going to win."[24]

As the contenders were announced, a confident Benton sat up, buttoned his jacket, adjusted his cuffs and started to stand—only to sit down fast when Rose was declared the winner.[25]

Academy of Motion Pictures Arts and Sciences voters awarded their top prize to Norman Jewison's *In the Heat of the Night*, a racially charged, Southern-set detective story starring Sidney Poitier and Rod Steiger (who outpolled both Gene Hackman and Michael J. Pollard as Best Supporting Actor) that satisfied the industry's craving for relevance in troubled times. "We was robbed,"[26] Beatty joked on his exit that night, prompting a flurry of not-always-complimentary responses. "Now, let's make it again!"[27] cabled Jean-Luc Godard, the onetime directorial stand-in for François Truffaut, who had suggested a winter shoot in New Jersey in contemporary dress.

In the Heat of the Night joined the list of noble, earnestly told films to receive the industry's ultimate approbation, but Beatty, Penn, and their collaborators could find solace in the fact that *Bonnie and Clyde* would leave the longer-lasting cultural legacy.

Like so many who had dismissed the film on its debut, *Time* critic Richard Schickel came to admit (albeit after five years) that its makers "sensed far better than I the basic shift in the basic mood of its basically youthful audience." Schickel went on to proclaim *Bonnie and Clyde* as "*the* major commercial discovery of the past five years [and] the largest single determinant of American film content in the late Sixties and early Seventies"[28]—more influential, he insisted, than Dennis Hopper's *Easy Rider* (1969), generally credited with ushering in the "New Hollywood." In 1980, social commentator Robert Kolker made Penn the principal case study in an analysis of what he called *A Cinema of Loneliness* that also included Stanley Kubrick, Francis Ford Coppola, Martin Scorsese, and Robert Altman. By breaking "a major cinematic contract between viewer and filmmaker that held that violent death on the screen would be swift and relatively clean," Kolker noted with disapproval, Penn "opened the bloodgates and our cinema has not stopped bleeding since."[29]

On December 19, 1968, Motion Picture Association of America (MPAA) president Jack Valenti appeared before the National Commission on the Causes and Prevention of Violence in Washington, DC, convened to address the underlying reasons for the breakdown in American society then convulsing the nation. The Texas native was barely eighteen months into a thirty-eight-year tenure as lobbyist and advocate for the motion picture and TV industry, but the considerable good will he had built up in his previous stint as special assistant to President Lyndon B. Johnson served him well. Employing the good-natured bombast and highfalutin rhetoric that became his trademark, Valenti began his opening remarks by noting, "There is a new breed of filmmaker. And mark you well this new filmmaker, because he's an extraordinary fellow. He's young. He's sensitive. He's dedicated. He's reaching out for new dimensions of expression. And he's not bound—not bound—by the conventions of a conformist past. I happen to think that's good. Moreover, this new style is matched by a new audience . . . seeking new fulfillment."[30]

Valenti knew going into the hearing room that *Bonnie and Clyde* would be Exhibit A, and he came prepared. In response to questioning by Judge Ernest W. McFarland, he acknowledged that "a number of people did think that *Bonnie and Clyde* was a picture of extreme violence with a tendency to cause people to think kindly of bandits and robbers and hoodlums." The MPAA chief reminded the panel that "I came from that part of the world, and as a young boy. . . . I must say my great hero was not Bonnie or Clyde, but Frank Hamer, who doesn't come out too well in the picture." Valenti noted that the National Catholic Office for Motion Pictures, successor to the dreaded Legion of Decency, called the film "a great morality play" and named it Best Mature Picture of 1967. "You've got to determine who you're going to follow," he suggested. "Those people who criticize *Bonnie and Clyde*, or the Catholics who are probably the most indefatigable monitors of the motion picture screen and whose integrity is almost impeccable."

"I would hate to think what a survey would show on this commission as to how many have [actually] seen *Bonnie and Clyde*," committee vice chairman Judge Leon A. Higginbotham interjected to general laughter.

Democratic Louisiana congressman Hale Boggs *had* seen the film, and he didn't hold back. "Those ... characters lived in my state," Boggs informed the witness. "They were reprehensible criminals. There was nothing about them that was commendable. They killed in cold blood, as the movie depicts."

Boggs had previously served as the youngest member of the Warren Commission investigating the assassination of John F. Kennedy and made the most of his allotted minutes. "I might tell [Mr. Valenti] that we had a murder in my town committed by an eighteen-year-old boy who had come out of *Bonnie and Clyde* one hour before [and] killed a young man who was running a drive-in grocery store. Now, whether or not what he saw in *Bonnie and Clyde* had any impact on the murder, I don't know. But I know that what I say to you is a fact—that he saw this movie which glorifies violence." (At this remove, it's impossible to substantiate the claim one way or the other.)

Before Valenti could interject, Boggs also took exception to the National Catholic Office's favorable opinion of the film. "I'm surprised you credit this type of omnipotence to a Catholic organization," he marveled. To which Valenti—agitated even in the transcripts—snapped back: "There are a great many clergymen—whose opinions I've read—who praise *Bonnie and Clyde*, saying that this is a picture of our time. I'm not saying they're right or wrong. I just want to illuminate that ... we are dealing in this very soggy ground of passing a judgment."

The bulk of the MPAA president's testimony centered on the newly imposed ratings system designed to replace the Production Code which *Bonnie and Clyde* had helped render obsolete. "G"—suitable for general audiences; "M" (now "PG")—suggested for mature audiences and mature young people, with parental discretion advised; "R"—restricted to audiences over sixteen unless accompanied by a parent or adult guardian; and "X"—"in which we say that this picture should not be shown to any child under sixteen regardless of anyone who accompanies him." Committee members evinced particular fascination with the "X" rating, judging from the starring role it plays in Valenti's testimony.

"No living man can tell you about the future of 'X' pictures," the MPAA chief conceded, with the caveat that "if the picture is an excellently made artistic picture which goes beyond the dimly lit boundaries we have set and it becomes an 'X' picture, I daresay it will draw an audience."

Less than a year later, a film influenced by *Bonnie and Clyde* would put that theory to the test.

In a letter to director Sam Peckinpah dated March 19, 1968, Warner Bros. confirmed that a print of Penn's film was on its way to Parras, Mexico, for a weekend screening just before the March 25 commencement of principal photography on *The Wild Bunch*, the story of end-of-the-line American mercenaries caught up in the wholesale slaughter of the Mexican Revolution. Peckinpah was determined to outdo Arthur Penn's use of squibs in the two sequences of indiscriminate mass killing that open and close the film. Writer W. K. Stratton's history of the film's making records how special effects technicians experimented on set by dressing up full-size cutouts in wardrobe, then standing them up against a corral fence and blowing holes in them with dummy rounds. Unimpressed with the results, Peckinpah picked up a revolver loaded with live ammunition and fired off a full cylinder, thoroughly shredding the cutout.

"That's the effect I want!" he barked. The crew set to work using "bigger squibs on both the front and back of the cutout, simulating the passage of a bullet through a body." For good measure, "they also added hamburger meat to give the illusion of tissue flying with the impact in addition to spreading stage blood."[31]

The results are on spectacular display in the film's climactic "Battle of Bloody Porch," in which the four-man bunch (played by William Holden, Ernest Borgnine, Ben Johnson, and Warren Oates) lay waste to the compound of a debauched Mexican general, martyring themselves in the process. As

Stratton recounts, "The images captured by [cinematographer Lucien] Ballard and his crew were more gruesome than anything ever before staged for a western."[32] Outdoing Penn's synchronized four-camera setup for *Bonnie and Clyde*'s concluding massacre, Peckinpah and Ballard employed six cameras shooting side by side. As edited by Lou Lombardo, the completed five-minute sequence contains 325 individual shots, with some as brief as three or four frames (one-eighth of a second, virtually subliminal), creating an impression of cataclysmic ferocity. The results nearly resulted in the MPAA issuing its first-ever "X" rating for violence, until a few judicious cuts, notably one of a full-frontal throat-slitting, resulted in a more palatable "R."

In later interviews, Peckinpah refused to acknowledge his debt to Penn, citing as his inspiration—as Penn did—Akira Kurosawa's *Seven Samurai*. (Even there, Peckinpah could be hugely uncharitable. At one liquor-fueled private get-together following a retrospective screening of *The Wild Bunch* at the University of Southern California, the director had the temerity to declare "Kurosawa stole that from *me!*"—never mind the fact that *Seven Samurai* preceded his own film by a decade.[33]) "All Peckinpah did was follow the technique I used ... and push it to the extreme," Penn countered, "and in this way his intention was to depict violence so fierce that people would be sickened." At least—"that's how he explained it, but I'm not convinced it's what he really wanted to achieve."[34]

Penn's doubts are borne out in the concluding moments of *The Wild Bunch*. Peckinpah not only appropriated Penn's groundbreaking technique in the depiction of violence, but also expanded on *Bonnie and Clyde*'s simultaneous glorification and debunking of the outlaw legend. "True mythic figures would not suffer the way [Bonnie and Clyde] do" in the final ambush scene, notes film historian Richard B. Jewell. "Anyone trying to encourage empathy between the audience and the characters would not make their injuries so brutal and graphic ... which is one of the ways that Penn reminds us that the life and death of these two itinerant criminals was savage, destructive and not something we should romanticize or view through rose-tinted glasses."[35] Peckinpah, in contrast, follows the carnage with a redemptive coda: as Mexican peasants make their way to the mountains with desperately needed firearms scavenged from the Battle of Bloody Porch, the director superimposes individual vignettes of the laughing bunch over the action. Moments after their self-inflicted martyrdom, the mercenaries have been enshrined as liberators.

The Wild Bunch disappointed Penn. "I think I resolved those issues beforehand with *Bonnie and Clyde*," he maintained. "Peckinpah is a true film director, no doubt about that. But I'm sure he can do better."[36]

For his part, Penn continued to be haunted by the specter of American violence. After the end of filming *Bonnie and Clyde*, the director fell into what he characterized to biographer Nat Segaloff as one of his periodic post-shoot depressions. "I don't want to go back into that dark area for a while because it's painful. . . . You're in it for a long, long time. It's a year, a year and half of immersing yourself in misery. . . . I feel very lonely during those films. I get so inside that I'm sure I'm a lousy father and husband at that point, because you end up touching personal, painful material."[37]

Penn took refuge from the darkness in his next—and most underrated—film, *Alice's Restaurant* (1969), a feature-length riff on Arlo Guthrie's eighteen-minute story song about the communal Thanksgiving Day refurbishment of a deconsecrated Massachusetts church. Debuted at the Newport Folk Festival in August 1967 while Penn was defending *Bonnie and Clyde* in Montreal, Guthrie's gently satirical ballad established the singer "as both an entertainer and a partisan who voiced the soul of the hippie generation just as his father [Woody Guthrie] had spoken for the disenfranchised thirty years earlier."[38] The film version provided a respite for the director to observe the fractures in American society without recourse to pyrotechnics.

"The only act of violence in the film is an act of nonviolence, that of draft dodging," Penn told interviewers. "If I wanted to, I could make a film about what's going on now in the United States that would be so violent you'd jump right out of your seat," he threatened. "There's enough material in newspapers every day to make two hundred films about violence. But even if I did make a film like this it would only show a fraction of what's going on in the country."[39]

When Penn *did* make that film, it was again in the guise of history.

Even as he was promoting *Bonnie and Clyde* to French New Wave organ *Cahiers du cinema* in December 1967, the director revealed, "I'm working on [a film] about the American Indian. Again, it's a comic story, but we'll have scenes that will be as terrible as . . . [it] really was."[40] Based on Thomas Berger's eponymous novel, *Little Big Man* (1970) emerged as the most epic of Penn's films. It is a sweeping, picaresque critique of Manifest Destiny from the first pioneer trains to the wiping out of George Armstrong Custer's Seventh Cavalry on the banks of the Little Big Horn River in June 1876, told through the eyes of that battle's lone survivor, 121-year-old Jack Crabb (a career-best performance for Dustin Hoffman).

"*Little Big Man* is a film about genocide," Penn said flatly at the time. Berger's novel "was written with a scalpel. In order to tell the story . . . he had to use razor sharp wit, something we emphasized in the film."[41] As with *Bonnie and Clyde*, and equally controversial at the time, humor and horror coexisted, often in the same frame.

"After *Bonnie and Clyde*, I [was] faced with the problem of depicting the Wild West on screen. . . . I could either make it physically painful for the audience or do it without showing a single drop of blood. I chose the latter. In [*Little Big Man*] nearly all the wars and killings are immaculately clean."[42] That's not entirely true. While a comedic tone prevails throughout much of the film, Penn seems more determined than ever to expose the unpleasantness underlying the frontier myth. *Little Big Man*'s major set piece depicts in graphic detail Custer's November 26, 1868, annihilation of a peaceful Cheyenne winter camp on the banks of the Washita River in what is now Oklahoma. Along with the concluding massacre in *Bonnie and Clyde*, it represents the finest and most wrenching of Penn's collaborations with editor Dede Allen.

The eight-minute sequence begins with a shot of restless horses in an encampment corral. "Grandfather, what's wrong with the ponies?" Little Big Man asks of his blind adoptive guardian, Old Lodge Skins (the memorable screen debut of indigenous actor Chief Dan George). "Don't you hear that, my son?" Old Lodge Skins asks, gesturing into the distance. As Little Big Man stares into the early morning fog, the silhouettes of riders gradually become visible. For a moment there is only the sound of the restless ponies in the corral and the hoof beats of the approaching riders. Then the merry fife-and-drum melody "Garry Owen," familiar to generations of Western viewers as the Seventh Cavalry anthem, rises on the soundtrack. Penn and Allen abruptly—and breathtakingly—shift the perspective to a series of panoramic long shots of Custer's troops about to descend on the village. The steady, monotonous drum rhythm grows ever louder, until it is finally overtaken and replaced by the first, withering volley of gunshots.

"It is a good day to die," Old Lodge Skins declares as Little Big Man desperately attempts to spirit him to safety across the river behind the camp. In trademark Penn fashion, the action alternates between their comical escape and horrific shots of men, women and children being killed at point-blank range. In one shocking telephoto image, a Cheyenne woman strips off a flaming robe, only to be shot in the back and fall naked into the snow. Little Big Man watches from hiding as Custer (a megalomaniac portrayal by Richard Mulligan) gives the order to "shoot the Indian ponies." Disorienting panning shots of cavalrymen firing into the corral and panicked horses combine to create an almost unwatchable butchery.

Worse is to come. From across the river, Little Big Man sees his wife, Sunshine, attempting to flee with their infant son strapped to a cradleboard on her back. The action, to this point all-encompassing, narrows to a single point of view. On the verge of safety, Little Big Man's wife is gunned down on the riverbank. Penn and Allen include one shot of the baby's head reduced to red pulp in the cradleboard the moment before Sunshine falls to the ground.

For an agonizing ten seconds—an eternity in screen time—all sound drops out entirely. Cavalrymen fire into the pony corral in silence; fires burn without sound; shadows of the withdrawing cavalrymen pass over the faces of the dead; the fife-and-drum band is unheard on the outskirts of the devastated village. The image fades to a blinding white.

Like so many Westerns of its era, *Little Big Man*'s treatment of the atrocity on the Washita owes more to then-contemporary events than actual frontier history. At the time of the film's production, the gruesome details of the March 1968 My Lai Massacre (known in Vietnam as the Sơn My Massacre after the village in which the killing occurred), when American soldiers shot and bayoneted women, children, and elderly men on an alleged search for Viet Cong guerrillas and "sympathizers," had only just begun to surface. Traditionalist genre critics remain eager to pounce on *Little Big Man* for this reason. "The box office shows that [Penn] really had his finger on the pulse of America," said Paul Andrew Hutton (the film became one of 1971's biggest hits). "[It's] a perfect representation of the Seventies in a way that *They Died With Their Boots On* is the perfect representation of America in December of 1941,"[43] he added, referring to Raoul Walsh's rah-rah version of the Custer story starring Errol Flynn, released on the eve of World War II.

Seen today, *Little Big Man* stands as an utter repudiation of the foundational myth of gun-toting frontier American individualism—not an alternative to, but an outright mocking of the legend printed indelibly on the national consciousness by John Ford and his contemporaries. The experience of making the film left Penn "out of gas. I was also rather depressed about the whole nature of where we were, politically and culturally."[44] Penn would never quite recapture the sensational energy and subversive inspiration that informs every frame of *Bonnie and Clyde* and *Little Big Man*, though his last truly groundbreaking film, the bitter detective thriller *Night Moves* (1975), comes close.

The exhaustion was perhaps inevitable. No other filmmaker of his era had done more to uproot and expose the fundamental contradictions in America's historical self-image. "With respect to *Bonnie and Clyde* and my other films," Penn noted at the movie's 1967 world premiere Montreal Film Festival press conference, "I would have to say that I think violence is a part of the American character."[45]

EPILOGUE

"MADE IN AMERICA"

"Hell of a ride" will be our epitaph.
—Clyde Barrow

If your legacy counts for anything in America, it will eventually become the subject of a musical.

On November 22, 2009, composer Frank Wildhorn and lyricist Don Black debuted their *Bonnie and Clyde* at the La Jolla Playhouse in San Diego, California. The authors echoed screenwriters David Newman and Robert Benton in their intention to be "as truthful as possible and inventive as necessary" in their efforts to "delve into the minds and hearts of two sociopathic lovers while exploring the world and conditions that fueled their deadly rampage." Clyde and Bonnie "saw the American Dream turn into a nightmare of bread lines and soup kitchens and became obsessed with celebrity, not only for the fame it brought, but for the freedom it delivered."[1]

Wildhorn and Black choose to place the couple's celebrity squarely in the context of America's outlaw culture. A rousing first-act curtain number, staged moments after Bonnie helps Clyde escape from prison with a smuggled-in gun—which Clyde employs to shoot a deputy at point-blank range—the couple sings jubilantly:

No need to rush,
Ev'rybody gets our autograph.
"Hell of a Ride"
Will be our epitaph.

* * * *

Ev'ry place we go the folks will turn their heads.
They'll be hollerin' from Dodge to Denver!
We are a pair they'll discuss.
Yes, the world will remember us!

The musical's book by Ivan Menchell wholeheartedly embraces the notion of Bonnie and Clyde as social bandits, ambitious kids from the sticks beaten down by the Depression and unwilling to settle for their parents' lot. "*What was good enough for you, pa / Will not satisfy your wayward son,*" Clyde sings in a lament. "*Jesse James had more fun / Building dreams with just a gun / That's how the west was won.*"

Firearms and onstage violence feature to an unusual degree for a mainstream musical. Prying open a cache of weapons raided from a National Guard armory, Clyde and brother Buck lovingly brandish their new BARs, celebrating: "*It's the end of small-town thinking / Say goodbye to .45s. / Now are dreams are so much bigger / These are gonna change our lives.*" The Barrow Gang's robbery of a failed bank prompts hilarity when a starstruck depositor asks for the couple's autograph, prompting Clyde and Bonnie to argue over who should receive top billing. In an abrupt tone shift worthy of the film, the spoken interlude ends with Clyde's killing of an overzealous teller with a sawed-off "whippit" shotgun.

A commercial and critical success in its California run, the musical version of *Bonnie and Clyde* transferred to Broadway in December 2011. Despite earning five Drama Desk and two Tony Awards nominations, the show closed after only thirty-six performances. In an uncanny replay of the Arthur Penn film's mistreatment by Warner Bros., original director and choreographer Jeff Calhoun lamented of his production, "I've never had a show close while it was still playing like a hit."[2]

As had happened more than forty years before, American reviewers couldn't reconcile the sordid subject matter livened up with soulful ballads, toe-tapping Western rhythms, and Broadway pop. "Wheel This Barrow

Out of Town," read the headline for Terry Teachout's review in the *Wall Street Journal*; the critic questioned the whole idea of a musical "based on a forty-four-year-old movie that is no longer well-remembered save by upper-middle-aged baby boomers."[3] Ben Brantley of the *New York Times* sounded the death knell with a snide dismissal that Bosley Crowther might have appreciated: "Clyde, honey, t'aint nothing you can do to raise the pulse of something that's as near to dead as the show you're now in."[4]

What a difference a decade makes.

In April 2022, informed by the alarming rise in mass shootings that plagued the United States since the musical's La Jolla premiere, *Bonnie and Clyde* opened to smash critical and popular acclaim on London's West End in a completely revamped production at the Theatre Royal Drury Lane; a definitive staging followed in March 2023 at the Garrick Theatre. Even before the curtain rose, director Nick Winston made clear that violence of a uniquely American sort would pervade everything that followed. A gunshot erupts in pitch darkness. A giant bullet hole appears in the center of the curtain, smoke issuing from the cavity—the first of many projections used to lend a cinematic feel to the staging. Over the ensuing two hours, the themes of outlawry, gunplay, and fame played out in an exhilarating display of stagecraft and performance regularly punctuated by bursts of rapturous applause from the largely youthful audience.[5]

The initial tableau presents an eerie nocturnal image of the death car. Inside, Bonnie and Clyde's bodies lie slumped over each other in a grotesque parody of a lovers' embrace. The musical's action transpires in front of a bullet-riddled American flag suspended vertically across the rear of the proscenium. In a spoken prologue not part of the original musical, Dallas deputy Ted Hinton leads a chorus of lawmen and townspeople who recite the grisly circumstances of the couple's death. "The automobile was hit with 167 steel-jacketed rounds fired from high-powered rifles in the hands of police officers," Frank Hamer states with pride. "Any one of those rounds would have been fatal to both," continues another chorus member, "but it did not seem advisable to fire just one bullet."

"Bonnie and Clyde died as they lived," Hinton pronounces. "By the gun."

Even more than Penn's film, stage director Winston's bold realization of Black and Waldman's musical[6] anchors the Barrow Gang's crime spree in a maelstrom of regenerative violence. The second-act curtain rises to reveal a historic billboard of a smiling American family encased in an automobile. Dad, mom, daughter and son, with the family dog leaning out of the rear window, stare ahead optimistically as a slogan pronounces, "There's No Way Like the American Way."[7] An onstage breadline files past a soup kitchen, singing the musical's signature number, a refrain that might have been heard in Warner Bros.' pre-Code *Gold Diggers of 1933*:

> *We may be in debt,*
> *Wake up in a sweat,*
> *But let's not forget:*
> *We were made in America.*
> *We were made in America!*

News of Clyde and Bonnie's larcenies travels among the chorus; the mood modulates from despair to anger and finally into rage, with the cast lifting the middle finger to the social and political establishment. The final curtain call doubles down on the image, backdropped by a projection of Bonnie and Clyde in silhouette, their firearms extended in opposite directions, the tattered Stars and Stripes waving behind them.

Gunshots resound.

The End.

Clyde Barrow and Bonnie Parker were American-made outlaws. *Bonnie and Clyde* remains a landmark American film.

"You guys caught lightning in a bottle with that one," screenwriters David Newman and Robert Benton remembered hearing "a thousand times" from studio executives, producers, agents, and "even aunts and uncles." In retrospect, they realized, "it seems a pretty accurate summary of what happened when you consider not only the success of the movie itself, but all the incredible stuff that followed: the fashion fad, the newspaper editorials, the hit songs, the cover stories, the satires, the posters, the amateur robberies 'in the style of,' and the pleasant, slightly spooky feeling of having coined three household words (if you include the 'and')." At the time, though, "we were just trying to sell the bottle."[8]

Arthur Penn turned that bottle into a Molotov cocktail hurled not only into the heart of the Hollywood studio system but also the dark soul of American identity. Confronted on the effects of his film's revolutionary violence, Penn never wavered in his answer. "I don't think art makes people do certain things," he said. "Art merely mirrors the era in which we live."[9]

For better or worse, *Bonnie and Clyde* still does.

 They Kill People

 Afterword and Acknowledgments

Neither a straightforward production history nor a traditional biography, *They Kill People* aims instead to center *Bonnie and Clyde* as the entry point to explore how fact is transformed into legend—even within the lives of the participants themselves—and what that fascination has to say about American society and culture. Rigorous historians may take issue with a certain reliance on anecdotal narratives, but our national inability to untangle self-propagating myth from verifiable fact is precisely the point.

My intention throughout has been to maintain a dispassionate tone in dealing with America's outlaw and firearms culture as refracted through the lens of Arthur Penn's film. So I will leave the last words on the subject to Arthur Schlesinger Jr.:

"We must remember how fragile the membranes of our civilization are, stretched so thin over a nation so disparate in its composition, so tense in its interior relationships, so cunningly enmeshed in underground fears and antagonisms, so entrapped by history in the ethos of violence,"[1] he wrote in 1968. "Unless we acknowledge the existence of the problem, unless we see the destructive impulse as rooted in our history, our society and ourselves, we will never be able to transcend the trouble within."[2]

~:·~

The *Bonnie and Clyde* production files occupy a single box in the Warner Bros. archives housed at the University of Southern California's Cinematic Arts Library. The collection spans the studio's history from its formative period in the early twenties through the mid-sixties, when "Colonel" Jack Warner sold his holdings to Seven Arts. *Bonnie and Clyde* is the very last of Warner Bros.' productions for which such documentation still exists. Thanks to the efforts of curator Bree Russell, in late May 2023 I spent a long but rewarding day poring over interoffice memos, budgets, daily call sheets, and otherwise unobtainable early drafts of the screenplay, including Warren Beatty's and Jack Warner's personal copies. No photography was permitted, and notes could only be taken in pencil, but Bree subsequently made available watermarked scans of crucial material, for which I am deeply grateful.

Two authors familiar with both the real and "reel" Barrow Gang stories deserve special mention for their assistance. Arthur Penn's biographer Nat Segaloff not only submitted to a long interview, but also graciously shared transcripts of unpublished conversations with Robert Benton and Dede Allen conducted by Philip Porcella; Nat's close friendship with Penn in the director's later years yielded many important insights. Jeff Guinn offered candid commentary on Clyde Barrow and Bonnie Parker's place in America's outlaw history both in interviews and over a monumental breakfast at Fort Worth's storied Paris Coffee Shop. He also provided support and encouragement for the book at a time when it was most sorely needed. Should you find yourself in Santa Fe after you've read these pages, Jeff, the next breakfast is on me—as long as you can handle New Mexico green chile.

My thanks to those experts in their respective fields who made time to answer my queries: Bob Boze Bell, Johnny D. Boggs, Samuel Kilborn Dolan, Loren Estleman, Mark Lee Gardner, Paul Andrew Hutton, Deborah Nadoolman Landis, David LeVay, Matthew and Molly Penn, John Neal Phillips, Betsy Gaines Quammen, Adam Winkler, and David Yazbeck. David's Tony Award–nominated musical *Dead Outlaw* debuted as *They Kill People* was being written and may represent the ultimate theatrical statement on the subject of American outlawry. It takes as its subject Elmer McCurdy, a notoriously inept bandit who achieved posthumous fame as a mummified corpse in an amusement park. "His career after he was shot and killed was more interesting than anything in his career before,"[3] says the composer.

Halfway through the writing of this book, I traveled to the Dallas-Fort Worth metroplex to visit locations frequented both by the Barrow Gang and the film crew that came thirty years after them. Steve Davis accompanied me to Hartgrave's Café, where Bonnie worked as a waitress; the Eagle Ford School, where she shared a classroom with the Mexican immigrants who now dominate her old neighborhood, and, most memorably, to Clyde's grave in the Western Heights Cemetery. Based on outdated website information warning of snakes and human varmints lurking in the supposedly overgrown plot, Steve brought along a .45-caliber sidearm, which fortunately proved unnecessary. The Barrow family's filling station home had been demolished shortly before my arrival, but a walk along the base of the Margaret Hunt Hill Bridge spanning the viaduct where Clyde grew up still conveyed a powerful sense of the marginal existence he lived.

On a scout of Red Oak, the site of *Bonnie and Clyde*'s pivotal murder of a bank official, my colleague Mike Farris wandered through a door bearing the name "Bonnie & Clyde's Salon, Spa and Barbershop." Proprietor Gabriel "The Magician" Mottu initially mistook us for building inspectors. Learning our true intent, he graciously offered up a trove of newspaper clippings dating from the location filming in the fall of 1966—and then asked if we might be interested in a DVD of eight-millimeter footage recorded by one of his client's grandparents. We were. As a result of Gabriel's generosity, a previously unknown chapter of *Bonnie and Clyde*'s making can now be told. I am forever grateful to Mike for making that detour on the way to our next destination.

For their Dallas hospitality, I am indebted to Sharon Sandell Goodwyn, her daughters Hannah and Sam, and their dogs Casper and Bella. My deepest apologies to the dogs for displacing them from some of their favorite resting places for what must have seemed an unendurable week. Thanks also to Dorothy Massey, owner of indispensable independent bookstore Collected Works in Santa Fe, New Mexico, and her event producer, Cecile Lipworth, for providing the space (and the endless cups of Iconik brand coffee) required to accomplish the final copyedit.

Stephen Hull, director of the University of New Mexico Press, first heard the pitch for these pages at the 2023 Tucson Festival of the Book (one of America's top literary celebrations and, unlike so many more elitist events, one free to the public). In contrast to my own agents, he immediately understood the subject's possibilities and championed the material throughout writing and publication. Jason and Jill Strykowski provided immeasurable assistance in collecting the photographic material to accompany the text.

Robert Nott read every chapter of *They Kill People* in its original draft and provided his usual journalist's insight. Richard B. Jewell, who inspired a generation of future film creators and scholars at the University of Southern California (and in whose "Film Genres: The Gangster Film" class at USC I first saw *Bonnie and Clyde* on the big screen), graciously agreed to review the completed manuscript and provided his usual measured advice.

David Morrell conducted a granular examination of the finished book, helping to eliminate what he likes to refer to as "overly familiar colloquial expressions" (and the rest of us call clichés). While he will be disappointed that only 99 percent of his suggestions are reflected in what I've now finished, every one of them represents an improvement.

Finally, to Sheila Ellis, my profoundest appreciation and love for your unwavering support and infallible judgment. Like Clyde Barrow and Bonnie Parker (minus the larceny and killing), we have traveled a long road together. And with no Frank Hamer to stop us, the V-8 is only picking up speed.

 Notes

INTRODUCTION

1. Lewis, "Oscar Wilde Bothered."
2. Lewis, "Oscar Wilde Bothered."
3. Lewis, "Oscar Wilde Bothered."
4. Interview with Bell. For dates of interviews, consult the selected bibliography, under Author Interviews.
5. Interview with Gardner.
6. Burrough, *Gunfighters*, 378–79.
7. Interview with Guinn.
8. Hartman, *Hidden History of Guns*, 7.
9. Rachel Weiner, "The Supreme Court Upended Gun Laws Nationwide. Mass Confusion Has Followed," *Washington Post*, July 11, 2024.
10. Dunbar-Ortiz, *Loaded*, 16.
11. Hofstadter and Wallace, *American Violence: A Documentary History*, 6.
12. Segaloff, *Arthur Penn*, 142.
13. Arthur Penn interview, in Arthur Penn, dir., *Bonnie and Clyde*, starring Warren Beatty and Faye Dunaway (Warner Bros., 1967), 40th anniversary, 2-disc special edition, DVD. Hereafter, Penn, *Bonnie and Clyde*.
14. Schlesinger, *Violence*, x.
15. Wake and Hayden, *Bonnie and Clyde Book*, 9.

CHAPTER 1

The epigraph is from Bonnie Parker, "The Story of Bonnie and Clyde," in Fortune, *Fugitives*, 247.

1. Hinton, *Ambush*, 167.
2. Hinton, *Ambush*.
3. Jenkins and Frost, *"I'm Frank Hamer,"* 206.
4. Brinkley, *Wheels for the World*, 421. The second letter rests in the collections of the Henry Ford Museum of American Innovation in Dearborn, Michigan; the handwriting is disputed.
5. Phillips, *Running with Bonnie and Clyde*, 53.
6. Phillips, *Running with Bonnie and Clyde*, 4.
7. Boessenecker, *Texas Ranger*, 432. Hinton credits himself with making the fatal identification (Hinton, *Ambush*, 168), but Hamer, Guinn and other give the "honors" to Alcorn.
8. Hinton, *Ambush*, 171.
9. Jenkins and Frost, *"I'm Frank Hamer,"* 206.
10. Hinton, *Ambush*, 169–70.
11. Burrough, *Public Enemies*, 361.
12. Boessenecker, *Texas Ranger*, 433.
13. Boessenecker, *Texas Ranger*, 437.
14. Hinton, *Ambush*, 173.
15. Chaiken and Cronin, *Arthur Penn Interviews*, 42.
16. Segaloff, *Arthur Penn*, 154.
17. Dunaway, *Looking for Gatsby*, 135.
18. Wake and Hayden, *Bonnie and Clyde Book*, 172.
19. Sherman and Rubin, *Director's Event*, 114.
20. John Baxter, *Hollywood in the Sixties* (Tantivy Press, 1972), 33.
21. Segaloff, *Arthur Penn*, 155.

CHAPTER 2

The epigraph is from Bob and Odette Blaisdell, eds., *The Wit and Wisdom of Oscar Wilde* (Courier Corporation, 2012), 155.

1. Fortune, *Fugitives*, 71.
2. Phillips, *Running with Bonnie and Clyde*, 81.
3. Fortune, *Fugitives*, 55.
4. Fortune, *Fugitives*, 23.
5. Interview with Guinn.
6. Haag, *Gunning of America*, 326.
7. Alan Mirken, ed., *The 1927 Edition of the Sears, Roebuck Catalogue: The Roaring Twenties*, 502–7 (Bounty Books, 1970).
8. Interview with Phillips
9. Fortune, *Fugitives*, 20.
10. Fortune, *Fugitives*, 28.
11. Interview with Hutton.
12. Bonnie Parker, "The Story of Bonnie and Clyde," in Fortune, *Fugitive*.
13. Marie Barrow interview, in *Remembering Bonnie and Clyde*.
14. Fortune, *Fugitives*, 68.
15. Guinn, *Go Down Together*, 47.
16. Fortune, *Fugitives*, 56.
17. Hinton, *Ambush*, xiii.
18. Fortune, *Fugitives*, 44.
19. Fortune, *Fugitives*.
20. Hinton, *Ambush*, 8.
21. Fortune, *Fugitives*, 62.
22. Boessenecker, *Texas Ranger*, 390; Guinn, *Go Down Together*, 51.
23. Fortune, *Fugitives*, 62–66.
24. Fortune, *Fugitives*.
25. Fortune, *Fugitives*, 76–77.
26. *Waco Times Herald*, March 24, 1930.
27. *Dallas Morning News*, January 30, 1930.
28. *Houston Press*, April 9, 1930.
29. Burrough, *Public Enemies*, 26.

CHAPTER 3

The epigraph is from something said to actor Matthew Modine after a take on *Full Metal Jacket* (as relayed at https://creativesamba.substack.com/p/real-is-good-interesting-is-better).

1. Finstad, *Warren Beatty*, 323.
2. Harris, *Pictures at a Revolution*, 12.
3. "Robert Benton Looks Back, Unwillingly, at a Brilliant Career," 27east, July 28, 2008, https://www.27east.com/arts/robert-benton-looks-back-unwillingly-at-a-brilliant-career-in-cinema-1377209/.
4. "Robert Benton Looks Back, Unwillingly, at a Brilliant Career."
5. Harris, *Pictures at a Revolution*, 11.
6. Harris, *Pictures at a Revolution*, 10–11.
7. *Esquire*, July 1, 1964, 25.
8. *Esquire*, July 1, 1964, 26–27.
9. David Newman, "What's It Really All About?," in Friedman, *Arthur Penn's Bonnie and Clyde*, 39.
10. Newman, "What's It Really All About?," 38–39.
11. Newman and Benton, "Lightning in a Bottle," 13.
12. Newman and Benton, "Lightning in a Bottle."
13. Newman and Benton, "Lightning in a Bottle," 13–14.
14. Toland, *Dillinger Days*, 38.
15. Toland, *Dillinger Days*, 39.
16. Newman, "What's It Really All About?," 39.
17. Biskind, *Easy Riders, Raging Bulls*, 48.
18. Newman and Benton, "Lightning in a Bottle."
19. Newman and Benton, "Lightning in a Bottle."
20. Newman and Benton, "Lightning in a Bottle," 14.
21. Newman and Benton, "Lightning in a Bottle."
22. Newman and Benton, "Lightning in a Bottle," 14–15.
23. Newman and Benton, "Lightning in a Bottle," 15.
24. Newman and Benton, "Lightning in a Bottle," 20.
25. Newman and Benton, "*Bonnie and Clyde* [screenplay]," 253.
26. Newman and Benton, "*Bonnie and Clyde* [screenplay]," 254.

27. Newman and Benton, "*Bonnie and Clyde* [screenplay]," 255.
28. All character descriptions appear in Newman and Benton, "*Bonnie and Clyde* [screenplay]," 253.
29. Newman and Benton, "*Bonnie and Clyde* [screenplay]," 256.
30. Newman and Benton, "*Bonnie and Clyde* [screenplay]," 270.
31. Newman and Benton, "*Bonnie and Clyde* [screenplay]," 263.
32. Newman and Benton, "*Bonnie and Clyde* [screenplay]."
33. Newman and Benton, "*Bonnie and Clyde* [screenplay]," 253.
34. Newman and Benton, "*Bonnie and Clyde* [screenplay]," 295.
35. Newman and Benton, "*Bonnie and Clyde* [screenplay]," 295.
36. Warren Beatty copy of *Bonnie and Clyde* script, n.d., 117.
37. Newman and Benton, "*Bonnie and Clyde* [screenplay]," 87.
38. Harris, *Pictures at a Revolution*, 18.
39. Producer Julia Phillips, who worked with Truffaut as an actor in *Close Encounters of the Third Kind*, regarded Truffaut's alleged English incomprehension "a ploy . . . to keep the world at bay and for his own private amusement." Phillips, *You'll Never Eat Lunch in This Town Again* (Random House, 1991), 244.
40. Newman and Benton, "Lightning in a Bottle," 20.
41. Harris, *Pictures at a Revolution*, 36.
42. Newman and Benton, "Lightning in a Bottle," 20.
43. Newman and Benton, "Lightning in a Bottle."
44. All Benton quotes are from in Newman and Benton, "Lightning in a Bottle," 21–22.
45. Newman and Benton, "Lightning in a Bottle."
46. Harris, *Pictures at a Revolution*, 63–64.
47. Newman and Benton, "Lightning in a Bottle," 24.
48. Newman and Benton, "Lightning in a Bottle."
49. Newman and Benton, "Lightning in a Bottle."
50. Newman and Benton, "Lightning in a Bottle."
51. Newman and Benton, "Lightning in a Bottle."
52. Harris, *Pictures at a Revolution*, 92.
53. Newman and Benton, "Lightning in a Bottle," 24; Harris, *Pictures at a Revolution*, 93.

CHAPTER 4

The epigraph is from D. H. Lawrence, *Studies in Classic American Literature* (Warbler Classics, 2023), 48.

1. Schlesinger, *Violence*, 30–31.
2. Murphy, *Violence Inside Us*, 157.
3. Murphy, *Violence Inside Us*, 41, 45.
4. Murphy, *Violence Inside Us*, 28–29.
5. Chaiken and Cronin, *Arthur Penn Interviews*, 14.
6. Murphy, *Violence Inside Us*, x–xi.
7. Kyle, *American Gun*, xiii.
8. Slotkin, *Gunfighter Nation*, 13, 77.
9. Bainbridge, *Gun Barons*, 1.
10. Haag, *Gunning of America*, 5.
11. Anderson, *Second*, 17.
12. Winkler, *Gun Fight*, 104.
13. Interview with Hutton.
14. Tony Horwitz, *Spying on the South: An Odyssey Across the American Divide* (Penguin, 2019), 235.
15. Horwitz, *Spying on the South*, 234.
16. Interview with Hutton.
17. Burrough, *Gunfighters*, 53.
18. Hulbert, *Ghosts of Guerrilla Memory*, 185, 243.
19. Interview with Bell.
20. Interview with Dolan.
21. Edwards, *Noted Guerrillas*, 450.
22. Edwards, *Noted Guerrillas*, 451.
23. Hulbert, *Ghosts of Guerrilla Memory*, 53.
24. Burns, *Saga of Billy the Kid*, 56.
25. Burns, *Saga of Billy the Kid*, 59.
26. Burns, *Saga of Billy the Kid*, 58.
27. Burns, *Saga of Billy the Kid*, 57–58.
28. Interview with Hutton.
29. Hobsbawm, *Bandits*, 46.
30. Hobsbawm, *Bandits*, 47–48.
31. Hobsbawm, *Bandits*, 51.

CHAPTER 5

The epigraph is from Doherty, *Pre-Code Hollywood*, 348.
1. Finstad, *Warren Beatty*, 345.
2. Newman and Benton, "Lightning in a Bottle," 17.
3. Haag, *Gunning of America*, 382.
4. Potter, *War on Crime*, 57.
5. Doherty, *Pre-Code Hollywood*, 150.
6. Doherty, *Pre-Code Hollywood*, 351.
7. Doherty, *Pre-Code Hollywood*.
8. Henry E. Scott, *Shocking True Story: The Rise and Fall of Confidential, "America's Most Scandalous Magazine"* (Pantheon, 2004).
9. Doherty, *Pre-Code Hollywood*, 2.
10. Doherty, *Pre-Code Hollywood*, 320.
11. Doherty, *Pre-Code Hollywood*, 321.
12. Doherty, *Hollywood Censor*, 199
13. Doherty, *Hollywood Censor*.
14. Behlmer, *Inside Warner Bros.*, 15.

CHAPTER 6

The epigraph is from Wake and Hayden, *Bonnie and Clyde Book*, 187.
1. Harris, *Pictures at a Revolution*, 17.
2. Finstad, *Warren Beatty*, 341.
3. Sherman and Rubin, *Director's Event*, 114.
4. *Guardian* interview, National Film Theatre, London, September 30, 1981.
5. Sherman and Rubin, *Director's Event*, 103.
6. Interview with Segaloff.
7. Wake and Hayden, *Bonnie and Clyde Book*, 183.
8. Wake and Hayden, *Bonnie and Clyde Book*, 11.
9. Andrew Sarris, *The American Cinema* (Da Capo Press, 1996), 123, 135–36.
10. Thomson, *Biographical Dictionary of Film*, 6th ed., 805–6.
11. Ted Sennet, *Great American Directors* (Harry N. Abrams, 1996), 195.

12. Chaiken and Cronin, *Arthur Penn Interviews*, 163, 176.
13. Segaloff, *Arthur Penn*, 18.
14. Chaiken and Cronin, *Arthur Penn Interviews*, 208.
15. Segaloff, *Arthur Penn*, 20.
16. Segaloff, *Arthur Penn*.
17. Segaloff, *Arthur Penn*, 21.
18. Segaloff, *Arthur Penn*.
19. Segaloff, *Arthur Penn*, 22.
20. Chaiken and Cronin, *Arthur Penn Interviews*, 69.
21. Chaiken and Cronin, *Arthur Penn Interviews*, 177–78.
22. Chaiken and Cronin, *Arthur Penn Interviews*, 207.
23. Segaloff, *Arthur Penn*, 61.
24. All preceding Arthur Penn quotes are from *The Left Handed Gun* DVD commentary track: Arthur Penn, dir., *The Left Handed Gun*, starring Paul Newman and John Dehner (Warner Bros., 1958). Hereafter, *Left Handed Gun* DVD commentary track. Astonishingly, the director's voice is absent from the commemorative release of *Bonnie and Clyde* and subsequent films.
25. *Guardian* interview, National Film Theatre, London, September 30, 1981.
26. Richard B. Jewell, email to author, July 31, 2024.
27. *Guardian* interview, National Film Theatre, London, September 30, 1981.
28. Segaloff, *Arthur Penn*, 65.
29. Segaloff, *Arthur Penn*, 65–66.
30. *Left Handed Gun* DVD commentary track.
31. *Left Handed Gun* DVD commentary track.
32. *Left Handed Gun* DVD commentary track.
33. *Guardian* interview, National Film Theatre, London, September 30, 1981.
34. Segaloff, *Arthur Penn*, 117.
35. Sarris, *American Cinema*, 135.
36. Finstad, *Warren Beatty*, 314.

37. *Guardian* interview, National Film Theatre, London, September 30, 1981.
38. Finstad, *Warren Beatty*, 317.
39. Segaloff, *Arthur Penn*, 122.
40. Harris, *Pictures at a Revolution*, 149.
41. Wake and Hayden, *Bonnie and Clyde Book*, 166.
42. Chaiken and Cronin, *Arthur Penn Interviews*, 183.
43. Finstad, *Warren Beatty*, 325.
44. Chaiken and Cronin, *Arthur Penn Interviews*, 183.
45. Finstad, *Warren Beatty*, 359.
46. Friedman, *Arthur Penn's Bonnie and Clyde*, 12.
47. Robert Benton interview, in Penn, *Bonnie and Clyde*.
48. Harris, *Pictures at a Revolution*, 207.
49. Newman and Benton, "Lightning in a Bottle," 28.
50. Friedman, *Arthur Penn's Bonnie and Clyde*, 20.
51. Wake and Hayden, *Bonnie and Clyde Book*, 171.
52. Wake and Hayden, *Bonnie and Clyde Book*.
53. Chaiken and Cronin, *Arthur Penn Interviews*, 184.
54. Richard B. Jewell, email to author, July 31, 2024.
55. Newman and Benton, "Lightning in a Bottle," 26.
56. Undated interview with Benton, late 1977 or early 1978. Transcript courtesy of Nat Segaloff.
57. Friedman, *Arthur Penn's Bonnie and Clyde*, 11.
58. Harris, *Pictures at a Revolution*, 153.
59. Wake and Hayden, *Bonnie and Clyde Book*, 185.
60. Chaiken and Cronin, *Arthur Penn Interviews*, 184.
61. Chaiken and Cronin, *Arthur Penn Interviews*, 22.
62. Geoff Boucher, "Remembering *Bonnie and Clyde*," *Los Angeles Times*, March 23, 2008.
63. Boucher, "Remembering *Bonnie and Clyde*."
64. Newman and Benton, "*Bonnie and Clyde*," 286.

CHAPTER 7

The epigraph is from Newman and Benton's *Bonnie and Clyde* screenplay, in Wake and Hayden, *Bonnie and Clyde Book*, 64.

1. Doherty, *Pre-Code Hollywood*, 161.
2. Doherty, *Pre-Code Hollywood*.
3. LeRoy, *Mervyn LeRoy*, 109.
4. Wikipedia, "I Am a Fugitive from a Chain Gang," last modified July 8, 2025, https://en.wikipedia.org/wiki/I_Am_a_Fugitive_from_a_Chain_Gang.
5. LeRoy, *Mervyn LeRoy*, 110.
6. LeRoy, *Mervyn LeRoy*, 111.
7. Wikipedia, "I Am a Fugitive from a Chain Gang."
8. Burns remained a felon until 1945, when Georgia finally commuted his sentence.
9. Marie Barrow interview, in *Remembering Bonnie and Clyde*.
10. Philips, *Running with Bonnie and Clyde*, 38.
11. Blumenthal, *Bonnie and Clyde*, 39.
12. Blumenthal, *Bonnie and Clyde*, 37.
13. Interview with Phillips.
14. Fortune, *Fugitives*, 101.
15. Fortune, *Fugitives*, 102.
16. Fortune, *Fugitives*, 103.
17. Fortune, *Fugitives*.
18. Egan, *Worst Hard Time*, 95.
19. Egan, *Worst Hard Time*, 114.
20. Interview with Phillips.
21. Fortune, *Fugitives*, 105.
22. Guinn, *Go Down Together*, 93.
23. Guinn, *Go Down Together*.
24. Schneider, *Bonnie and Clyde*, 156.
25. Hinton, *Ambush*, 112.
26. Philips, *Running with Bonnie and Clyde*, 78.
27. Modern historians mostly validate Clyde's claims, placing him as the driver in the Bucher killing and nowhere to be seen in Hall's murder.

28. Fortune, *Fugitives*, 115.
29. Fortune, *Fugitives*, 105.
30. Philips, *Running with Bonnie and Clyde*, 90.
31. Phillips, *Running with Bonnie and Clyde*, 91.
32. Fortune, *Fugitives*, 105.
33. Fortune, *Fugitives*, 107.
34. Guinn, *Go Down Together*, 110. Guinn's citations of the poem derive from Bonnie's original notebooks, obtained from a private collection; all other references rely on the revised version found and published after the raid in Joplin, Missouri, over a year later.
35. Guinn, *Go Down Together*, 110.
36. Fortune, *Fugitives*, 108–9.
37. Chaiken and Cronin, *Arthur Penn Interviews*, 40.
38. Chaiken and Cronin, *Arthur Penn Interviews*, 41.
39. Chaiken and Cronin, *Arthur Penn Interviews*, 42.
40. Chaiken and Cronin, *Arthur Penn Interviews*, 44.
41. Chaiken and Cronin, *Arthur Penn Interviews*, 46.
42. Chaiken and Cronin, *Arthur Penn Interviews*, 47.
43. Wake and Hayden, *Bonnie and Clyde Book*, 7–8.
44. Fortune, *Fugitives*, 247.
45. Fortune, *Fugitives*, 249.
46. Fortune, *Fugitives*, 248.
47. Fortune, *Fugitives*, 250.

CHAPTER 8

1. FBI File No. 26-4397, in Bonnie and Clyde: The Dallas Field Office Files.
2. Potter, *War on Crime*, 96.
3. FBI File No. 25-5501, in Bonnie and Clyde: The Dallas Field Office Files.
4. Hoover letter, dated September 8, 1933, in FBI File No. 25-5501, in Bonnie and Clyde: The Dallas Field Office Files.
5. Hobsbawm, *Bandits*, 184.

6. Hobsbawm, *Bandits*.
7. Cawelti, *Six-Gun Mystique Sequel*, 38–39.
8. Trefethen and Serven, *Americans and Their Guns*, 13.
9. Interview with Winkler.
10. Waldman, *Second Amendment*, xiii.
11. Halbrook, *That Every Man Be Armed*, 57.
12. Interview with Hutton.
13. Frederick Jackson Turner, "The Significance of the Frontier in American History (excerpts)," accessed June 19, 2025, http://nationalhumanitiescenter.org/pds/gilded/empire/text1/turner.pdf.
14. Erdozian, *One Nation Under Guns*, 91.
15. Program for the 1886 Wild West Show, quote in Slotkin, *Gunfighter Nation*, 67.
16. Schlesinger, *Violence*, 47.
17. Slotkin, *Gunfighter Nation*, 192–93.
18. Slotkin, *Gunfighter Nation*, 154
19. Interview with Winkler.
20. Dykstra, *Cattle Towns*, 122n1.
21. Dykstra, *Cattle Towns*, 116.
22. Interview with Boggs.
23. Sonnichsen, *From Hopalong to Hud*, 23–24.
24. Winkler, *Gun Fight*, 160.
25. Winkler, *Gun Fight*.
26. Interview with Boggs.
27. Winkler, *Gun Fight*, 173.
28. Winkle, *Gun Fight* r, 63.
29. Smyth, *NRA*, 24.
30. Trefethen, 291.
31. Smyth, *NRA*, 50.
32. Schlesinger, *Violence*, 46.
33. HR 1 (known as the "One Big, Beautiful Bill"), signed into law by President Donald J. Trump on July 4, 2025, reduced the National Firearms Act's excise tax on noise suppressors and short-barreled weapons from $200 to

$0, but fell short of outright removal from the list of proscribed firearms and accessories.
34. Smyth, *NRA*, 51.
35. Smyth, *NRA*, 51; see also Winkler, *Gun Fight*, 210–11.
36. Winkler, *Gun Fight*, 210–11.
37. Winkler, *Gun Fight*, 212.
38. Smyth, *NRA*, 53.
39. Winkler, *Gun Fight*, 214.
40. Winkler, *Gun Fight*, 215.
41. Waldman, *Second Amendment*, 83.
42. Halbrook, *That Every Man Be Armed*, 185.
43. In 2008, the US Supreme Court ruled in *District of Columbia v. Heller* that the Second Amendment applied to an individual right to bear arms outside militia service. Justice Antonin Scalia wrote the landmark decision, which divided the court by a vote of 5 to 4.
44. Schlesinger, *Violence*, ix.
45. Schlesinger, *Violence*, 47.

CHAPTER 9

The epigraph is from a Warren Beatty interview with Curtis Hanson, in Wake and Hayden, *Bonnie and Clyde Book*, 179.
1. Robert Benton interview, in Penn, *Bonnie and Clyde*.
2. Harris, *Pictures at a Revolution*, 95.
3. Harris, *Pictures at a Revolution*.
4. Finstad, *Warren Beatty*, 344.
5. Harris, *Pictures at a Revolution*, 95.
6. Harris. In interviews with Finstad, Segaloff, and others, Benton's page count differed.
7. Warren Beatty copy of *Bonnie and Clyde* script, n.d., 33.
8. Warren Beatty copy of *Bonnie and Clyde* script, n.d.
9. Warren Beatty copy of *Bonnie and Clyde* script, n.d.
10. Warren Beatty copy of *Bonnie and Clyde* script, n.d., 34.
11. Warren Beatty copy of *Bonnie and Clyde* script, n.d.
12. Warren Beatty interview, in Penn, *Bonnie and Clyde*.

13. Warren Beatty interview, in Penn, *Bonnie and Clyde*.
14. Wake and Hayden, *Bonnie and Clyde Book*, 178.
15. Finstad, *Warren Beatty*, 232.
16. Finstad, *Warren Beatty*, 71.
17. Finstad, *Warren Beatty*, 3.
18. Finstad, *Warren Beatty*, 54.
19. Finstad, *Warren Beatty*, 197.
20. Finstad, *Warren Beatty*.
21. Kazan, *Elia Kazan: A Life* (Knopf, 1988), 603.
22. Finstad, *Warren Beatty*, 303.
23. Finstad, *Warren Beatty*, 302.
24. Finstad, *Warren Beatty*, xiii–xiv. Rossen collapsed from exhaustion during production and never directed another picture; Seberg attributed his death less than two years later in part to tensions on the *Lilith* set.
25. Wake and Hayden, *Bonnie and Clyde Book*, 178.
26. Finstad, *Warren Beatty*, 319.
27. Boucher, "Remembering *Bonnie and Clyde*."
28. De Baecque and Toubiana, *Truffaut*, 212.
29. Finstad, *Warren Beatty*, 343.
30. Robert Towne interview, in Penn, *Bonnie and Clyde*.
31. Harris, *Pictures at a Revolution*, 153.
32. Wake and Hayden, *Bonnie and Clyde Book*, 179.
33. Harris, *Pictures at a Revolution*, 154.
34. Chaiken and Cronin, *Arthur Penn Interviews*, 45.
35. Finstad, *Warren Beatty*, 359.
36. Harris, *Pictures at a Revolution*, 193.
37. Finstad, *Warren Beatty*, 281.
38. Boucher, "Remembering *Bonnie and Clyde*."
39. Warren Beatty interview, in Penn, *Bonnie and Clyde*.
40. Harris, *Pictures at a Revolution*, 194.
41. These and all subsequent contractual and budget numbers are from the Warner Bros. files, at the University of Southern California's Cinematic Arts Library.
42. Biskind, *Easy Riders, Raging Bulls*, 29–30.

43. Wood and Wagner reunited in 1972 and remained married until Wood's death by drowning in November 1981, at age 43.
44. Finstad, *Warren Beatty*, 362.
45. Finstad, *Warren Beatty*, 363. A few years earlier, in 1962, Weld had guest-starred in " A Case Study of Two Savages," an episode of ABC's one-hour police drama, *Naked City*. The disturbing plot followed the murder rampage of a young Southern couple throughout New York City, intended to remind viewers of a similar rampage by Charles Starkweather and Carol Ann Fugate throughout Nebraska and Wyoming in 1958.
46. Finstad, *Warren Beatty*, 363.
47. Dunaway, *Looking for Gatsby*, 122.
48. Dunaway, *Looking for Gatsby*, 11.
49. Dunaway, *Looking for Gatsby*, 132.
50. Laurent Bouzereau, dir., *Faye: The Many Lives of Faye Dunaway* (HBO Documentary Films, 2024).
51. Dunaway, *Looking for Gatsby*, 13
52. Dunaway, *Looking for Gatsby*, 95.
53. Dunaway, *Looking for Gatsby*, 99.
54. Dunaway, *Looking for Gatsby*, 96.
55. Dunaway, *Looking for Gatsby*, 111–12.
56. Dunaway, *Looking for Gatsby*, 96.
57. Harris, *Pictures at a Revolution*, 248.
58. Finstad, *Warren Beatty*, 368.
59. Dunaway, *Looking for Gatsby*, 122.
60. Harris, *Pictures at a Revolution*, 248.
61. Dunaway, *Looking for Gatsby*, 58.
62. Harris, *Pictures at a Revolution*, 248.
63. Dunaway, *Looking for Gatsby*, 115.
64. Finstad, *Warren Beatty*, 367; Warren Beatty interview, in Penn, *Bonnie and Clyde*.
65. Gene Hackman interview, in Penn, *Bonnie and Clyde*.
66. Harris, *Pictures at a Revolution*, 209.
67. Estelle Parsons interview, in Penn, *Bonnie and Clyde*.
68. Biskind, *Easy Riders, Raging Bulls*, 30.

69. Finstad, *Warren Beatty*, 367.
70. Harris, *Pictures at a Revolution*, 214.
71. Finstad, *Warren Beatty*, 349.
72. Finstad, *Warren Beatty*, 350.
73. Biskind, *Easy Riders, Raging Bulls*, 50.
74. Chaiken and Cronin, *Arthur Penn Interviews*, 168.
75. Penn, "Making Waves," 23–24.
76. Newman and Benton (and Towne),"*Bonnie and Clyde* [screenplay]," 122.
77. Biskind, *Easy Riders, Raging Bulls*, 50.
78. Harris, *Pictures at a Revolution*, 215.
79. Harris, *Pictures at a Revolution*.
80. Segaloff, *Arthur Penn*, 154.
81. Sherman and Rubin, *Director's Event*, 106–7.
82. Sherman and Rubin, *Director's Event*, 107. Italics in original.
83. The *AFI Catalog of Feature Films* lists October 4, 1966, as the production's start date, but call sheets and memos in the Warner Bros. archives at the University of Southern California Cinematic Arts Library are all dated October 11.
84. Leff and Simmons, *Dame in the Kimono*, 264.
85. Shurlock letter to Jack L. Warner, October 13, 1966, Warner Bros. archives.
86. MacEwen note, Warner Bros. archives.
87. Jack L. Warner telegram to Beatty, October 11, 1966, Warner Bros. archives.
88. Jack L. Warner interoffice memorandum to MacEwen, n.d., Warner Bros. archives.
89. Finstad, *Warren Beatty*, 369; Harris, *Pictures at a Revolution*, 195.

CHAPTER 10

The epigraph is from Blumenthal, *Bonnie and Clyde*, 7. A Texas native and long-time Democratic congressman, Wright served as Speaker of the US House of Representatives from 1987 to 1989.

1. Interview with Guinn.
2. Guinn, *Go Down Together*, 172.
3. Hinton, *Ambush*, 39.
4. Interview with Guinn.
5. Interview with Guinn.
6. Fortune, *Fugitives*, 163.
7. Fortune, *Fugitives*, 239.
8. Interview with Guinn.
9. Interview with Guinn.
10. Interview with Guinn.
11. Interview with Guinn.
12. Blumenthal, *Bonnie and Clyde*, 167.
13. Potter, *War on Crime*, 8.
14. Interview with Guinn.
15. Guinn, *Go Down Together*, 241.
16. Knight and Davis, *Bonnie and Clyde*, 141.
17. Fortune, *Fugitives*, 126.
18. Fortune, *Fugitives*.
19. Fortune, *Fugitives*, 211.
20. Fortune, *Fugitives*, 191.
21. Potter, *War on Crime*, 93.
22. Potter, *War on Crime*, 223.
23. Newman and Benton, "*Bonnie and Clyde*," 280. The writers likely took their inspiration from a nearly identical moment in *Fugitives* when Emma Parker asks, "Where you going now, Clyde?" "Driving," he says. "Just driving from now till they get us." Fortune, *Fugitives*, 132.
24. Interview with Guinn.
25. Richard B. Jewell, email to author, July 31, 1924.
26. Interview with Phillips.
27. Guinn, *Go Down Together*, 131.

28. Fortune, *Fugitives*, 213.
29. Fortune, *Fugitives*, 165.
30. Fortune, *Fugitives*, 156.
31. Fortune, *Fugitives*, 157.
32. Newman and Benton, "Bonnie and Clyde," 267.
33. Guinn, *Go Down Together*, 364.
34. Interview with Phillips.
35. Barrow, *My Life with Bonnie and Clyde*, 183.
36. Barrow, *My Life with Bonnie and Clyde*, 62.
37. Fortune, *Fugitives*, 157.
38. Interview with Phillips.
39. Blumenthal, *Bonnie and Clyde*, 124.
40. Interview with Phillips.
41. Interview with Guinn.
42. Interview with Guinn.
43. Interview with Phillips.
44. Barrow, *My Life with Bonnie and Clyde*, 43.
45. Barrow, *My Life with Bonnie and Clyde*.
46. Barrow, *My Life with Bonnie and Clyde*, 42.
47. Barrow, *My Life with Bonnie and Clyde*, 44.
48. Barrow, *My Life with Bonnie and Clyde*, 45.
49. FBI File No. 26-4397, in Bonnie and Clyde: The Dallas Field Office Files.
50. Fortune, *Fugitives*, 157.
51. Schneider, *Bonnie and Clyde*, 233.
52. Interview with Phillips.
53. Newman and Benton, "Bonnie and Clyde," 269.
54. Newman and Benton, "Bonnie and Clyde," 270.
55. Barrow, *My Life with Bonnie and Clyde*, 42.
56. Fortune, *Fugitives*, 151.
57. Newman and Benton, "Bonnie and Clyde," 270.
58. Barrow, *My Life with Bonnie and Clyde*, 56.
59. Barrow, *My Life with Bonnie and Clyde*, 54–55.
60. Barrow, *My Life with Bonnie and Clyde*, 56–57.
61. Barrow, *My Life with Bonnie and Clyde*, 55.

62. Wake and Hayden, *Bonnie and Clyde Book*, 9.
63. Guinn, *Go Down Together*, 210.
64. Letter dated June 27, 1933, in Bonnie and Clyde: The Dallas Field Office Files.
65. Letter dated June 27, 1933, in Bonnie and Clyde: The Dallas Field Office Files.
66. Guinn, *Go Down Together*, 210.

CHAPTER 11

1. Haag, *Gunning of America*, xviii.
2. Haag, *Gunning of America*.
3. Haag, *Gunning of America*, 163.
4. Bainbridge, *Gun Barons*, 42.
5. Bainbridge, *Gun Barons*, 30.
6. Haag, *Gunning of America*, xiii.
7. Murphy, *Violence Inside Us*, 47.
8. Interview with Winkler.
9. Slotkin, *Gunfighter Nation*, 352.
10. Haag, *Gunning of America*, 201.
11. Dunbar-Ortiz, *Loaded*, 79.
12. Cramer, *Armed America*, 56.
13. Cramer, *Armed America*, 63.
14. Interview with Winkler.
15. Haag, *Gunning of America*, 33.
16. Haag, *Gunning of America*, 69.
17. Phil Klay, "How Did Guns Get So Powerful?" *New Yorker*, June 11, 1922.
18. The structure remained intact until 1936, when it was destroyed by fire; a rail stop still bears the name.
19. Bainbridge, *Gun Barons*, 118–19.
20. Rasenberger, *Revolver*, 275.
21. Rasenberger, *Revolver*.
22. Rasenberger, *Revolver*, 287.
23. Bainbridge, *Gun Barons*, 116.

24. Rasenberger, *Revolver*, 276.
25. Haag, *Gunning of America*, 40.
26. Rasenberger, *Revolver*, 286.
27. Bainbridge, *Gun Barons*, 275.
28. Bainbridge, *Gun Barons*, 377.
29. Bainbridge, *Gun Barons*, 188.
30. Rasenberger, *Revolver*, 380.
31. Rasenberger, *Revolver*, 379–80.
32. Haag, *Gunning of America*, 388.
33. Haag, *Gunning of America*, 198.
34. Schlesinger, *Violence*, 58.
35. Interview with Winkler.
36. Haag, *Gunning of America*, 89.
37. Haag, *Gunning of America*, 339.
38. Haag, *Gunning of America*, 146.
39. Haag, *Gunning of America*, 339.
40. Company records indicate that Winchester sold precisely eighteen of 126 rifles manufactured in 1873.
41. Haag, *Gunning of America*, 186.
42. Haag, *Gunning of America*, 362.
43. Haag, *Gunning of America*, 181–82.
44. Cawelti, *Six-Gun Mystique Sequel*, 39.
45. Haag, *Gunning of America*, 333.
46. Haag, *Gunning of America*, 324.
47. Haag, *Gunning of America*.
48. Knight and Davis, *Bonnie and Clyde*, 7.
49. Haag, *Gunning of America*, 330.
50. Haag, *Gunning of America*.
51. Colt ad reproduced in Haag, *Gunning of America*, 331.
52. Interview with Hutton.
53. Harris, *Pictures at a Revolution*, 60.
54. Guinn, *Go Down Together*, 13.
55. Doherty, *Pre-Code Hollywood*, 356.
56. Doherty, *Pre-Code Hollywood*, 362.

CHAPTER 12

1. The actor has since been identified as one Justus D. Barnes, a classically trained stage performer with a name and face straight out of a "WANTED!" poster.
2. George C. Pratt, *Spellbound in Darkness: A History of the Silent Film* (New York Graphic Society, 1973), 36.
3. Pratt, *Spellbound in Darkness*, 34.
4. George Fenin and William K. Everson, *The Western: From Silents to the Seventies* (Penguin Books, 1973), 47.
5. Pratt, *Spellbound in Darkness*, 34.
6. Segaloff, *Arthur Penn*, 153.
7. Segaloff, *Arthur Penn*.
8. Newman and Benton, "Bonnie and Clyde," 263.
9. Jack L. Warner copy of *Bonnie and Clyde* script, dated September 6, 1966.
10. Chaiken and Cronin, *Arthur Penn Interviews*, 199.
11. Newman and Benton (and Towne), "Bonnie and Clyde," 70.
12. Imagine that in today's media environment.
13. "Red Oak Turns Back: Town Provides Background for Depression," *Dallas Morning News*, October 23, 1966.
14. Boucher, "Remembering 'Bonnie and Clyde.'"
15. "Shooting Too Real for Man," *Dallas Morning News*, n.d.
16. Hollywood vocabulary is loaded with firearm vernacular. An actor "looks down the barrel" of a lens, while the ritual countdown of "Speed!—Set!—Action!" bears the same cadence as "Ready!—Aim!—Fire!"
17. "Bonnie and Clyde Movie Recalled by Residents," *News-Texas Special from Garland*, n.d.
18. "Bonnie and Clyde Movie Recalled by Residents," *News-Texas Special from Garland*, n.d.
19. Harris, *Pictures at a Revolution*, 250.
20. Harris, *Pictures at a Revolution*.
21. Warren Beatty interview, in Penn, *Bonnie and Clyde*.
22. Harris, *Pictures at a Revolution*, 210.
23. Harris, *Pictures at a Revolution*, 258.
24. Memo from Reddish, n.d., Warner Bros. archives.

25. Robert Benton interview, in Penn, *Bonnie and Clyde*.
26. Robert Towne, "A Trip with Bonnie and Clyde," in Wake and Hayden, *Bonnie and Clyde Book*, 174.
27. Towne, "A Trip with Bonnie and Clyde," 174.
28. Five years later, Benton and Newman's mentor Peter Bogdanovich and his cinematographer Laszlo Kovacs would demonstrate how the same nostalgia could be reclaimed in monochrome in *Paper Moon*.
29. Chaiken and Cronin, *Arthur Penn Interviews*, 124.
30. Sherman and Rubin, *Director's Event*, 112.
31. Segaloff, *Arthur Penn*, 148.
32. Segaloff, *Arthur Penn*.
33. Mintzer, *Conversations with Dean Tavoularis*, 31.
34. Mintzer, *Conversations with Dean Tavoularis*, 51.
35. Mintzer, *Conversations with Dean Tavoularis*, 51–52.
36. Warner Bros. archives.
37. Dean Tavoularis interview, in Penn, *Bonnie and Clyde*.
38. Harris, *Pictures at a Revolution*, 253.
39. Mintzer, *Conversations with Dean Tavoularis*, 57. Visiting these same places today, a traveler is struck by how camera-ready the locations remain.
40. Towne, "A Trip with Bonnie and Clyde," 174.
41. Mintzer, *Conversations with Dean Tavoularis*, 54.
42. Lightman, "Raw Cinematic Realism."
43. "Red Oak Turns Back: Town Provides Background for Depression," *Dallas Morning News*, October 23, 1966
44. Finstad, *Warren Beatty*, 366.
45. Finstad, *Warren Beatty*.
46. Finstad, *Warren Beatty*.
47. Finstad, *Warren Beatty*.
48. Arthur Penn interview, in Penn, *Bonnie and Clyde*.
49. Arthur Penn interview, in Penn, *Bonnie and Clyde*, 266.
50. Arthur Penn interview, in Penn, *Bonnie and Clyde*.
51. Interview with David LeVay.
52. Interview with Deborah Nadoolman Landis.
53. Interview with David LeVay.
54. Finstad, *Warren Beatty*, 369.

55. Finstad, *Warren Beatty*.
56. Finstad, *Warren Beatty*.
57. Theadora Van Runkle interview, in Penn, *Bonnie and Clyde*.
58. Harris, *Pictures at a Revolution*, 250–51.
59. Theadora Van Runkle interview, in Penn, *Bonnie and Clyde*.
60. Chaiken and Cronin, *Arthur Penn Interviews*, 36.
61. Chaiken and Cronin, *Arthur Penn Interviews*, 39.
62. Chaiken and Cronin, *Arthur Penn Interviews*.
63. Chaiken and Cronin, *Arthur Penn Interviews*, 57.
64. Arthur Penn interview, in Penn, *Bonnie and Clyde*.
65. Chaiken and Cronin, *Arthur Penn Interviews*, 38.
66. Gene Hackman interview, in Penn, *Bonnie and Clyde*.
67. Chaiken and Cronin, *Arthur Penn Interviews*, 36.
68. Segaloff, *Arthur Penn*, 152.
69. Segaloff, *Arthur Penn*.
70. Boucher, "Remembering 'Bonnie and Clyde.'"
71. Dunaway, *Looking for Gatsby*, 123.
72. Dunaway, *Looking for Gatsby*.
73. Towne, "A Trip with Bonnie and Clyde," 175–76.
74. Towne, "A Trip with Bonnie and Clyde," 175–76.
75. *Dallas Morning News*, n.d.
76. Boucher, "Remembering 'Bonnie and Clyde.'"
77. Finstad, *Warren Beatty*, 370.
78. Harris, *Pictures at a Revolution*, 251.
79. Harris, *Pictures at a Revolution*.
80. Finstad, *Warren Beatty*, 371.
81. Harris, *Pictures at a Revolution*, 251.
82. Finstad, *Warren Beatty*, 371.
83. Harris, *Pictures at a Revolution*, 250.
84. Harris, *Pictures at a Revolution*.
85. Boucher, "Remembering 'Bonnie and Clyde.'"
86. Harris, *Pictures at a Revolution*, 246.
87. Boucher, "Remembering 'Bonnie and Clyde.'"
88. Harris, *Pictures at a Revolution*, 247.
89. Faye Dunaway interview, in Penn, *Bonnie and Clyde*.

90. Arthur Penn interview, in Penn, *Bonnie and Clyde*.
91. Interview with Matthew and Molly Penn.
92. Boucher, "Remembering "Bonnie and Clyde."
93. Wake and Hayden, *Bonnie and Clyde Book*, 182.
94. Harris, *Pictures at a Revolution*, 246.
95. Harris, *Pictures at a Revolution*, 216.
96. Harris, *Pictures at a Revolution*, 246.
97. Harris, *Pictures at a Revolution*.
98. Segaloff, *Arthur Penn*, 149.
99. Segaloff, *Arthur Penn*.

CHAPTER 13

The epigraph is from Fortune, *Fugitives*, 150.

1. Phillips, *Running with Bonnie and Clyde*, 135.
2. Burrough, *Public Enemies*, 28.
3. Burrough, *Public Enemies*; Phillips, *Running with Bonnie and Clyde*, 135.
4. Guinn, *Go Down Together*, 193.
5. Guinn, *Go Down Together*.
6. Burrough, *Public Enemies*, 30.
7. Barrow, *My Life with Bonnie and Clyde*, 95.
8. Burrough, *Public Enemies*, 30.
9. David Newman, "What's It Really All About?," in Friedman, *Arthur Penn's Bonnie and Clyde*, 38.
10. Sherman and Rubin, *Director's Event*, 113.
11. Fortune, *Fugitives*, 150.
12. Fortune, *Fugitives*, 113.
13. Fortune, *Fugitives*, 141.
14. Newman and Benton, "Bonnie and Clyde," 260.
15. Newman and Benton, "Bonnie and Clyde."
16. Newman and Benton, "Bonnie and Clyde," 263.
17. Barrow, *My Life with Bonnie and Clyde*, 109.
18. Guinn, *Go Down Together*, 212–13.
19. Guinn, *Go Down Together*, 211.

20. Phillips, *Running with Bonnie and Clyde*, 141.
21. Barrow, *My Life with Bonnie and Clyde*, 111.
22. Guinn, *Go Down Together*, 213.
23. Guinn, *Go Down Together*, 215.
24. Toland, *Dillinger Days*, 79.
25. US Bureau of Investigation File No. 26-4397, August 17, 1933.
26. Phillips, *Running with Bonnie and Clyde*, 143.
27. Guinn, *Go Down Together*, 215.
28. Barrow, *My Life with Bonnie and Clyde*, 119.
29. Toland, *Dillinger Days*, 80.
30. Bryan Burrough recounts the mattress story in *Public Enemies*, maintaining that Buck's wound was self-inflicted, sustained when his BAR continued to fire as he stumbled; Burrough, *Public Enemies*, 63.
31. Guinn, *Go Down Together*, 216.
32. Barrow, *My Life with Bonnie and Clyde*, 119.
33. Barrow, *My Life with Bonnie and Clyde*, 121.
34. Knight and Davis, *Bonnie and Clyde*, 102.
35. Newman and Benton, "Bonnie and Clyde," 284.
36. Barrow, *My Life with Bonnie and Clyde*, 128.
37. Newman and Benton, "Bonnie and Clyde," 284.
38. Newman and Benton, "Bonnie and Clyde," 284–85.
39. Warren Beatty copy of *Bonnie and Clyde* script, n.d., 117.
40. Newman and Benton, "Bonnie and Clyde," 285.
41. Harris, *Pictures at a Revolution*, 251.
42. The site today is one of South Dallas's largest waste management facilities.
43. Guinn, *Go Down Together*, 223.
44. Blumenthal, *Bonnie and Clyde*, 129.
45. Piper interview, in *Remembering Bonnie and Clyde*.
46. Guinn, *Go Down Together*, 224.
47. Guinn, *Go Down Together*, 225.
48. Phillips, *Running with Bonnie and Clyde*, 151.
49. Fortune, *Fugitives*, 203.
50. Fortune, *Fugitives*, 202.
51. Barrow, *My Life with Bonnie and Clyde*, 133.
52. Phillips, *Running with Bonnie and Clyde*, 155.

53. Guinn, *Go Down Together*, 225.
54. US Bureau of Investigation File No. 26-4397, August 17, 1933.
55. US Bureau of Investigation File No. 26-4397, August 17, 1933.
56. Newman and Benton, "*Bonnie and Clyde*," 286. The sequence appears with only minor changes in the revised version published in Wake and Hayden, *Bonnie and Clyde Book*, 135–37, reinforcing the notion that Penn made his changes on the spot and later in editing.
57. Newman and Benton, "*Bonnie and Clyde*," 286.
58. Newman and Benton, "*Bonnie and Clyde*."
59. Newman and Benton, "*Bonnie and Clyde*."
60. Newman and Benton, "*Bonnie and Clyde*."

CHAPTER 14

The epigraph is from Boessenecker, *Texas Ranger*, 135.
1. Newman and Benton, "*Bonnie and Clyde*," 253.
2. Newman and Benton, "*Bonnie and Clyde*," 272.
3. Newman and Benton, "*Bonnie and Clyde*."
4. Newman and Benton (and Towne), "*Bonnie and Clyde*," 95.
5. Newman and Benton, "*Bonnie and Clyde*," 272.
6. Newman and Benton, "*Bonnie and Clyde*," 272–73.
7. Newman and Benton, "*Bonnie and Clyde*," 273.
8. Newman and Benton, "*Bonnie and Clyde*."
9. Interoffice communication, September 12, 1966. Warner Bros. archives.
10. Interoffice communication, September 12, 1966. Warner Bros. archives.
11. Undated telegram from attorney Jose (Joseph) D. Jamail, Warner Bros. archives.
12. Boessenecker, *Texas Ranger*, 461.
13. Utley, *Lone Star Lawmen*, 164.
14. Boessenecker, *Texas Ranger*, 5.
15. Swanson, *Cult of Glory*, 307.
16. Sherman and Rubin, *Director's Event*, 114.
17. Interview with Guinn.
18. Jenkins and Frost, "*I'm Frank Hamer*," 51–52.

19. Jenkins and Frost, "I'm Frank Hamer," 52; Swanson, Cult of Glory, 280.
20. Jenkins and Frost, "I'm Frank Hamer," 51.
21. Boessenecker, Texas Ranger, 77.
22. Boessenecker, Texas Ranger.
23. Boessenecker, Texas Ranger, 11.
24. Boessenecker, Texas Ranger, 13.
25. In The Gunfighters: How Texas Made the West Wild, Bryan Burrough makes a convincing case for the state's honor culture as the foundation for all the West's gunslinger legends. The book can be read as prequel to his essential account of the thirties crime wave, Public Enemies.
26. Guinn, Go Down Together, 252.
27. Boessenecker, Texas Ranger, 244.
28. Walter Prescott Webb, The Texas Rangers: A Century of Frontier Defense (University of Texas Press, 1935), 524.
29. Boessenecker, Texas Ranger, 104–5.
30. Swanson, Cult of Glory, 283; Boessenecker, Texas Ranger, 184–85; Utley, Lone Star Lawmen, 73.
31. Arelis R. Hernandez and Frank Holley Jones, "After a Borderland Shootout, a 100-Year-Old Battle for the Truth," Washington Post, May 15, 1924.
32. Swanson, Cult of Glory, 64.
33. Swanson, Cult of Glory, 65.
34. Rasenberger, Revolver, 193.
35. Swanson, Cult of Glory, 65–66.
36. Swanson, Cult of Glory, 66.
37. Rasenberger, Revolver, 234.
38. Rasenberger, Revolver, 238.
39. Fehrenbach, Lone Star, 482.
40. Swanson, Cult of Glory, 112.
41. Utley, Lone Star Lawmen, 6.
42. Swanson, Cult of Glory, 249.
43. Boessenecker, Texas Ranger, 22.
44. Boessenecker, Texas Ranger.
45. Utley, Lone Star Lawmen, 28; Boessenecker, Texas Ranger, 123.
46. Utley, Lone Star Lawmen, 27.

47. Monica Muñoz Martinez, "How 'The Highwaymen' Whitewashes Frank Hamer and the Texas Rangers," March 31, 2019, www.washingtonpost.com/outlook/2019/03/31/how-highwaymen-whitewashes-frank-hamer-texas-rangers/.
48. Boessenecker, *Texas Ranger*, 130.
49. Boessenecker, *Texas Ranger*, 135.
50. Swanson, *Cult of Glory*, 254.
51. Boessenecker, *Texas Ranger*, 134.
52. Boessenecker, *Texas Ranger*, 228.
53. Utley, *Lone Star Lawmen*, 88.
54. Boessenecker, *Texas Ranger*, 84.
55. Boessenecker, *Texas Ranger*, 376.
56. Utley, *Lone Star Lawmen*, 136–37; Boessenecker, *Texas Ranger*, 363; Swanson, *Cult of Glory*, 301.
57. Swanson, *Cult of Glory*, 302.
58. Swanson, *Cult of Glory*, 304.
59. Utley, *Lone Star Lawmen*, 140.
60. Despite Governor Moody's pronouncement that all guilty parties would be brought to justice, only the arsonist was ever convicted, to a two-year sentence.
61. Swanson, *Cult of Glory*, 305.
62. Swanson, *Cult of Glory*, 314.
63. Boessenecker, *Texas Ranger*, 386.
64. Potter, *War on Crime*, 97.
65. Burrough, *Public Enemies*, 352.
66. Boessenecker, *Texas Ranger*, 431.
67. Jenkins and Frost, *"I'm Frank Hamer,"* 206.
68. Utley, *Lone Star Lawmen*, 165.
69. Webb, *Texas Rangers*, 519–21.
70. Webb, *Texas Rangers*, 319.

CHAPTER 15

The epigraph is from Lightman, "Raw Cinematic Realism."

1. Dunaway, *Looking for Gatsby*, 118.
2. Dunaway, *Looking for Gatsby*, 119.
3. Dunaway, *Looking for Gatsby*.
4. Dunaway, *Looking for Gatsby*.
5. Harris, *Pictures at a Revolution*, 249.
6. Harris, *Pictures at a Revolution*, 248.
7. Dunaway, *Looking for Gatsby*, 125.
8. Harris, *Pictures at a Revolution*, 248.
9. Harris, *Pictures at a Revolution*, 249.
10. Dunaway, *Looking for Gatsby*, 132.
11. "Red Oak Turns Back: Town Provides Background for Depression," *Dallas Morning News*, October 23, 1966. Regarding that cigar bit: Dunaway put the stogie in the center of her mouth, not the side, as Bonnie did in the Joplin snapshots. "That's how Jeanne Moreau did it in *The Lovers*," the actress wrote of her inspiration from 1959 Louis Malle film. "It's very sexual." See Dunaway, *Looking for Gatsby*, 130.
12. Dunaway, *Looking for Gatsby*, 119.
13. Harris, *Pictures at a Revolution*, 249.
14. Finstad, *Warren Beatty*, 373.
15. Dunaway, *Looking for Gatsby*, 133.
16. Dunaway, *Looking for Gatsby*.
17. Dunaway, *Looking for Gatsby*.
18. Newman and Benton (and Towne), "*Bonnie and Clyde*," 48–49.
19. Dunaway, *Looking for Gatsby*, 133. Working with director Robert Altman a few years later on *McCabe and Mrs. Miller* (1971), Beatty pushed the count to more than sixty takes on a simple transitional shot of his character sitting at a desk.
20. Newman and Benton, "*Bonnie and Clyde*," 278.
21. Newman and Benton, "*Bonnie and Clyde*," 279.
22. Newman and Benton, "*Bonnie and Clyde*."
23. Harris, *Pictures at a Revolution*, 254.
24. Chaiken and Cronin, *Arthur Penn Interviews*, 50.

25. Chaiken and Cronin, *Arthur Penn Interviews*, 50.
26. Chaiken and Cronin, *Arthur Penn Interviews*.
27. Mintzer, *Conversations with Dean Tavoularis*, 54–57.
28. Harris, *Pictures at a Revolution*, 253.
29. Wake and Hayden, *Bonnie and Clyde Book*, 192.
30. Wake and Hayden, *Bonnie and Clyde Book*.
31. Chaiken and Cronin, *Arthur Penn Interviews*, 124.
32. Wake and Hayden, *Bonnie and Clyde Book*, 192.
33. Robert Towne interview, in Penn, *Bonnie and Clyde*.
34. The building still stands, now an antique emporium but instantly recognizable.
35. Warren Beaty interview, in Penn, *Bonnie and Clyde*.
36. Richard Matlby, *Hollywood Cinema*, 2nd ed. (Blackwell, 2003), 164, 186.
37. Warren Beatty interview, in Penn, *Bonnie and Clyde*.
38. Harris, *Pictures at a Revolution*, 254.
39. Harris, *Pictures at a Revolution*.
40. Warren Beatty copy of *Bonnie and Clyde* script, n.d., 87.
41. Arthur Penn interview, in Penn, *Bonnie and Clyde*.
42. Arthur Penn interview, in Penn, *Bonnie and Clyde*.
43. The ice cream parlor continues to do business in Crandall, Texas.
44. Sherman and Rubin, *Director's Event*, 106.
45. Lightman, "Raw Cinematic Realism."
46. Lightman, "Raw Cinematic Realism."
47. Lightman, "Raw Cinematic Realism."
48. Lightman, "Raw Cinematic Realism."
49. MacEwen letter to Warren Beatty, November 2, 1966, Warner Bros. archives.

CHAPTER 16

The epigraph is from Hobsbawm, *Bandits*, 196.
1. Interview with Gardner.
2. Gardner, *To Hell on a Fast Horse*, 120.
3. Interview with Gardner.
4. Gardner, *To Hell on a Fast Horse*, 98. The photograph is also responsible for the erroneous belief that William Bonney was left-handed. Tintype cameras flipped the recorded image.
5. Newman and Benton, "Lightning in a Bottle," 18.
6. Dunaway, *Looking for Gatsby*, 125.
7. Harris, *Pictures at a Revolution*, 245. In a case of life imitating art imitating life, Pilot Point continues to celebrate "Bonnie and Clyde Days" every November.
8. Sherman, *Directing the Film*, 81.
9. Sherman, *Directing the Film*.
10. Interview with Guinn.
11. Newman and Benton (and Towne), "*Bonnie and Clyde*," 34; Newman and Benton, "*Bonnie and Clyde*," 253.
12. Blumenthal, *Bonnie and Clyde*, 159.
13. Latter-day depictions of the story, including *The Highwaymen* (2019) and the two-part A&E miniseries *Bonnie and Clyde* (2013), print this discredited legend.
14. Guinn, *Go Down Together*, 284.
15. Interview with Guinn.
16. Guinn, *Go Down Together*, 5. In an interview, Guinn noted drily that fiancée Marie Tullis "had a keen sense of theater herself."
17. Associated Press report, n.d.
18. Fortune, *Fugitives*, 80.
19. Fortune, *Fugitives*, 243.
20. Fortune, *Fugitives*.
21. Harris, *Pictures at a Revolution*, 255.
22. Biskind, *Easy Riders, Raging Bulls*, 34.
23. The scene appears on pages 282–83 in the version of the script published in Thomas's 1986 compendium *Best American Screenplays*, which includes,

among others, *All Quiet on the Western Front* (1930), *Meet John Doe* (1941), *Casablanca* (1942), *Rebel Without a Cause* (1955), *The Graduate* (1967), and *Butch Cassidy and the Sundance Kid* (1969).

24. All citations in this extended passage are from Newman and Benton, "*Bonnie and Clyde,*" 282–83.
25. Newman and Benton (and Towne), "*Bonnie and Clyde,*" 125.
26. Dunaway, *Looking for Gatsby*, 131.
27. Harris, *Pictures at a Revolution*, 254.
28. Newman and Benton, "*Bonnie and Clyde,*" 295.
29. Arthur Penn interview, in Penn, *Bonnie and Clyde*.
30. Chaiken and Cronin, *Arthur Penn Interviews*, 42.
31. Friedman, *Arthur Penn's Bonnie and Clyde*, 138.
32. Chaiken and Cronin, *Arthur Penn Interviews*, 56.
33. Richard Gilman, the *New Republic*, quoted in Harris, *Pictures at a Revolution*, 256.
34. Biskind, *Easy Riders, Raging Bulls*, 35.
35. Friedman, *Arthur Penn's Bonnie and Clyde*, 130.
36. Chaiken and Cronin, *Arthur Penn Interviews*, 74.
37. Harris, *Pictures at a Revolution*, 257.
38. Harris, *Pictures at a Revolution*.
39. Jack L. Warner interoffice memo to MacEwen, 5/15/67.
40. Parnell interview, in *Remembering Bonnie and Clyde*.
41. Hinton, *Ambush*, 166.
42. Boessenecker, *Texas Ranger*, 431.
43. Guinn, *Go Down Together*, 339.
44. Phillips, *Running with Bonnie and Clyde*, 198–99.
45. Boessenecker, *Texas Ranger*, 434.
46. Dunaway, *Looking for Gatsby*, 139.
47. Newman and Benton (and Towne), "*Bonnie and Clyde,*" 161.
48. Newman and Benton, "*Bonnie and Clyde,*" 295.
49. Mintzer, *Conversations with Dean Tavoularis*, 57, 61.
50. Mintze, *Conversations with Dean Tavoularis* r, 61.
51. Segaloff, *Arthur Penn*, 155.
52. Segaloff, *Arthur Penn*.
53. Prior accounts of the filming of *Bonnie and Clyde* maintain the ambush scene occupied three shooting days, but call sheets in the Warner Bros.

archives are dated December 29, 1966, December 30, 1966, January 2, 1967, and January 3, 1967—four days.
54. Harris, *Pictures at a Revolution*, 258.
55. Harris, *Pictures at a Revolution*, 258–59.
56. Harris, *Pictures at a Revolution*, 259.
57. Penn, "Making Waves," 28.

CHAPTER 17

The epigraph is from Winkler, *Gun Fight*, 234.
1. Hobsbawm, *Bandits*, 39–40.
2. Hobsbawm, *Bandits*, 95.
3. Potter, *War on Crime*, 78.
4. Newman and Benton, "*Bonnie and Clyde*," 288.
5. Chaiken and Cronin, *Arthur Penn Interviews*, 22.
6. Winkler, *Gun Fight*, 233.
7. Seale, *Seize the Time*, 80–81.
8. Seale, *Seize the Time*.
9. Winkler, *Gun Fight*, 234.
10. Seale, *Seize the Time*, 88–90.
11. Seale, *Seize the Time*, 90.
12. Winkler, *Gun Fight*, 237.
13. Winkler, *Gun Fight*, 246.
14. Anderson, *Second*, 140.
15. Seale, *Seize the Time*, 153.
16. Seale, *Seize the Time*, 164.
17. Winkler, *Gun Fight*, 138.
18. Seale, *Seize the Time*, 157.
19. Seale, *Seize the Time*, 159.
20. Anderson, *Second*, 133.
21. Anderson, *Second*, 139.
22. Winkler, *Gun Fight*, 245.
23. Winkler, *Gun Fight*.
24. Ronald Reagan, "Remarks at the Annual Members Banquet of the National Rifle Association," Ronald Reagan Presidential Library, May 6, 1983, accessed

June 20, 2025, www.reaganlibrary.gov/archives/speech/remarks-annual-members-banquet-national-rifle-association-phoenix-arizona.
25. Waldman, *Second Amendment*, 90.
26. Erdozian, *One Nation Under Guns*, 132.
27. Lyndon Johnson, "Remarks Upon Signing the Gun Control Act of 1968," The American Presidency Project," October 22, 1968, accessed June 20, 2025, www.presidency.ucsb.edu/documents/remarks-upon-signing-the-gun-control-act-1968.
28. Winkler, *Gun Fight*, 153.
29. Chaiken and Cronin, *Arthur Penn Interviews*, 75.
30. Cawelti, *Focus on Bonnie and Clyde*, 19.
31. Cawelti, *Focus on Bonnie and Clyde*, 19.
32. Chaiken and Cronin, *Arthur Penn Interviews*, 75.
33. Jonathan Thompson, "Sagebrush Sheriffs: How Rural Peace officers are joining the radical right's war against the feds," *High Country News*, February 8, 2016.
34. Thompson, "Sagebrush Sheriffs."
35. Thompson, "Sagebrush Sheriffs."
36. Interview with Hutton.
37. Toobin, *Homegrown* 97.
38. Toobin, *Homegrown*, 70.
39. Toobin, *Homegrown*, 97.
40. Toobin, *Homegrown*, 70.
41. Toobin, *Homegrown*.
42. Interview with Quammen.
43. Interview with Quammen.
44. Slotkin, *Gunfighter Nation*, 154.
45. Slotkin, *Gunfighter Nation*, 352.
46. Temple, *Up in Arms*, 32.
47. Temple, *Up in Arms*.
48. Keeler, *Standoff*, 152.
49. Quammen, *American Zion*, 228.
50. Keeler, *Standoff*, 125.
51. Temple, *Up in Arms*, 161.
52. Rhodes drew an eighteen-year sentence for seditious conspiracy for his role in the January 6, 2021, riots at the US Capitol, the longest sentence

received by any such defendant. President Donald J. Trump commuted Rhodes's sentence on January 20, 2025, the first day of his second term in office. That same day, Trump issued blanket commutations or pardons to all the 1,500-plus January 6 rioters.
53. Quammen, *True West*, 65.
54. Quammen, *American Zion*, 193.
55. Quammen, *American Zion*, 194.
56. Quammen, *American Zion*.
57. Interview with Quammen.
58. Interview with Quammen.
59. https://www.facebook.com/hccommitteeofsafety/.
60. Hal Herring, "Making Sense of Malheur," *High Country News*, March 21, 2016.
61. Quammen, *American Zion*, 206.
62. Interview with Quammen. After the re-establishment of legal authority and the arrest of both Bundy brothers and their cohorts, Sheriff Ward's investigation of the site recovered twenty-two long guns, twelve handguns, 16,636 live rounds of ammunition, and another 1,695 spent casings from target practice.
63. McCann, *Shadowlands*, 164.
64. Tony Dokoupil, "Oregon Occupier LaVoy Finicum Warns FBI He'd Take Death Over Jail," *NBC News*, January 6, 2016.
65. Finicum, *Only by Blood and Suffering*, vii.
66. Finicum, *Only by Blood and Suffering*, 276.
67. The Oregonian, "Shawna Cox Cell Phone Video from Inside LaVoy Finicum's Truck," YouTube video, 12 minutes, 28 seconds, www.youtube.com/watch?v=eEswP_HSFV4&pp=ygUbc2hhd25hIGNveCBjZWxsIHBob25lIHZpZGVv.
68. Finicum's name continues to be invoked as that of a martyr to a peculiarly American cause and has even found its way into popular media culture. In the fifth season of the FX anthology series *Fargo* (inspired by the 1996 film), a Constitutional Sheriff played with relish by Jon Hamm issues a live-stream call to arms as "Deep State" forces converge on his ranch. "They're comin' for me the way they came for Ammon and LaVoy," he intones gravely. "And don't be fooled. After they murder me, they're coming for you next."

CHAPTER 18

The epigraph is from Penn, "Making Waves," 28.
1. Penn, "Making Waves," 29.
2. Penn, "Making Waves."
3. Finstad, *Warren Beatty*, 378.
4. Penn, "Making Waves," 29.
5. Harris, *Pictures at a Revolution*, 327.
6. Harris, *Pictures at a Revolution*, 325.
7. Lederer interoffice communication to MacEwen, June 5, 1967. Warner Bros. archives.
8. Penn, "Making Waves," 28.
9. Harris, *Pictures at a Revolution*, 325.
10. Jack L. Warner interoffice communication to MacEwen, March 14, 1967, Warner Bros. archives.
11. MacEwen letter to Beatty, November 2, 1966. Warner Bros. archives.
12. Transcript, Segaloff interview with Allen, July 16, 2008.
13. Transcript, Porcella interview with Allen, 1976.
14. Transcript, Porcella interview with Allen, 1976.
15. Transcript, Segaloff interview with Allen, July 16, 2008.
16. Chaiken and Cronin, *Arthur Penn Interviews*, 197.
17. Chaiken and Cronin, *Arthur Penn Interviews*, 170.
18. Interview with Matthew and Molly Penn.
19. Transcript, Porcella interview with Allen, 1976.
20. Chaiken and Cronin, *Arthur Penn Interviews*, 170.
21. Harris, *Pictures at a Revolution*, 286.
22. Chaiken and Cronin, *Arthur Penn Interviews*, 170.
23. Chaiken and Cronin, *Arthur Penn Interviews*, 170–71.
24. Transcript, Segaloff interview with Allen, July 16, 2008.
25. Sherman, *Directing the Film*, 114.
26. Transcript, Segaloff interview with Allen, July 16, 2008.
27. Sherman, *Directing the Film*, 114.
28. Harris, *Pictures at a Revolution*, 258.
29. And he apparently held no serious grudges. For the role of the undertaker's girlfriend, Penn cast Frankenheimer's wife, Evans Evans, who teams wonderfully with Gene Wilder.

30. Sherman, *Directing the Film*, 114.
31. Dede Allen interview, in Penn, *Bonnie and Clyde*.
32. Robert Benton interview, in Penn, *Bonnie and Clyde*.
33. Friedman, *Arthur Penn's Bonnie and Clyde*, 106.
34. Transcript, Segaloff interview with Allen, July 16, 2008.
35. Chaiken and Cronin, *Arthur Penn Interviews*, 22.
36. Transcript, Segaloff interview with Allen, July 16, 2008.
37. Segaloff, *Arthur Penn*, 158.
38. Transcript, Segaloff interview with Allen, July 16, 2008.
39. Finstad, *Warren Beatty*, 378.
40. Finstad, *Warren Beatty*, 384.
41. Sonny Burke interoffice communication to MacEwen. Warner Bros. archives.
42. Transcript, Porcella interview with Allen, 1976.
43. Harris, *Pictures at a Revolution*, 325.
44. Chaiken and Cronin, *Arthur Penn Interviews*, 207.
45. Finstad, *Warren Beatty*, 279.
46. Patrick Goldstein, "Blast from the Past," *Los Angeles Times*, August 24, 1997.
47. Harris, *Pictures at a Revolution*, 327.
48. Finstad, *Warren Beatty*, xiv.
49. Finstad, *Warren Beatty*.
50. Finstad, *Warren Beatty*, 379.
51. Finstad, *Warren Beatty*.
52. Finstad, *Warren Beatty*.
53. Finstad, *Warren Beatty*, 381.
54. MacEwen to AP, n.d., Warner Bros archives
55. Finstad, *Warren Beatty*, 382.
56. Wake and Hayden, *Bonnie and Clyde Book*, 9–10.
57. Wake and Hayden, *Bonnie and Clyde Book*, 11.
58. Wake and Hayden, *Bonnie and Clyde Book*.
59. Bosley Crowther, "Shoot-Em-Up Film Opens World Fete; 'Bonnie and Clyde' Cheered by Montreal First-Nighters," *New York Times*, August 7, 1967.
60. Crowther, "Shoot-Em-Up Film."

61. Segaloff, *Arthur Penn*, 159.
62. Crowther, "Shoot-Em-Up Film."
63. Quoted in Wake and Hayden, *Bonnie and Clyde Book*, 221.
64. Harris, *Pictures at a Revolution*, 339.
65. Bosley Crowther, "Brutal Tale of 12 Angry Men," *New York Times*, June 16, 1967.
66. Bosley Crowther, "Movies to Kill People By," *New York Times*, July 9, 1967.
67. Crowther, "Movies to Kill People By."
68. Harris, *Pictures at a Revolution*, 338.
69. Segaloff, *Arthur Penn*, 159.
70. Dunaway, *Looking for Gatsby*, 140.
71. Dunaway, *Looking for Gatsby*.
72. Dunaway, *Looking for Gatsby*.
73. Dunaway, *Looking for Gatsby*.
74. Dunaway, *Looking for Gatsby*.
75. Dunaway, *Looking for Gatsby*.
76. Segaloff, *Arthur Penn*, 159.
77. Wake and Hayden, *Bonnie and Clyde Book*, 218.
78. Wake and Hayden, *Bonnie and Clyde Book*.
79. Wake and Hayden, *Bonnie and Clyde Book*.
80. Harris, *Pictures at a Revolution*, 341.
81. Wake and Hayden, *Bonnie and Clyde Book*, 218.
82. Harris, *Pictures at a Revolution*, 341.
83. Jay Jacobs, "Bloody Murder," *National Catholic Reporter*, October 5, 1967.
84. Harris, *Pictures at a Revolution*, 368.
85. Segaloff, *Arthur Penn*, 159.

CHAPTER 19

The epigraph is from a Marie Barrow interview, in *Remembering Bonnie and Clyde*.

1. Interview with Phillips.
2. Hinton, *Ambush*, 179.
3. Guinn, *Go Down Together*, 343.
4. Hinton, *Ambush*, 179.
5. Phillips, *Running with Bonnie and Clyde*, 209.
6. Guinn, *Go Down Together*, 344.
7. Phillips, *Running with Bonnie and Clyde*, 209.
8. Phillips, *Running with Bonnie and Clyde*, 210.
9. Phillips, *Running with Bonnie and Clyde*.
10. Fortune, *Fugitives*, 251.
11. Blumenthal, *Bonnie and Clyde*, 184.
12. Guinn, *Go Down Together*, 255.
13. Fortune, *Fugitives*, 251.
14. Phillips, *Running with Bonnie and Clyde*, 214.
15. Phillips, *Running with Bonnie and Clyde*, 214–15.
16. Phillips, *Running with Bonnie and Clyde*, 216.
17. Fortune, *Fugitives*, 257.
18. Fortune, *Fugitives*, 258.
19. Phillips, *Running with Bonnie and Clyde*, 215–16
20. Fortune, *Fugitives*, 256.
21. muddbosss, "Bonnie and Clyde Funerals . . . ," YouTube video, 2 minutes, 51 seconds, www.youtube.com/watch?v=zMDImoPgA0A&pp=ygUZYm9ubmllIGFuZCBjbHlkZSBmdW5lcmFscw%3D%3D.
22. Phillips, *Running with Bonnie and Clyde*, 216.
23. muddbosss, "Bonnie and Clyde Funerals."
24. Phillips, *Running with Bonnie and Clyde*, 219.
25. All above citations are from *The Retribution of Clyde Barrow and Bonnie Parker*, as preserved at footagefarm, "The Retribution of Clyde Barrow and Bonnie Parker 1/2 - 220668-06 | Footage Farm", YouTube video, 9 minutes, 37 seconds, www.

youtube.com/watch?v=aq7uBsuqImY&pp=ygUiYm9iYmlIIGFu
ZCBjbHlkZSBkZWF0aCBjYXIgZm9vdGFnZQ%3D%3D.

26. Blumenthal, *Bonnie and Clyde*, 191. The mothers ultimately served a thirty-day sentence for harboring their children while Clyde and Bonnie were federal fugitives.
27. *True Detective Mysteries*, June 1934, 26.
28. Toland, *Dillinger Days*, 39.
29. Potter, *War on Crime*, 101.
30. Potter, *War on Crime*.
31. Fortune, *Fugitives*, 13.
32. Fortune, *Fugitives*, 14. Not surprisingly, Fortune became a Hollywood screenwriter, notably on *Dark Command* (1940), a heavily fictionalized account of Quantrill's Raiders featuring John Wayne and Claire Trevor.
33. "About the Book," in Fortune, *Fugitives*, 11.
34. Guinn, *Go Down Together*, 360.
35. Knight and Davis, *Bonnie and Clyde*, 2.
36. Guinn, *Go Down Together*, 355.
37. Jenkins and Frost, "*I'm Frank Hamer*," 220.
38. Boessenecker, *Texas Ranger*, 441.
39. Jenkins and Frost, "*I'm Frank Hamer*," 220.
40. Jenkins and Frost, "*I'm Frank Hamer*."
41. Boessenecker, *Texas Ranger*, 441.
42. J. Edgar Hoover, *Persons in Hiding* (Boston: Little, Brown, 1938), xviii.
43. Burrough, *Public Enemies*, 509.
44. Bryan Burrough's definitive 2004 history, *Public Enemies: America's Greatest Crime Wave and the Birth of the FBI*, thoroughly dismantles Hoover's claims.
45. Letter from Joseph Breen to Jack Jungmeyer, August 7, 1945. Production Code Administration Records, Academy of Motion Picture Arts and Sciences, Margaret Herrick Library, Beverly Hills, CA.
46. Letter from Joseph Breen to Jack Jungmeyer, August 7, 1945. Production Code Administration Records, Academy of Motion Picture Arts and Sciences, Margaret Herrick Library, Beverly Hills, CA.
47. Marvin H. Alpert, "Killer in Skirts," *Argosy*, March 1956.
48. Muller, *Gun Crazy*, 109.

49. Muller, *Gun Crazy*, 118.
50. Muller, *Gun Crazy*.
51. Muller, *Gun Crazy*, 165.

CHAPTER 20

The epigraph is from Gitlin, *Sixties*, 318.

1. Chaiken and Cronin, *Arthur Penn Interviews*, 141.
2. Gitlin, *Sixties*, 318.
3. Murphy, *Violence Inside Us*, 107.
4. Hofstadter and Wallace, *American Violence*, 35.
5. Transcript, Segaloff interview with Allen, July 16, 2008.
6. Wake and Hayden, *Bonnie and Clyde Book*, 9–10.
7. Chaiken and Cronin, *Arthur Penn Interviews*, 22.
8. "Low-Down Hoedown," *Time* magazine, August 25, 1967.
9. Stefan Kanter, "The Shock of Freedom in Films," *Time* magazine, December 8, 1967.
10. Harris, *Pictures at a Revolution*, 391.
11. Dunaway, *Looking for Gatsby*, 117.
12. Harris, *Pictures at a Revolution*, 391.
13. Harris, *Pictures at a Revolution*.
14. Harris, *Pictures at a Revolution*, 371.
15. Bosley Crowther, *Reruns: Fifty Memorable Films* (G.P. Putnam, 1978).
16. Finstad, *Warren Beatty*, 385.
17. Reprinted in Wake and Hayden, *Bonnie and Clyde Book*, 195. To put that statistic in perspective, seven thousand words exceeds the length of an average chapter of this book.
18. Wake and Hayden, *Bonnie and Clyde Book*.
19. Wake and Hayden, *Bonnie and Clyde Book*, 205.
20. Wake and Hayden, *Bonnie and Clyde Book*, 195–200.
21. Wake and Hayden, *Bonnie and Clyde Book*, 211.
22. Wake and Hayden, *Bonnie and Clyde Book*, 213.
23. Chaiken and Cronin, *Arthur Penn Interviews*, 36–37. Contrary to Kael's later claims, her review had nothing to do with *Bonnie and Clyde*'s box

office turnaround. By the time her piece appeared, the movie had already been pulled from theaters in New York and Los Angeles and replaced by John Huston's sexual passions-on-a-military-base melodrama, *Reflections in a Golden Eye*, starring Elizabeth Taylor and Marlon Brando. Penn's daughter Molly told the author in an interview that "Dad was deeply hurt [by Kael's review] because he'd put everything he had into the film."

24. Harris, *Pictures at a Revolution*, 413.
25. Beatty and Dunaway reunited to present the Best Picture Oscar at the 89th Annual Academy Awards in 2017, precipitating what may be the greatest gaffe in Oscar history. Handed the wrong ballot, they mistakenly announced *La La Land* as the winner. Director Damien Chazelle and his cast took the stage for more than two minutes before the actual winner, Barry Jenkins's *Moonlight*, could claim its rightful trophy.
26. Harris's *Pictures at a Revolution: Five Movies and the Birth of the New Hollywood* offers the definitive account of this contest.
27. Harris, *Pictures at a Revolution*, 416.
28. Richard Schickel, *Second Sight: Notes on Some Movies 1965–1970* (Simon and Schuster 1972), 143.
29. Kolker, *Cinema of Loneliness*, 44–47.
30. All citations in this section from *Mass Media Hearings: A Report to the National Commission on the Causes and Prevention of Violence, December 1969* (U.S. Government Printing Office, 1970), vol. 9A, 192–225.
31. Stratton, *Wild Bunch*, 184.
32. Stratton, *Wild Bunch*, 262.
33. The author was part of Peckinpah's entourage that night.
34. Chaiken and Cronin, *Arthur Penn Interviews*, 69.
35. Richard B. Jewell, email to author, July 31, 2024.
36. Chaiken and Cronin, *Arthur Penn Interviews*, 69. As proof, Penn pointed to *Ride the High Country*, Peckinpah's elegiac 1962 Western that marked the final screen appearance of Randolph Scott.
37. Segaloff, *Arthur Penn*, 208.
38. Segaloff, *Arthur Penn*, 182.
39. Chaiken and Cronin, *Arthur Penn Interviews*, 66.
40. Wake and Hayden, *Bonnie and Clyde Book*, 172.
41. Chaiken and Cronin, *Arthur Penn Interviews*, 67.

42. Chaiken and Cronin, *Arthur Penn Interviews*, 68.
43. Johnny D. Boggs, *The American West on Film* (Santa Barbara, CA: ABC-CLIO), 159.
44. Chaiken and Cronin, *Arthur Penn Interviews*, 210.
45. Harris, *Pictures at a Revolution*, 337.

EPILOGUE

The epigraph is a lyric by Don Black from the musical *Bonnie and Clyde* (2009).

1. "Letter from the Authors," *Bonnie and Clyde* program (2023), Garrick Theatre, London.
2. See "Broadway (2011)," under "*Bonnie & Clyde* (musical)" Wikipedia, last modified June 20, 2025, https://en.wikipedia.org/wiki/Bonnie_%26_Clyde_(musical).
3. *Wall Street Journal*, December 2, 2011. Teachout subsequently served as librettist for the 2009 opera *The Letter*, an adaptation of a less remembered film, *The Letter* (1940), which failed to achieve a follow-up production after its Santa Fe Opera debut.
4. *New York Times*, December 1, 2011.
5. The author attended the April 5, 2023, evening performance.
6. A filmed version of the show's January 2022 production at the Theatre Royal Drury Lane remains available for pay-per-view streaming.
7. Erected across the country by the National Association of Manufacturers in January 1937, the billboards sought to advertise that Americans enjoyed "THE WORLD'S HIGHEST STANDARD OF LIVING," yet photographers such as Dorothea Lange, Margaret Bourke-White, and others tended to juxtapose the multiracial breadlines extending beyond the hopeful graphic.
8. Newman and Benton, "Lightning in a Bottle," 13.
9. Chaiken and Cronin, *Arthur Penn Interviews*, 13.

AFTERWORD AND ACKNOWLEDGMENTS

1. Schlesinger, *Violence*, 62.
2. Schlesinger, *Violence*, 90.
3. Interview with Yazbeck.

Selected Bibliography

BONNIE AND CLYDE

Biskind, Peter. *Easy Riders, Raging Bulls: How the Sex-Drugs-and-Rock 'n'-Roll Generation Saved Hollywood*. Simon and Schuster, 1998.

Cawelti, John G., ed. *Focus on Bonnie and Clyde*. Prentice-Hall, 1973.

Chaiken, Michael, and Paul Cronin, eds. *Arthur Penn Interviews*. University of Mississippi Press, 2008.

De Baecque, Antoine, and Serge Toubiana. *Truffaut: A Biography*. University of California Press, 2000.

Dunaway, Faye, with Betsy Sharkey. *Looking for Gatsby: My Life*. Pocket Books, 1995.

Finstad, Suzanne. *Warren Beatty: A Private Man*. Three Rivers Press, 2005.

Fraser-Cavassoni, Natasha. *Sam Spiegel*. Simon and Schuster, 2003.

Friedman, Lester, ed. *Arthur Penn's Bonnie and Clyde*. Cambridge University Press, 2000.

Gitlin, Todd. *The Sixties: Years of Hope, Days of Rage*. Bantam Books, 1993.

Harris, Mark. *Pictures at a Revolution: Five Movies and the Birth of the New Hollywood*. Penguin Press, 2008.

Kael, Pauline. "Crime and Poetry." In *The Bonnie and Clyde Book*, edited by Sandra Wake and Nicole Hayden, 195–215. Simon and Schuster, 1972.

Kolker, Robert. *A Cinema of Loneliness*. 4th ed. Oxford University Press, 2011.

Lightman, Herb A. "Raw Cinematic Realism in the Photography of 'Bonnie and Clyde.'" American Cinematographer. August 7, 2017. https://theasc.com/articles/flashback-bonnie-and-clyde.

Mintzer, Jordan. *Conversations with Dean Tavoularis*. Synecdoche, 2022.

Muller, Eddie. *Gun Crazy: The Origin of American Outlaw Cinema*. Black Pool Productions, 2014.

Newman, David, and Robert Benton. "Bonnie and Clyde [screenplay]." In *Best American Screenplays*, by Sam Thomas, 251–95. Crown, 1986.

Newman, David, and Robert Benton. "Lightning in a Bottle." In *The Bonnie and Clyde Book*, edited by Sandra Wake and Nicole Hayden, 13–30. Simon and Schuster, 1972.

Newman, David, and Robert Benton (and Robert Towne). *"Bonnie and Clyde* [screenplay]." In *The Bonnie and Clyde Book*, edited by Sandra Wake and Nicole Hayden, 31–164. Simon and Schuster, 1972.

Penn, Arthur. "Making Waves." In *Arthur Penn's Bonnie and Clyde*, edited by Lester Friedman, 11–31. Cambridge University Press, 2000.

Seale, Bobby. *Seize the Time: The Story of the Black Panther Party and Huey Newton*. Black Classic Press, 1991.

Segaloff, Nat. *Arthur Penn: American Director*. University Press of Kentucky, 2011.

Sherman, Eric. *Directing the Film: Film Directors on Their Art*. Little, Brown, 1976.

Sherman, Eric, and Martin Rubin. *The Director's Event: Interviews with Five American Film-Makers*. Atheneum, 1970.

Stratton, W. K. *The Wild Bunch: Sam Peckinpah, a Revolution in Hollywood and the Making of a Legendary Film*. Bloomsbury, 2019.

Thomas, Sam, ed. *Best American Screenplays*. Crown, 1986.

Wake, Sandra, and Nicole Hayden, eds. *The Bonnie and Clyde Book*. Simon and Schuster, 1972.

PRE-CODE HOLLYWOOD

Behlmer, Rudy. *Inside Warner Bros. (1935–1951)*. Viking, 1985.

Doherty, Thomas. *Pre-Code Hollywood: Sex, Immorality and Insurrection in American Cinema, 1930–34*. Columbia University Press, 1999.

Doherty, Thomas. *Hollywood Censor: Joseph I. Breen and the Production Code Administration*. Columbia University Press, 2017.

Leff, Leonard J., and Jerold L. Simmons. *The Dame in the Kimono: Hollywood, Censorship and the Production Code from the 1920s to the 1960s*. Weidenfeld and Nicholson, 1990.

LeRoy, Mervyn, with Dick Kleiner. *Mervyn LeRoy: Take One*. Hawthorn Books, 1974.

THE BARROW GANG

Barrow, Blanche Caldwell. *My Life with Bonnie and Clyde*. Edited by John Neal Phillips. University of Oklahoma Press, 2004.

Blumenthal, Karen. *Bonnie and Clyde: The Making of a Legend*. Viking, 2018.

Brinkley, Douglas. *Wheels for the World: Henry Ford, His Company and a Century of Progress*. Penguin Books, 2003.

Burrough, Bryan. *Public Enemies: America's Greatest Crime Wave and the Birth of the FBI, 1933–34*. Penguin Press, 2004.

Egan, Timothy. *The Worst Hard Time: The Untold Story of Those Who Survived the Great American Dust Bowl*. Houghton Mifflin, 2006.

Federal Bureau of Investigation. Bonnie and Clyde: The Dallas Field Office's Files from 1933 to 1934. Vol. 1. N.d. A two-volume, unpaginated compendium of memos, haphazardly arranged.

Fortune, Jan B. *Fugitives: The Story of Clyde Barrow and Bonnie Parker, as Told by Bonnie's Mother and Clyde's Sister*. Wild Horse Press, 2013. Reprint of the 1934 edition.

Guinn, Jeff. *Go Down Together: The True, Untold Story of Bonnie and Clyde*. Simon and Schuster, 2009.

Hinton, Ted, as told to Larry Grove. *Ambush: The Real Story of Bonnie and Clyde*. Eakin Press, 1979.

Knight, James R., and Jonathan Davis. *Bonnie and Clyde: A 21st-Century Update*. Eakin Press, 2003.

Phillips, John Neal. *Running with Bonnie and Clyde: The Ten Fast Years of Ralph Fults*. University of Oklahoma Press, 1996.

Potter, Claire Bond. *War on Crime: Bandits, G-Men and the Politics of Mass Culture*. Rutgers University Press, 1998.

Schneider, Paul. *Bonnie and Clyde: The Lives Behind the Legend*. Henry Holt, 2009.

Toland, John. *The Dillinger Days*. Random House, 1963.

OUTLAWS

Burns, Walter Noble. *The Saga of Billy the Kid: The Thrilling Life of America's Original Outlaw*. Skyhorse, 2014. Facsimile reprint of the original 1925 edition.

Burrough, Brian. *The Gunfighters: How Texas Made the West Wild*. Penguin, 2025.

Cawelti, John G. *The Six-Gun Mystique Sequel*. Bowling Green State University Popular Press, 1999.

Dykstra, Robert R. *The Cattle Towns*. University of Nebraska Press, 1968.

Edwards, John Newman. *Noted Guerrillas, or The Warfare of the Border*. H. W. Baird, 1879.

Gardner, Mark Lee. *To Hell on a Fast Horse: The Untold Story of Billy the Kid and Pat Garrett*. William Morrow, 2020.

Hobsbawm, Eric. *Bandits*. York Press, 2020.

Hulbert, Matthew Christopher. *The Ghosts of Guerrilla Memory: How Civil War Bushwhackers Became Gunslingers in the American West*. University of Georgia Press, 2016.

Hulbert, Matthew Christopher. *Oracle of Lost Causes: John Newman Edwards and His Never-Ending Civil War*. University of Nebraska Press, 2023.

Lake, Stuart N. *Wyatt Earp: Frontier Marshall*. Houghton Mifflin, 1931.

Olmstead, Frederick Law. *A Journey Through Texas; or, A Saddle-Trip on the Western Frontier*. Dix, Edwards, 1857.

Slotkin, Richard. *Gunfighter Nation: The Myth of the Frontier in Twentieth-Century America*. University of Oklahoma Press, 1992.

Sonnichsen, C. L. *From Hopalong to Hud: Thoughts on Western Fiction*. Texas A&M University Press, 1978.

Waters, Frank. *The Earp Brothers of Tombstone*. University of Nebraska Press, 1960.

FIREARMS AND THE SECOND AMENDMENT

Anderson, Carol. *The Second: Race and Guns in a Fatally Unequal America.* Bloomsbury, 2021.

Bainbridge, John, Jr. *Gun Barons: The Weapons That Transformed America and the Men Who Invented Them.* St. Martin's Press, 2022.

Cornell, Saul. *A Well-Regulated Militia: The Founding Fathers and the Origins of Gun Control in America.* Oxford University Press, 2006.

Cramer, Clayton E. *Armed America: The Story of How and Why the Gun Became as American as Apple Pie.* Nelson Current, 2006.

Dunbar-Ortiz, Roxanne. *Loaded: A Disarming History of the Second Amendment.* City Lights Books, 2018.

Erdozian, Dominic. *One Nation Under Guns: How Gun Culture Distorts Our History and Threatens to Destroy Democracy.* Crown, 2024.

Haag, Pamela. *The Gunning of America: Business and the Making of American Gun Culture.* Basic Books, 2016.

Halbrook, Stephen P. *That Every Man Be Armed: The Evolution of a Constitutional Right.* University of New Mexico Press, 2013.

Halbrook, Stephen P. *America's Rifle: The Case for the AR-15.* Post Hill Press, 2022.

Hartman, Thom. *The Hidden History of Guns and the Second Amendment.* Berreti-Koehler, 2019.

Kyle, Chris. *American Gun: A History of the U.S. in Ten Firearms.* William Morrow, 2013.

Lavergne, Gary M. *A Sniper in the Tower: The Charles Whitman Murders.* University of North Texas Press, 1997.

Murphy, Chris. *The Violence Inside Us: A Brief History of an Ongoing American Tragedy.* Random House, 2020.

Rasenberger, Jim. *Revolver: Sam Colt and the Six-Shooter That Changed America.* Scribner, 2020.

Schlesinger, Arthur, Jr. *Violence: America in the Sixties.* Signet Books, 1968.

Smyth, Frank. *The NRA: An Unauthorized History.* Flatiron Books, 2020.

Trefethen, James B., and James E. Serven, eds. *Americans and Their Guns.* Stackpole Books, 1967.

Waldman, Michael. *The Second Amendment: A Biography.* Simon and Schuster, 2014.

Winkler, Adam. *Gun Fight: The Battle Over the Right to Bear Arms in America*. Norton, 2013.

Wills, Gary, ed. *The Federalist Papers by Alexander Hamilton, James Madison and John Jay*. Bantam Books, 1982.

TEXAS RANGERS

Boessenecker, John. *Texas Ranger: The Epic Life of Frank Hamer, the Man Who Killed Bonnie and Clyde*. Thomas Dunne Books, 2016.

Fehrenbach, T. R. *Lone Star: A History of Texas and the Texans*. American Legacy Press, 1968.

Jenkins, John H., and Gordon Frost. *"I'm Frank Hamer": The Life of a Texas Peace Officer*. State House Press, 2015.

Swanson, Doug J. *Cult of Glory: The Bold and Brutal History of the Texas Rangers*. Penguin Books, 2020.

Utley, Robert M. *Lone Star Lawmen: The Second Century of the Texas Rangers*. Vol. 2. Berkley Books, 2007.

SAGEBRUSH REBELLION

Finicum, LaVoy. *Only by Blood and Suffering: Regaining Lost Freedom*. Perpetua Printing, 2017.

Keeler, Jacqueline. *Standoff: Standing Rock, the Bundy Movement and the American Story of Sacred Lands*. Torrey House Press, 2021.

Mack, Richard. *The County Sheriff: America's Last Hope*. Self-published, 2009.

Mack, Richard, and Timothy Roberts Walters. *From My Cold, Dead Fingers: Why America Needs Guns*. Rawhide Western Publishing, 1994.

McCann, Anthony. *Shadowlands: Fear and Freedom in the Oregon Standoff*. Bloomsbury, 2009.

Pogue, James. *Chosen Country: A Rebellion in the West*. Henry Holt, 2018.

Quammen, Betsy Gaines. *American Zion: Cliven Bundy, God and Public Lands in the West*. Torrey House Press, 2020.

Quammen, Betsy Gaines. *True West: Myth and Mending on the Far Side of America*. Torrey House Press, 2023.

Temple, John. *Up in Arms: How the Bundy Family Hijacked Public Lands, Outfoxed the Federal Government, and Ignited America's Patriot Militia Movement.* BenBella Books, 2019.

Toobin, Jeffrey. *Homegrown: Timothy McVeigh and the Rise of Right-Wing Extremism.* Simon and Schuster, 2023.

FILMS AND DOCUMENTARIES

Hancock, John Lee, dir. *The Highwaymen*. Starring Kevin Costner and Woody Harrelson. Netflix, 2019.

King, Louis, dir. *Persons in Hiding*. Starring Patricia Morison and J. Carrol Naish. Paramount Pictures, 1939.

Lewis, Joseph H, dir. *Gun Crazy*. Starring John Dall and Peggy Cummins. King Brothers/United Artists, 1950.

Peckinpah, Sam, dir. *The Wild Bunch*. Starring William Holden and Ernest Borgnine. Warner Bros., 1969.

Penn, Arthur, dir. *Alice's Restaurant*. Starring Arlo Guthrie and Patricia Quinn. United Artists, 1969.

Penn, Arthur, dir. *Bonnie and Clyde*. Starring Warren Beatty and Faye Dunaway. Warner Bros., 1967. Fortieth anniversary edition. 2-disc special edition, 2008. DVD. Still the most comprehensive version ever released, including exclusive interviews, deleted scenes and a wealth of original promotional material.

Penn, Arthur, dir. *The Chase*. Starring Marlon Brando, Jane Fonda and Robert Redford. Columbia Pictures, 1966.

Penn, Arthur, dir. *The Left Handed Gun*. Starring Paul Newman and John Dehner. Warner Bros., 1958.

Penn, Arthur, dir. *Little Big Man*. Starring Dustin Hoffman and Chief Dan George. National General Pictures, 1971.

Penn, Arthur, dir. *Mickey One*. Starring Warren Beatty and Alexandra Stewart. Columbia Pictures, 1965.

Remembering Bonnie and Clyde. Turquoise Film and Video Productions, 2004.

Witney, William, dir. *The Bonnie Parker Story*. Starring Dorothy Provine and Jack Hogan. American International Pictures, 1958.

AUTHOR INTERVIEWS

Bob Boze Bell, September 7, 2023.
Johnny D. Boggs, August 24, 2023.
Samuel Kilborn Dolan, June 10, 2024.
Mark Lee Gardner, December 15, 2023.
Jeff Guinn, September 9, 2023.
Paul Andrew Hutton, September 14, 2023.
Richard B. Jewell, July 31, 2024.
Deborah Nadoolman Landis, March 13, 2025.
David LeVay, May 6, 2023.
Matthew and Molly Penn, April 30, 2025.
John Neal Phillips, September 11, 2023.
Betsy Gaines Quammen, October 18, 2023.
Nat Segaloff, September 8, 2023.
Adam Winkler, October 30, 2023.

 Index

Adams, John: coined the phrase of US as a nation of laws, xvii; cousin of Adams, Samuel, 35; defended Preston, Thomas (British captain), for murder charges, 35

Adams, Samuel: directed the Sons of Liberty, 35; fostered the harassment of a British sentry (1770), 35

Allen, Dede (film editor): Robert Benton credited her for the tempo in the movie, 246–47; butcher scene removed by Penn, Arthur, and, 168–69; career in film editing, 244–45, 247; complimented by Penn, Arthur, for her selection of takes, 245–47; considered herself a "gut editor," 244; earned her first feature editing credit for work on *Odds Against Tomorrow* (1959), 244; edited Penn's, Arthur, *Little Big Man* (1970), 290; edited six films for Penn, Arthur, 244; initially intimidated by Penn, Arthur, 245; left the cutting of the ambush to her assistant (Jerry Greenberg), 248; noted that adult viewers of *Bonnie and Clyde* may not understand that the US is a country of assassins, 278; regarded *Bonnie and Clyde* as her best work, 247; strong visual memory for dailies, 246; trusted by Penn, Arthur, 245; used a cutting style that emphasized momentum over continuity, 247

Barrow, Blanche (Barrow's, Buck, wife; *née* Caldwell Callaway): a member of the Barrow Gang, 130; as the only real-life person in the story that was alive to see the film, 110, 131; Beatty, Warren, met with her in Texas, 130; considered as formidable and more attractive than Bonnie, 130; daughter of an Oklahoma preacher, 127; displeased with her portrayal in the film, 129; her camera made possible the Joplin (Missouri) photographs of Bonnie and Clyde, 27; imprisoned in Missouri (1933), 129; lobbied for a pardon for Barrow, Buck, 127; met Barrow, Marvin (Buck), an escaped convict, 127, 129; served as the front woman for the Barrow Gang, 130, 171; suffered eye damage from flying glass at the shooting near Platte City (Iowa), 27, 158, 177; was the only member whose photograph had not appeared in newspapers, 171

Barrow, Cumie (Clyde's mother): lobbied for a pardon for Barrow, Buck, 127; lobbied the Texas governor for leniency for Clyde, 69; participated in the road show organized by Stanley, Charles (the "Crime Doctor"), 268; protested showing of *The Retribution of Clyde Barrow and Bonnie Parker* (1934), 266; was offered $50,000 for Clyde's body, 263

Barrow, Marvin "Buck" (Clyde's older brother): imprisoned for a 1929 failed safe-cracking job, 127; member of the Barrow Gang, 26; rejoined the Barrow Gang in Joplin (Missouri), 128; shot in the head near Platte City (Iowa), 27, 158, 178; tensions with Clyde and Bonnie, 170; voluntarily surrendered to prison officials in 1931, 127; walked out of the prison in 1930, 127; was granted a full pardon in 1932, 127

Barrow Cowan, Nell (Clyde's sister): Barrow and Parker families minimized Blanche Barrow's involvement with Barrow Gang, 129; co-contributor to *Fugitives: The Story of Clyde Barrow and Bonnie Parker* (1934), 268; disavowed content of the *Fugitives* book, 268

Barrow Gang: ambush by cops and vigilantes at Dexfield Park (Dexter, Iowa,), 170; after release from Eastham Prison (Texas), Methvin, Henry, joined the, 213; and robbery of weapons from National Guard armories, 82–83, 170; characterized by *True Detective Mysteries* tabloid as trigger-happy degenerates, 267; constant motion as defining feature of, 124; escape from well-armed cops and shootout near Platte City (Iowa), 170; FBI inventory of weapons stolen from the National Guard armory in Enid (Oklahoma), 82; foiled police raid in Joplin (Missouri), 27, 77; inaccurate sightings of their whereabouts and robberies across multiple states, 125; involved in the killing of nine lawmen, 3; its crime journey lasted close to two years, 3, 215, 247; Joplin photographs made Clyde and Bonnie national celebrities, 210; killing of two Texas highway officers in Grapevine (Texas), 213–14; perpetrated a string of small-town robberies and ransom-less kidnappings, 3; prompted enactment of the 1934 National Firearms Act, 230–31; seventeen year old Jones, W.D., joined the, 125–26; story inspired several films, 273–74; strategic location of Joplin, 118; the name for Clyde Barrow and associates, 3; viewed by Benton, Robert, as outlaws and outcasts, 24; were no longer considered amateurs after the failed Joplin police raid, 135

Beatty, Warren: acquired rights to the script (1965), 50, 61; an accomplished piano player, 98; commented on problem with Dunaway's, Faye, face, 108; considered a perfectionist, 200; credited with Crowther's, Bosley, demotion, 281; decided to film on location (Texas), 151; described what a healthy situation is in movie making, 101; hesitated purchasing script, 42; insistence on Penn, Arthur, as director, 61; maintained commitment to avoid sexual relations with co-star and staff, 160; offered to buy the film back from Warner Bros., 249–50; mutual respect for Penn, Arthur, 60; off-screen tensions with Dunaway, Faye, 7–8; on importance of control and meticulous planning, 97–98; produced and stared in

Bonnie and Clyde, 6; played the role of Clyde, 7–8; similarity with Hughes, Howard, as control freaks, 98; *Splendor in the Grass* (1961) launched his stardom, 99, 102; tensions with Penn, Arthur, 59–60; turned down the offer to play the role of Kennedy, John F., in *PT 109* (1963), 102–3

Benton, Robert: accepted at Columbia University, but dropped out after the first semester, 22; and full shooting treatment for *Bonnie and Clyde*, 25–26; a talented graphic designer, 22; attended meetings with Beatty, Warren, Penn, Arthur, and Warner Bros. executives, 111; collaborated with Newman, David, in writing the script for the film, 23; confronted dyslexia, 22; developed a close relationship with Newman, David, at *Esquire*, 22; early insistence on a ménage à trois strand for the film, 61; earned a bachelor's degree , 22; grew-up in Ellis County (Texas), 21; hired by *Esquire*, 22; his father attended Clyde's and Bonnie's funerals, 21–22; inspired by *The Dillinger Days* (1963), 122, 267; on Bonnie and Clyde seeking celebrity status, 24–25; Steinem, Gloria, broke relationship with, 21; suggested Penn, Arthur, deserved a writing credit for the film, 114; understood the film as par of the New Sentimentality filmmaking, 24, 25

Bergman, Ingmar (film director/screen writer): influence on the film treatment for *Bonnie and Clyde*, 28, 206

Billy the Kid (Bonney, William), xvii, 13; as a psychopath, xvii; as a Robin Hood, 40; character included in Penn's, Arthur, *The Left Handed Gun* (1958), 51; Garrett, Pat (Lincoln County sheriff) shot and killed, 39; Hayes, Rutherford B. (president) ordered the termination of the New Mexico range war, and capture of, 39; idolized by Clyde, 13, 37, 143; killing of Tunstall, John (surrogate father) led to revenge against Chisum, John (cattleman) by, 39; other names used by, 39; relished Eastern media coverage, 209; *The Saga of Billy the Kid* (1925) a biographical account of, 3; Vidal, Gore, incorporated the character in a television production, 55. *See also* Burns, Walter Noble; Gardner, Mark Lee; Hutton, Paul Andrew

Black Panther Party: accumulation of weapons, 228; and the armed "Sacramento Invasion" (1967), 229–30; began to shadow police in Oakland (California), 228; belief in the liberating and equalizing power of guns, 228; emergence of (1966), 227; federal and state legislation to control Blacks by controlling guns, 229; National Rifle Association (NRA) agreed with editorial calling for gun control, 230; Reagan, Ronald (governor, California), enacted the Mulford Act to prohibit the open carrying of a firearm without a permit, 230; were in Penn's, Arthur, mind during the making of *Bonnie and Clyde*, 231–32

Boessenecker, John (historian): considers Hamer, Frank, a great lawman, 183; credits Hamer, Frank, for eliminating the troublesome elements in Navasota (Texas), 184; Hamer's, Frank, biographer, 183; notes Texas expectation that boys should know how to load, shoot and clean guns, 184; on Dallas police knowing Bonnie was a streetwalker, 17; on postcard of dead Mexicans, 189

Bogdanovich, Peter (director/actor/writer): advised Benton, Robert, and Newman, David, on filmmaking, 25; and reflection on Hitchcock, Alfred, 25

Boggs, Johnny D. (historian): asserts most of those killed at the O.K. Corral were meant to be arrested for possession of a firearm, 89; interprets the Gunfight at the O.K. Corral as an arrest gone bad, 89; notes gun control ordinances were stricter in towns in the West, than contemporary cities, 87

Bonnie (Elizabeth Parker): allegation of being a streetwalker, 17; and deprived upbringing and desire to improve her class status, 12; an estimated twenty-thousand persons attended the funeral service for, 264; aspired to be a celebrity actor, 15; authored the ballad "End of the Line," 263, 267; central to the creation of the legend of Bonie and Clyde, 122, 214; cigar in staged Joplin (Missouri) photograph, 119–20; compared to pre-Code heroines, 16; considered short and thin, 16; craved attention, 15–16; described as "Killer in Skirts," in the magazine *Argosy*, 272; early poems about heroin addicts and prostitutes, 76–77; expressed her loneliness in letters to Clyde, 18; fragments of a typed manuscript written by, 267; held waitressing and housekeeping jobs when she met Clyde, 11–12; jailed in Kaufman (Texas), 74; joined Clyde's Lake Dallas Gang, 74; married to Thornton, Roy, when she met Clyde, 12; met Clyde in West Dallas (1930), 11–12; newspapers invented the smoking of cigars by Bonnie, 120, 214; police found the notebook "Suicide Sal" after the Joplin escape, 119; rarely used a firearm during her life, 13; smuggled a gun to Clyde while in jail, 11–13, 18; stylish and trendy, 16; the focus of *The Bonnie Parker Story* (1958), 272–73; told kidnapped Boyd, Percy (police chief in Commerce, Oklahoma), to tell the press she did not smoke cigars, 121; transformed into a celebrity after Joplin (Missouri) photographs, 210

Bonnie (Parker) and Clyde (Barrow): alleged theft of cash from ambushed car by Jordan, Henderson (Bienville Parish sheriff), 161; and phrase "They Kill People," xviii, 250; as folk heroes, 212–13; as frontier outlaws, 41; Bonnie was twenty-three when killed, 3; carried out multiple small-town robberies, 3, 121; Clyde was twenty-four when killed, 3; demand for photos of their dead bodies, 262; failed Joplin (Missouri) police raid and framing of outlaws, 27, 119; frantic public effort to collect memorabilia, including body parts, from the ambushed car, 261; large frenzied crowd effort to access the autopsy, 262; *Fugitives: The Story of Clyde Barrow and Bonnie Parker* (1934) as the beginning of the legend of, 268; importance of Joplin photographs for her popular attraction, 119; included as characters in *Wanted for Murder* (1945), 271; inspired several movies, 272–74; involved in the murder of nine lawmen across four states, 3; killed on 23 May 1934 in Louisiana, 4; near-carnival atmosphere at the site of the ambush, 261; origins in West Dallas (Texas), 3; premonitions of their mortality, 215; sex appeal and their popular celebrity status, 122; stage photographs of themselves in Joplin, 27, 119–20; tensions with Barrow, Buck, and Barrow, Blanche, 170; tow truck with the "death car," stopped by a school, 261–62; *True Detective Mysteries* published a six-part serial after their death (1934), 266

Bonnie and Clyde, film (1967): ambush scene filmed in California, 220; and the linking of celebrity status and crime, 210; attracted younger audiences, 257, 284; Benton, Robert, and Newman, David, listened to "Foggy Mountain Breakdown" during writing of script, 25–26; Black audiences embraced, 232; budget of $1.8 million, 7; competition with *The Graduate* for the 1968 Academy Awards, 283; debut on 13 August 1967, 251, 255; Denton (Texas) school district dismissed classes for "Bonnie and Clyde Day," 256; early screenings, 251–52; elements in the film represented defiance of the early moralistic Motion Picture Production Code, 169, 203–4; filmed in Pilot Point and Red Oak (Texas), 210, 227; "Foggy Mountain Breakdown" (1949) as the music theme for, 211, 249; grossed $70 million worldwide, 280; historically significant stage direction in filmmaking, 27; importance of exclusions in the art of storytelling, 26; inspired the production of "The Ballad of Bonnie and Clyde," 279; Jamieson Film Co. produced the *The Retribution of Clyde Barrow and Bonnie Parker* (1934), 265; labeled the best movie of the year, 279; lack of interest in directing or producing, 31; Lewis's, Joseph H., *Gun Crazy* (1950) as antecedent to, 274; local residents played one-line walk-on roles, 211; love and hate among Warner Bros. executives for, 232–42, 249; included as an advance premier at the Montreal Film Festival, 251; Moss, C. W., character a composite of crime associates, 26; multiple rejections to produce, 31; parallel scene to *The Grapes of Wrath*, 227; perceived as a western, 42, 155; preceded by the assassination of Kennedy, John F., (1963) and the shooting at The University of Texas at Austin (1966), 7–8; production and release coincided with emergence of the

Index 361

Bonnie and Clyde (continued)
  Black Panther Party (1966), 227; production of musical *Bonnie and Clyde* (2009), 294–95; received ten Oscar nominations, xx, 280; stimulated the consumer purchase of French berets, 280; Warner Bros. hesitated in publicizing, 255; Warner, Jack, may have considered Bonnie and Clyde as somewhat un-American, 249; won the Best Supporting Actress and Best Cinematography Academy Awards (1968), 283
Brown, H. Rap (Black Panther): on the necessity of violence and its saliency in US history, 278
Bundy, Ammon (son of Bundy, Clive): Hammond, Dwight (father) and Hammond, Steven (son) charged with arson on federal land, 239; led armed occupation of Malheur National Wildlife Refuge (Oregon, 2016), 239; media labels for occupiers/occupation, 239; Rhodes, Stewart (founder, Oath Keepers), opposed occupation, 229
Bundy, Cliven (Nevada cattle rancher and farmer): accumulated over one million dollars in unpaid grazing fees and fines, 236; Bureau of Land Management (BLM) released cattle and retreated, 237–38; BLM ordered that grazing must stop and notified him of possible confiscation of cattle, 236; confrontation with BLM officers ("Battle of Bunkerville"), 236–37; federal court found him in violation of law, and ordered him to remove the cattle from public land, 236; grazed hundreds of heads of cattle on public lands, 236; grazing on public lands administered by BLM, 236; grew casaba melon, 235; importance of ranching in appeal to the public, 238; submitted notice to the Nevada Clark County Sheriff (Gillespie, Douglas) seeking protection from federal authorities, 236; supported by Idaho III% and other militia groups, 236–37
Burns, Walter Noble (historian): author of *The Saga of Billy the Kid* (1925), 3, 39; on Billy the Kid's revenge against corporations, 39; viewed Billy the Kid as a perfect teenage rebel and fearless, 40

Cavitt, Mabel: a sixty-six-year-old teacher in Red Oak (Texas), 212; noted for the most memorable face in the film, 212; played the role of Bonnie's mother in *Bonnie and Clyde*, 212
Clyde (Chestnut Barrow): admired Jesse James and Billy the Kid, 13; adopted the middle name "Champion," 14; also known as Williams, Elvin, Hale, Jack, and Bailey, Roy, 11; amassed a large cache of weapons, 82, 135, 165; and deprived upbringing and desire to improve his class status, 12; an estimated ten-thousand persons attended the funeral service, 264; a "person of interest" to the Dallas and Fort Worth police, 14–15; as a "control freak," 13; a victim of repeated rape and

torture in prison, 68, 78; avoided robbing larger banks, 125–26; burned a mail delivery truck, 73; carried *The Saga of Billy the Kid* (1925) on the day of the ambush, 3; collaborated with Fults, Ralph, on a string of robberies (1932), 71; considered short and skinny, 14; convinced a fellow inmate in prison to cut two toes on his left foot, 68; desired material things he could not afford, 15; disguised as a woman to evade surveillance, 124; driving skills of, 123, 124; family worked as sharecroppers in Ellis County (Texas), 21; formed Lake Dallas Gang, 71; found the payroll safe empty at the Simms Oil Refinery (Dallas), 71; jobs held by, 14; killed his rapist in prison, 68; label of dumbbell bandits applied to a cellmate and, 19; liked Fords, 14; loved guns since childhood, 13, 132; physical mistreatment of Bonnie and her physical resistance, 127; regarded as a fashionable dresser, 14; treated weapons with fetishistic reverence, 132; *Waco Times–Herald* assigned the nickname of "Schoolboy" Barrow to, 15; was the driver on the day of the ambush, 4–5

Crowther, Bosley (film critic): and Warner Bros. response to negative review by, 255; as a conservative moralist, 254; enraged by Penn's, Arthur, characterization of the US as a violent society, 277; negative review of *Bonnie and Clyde*, 253–54; removed as film critic by the *New York Times*, 280–81; retired from the *New York Times* and hired by Columbia Pictures, 281; was also critical of the filmmakers and audience attraction to the film, 253

Dillinger, John: focus of true crime biography *The Dillinger Days* (1963), 24; Hamer, Frank (Texas Ranger) viewed Clyde as a more clever and reckless outlaw than, 123; named Public Enemy No. 1 by the FBI, 123; penchant for Ford V-8 automobiles, 3; robbed twelve banks in four states, 123; stole $300,000 in one year, 123; viewed Bonnie and Clyde as "kids stealing grocery money," 123

drive-in theaters: accounted for close to a third of movie screens in the mid 1960s, 204; and importance of lighting in films to improve their view in, 204–5

Dunaway, Faye: *Bonnie and Clyde* was her third film in 1966, 85; close friend of Pollard, Michael J., on the production of the film, 199; considered herself a perfectionist, 200; disliked how she appeared as Bonnie in the early rushes/dailies, 198; earned $30,000 for her role as Bonnie, 108; insecurities, 108, 199; maintained professional relationship with Beatty, Warren, 160; noted the lack of interest by Warner Bros. in publicizing the film, 255; off-screen tensions with Beatty, Warren, 7–8; recognized as talented, was offered a non-exclusive five-picture contract by Spiegel, Sam (producer),

Dunaway, Faye (*continued*)
and six-picture contract by Preminger, Otto (director/producer), 107; played the role of Bonnie in the film, 7–8; reliance on Cokes and appetite suppressors during filming, 198; sought lead female role in *Hurry Sundown*, but Fonda, Jane, was selected instead, 107

Dunbar-Ortiz, Roxanne (historian): on the presence of firearms and organized violence in US colonization, 138

Dutton, John (script supervisor): noted the film being weeks over schedule and over budget, 220; recalls tensions in the making of *Bonnie and Clyde*, 161, 162

Dykstra, Robert R. (historian): author of *The Cattle Towns* (1968), 87; corrected the history of cattle towns as violent due to guns, 87; noted local prohibitions on discharging of firearms and possession of weapons by civilians, 87; tabulated the low number of homicides from 1870 to 1885, 87

Earp, Wyatt: ABC TV broadcasted *The Life and Legend of Wyatt Earp* (1955–1961) based on Lake's, Stuart N. (writer), *Wyatt Earp: Frontier Marshall* (1931), 89; as an entrepreneur and brothel-keeper, xvi; book by Lake, Stuart N., considered a fabrication, 88; studied by Hutton, Paul Andrew (historian), 36; survived the Shootout at the O.K. Corral unharmed, 88; the focus of the "biography" by Lake, Stuart N., 88; *Wyatt Earp* "biography" became the basis for subsequent film and video representations of the Gunfight at the O.K. Corral and mythical legend of, 88–89. *See also* O.K. Corral, Gunfight/Shootout

Ebert, Roger (film critic): declared *Bonnie and Clyde* a "masterpiece," 258

Edwards, John Newman (writer): fostered the legend of Jesse James, 38; noted the link between and outlaw and his gun, 39; set the legend-making pattern of framing outlaws as not criminals in *Noted Guerillas* (1879), 38–39

Federal Bureau of Investigation (FBI): agency role in contesting the representation of criminals as heroes, 270; agents found a Browning automatic rifle at the Joplin (Missouri) raid site, 119; Bundy, Cliven, reported as not a threat by, 236; Finicum, La Voy, killed by Oregon state police and, 240–41; labeled the Barrow Gang as toughest outlaws, 236; participated in the raid of the Branch Davidians (Waco, Texas), 234; reported high level of gun assaults from 1964 through 1967, 32–33; robbery of National Guard armories a concern for Hoover, J. Edgar, head of, 82–83, 165; Schlesinger Jr., Arthur (historian/consultant) examined crime data from, 32; testimony provided by Barrow, Blanche, regarding cache of firearms, 132; wanted posters

for Clyde show the middle name as "Champion," 14
Ferguson, James (governor, Texas): ended summary execution of Mexicans, 190; ordered the Texas Rangers to eliminate Mexicans associated with El Plan de San Diego, 189
Ferguson, Miriam "Ma" (governor, Texas): approved the hiring of Hamer, Frank, to pursue and kill Bonnie and Clyde, 193; authorized the order to kill Bonnie and Clyde, 3–4; granted Methvin, Henry, amnesty in exchange for assistance in ambushing Bonnie and Clyde, 220–21; on alleged pardon of Barrow, Buck, 128; wife of Ferguson, James (governor, Texas), 192
Finicum, La Voy (rancher, Arizona): and occupation of the Malheur National Wildlife Refuge (Oregon), 240; an observer at BLM confrontation in Nevada, 240; authored a self-published novel, 240; became a self-appointed spokesman for the occupation, 240; killed while attempting to outrun an FBI roadblock (2016), 240–41; posthumously attained cowboy folk hero status, 241
Flowers, A. D.: special effects technician for *Bonnie and Clyde*, 7, 9
Fredericks, Ellsworth: filming career, 205; second cinematographer for *Bonnie and Clyde*, 205
Fults, Ralph: after release from prison joined the Barrow Gang, 67; a member of Clyde's Lake Dallas Gang, 71; burned a mail delivery truck, 73; collaborated with Clyde on a string of robberies (1932), 71; fellow inmate with Clyde at Eastham Prison (Texas), 67; his memoir is the only eyewitness account of Clyde's prison period, 67; noted that there was nothing romantic about the actions of the Barrow Gang, 125; reported rapes of Clyde in prison, 68

Gardner, Mark Lee (historian): examined the stories of James, Jesse and Billy the Kid, xvii–xviii; on the tenuous link between myths and reality, xvii; outlaws and audaciousness of crimes, 209
Gillespie, Douglas (sheriff, Clark County, Nevada): considered a "red coat" by members of the Sagebrush Sheriffs group, 236; declined Bundy's, Cliven, request to intervene on his behalf against the US Bureau of Land Management (BLM), 236–37; was not part of the Sagebrush Sheriffs, 236
Godard, Jean-Luc: declined invitation to direct *Bonnie and Clyde*, 30–31; directed *Breathless* (1960), 23; directed *Contempt* (*Le mepris*, 1963), 30–31; liked the *Bonnie and Clyde* script but suggested filming in January in New Jersey, 30, 284
Greenberg, Jerry (assistant editor): assisted Allen, Dede, in the editing of *Bonnie and Clyde*, 248; edited *The French Connection* (1970) and *Apocalypse Now* (1979), 248; Warner Bros. did not list assistant editors in the film credits, 248

Guffey, Burnett (Bernie): after heart attack returned to filming *Bonnie and Clyde*, 205; became Columbia Pictures premier director of photography, 202; disagreement with Penn, Arthur, related to "source" lighting, 204–5; filming career, 202, 307; innovated use of window screen to diffuse light, 206, 212; integrated a "Sun Gun" spotlight, 206; received the Academy Award for Best Cinematography, 283; served as president of the American Society of Cinematographers, 202; suffered a heart attack during filming of *Bonnie and Clyde*, 202; tensions with Penn, Arthur, 203; veteran cinematographer, 7, 9

Guinn, Jeff (Bonnie and Clyde biographer): Bonnie and Clyde as bungling bandits, 121; Bonnie and Clyde cherished their celebrity status, 121; Bonnie and Clyde misadventures as comedy, 71; Bonnie and Clyde's actions as a vicarious sense of revenge against the rich and powerful, 121; considers Bonnie as the more dangerous of the couple, 214; considers Hamer, Frank, as a thug concerned with his image, 183–84; on the importance of 13 April 1933 in US popular culture, 118; on their effort to fight back and aid some people in need, 13; on US obsession with mythology of outlaws, 122; suggests Bonnie engaged with crime before meeting Clyde, 77

guns: and enactment of the 1934 National Firearms Act, 230–31; and gun rights, 233; and high popular valuation of automobiles and, 14; association between freedom and, 233; Beatty, Warren, wore his shoulder-holstered Colt .45 throughout the production, 159; Clyde took great care of his guns and had a pet name for each one, 265; connection between masculinity and mystique surrounding, 143; COVID-19 and rush to purchase of, xix; cultural and symbolic importance of Western gunfighters in, xvii; disproportionate ownership in US of, xix; glorified notion of "a man with a gun," 35; Johnson, Lyndon B. (president), sought to enact a firearms registry and a universal licensing requirement, 231; link between sex and, 26; Mack, Richard (sheriff, Graham County, Arizona), led challenge to Brady Act of 1993, 233; McVeigh, Timothy, sold pro-gun bumper stickers at the Waco confrontation (1993), 234; National Rifle Association (NRA) argument that white Americans need guns to protect themselves from armed Blacks, 231; on enactment of the Federal Assault Weapons Ban (1994), 233; on the mythical link between the West, the cowboy, and, 234–35; outlaw notions appropriated in advertising of, 144; public health crisis related to violence and, xix; qualified endorsement by the NRA of the Gun Control Act of 1968, 230–31; Reagan, Ronald (president), assertion about guns not making criminals, 230; references in everyday speech, xvii; Sagebrush Sheriffs' opposition to restrictions on gun ownership, 233; Supreme Court sided with challengers to the Brady Act, 233

Haag, Pamela (historian): and targeting of marketing to preteen and teenage males, 144; authored *The Gunning of America* (2016), 136; importance of creating a demand by military, and civilians, 139; on the 'amorality of business' in the creation of a gun market, 137; on the marketing and production of a gun culture and gun consuming market, 136–37, 142; personal use of firearms limited among firearm barons (Winchester, Oliver, and Remington, Eliphalet), 137; promotion of firearms integrated violence, 138; strategy to market firearms as both commodities of instinct, and as luxury goods, 142; Winchester and Remington corporations labeled their advance sales men as "missionaries," 137

Hackman, Gene (actor): asserts he owed his acting career to Beatty, Warren, for inclusion in *Bonnie and Clyde*, 110; fired from *The Graduate*, 110; on Penn's, Arthur, trust of actors and knowing what an actor needed, 158–59; played the role of Barrow, Buck, 109; previously collaborated with Beatty, Warren, 109

Hamer, Frank (Francis A., Texas Ranger): appears as Bryce, Frank in *Bonnie and Clyde*, 181; as a white supremacist, 191; boasted of his prowess with firearms, 185; city marshal of Navasota (Texas), 184; Colt .45 gun inscribed with the phrase "Old Lucky," 4, 185; first Texas Ranger to lose a black prisoner to a lynch mob (Sherman, Texas), 191; led the pursuit and killing of Bonnie and Clyde, 1–4, 191; prevented the lynching of some prisoners, 191; regarded by the Texas Ranger Museum as the greatest Ranger, 183; responded to a reporter that he had killed twenty-three individuals, "not counting Mexicans," 185; role as a for-hire strikebreaker, 196; said to be one of the Texas Rangers in the photograph with dead Mexicans on the ground, 189; threatened Texas state representative regarding an investigation of Texas Ranger atrocities, 186; viewed Bonnie and Clyde as more clever than Dillinger, John, 123

Hobsbawm, Eric (historian): and the concept of "social bandit," 40, 226; description of the "noble robber," 40

Hofstadter, Richard (historian): commented on Brown's, H. Rap (Black Panther), assertion about violence in the US, 278; on simultaneous existence of gun culture and identity as "best-behaved and best-regulated peoples" in the US, xix; recognized "gun culture" in the US, xix

Hoover, J. Edgar (FBI director): authored *Persons in Hiding* (1938), 270; concerned with the production of gangster films, 43; confronted nationwide crime spree, 43; on importance of powerful weapons for police to confront criminals, 135

Hutton, Paul Andrew (Western history writer/historian): and dual obsession for cars and guns in the US, 14; and US elevation of individualism, 36; authored works on Custer, Earp, and Billy the Kid, 36; on Billy the Kid as a perfect teenage rebel and later Robin Hood, 40; on the enshrinement of gun ownership in the Constitution, 85; on US emergence from rebellion and violence, 36; praises Penn's, Arthur, appreciation of the social context in the making of *Little Big Man* (1970), 292; suggested the Civil War produced a generation of "alienated killers," 37; suggests the Second Amendment aims to allow residents to overthrow a tyrannical government, 233

James, Jesse, xvii, 37–39; Bonnie and Clyde as heirs of, 40; idolized by Clyde, 13, 37, 83; noted by Bonnie, 1; would be labeled terrorist in the present, 38. *See also* Edwards, John Newman; Gardner, Mark Lee
Jewell, Richard B. (film scholar): *Bonnie and Clyde* and the production of the Bonnie and Clyde legend, 125; observation on the ambush of Bonnie and Clyde, 288
Jones, Elinor Wright (producer/playwright), 30; optioned the treatment for *Bonnie and Clyde*, 28

Kael, Pauline (film critic): became the *New Yorker*'s most prominent film critic, 281; viewed *Bonnie and Clyde* as the most exciting US film since *The Manchurian Candidate* (1962), 281
Kalmenson, Ben (Warner Bros. head of distribution): all bookings for Bonnie and Clyde film stopped, 259; and low budget allocated for the film, 104; booked the film in thirty-five theaters in Kansas City, Omaha, and surrounding area, 250–59; consigned the film to second-rate theaters, and Southern drive-ins, 249; described as a "crochety, opinionated guy" and "jumped-up salesman," 243; dismissive of the film, 249; left the film out from the list of summer releases, 243; opined that the film was "a piece of shit," 242, 243

La Matanza (The Killing Time): Texas Rangers' Mexican killing spree (1915–1919), 189
Lederer, Richard (head of advertising at Warner Bros.): campaigned for a red-carpet premier in Manhattan, 249; with input from the screenwriters, developed the advertising tagline of "They're Young. They're in Love. And They Kill People." 250; early champion of the script, 243; observed that Warner Bros. was a very conservative studio in the mid-sixties, 104; recognized the potential of a *Bonnie and Clyde* film with a younger audience, 104

MacEwen, Walter (studio head of production at Warner Bros.): championed the film over

Warner's, Jack, objections, 107–8; communicated Warner's, Jack, demand to move the production to the studios, to Beatty, Warren, 243–44; conversation with Shurlock, Geoffrey (head of Production Code Administration), on prohibited sexual depictions, 116; pressured by Warner, Jack, to complete the production of the film, 220; recognized the potential of a *Bonnie and Clyde* film with a younger audience, 82; strongly supported the film, 116; telegrammed Beatty, Warren, that the studio was no longer going to cover the cost of editing in New York, 244

McVeigh, Timothy (domestic terrorist): his bombing of the Oklahoma City federal building killed 168 people, and injured 680 others (1995), 234; observed the confrontation at the Branch Davidian complex (Waco, 1993), 234; Oklahoma City bombing remains the deadliest act of domestic terrorism, 234; on how outlawing guns made him an outlaw, 233; regarded guns as instruments of freedom, 234

Methvin, Henry (son of Methvin, Iverson "Ivy"): kills Texas Highway Patrolmen, 213; offered a governor's reprieve by Hamer, Frank (Texas Ranger) and Simmons, Lee (general manager of Texas prisons), if his father aided in the ambush of Bonnie and Clyde, 220–21; wanted for a related murder in Oklahoma, 221

Methvin, Iverson "Ivy": agreed to help lawmen in arranging the ambush for Bonnie and Clyde, in exchange for amnesty for son (Henry), 220–21; handcuffed to a tree by Hamer, Frank, to force his cooperation, 221

Morgenstern, Joseph (film critic): authored negative reviews of *Bonnie and Clyde*, 257; retracted his initial review, 257–58

Motion Picture Production Code (1927): Bonnie's pre-Code talk, 18; Breen, Joseph I., appointed as director of Production Code Administration (PCA), 48; Breen, Joseph I., held moralistic and anti-Jewish views, 48–49; Catholic clergy called for boycott of all films, 48; Code of 1930 noted that criminals should not be made heroes, 145; collapsed with new generation of filmmakers and changes in society (1960s), 6; dictated on-screen morality, 6, 42, 44; early code specified that firearms should be limited, 146; establishment of the PCA, (1934), 48; films produced before July 1934 as pre-Code films, 45–48; included the "use of firearms" and "sympathy for criminals," 44; members of Congress raise the issue of national censorship and regulation of films, 48; Motion Picture Association of America (MPAA) revised the 1934 Code (1966), 115–16; new film rating system, 286–87; PCA controlled content for over two decades, 49; PCA objected to Penn's, Arthur, *The Left Handed Gun* (1958), 58; PCA rejected *Wanted for Murder* (1945), which included characters named Clyde and Bonnie, 271–72;

Motion Picture Production Code (*continued*)
pre-Code films, described, 16–17, 27; revisions included in the 1929 version, 44–45; sex and violence represented in pre-Code films, 47–48, 120; Shurlock, Geoffrey, head of PCA in the early 1960s, 116; transitional era, 205; Valenti, Jack (president of MPAA) appeared at a meeting of the National Commission on the Causes of and Prevention of Violence (1968), 285–87

New Sentimentality: as a filmmaking theme that emphasized style over content, 23, 210; Benton, Robert, and Newman, David, authored "The New Sentimentality" article for *Esquire* (1964), 23; later known as "the Sixties," 23; motif reflected in *Bonnie and Clyde*, 23

Newman, David: and full shooting treatment for *Bonnie and Clyde*, 25–26; attended meetings with Penn, Arthur, 111; collaborated with Benton, Robert, in writing the script for the film, 23; early insistence on a ménage à trois strand in the film, 61; inspired by *The Dillinger Days* (1963), 121, 267; on Bonnie and Clyde seeking celebrity status, 24–25; understood the film as part of the New Sentimentality filmmaking, 24, 25; worked at *Esquire*, 33

O.K. Corral, Gunfight/Shootout at (1881): a confrontation between a US Marshall (Earp, Virgil) and his associates, against the Clanton and McLaury brothers, 88; a deadly confrontation about a Tombstone ordinance on firearm possession in the city, 89; as example of "printing the legend," 36; as the most celebrated armed encounter in the "Wild West," 87; its mythical value exceeds the particular significance of the event at the time, 89; shootout took place in less than thirty seconds, 87; *Star Trek* episode (1968) recycled the mythical legend about, 88–89; the publishing of *Wyatt Earp: Frontier Marshall* (1931) cemented the mythical legend about, 88

Parker, Emma (Bonnie's mother): collaborated with Barrow Cowan, Nell (Clyde's sister) and a reporter to publish a book (*Fugitives: The Story of Clyde Barrow and Bonnie Parker, 1934*), 128, 268; disavowed contents of *Fugitives*, 268; filed a lawsuit against the producers of *The Retribution of Clyde Barrow and Bonnie Parker*, 266

Parsons, Estelle (actor): awarded the Best Supporting Actress for role in *Bonnie and Clyde*, 129, 283; played the role of Barrow, Blanche (wife of Barrow, Buck), 110; received the lowest salary among the principal actors in the film, 110; tensions with Dunaway, Faye, 199; wore recycled studio costumes, 157

Peckinpah, Sam (film director): cited influence of Kurosawa's, Akira, *Seven Samurai* (1954), 288;

did not acknowledge his debt to Penn, Arthur, 288; directed *The Wild Bunch* (1969), 36, 288; outdid the ambush scene in *Bonnie and Clyde* by using six cameras, rather than four, 288; was determined to outdo Penn's, Arthur, use of squibs, 287

Penn, Arthur (film director): ambush scene inspired by Kurosawa's, Akira, *Seven Samurai* (1954), 6, 218; *Bonnie and Clyde* (1967) and *Little Big Man* (1970) as finest collaboration with editor Allen, Dede, 290; born to a Russian-Jewish family in Philadelphia, 52; challenge in filming ambush, 7, 224; cinematic capturing of propensity to violence and obsession with guns, xx, 8–9, 219; commented that he liked violence and that it makes good movies, 50; congruence between humor and violence, 252; converted Bonnie and Clyde into romantic martyrs, 8; credited his wife for an important structural change in the script, 113; decided to film on location (Texas), and defended the decision, 151, 244; directed *Bonnie and Clyde* (1967), xx, 6; disagreement with Guffey, Burnett, related to "source" lighting, 204; drew ballistic sound effects from *Shane* (1952), 248; experienced a period of post-shoot depression after *Bonnie and Clyde*, 289; filmmaking importance of ambush scene, 6; film produced and released during domestic upheavals in the US, xx; filming career drawn to "outsider" protagonists, 51; fired by Lancaster, Burt, while filming *The Train* (1963), 246; insight about the element of fatalism in the couple, 216; labeled "the American Truffaut" after the release of *Bonnie and Clyde*, 59; mutual respect for Beatty, Warren, 60; noted persistence of violent periods in US history, 33; on film technicians' power over films, 203; part of infantry division during World War II, 52; productions by, 51, 289–92; reflection on coexistence of a churchgoing, moralistic, puritanical society and acceptance of human violence, 253; quoted Moses, Robert Parris, regarding the issue of law becoming outlaw, 232; shot much footage to have more options in editing, 246; tensions with Beatty, Warren, 59–60; *The Left Handed Gun* (1958) as prequel to *Bonnie and Clyde*, 57–58, 205; viewed the actual ambush as worse than crimes by the couple, 8; violence as part of the American character, 293; wanted gunshots to be played at high volume, 248; wanted to make Bonnie and Clyde into legends, 6, 218

Phillips, John Neal (historian): celebrations held at the location of the ambush and cemetery, 260; characterized Clyde as a control freak, 13; edited Barrow's, Blanche, memoir, 129; interviewed Fults, Ralph, 68, 125; general-public held banks, politicians, and police officers as responsible for the Great Depression, 70; support for those who resist authority, 70

Pollard, Michael J. (actor): close friend of Dunaway, Faye, on the production of *Bonnie and Clyde*, 199; consumed nightly doses of acid, 199; did not know how to drive when hired, 89, 155; noted applause and screams for the film, 251–52; played the role of Moss, C.W., in the film, 88–89, 155

Posse Comitatus Act (1878): aimed at restricting federal authorities from interfering with local police matters, 232; invoked by Bundy, Clive, 236

Potter, Claire Bond (crime historian): Bonnie and Clyde revived popular fascination with bandits, 122; on class views regarding the killing of police officers, 226; on erroneous identification of other couples as Bonnie and Clyde, 124

Quammen, Betsy Gaines (historian): argues that to understand "the West is to understand America," 234–35; on the importance of the "cowboy" to national and regional imaginaries, 235; on the ironical myths about the "cowboy," 235; observes that support for Bundy's, Cliven, anti-government actions were driven by his role as rancher, 238; on transformation of occupation of Malheur National Wildlife Refuge from a farce to a tragedy, 239–40; suggests the *Yellowstone* TV series negatively impacted Montana, 238

Ransom, Henry Lee (Texas Ranger commander): and consideration of pardons by the Texas governor, 189; involved in the extrajudicial executions of Mexicans in South Texas, 189; participated in suppression of Philippine Insurrection, 189

Reddish, Jack: assistant director in *Bonnie and Clyde*, 9

Rhodes, Stewart (founder, Oath Keepers): dissuaded Oath Keepers from overt display of weapons at Bunkerville (Nevada), 237; encouraged supporters to attend the confrontation between Bundy, Cliven, and the Bureau of Land Management (BLM) at Bunkerville, 237; on the hypermasculinity of recruits among Oath Keepers, 237; recruited lonely males to be part of a militia, 237; rejected invitation to participate in the Malheur National Wildlife Refuge occupation (Oregon), 239

Robin Hood: and contemporary fantasies, xviii; Billy the Kid as a parallel to, 40; Bonnie and Clyde as a kind of, 83

Schlesinger Jr., Arthur (historian/consultant): authored the essay "Violence as an American Way of Life" (1968), 32; common self-identification in the US as peaceful, tolerant people living under a government of laws, 32; concern with the US "Gunsmoke ethos," 142; examined FBI. data on crime, 32–33; on US identification with violent impulses, xx; recognized a destructive impulse linked to historical tensions, 33, 108, 94

Segaloff, Nat: attraction of *Bonnie and Clyde* to younger audiences, 257; noted Penn's, Arthur, pre-occupation with US characters, 51; Penn's, Arthur, biographer, 51–52, 148

Sheridan, Taylor (director/producer): impact of *Yellowstone* series on purchase of ranching/farming land in Montana, 238; produced the neo-Western *Yellowstone* TV series (2018–2024), 238

Stanley, Charles (the "Crime Doctor"): assaulted by Hamer, Frank, 270; Hamer, Frank, was enraged with the travelling show, 269–70; organized a traveling show with the car in which Bonnie and Clyde were killed, 269–70

Steinem, Gloria: broke relationship with Benton, Robert (*Esquire* editor), 21

Tavoularis, Dean: art director for *Bonnie and Clyde*, 7; career experience of, 155; critical of the big-studio system, 153–54; introduced the idea of the release of birds for the film, 223, 224, 247–48; Penn, Arthur, appreciated his contribution to the film, 152; responsible for locating the needed cars, 155; tensions with Guffey, Burnett (cinematographer), 203

Texas Rangers: atrocities committed by Texas Rangers/soldiers in Mexico, 188; confrontation with Comanches known as "Hays' Big Fight," or "The Battle of Walker's Creek," 187; created by Austin, Stephen F., to patrol Indigenous people and Mexicans, and protect White settlers, 186; Hamer, Frank, 1–2; Hamer, Frank aided by Alcorn, Bob, Gault, Maney, Hinton, Ted, and Henderson, Jordan, 2, 4; Hays and Walker participated in the Mexican-American War (1846–1848), 187; Hays, Jack "Coffee" (Ranger), confronted Comanches with the advantage of the new Patterson Colt, 186; Hays praised the new Colt gun, 187; Hinton, Ted, brought a movie camera to the ambush, 5; killing of Mexicans in La Matanza, 189; linked reputation of the Colt revolver and ascendancy of, 186; officers carried two Colts, 186–87; officers fired one hundred and sixty-seven rounds in the execution of Bonnie and Clyde, 4; Swanson, Doug J. (historian) and the "cult of glory" in, 186; US Senate investigation concluded that one hundred Mexicans were killed without due process by, 190; Walker, Samuel (Ranger) credited his survival at Walker's Creek to the Colt weapon, 187; Walker's suggestions for improving the gun led to production of the Colt Walker, 187–88; Walker viewed the Colt as "the most perfect weapon" to confront Indians and Mexicans, 187; Zachary Taylor (general) noted that Texas Rangers and soldiers were "too hard to control," 188

Toland, John: alleged Clyde held homosexual tendencies, 24, 267; authored *The Dillinger Days* (1963), 24; inspiration for

Toland, John (*continued*)
Benton, Robert, and Newman, David, 122; integrated the characters of Bonnie and Clyde in *The Dillinger Days*, 24; on Clyde's "effeminate appearance," 267; on his sloppy scholarship, 24, 173, 267

Towne, Robert (screenwriter): asked to write the scene where Bonnie and Clyde enact their own funeral, 215; contributions to dialogue, 175, 182, 216; credited as a "special consultant" on *Bonnie and Clyde*, 112; developed a creative partnership with Beatty, Warren, 101; held the role of unofficial adviser to Beatty, Warren, 111; notes that he persuaded Beatty, Warren, to buy the rights to the film script, 111–12; Production Code official opposed the sexual representations in the film, 116; revised the sexual relationship between Clyde and Bonnie in the film, 114–15; rewrote the family reunion scene, 113–14; writing career, 112; wrote the script for *Chinatown* (1974), 111

Truffaut, François (film director): advised Benton, Robert, and Newman, David, on improvements to their treatment, 29; directed and scripted *Fahrenheit 451*, 30; directed *Jules et Jim* (1962), 21; indicated that he would not direct films with Beatty, Warren, or Brando, Marlon, 100; noted the important dynamic in the Bonnie and Clyde characters in the script, 29; turned down the invitation to direct *Bonnie and Clyde*, 30, 61; urged the highlighting of sex and violence in the film, 29

Utley, Robert M. (historian): characterizes Hamer, Frank, as a white supremacist, 191; credits Jordan, Henderson (Bienville Parish sheriff), with the success of the Bonnie and Clyde ambush, 183; on the "six-shooter mindset" in the Texas Rangers, 188; suggests Hamer's, Frank, participation in the killing of Bonnie and Clyde restored the reputation of Texas Rangers, 194

Van Runkle, Theadora, 155–56, 198; Beatty, Warren, intervened to hire her, 156; concluded that *Bonnie and Clyde* would be a hit, and that she would be nominated for an Oscar, 155–56; considered attractive, elegant, hip, and stylish, 156; costume designer for the film, 7; Dunaway, Faye, and Beatty, Warren, rejected her hair style suggestions, 157; had to use some stock costumes from the Warner Brothers' warehouse, 157; impressed Penn, Arthur, with her sketches, 156; Jeakins, Dorothy, her mentor, 155; not able to be on location during the filming, 157; on site wardrobing carried out by her assistant, Brown, Norma, 157

Waldman, Michael (president of the Brennan Center for Justice): on challenge in interpreting the Second Amendment related to protecting militias and individual rights to a gun, 84

Warner, Jack L. (the "Colonel"): anticipated a total financial loss with *Bonnie and Clyde*, 117; contested Production Code Administration over *Who's Afraid of Virginia Woolf?* (1966), 116; deleted material from musical at the request of Nixon, Richard M. (president), 249; did not like Beatty, Warren, 102–3; disagreed with the production of the film in Texas, 151; displeased with cutting of film in New York, 243; embraced the Israeli war against Arab nations, 250; expressed his dislike of the *Bonnie and Clyde* script after production had started and when screened, 116, 243; head of Warner Bros. studios, 49, 65; known for asserting his authority to demand the ending of a film, 225; on wish to bury the film, 249; ordered that the production return to the studio, 219; raised substantial money for Israel, 250; resistance to a general US release of the film, 258; response to Production Code revisions, 49; sold Warner Bros. to Seven Arts, but remained president, 102; sought to recoup production costs from Southern drive-ins, 249; suggestion that he wanted to prove he was the most American mogul, 249; wanted *Bonnie and Clyde* filmed in the Warner Bros. studios, 151

Whitman, Charles: killed sixteen people from the University of Texas at Austin Tower (1966), 8, 179; wounded thirty-one individuals, 8

Wilde, Oscar: invitation by Tabor, Horace A. W., xv–xvi; trip to the US west, xv–xvi

Wilder, Gene (actor): played the role of Grizzard, Eugene (undertaker), 201; screen debut in *Bonnie and Clyde*, 161, 262

Winkler, Adam (professor of law): argues the Shootout at the O.K. Corral as a story about gun culture and gun control culture, 112; author of *Gun Fight: The Battle Over the Right to Bear Arms in America* (2013), 111; considerable regulation of firearms before the Civil War, 138; guns noted in the formation of the Constitution, but only in reference to arm militias for the defense of the states and nation, 106; impact of the emergence of the Black Panthers on gun control, 229; notes the presence of strict gun-control laws in frontier towns, 108; on association of masculinity and gun ownership, 142; on assumptions about the presence of guns and gunfights in the Wild West, 108, 111, 137